D1231812

Why Aren't Jewish Women Circumcised?

Why Aren't Jewish Women Circumcised?

Gender and Covenant in Judaism

Shaye J. D. Cohen

UNIVERSITY OF CALIFORNIA PRESS
Berkeley • *Los Angeles* • *London*

The publisher gratefully acknowledges the generous
contribution to this book provided by the Jewish Studies
Endowment Fund of the University of California Press
Associates, which is supported by a major gift from the
S. Mark Taper Foundation.

University of California Press
Berkeley and Los Angeles, California

University of California Press, Ltd.
London, England

Library of Congress Cataloging-in-Publication Data

Cohen, Shaye J. D.
   Why aren't Jewish women circumcised? : gender and
covenant in Judaism / Shaye J.D. Cohen.
      p.   cm.
   Includes bibliographical references and index.
   ISBN 0-520-21250-9 (cloth : alk. paper).
      1. Berit milah—History.   2. Circumcision—Reli-
gious aspects—Judaism.   3. Women in rabbinical literature.   4. Rabbinical literature—History and criticism.
5. Jews—Identity.   I. Title.

BM705.C65   2005
296.4'422—dc22   2004030699

Manufactured in the United States of America

14   13   12   11   10   09   08   07   06   05
10   9   8   7   6   5   4   3   2   1

Printed on Ecobook 50 containing a minimum 50%
post-consumer waste, processed chlorine free. The bal-
ance contains virgin pulp, including 25% Forest Stew-
ardship Council Certified for no old growth tree cutting, processed either TCF or ECF. The sheet is
acid-free and meets the minimum requirements of
ANSI/NISO Z39.48–1992 (R 1997) (Permanence of
Paper).♾

For Miriam

Who daily demonstrates the truth of
the rabbinic statement "The Holy One,
Blessed be He, gave greater discernment
to women than to men" (B. Niddah 45b)

Contents

Illustrations

Preface

Why aren't Jewish women circumcised? At first glance, the question seems silly: circumcision is the surgical removal of the foreskin from the penis, and a woman does not have a penis. But the question is not silly and the answers it elicits are neither obvious nor trivial, and this for several reasons. First, many other cultures do (or did) circumcise women. Second, classical Judaism has invested the circumcision of males with so much meaning and importance that its failure to promote a parallel ritual for women is a striking fact that requires analysis. Third, Jewish circumcision has long played an important role in the debate between Judaism and Christianity, and the inability of one half of the Jews to be circumcised would seem to call into question the Jewish position that circumcision is an essential sign of the covenant between God and Israel. So, I repeat, why aren't Jewish women circumcised? The question is well posed by Debra Orenstein:

> *Brit Milah* [Jewish ritual circumcision] is the ultimate case-study for women's perspectives on the Jewish lifecycle because it raises questions that are supremely challenging and rich with potential: What is the purpose of this most ancient and basic—some would say primitive—mark of the covenant? What does it mean that women can never have it?. . . How shall we understand the fact that God made a covenant with Abraham and not Sarah, that the covenant is "cut" on males and not females, that Moses addressed men, and not women in preparing the people to receive Torah and covenant at Sinai (Exodus 19:15)? Given the scriptural and biological impediments, is it now possible for women to be full partners in the covenant, and, if so, how?[1]

Or, in a slightly more polemical formulation, if circumcision is an essential marker of Jewishness, what are women? Can women be Jews? And, if we conclude from the non-circumcision of women that circumcision is not an essential marker of Jewishness, then what exactly is circumcision? And why is there so much fuss about it? These are the questions that drive this book.

In this book I am interested not only in the history of Jewish circumcision but also, and perhaps even more so, in the history of Jewishness. What makes a Jew a Jew? Christians have long tended to look at Jewish circumcision as akin to Christian baptism. Without baptism one is not a member of the church; without baptism one is not saved from the effects of original sin; without baptism one is not really a Christian. If circumcision is truly analogous to Christian baptism, then circumcision is as essential to Jewishness as baptism is to Christianness. As we shall see, some strands of Jewish thought, notably the mystic, do conceive of circumcision much as Christians conceive of baptism, but other strands, notably the legal (in Hebrew, the *halakhic*), do not. But either way we have a problem. If circumcision is the baptismlike essential marker of Jewishness, how do we explain the absence of this essential mark from women? This question was raised by Christian authors in ancient and medieval times, as we shall see. If circumcision does not function like baptism—and for most of the Jewish thinkers treated in this book it does not—what makes a Jew a Jew?

Throughout this book I refer to the "circumcision" of women. Not for a moment and not even in jest am I suggesting or implying that Jewish women *should* be circumcised. On the contrary; I am delighted that Jewish tradition knows nothing of this procedure, which, if we may believe its opponents, is far more painful, dangerous, and deleterious than is the circumcision of men. I shall return to this in chapter 2 and in the concluding chapter. In any case, the subject of this book is not the circumcision of women but the non-circumcision of women.

This book is about Jewish women, but is not about Jewish women. Jewish women are everywhere but nowhere in this book. The Jewish women who figure on every page are women as imagined, constructed, and classified by Jewish men. When Jewish men say that women's exemption from the commandment of circumcision betokens their exclusion from the life of Torah study and prayer (see chapter 5), they are speaking *about* women. What the women themselves would have said, and did say, we do not know. No Jewish woman before early modern times wrote a memoir or autobiography; no Jewish woman before our own times has written a book of Jewish law. Whether Jewish women in the rabbinic societies of Late Antiquity and the high Middle Ages were content with their lot or sad, spiritually fulfilled or malnourished, feted or oppressed, we do not know.[2] This book is not a history of women's Judaism; it is at best a small contribution to the history of women in men's Judaism.

The form "preface" requires an author to give a brief synopsis of the prefaced book, and this I shall now do.[3] Since this book is about what men have that women do not, I begin in chapter 1 with a history of Jewish male circumcision, from the Bible to the Talmud to the high Middle Ages. I analyze changes in meaning, ritual, and surgical practice. Chapter 2 is devoted to female circumcision. Some cultures of the world practice female circumcision, what opponents call female genital mutilation, but Jewish culture is not one, nor has it ever been. The Jewish philosopher Philo explicitly says that Jewish women are not circumcised, whereas Egyptian women are; he also attempts to answer the question why God demanded circumcision only of Israelite men, and not of Israelite women. Chapter 3 is a history of that question, which brings us to Christianity. Beginning in the second century CE, Christians used the non-circumcision of Jewish women as an anti-Jewish argument: we Christians baptize our girls and our boys, but you Jews circumcise only your boys—how do your girls become Jews? This question, in any of three different formulations, became a standard argument in the anti-Jewish tracts written in the Latin West from Late Antiquity through the high Middle Ages. These same Christian thinkers also had to explain why God in Genesis 17 failed to demand of women circumcision or any functional equivalent. The fact that Jews circumcised only men was, from the Christian perspective, a problem that Jews needed to explain; the fact God asked Abraham to circumcise only men was, from the Christian perspective, a problem that Christians needed to explain.

In chapter 4 I try to explain why the rabbinic sages of antiquity ignored the Christian arguments. The sages recognized the gender divide represented by circumcision but were not concerned about it. The first rabbinic Jews to respond explicitly to the problem posed by the Christians on the basis of the non-circumcision of women were the anti-Christian polemicists of the high Middle Ages (ca. 1100–1400). In the absence of any canonical response handed down from ancient times, these writers were free to invent any response that they wished, and their varied responses constitute the heart of this book (chapters 4 through 8).

Chapter 5 presents what I take to be the "real" answer to the question, that is, the answer that is implicit in all of rabbinic culture from antiquity until recent times, and in some circles even to our own day. This is the answer that the rabbis of antiquity would have given to the Christian question had they deigned to do so, the answer that any defender of traditional rabbinic Judaism will hit upon instantly and inevitably: the absence of circumcision from Jewish women bespeaks their secondary, anomalous, problematic place in the rabbinic hierarchy. They are Jews, of course, but they are Jews who are not obligated to study the Torah or to observe all of its commandments. They are Jews, yet they are uncircumcised; they are like us, yet they are not like us; they are essential to our existence, yet they are marginal. This answer is presented by two thinkers of the thirteenth century but is to be found in one form or another in numerous other works before (implicitly) and since (both explicitly and implicitly).

Chapters 6 and 7 are devoted to interpreting Maimonides' view of circumcision. Nowhere in his voluminous writings does Maimonides treat the non-circumcision of women, but he provides ideas and material for later thinkers who do. Maimonides says that the purpose of circumcision is to weaken the male organ, in order to minimize lust and diminish sexual pleasure. In other words, circumcision makes men a little less manly. This theory, which was quite popular among medieval Jewish philosophers, could be used to explain the non-circumcision of women since they do not need to be made less manly and since they, apparently, are not troubled, as men are, by excessive lust and sexual cravings. Maimonides does not say this, of course, but some of his later followers did. This is the theme of chapter 6, in which I also discuss the Christian idea that circumcision effeminates Jewish men. Chapter 7 develops the Maimonidean idea that circumcision is not covenantal: circumcision is no different from any other commandment, and its absence does not betoken absence from the covenant or second-tier status. What makes a Jew a Jew, according to Maimonides, is proper faith, and this, not circumcision, determines who is "in" the people of Israel and who is "out." This view will allow one thinker to explain that the non-circumcision of Jewish women is simply a function of the fact that not every individual Jew is obligated to observe all the commandments. Women are exempt from some commandments, men are exempt from some commandments. As long as they believe properly, Jewish women can and do attain the same level of Jewishness as men.

In contrast with chapter 5, which presents the non-feminist, perhaps anti-feminist, canonical answer of Jewish tradition, and in contrast with chapters 6 and 7, which develop two answers in the Maimonidean tradition, chapter 8 brings us to a medieval proto-feminist response. This medieval author (actually the earliest of the authorities considered here) argues that women have a covenantal ritual of their own paralleling the circumcision of men. This ritual is the proper observance of the rabbinic laws governing the impurity of menstruation. Through the observation of these rules, a woman's menstrual blood becomes covenantal blood, akin to the covenantal blood of circumcision. This amazing view is based on the homology of circumcision and menstruation, a point that is argued or assumed by many modern anthropologists and psychologists and that finds a uniquely feminine equivalent to the uniquely male ritual of circumcision.

In the concluding chapter I discuss the circumcision controversies of modern times, beginning with the Frankfurt circumcision controversy of 1843. The advocates of Reform and the defenders of tradition fought a protracted battle over the necessity of circumcision for the maintenance of one's place in the Jewish community. Among the arguments advanced by the Reform party was the non-circumcision of women: circumcision cannot be essential to Jewish identity, they said, for otherwise how do our daughters enter our community? The Reformers did not realize that they were rehearsing a Christian argument, and their Orthodox respondents did not realize that they were independently producing some of the same arguments that had been advocated several hundred years before. In some Jewish circles the imparity between the treatment of newborn boys and the treatment of newborn girls rankles still. And a new argument against the circumcision of Jewish men is now on the horizon: this argument is based on the circumcision of non-Jewish women. If progressive individuals condemn female circumcision on humanitarian grounds, should they not also oppose male circumcision? Why is the circumcision of men privileged over the circumcision of women? This is an argument that medieval Jewish thinkers did not have to deal with, but it is an argument that soon will be on the Jewish agenda; perhaps it already is. And here the book concludes.

Having fulfilled my responsibility of summarizing the book, I now discharge the next obligation that befalls any preface writer. This project has had a long gestation, too long actually, and my list of debts is substantial. I began to work on this book in the early 1990s while I was at Brown University; I continued working on it during a stint as visiting

professor at Williams College (1995) and during a sabbatical in Jerusalem (1998–99)[4]; I am finally bringing this project to a close after having moved to Harvard University. I am grateful to Williams College for
honoring me with an appointment as Croghan Bicentennial Visiting
Professor, and I am grateful to the Lady Davis Foundation for having
facilitated my sabbatical in Jerusalem. I feel honored to have been invited to lecture on the themes of this book at Ben Gurion University of
Beer Sheva, Brown University, Haifa University, Harvard University,
Hebrew University, Indiana University, Jewish Theological Seminary,
Oxford University, Rutgers University, Stanford University, and the
University of Virginia. Many friends and colleagues over the years have
read drafts of chapters, provided bibliographical help, answered ques-
tions, or supplied important references. I regret that I have not been
more careful in keeping track of my debts, and at the great risk of omit-
ting someone's name, I should like to thank the following people:
Jonathan Berkey, David Biale, Jeremy Cohen, Uri Cohen, Theo Dagi,
William Darrow, Eva Frojmovic, Isaiah Gafni, Daniel Gordis, Daniel
Haberman, Michael Hammer, Jay Harris, Tal Ilan, Robin Judd, Bonnie
Kent, Gwen Kessler, Ora Limor, Kevin Madigan, Ivan Marcus, Saul
Olyan, Moshe Rosman, Jonathan Sarna, Michael Satlow, Menahem
Schmelzer, Bernard Septimus, David Sklare, Karen Stern, Mark Swan-
son, Elliot Wolfson, Abby Wyschogrod, and Mohammad Qasim Za-
man. To one and all, my deepest thanks. To those whose names I have
omitted, my deepest thanks and my sincerest apologies.

A few final notes. I use the masculine pronoun when referring to
God, because the Jews and Christians who are at the center of my work
regularly did so. All translations are mine unless otherwise noted. My
translations of the Tanakh are based on the New Jewish Version published by the Jewish Publication Society; verse numeration always follows the Hebrew. My translations of the New Testament are based on
the Revised Standard Version; my translations of ancient rabbinic literature are based on those published by the Soncino Press. In all cases I
have modified the underlying translations as I saw fit. Biblical translations, whether whole sentences or isolated words, whether from the
Jewish or the Christian Scriptures, are presented in *italics*. All dates in
this book are of the Common Era (CE) unless otherwise specified as before the Common Era (BCE).

An amusing anecdote. Over the years I have spoken about this project with many people. I explain to them that I am trying to understand
the significance of circumcision in Judaism given the fact that one half

of the Jewish people are not circumcised. One colleague, a learned and intelligent woman, at first reacted with the words "I did not know that so many Jews were uncircumcised!" After a long pause she said, "Oh, you mean women."

This book is dedicated to my wife, Miriam, who sustains me in all that I do.

PART ONE

Jewish Circumcision
and Christian Polemics

CHAPTER I

A Canonical History of Jewish Circumcision

The Caesar said to R. Tanhum, "Come, let us all become one people." R. Tanhum replied, "Very well! We who are circumcised cannot be like you. You become circumcised and be like us."

B. Sanhedrin 39a

What happens at a Jewish circumcision? A detailed account is provided by the famous essayist Michel de Montaigne (1533–1592), who, after witnessing a circumcision in Rome on January 30, 1581, wrote the following in his *Travel Journal:*

(1) On the 30th, he [Montaigne] went to see the most ancient religious ceremony there is among men, and watched it very attentively and with great profit: that is, the circumcision of the Jews.

(2) [A paragraph on the Sabbath services at the synagogue.]

(3a) But as for the circumcision, it is done in private houses, in the most convenient and lightest room in the infant's house. Where he [Montaigne] was, because the house was inconvenient, the ceremony was performed at the entrance door. They give the infants a godfather and a godmother, as we do; the father names the infant. They circumcise them on the eighth day from their birth. (3b) The godfather sits down on a table and puts a pillow on his lap; the godmother brings him the infant and then goes away. The infant is wrapped in our style; the godfather unwraps him below, and then those present and the man who is to do the operation all begin to sing, and accompany with songs all this action, which lasts a short quarter of an hour. (3c) The minister may be other than a rabbi, and whatever he may be among them, everyone wishes to be called to this office, for they hold that it is a great blessing to be employed at it often; indeed, they pay to be invited to do it, offering, one a garment, another some other useful thing for the infant; and they hold that he who has circumcised up to a certain number, which they know, when he is dead has this privilege, that the parts of his mouth are never eaten by worms.

3

(4a) On the table where the godfather is seated, there is at the same time a great preparation of all the instruments necessary for this operation. Besides that, a man holds in his hands a phial full of wine and a glass. There is also a brazier on the ground at which brazier this minister first warms his hands and then, finding the child all stripped, as the godfather holds him on his lap with his head toward him, he takes hold of his member and with one hand pulls back toward himself the skin that is over it, with the other pushing the glans and the member within. To the end of this skin, which he holds toward the said glans, he applies a silver instrument which stops the said skin there and keeps the cutting edge from injuring the glans and the flesh. After that, with a knife he cuts off this skin, which is immediately buried in some earth, which is there in a basin among the other preparations for this mystery. (4b) After that the minister with his bare nails plucks up also some other particle of skin which is on this glans and tears it off by force and pushes the skin back beyond the glans.

(5a) It seems that there is much effort in this, and pain; however they find no danger in it, and the wound always heals in four or five days. The infant's cry is like that of ours when they are baptized. (5b) As soon as this glans is thus uncovered, they hastily offer some wine to the minister, who puts a little in his mouth and then goes and sucks the glans of this child, all bloody, and spits out the blood he has drawn from it, and immediately takes as much wine again, up to three times. (5c) This done, he is offered, in a little paper cup, some red powder which they say is dragon's blood, with which he salts and covers the whole wound; and then he very tidily wraps this boy's member with cloths cut specially for this. (5d) That done, he is given a glass full of wine, which wine they say he blesses by some prayers that he says. He takes a swallow of it, and then by dipping his finger in it he three times takes a drop of it with his finger to the boy's mouth to be sucked; and afterward this same glass, just as it is, is sent to the mother and the women, who are in some other part of the house, to drink what wine is left. (5e) Besides that, another person takes a silver instrument, round as a tennis ball, held by a long handle (which instrument is pierced with little holes, like our perfuming pans), and carries it to the nose, first of the minister, and then of the infant, and then of the godfather: they suppose that these are odors to confirm and enlighten minds for devotion. He meanwhile still has his mouth all bloody.[1]

Montaigne knew no Hebrew and had little familiarity with Jews and Judaism, yet his account of the circumcision ceremony is extraordinarily accurate—in rigorously traditional circles it is still carried out almost exactly as Montaigne described it over four centuries ago. As Montaigne describes it, the ceremony takes place before a congregation of men; a female intermediary (the "godmother") takes the baby from the mother and brings him to the man (the "godfather") upon whose lap the circumcision will take place; she immediately retreats to the place of the women (3b, 5d). The minister, that is, the circumciser (in Jewish circles generally known as the *mohel*), is not necessarily the rabbi of the community, or indeed, a rabbi at all (3c). The ritual is accompanied by prayers (5d), wine (5d), and fragrance (5e). The act of circumcision takes place in three stages: first, the actual cutting of the foreskin (4a); second, the removal of the membrane under the foreskin (4b); third, the suctioning (5b) and dressing (5c) of the wound. The baby is named by the father (3a).

Montaigne based his account not only on what he saw but also on what he heard. Twice he tells the reader that the Jews have explained something to him: "they say" that the red powder is dragon's blood (5c), and "they say" that the wine is blessed by some prayers (5d). Other parts of the account, too, undoubtedly are based on oral information: how else, for example, could Montaigne have known that the Jews believe that circumcision protects the mouth of the circumciser from corruption after death (3c)? At least two points Montaigne seems to know on his own: He knows that a Jewish circumcision takes place on the eighth day and he knows that a boy receives his name at his circumcision. Montaigne knows these two points from the Bible and does not need to ask his informants about them.[2] The result is that he does not know precisely when in the ceremony the baby is named, and this point is narrated out of sequence (3a).

Montaigne's account is remarkable not only for its accuracy but also for its sympathy. Despite centuries of Christian polemic against Judaism, Jewish law, and Jewish circumcision, Montaigne approaches Jewish circumcision, "the most ancient religious ceremony there is among men" (1), sympathetically and without prejudice.[3] In describing this ritual, *the* most celebrated mark of Jewish difference vis-à-vis Christians, he remarks on the commonalities that link Jew and Christian.[4] The Jews "give the boys a godfather and a godmother, as we do" (3a), and the infant "is wrapped in our style" (3b). Montaigne assimilates Jewish circumcision to Christian baptism. Circumcision, like baptism and the other sacraments of the church, is a "mystery" (4a). "The boy's outcry is like that of ours when they are baptized" (5a). He attributes to the Jews an understanding of the power of incense ("they suppose that these are odors to confirm and enlighten minds for devotion" [5e]) that is identical with his own.[5] The only aspect of the ritual that appears to bother Montaigne is the *metzitzah*, the suctioning of the circumcision wound by the circumciser (5b). The last sentence of the account is "He [the circumciser] meanwhile still has his mouth all bloody." Montaigne was not the first or last Christian to be shocked by this practice.

Montaigne gives an accurate description of the circumcision of an eight-day-old Jewish boy but says nothing about the meaning of the ritual. This did not concern him in his *Travel Journal,* written in 1581. No doubt if asked why the Jews circumcise their sons he would have replied that they do so in the first instance because the Lord in Genesis 17 commanded them, and Jews, not being Christians, observe the commandments of the "Old Testament." But this explanation was not sufficient, as Montaigne himself and other scholars of his time realized. In the sixteenth century explorers and missionaries brought back to Europe the amazing news that many of the native peoples of Africa, the Americas, Australia, and Polynesia, peoples who knew nothing whatever about God, about the Bible, or about the Jews, also circumcised their sons. In some of his *Essays,* written in 1588, Montaigne discusses the diversity of humanity's habits and the curious fact that distant peoples sometimes have customs that mimic those of Europeans. He observes:

> We have newly discovered peoples who, as far as we know, have never heard of us, yet where they believe in circumcision.[6]

A page or two later he writes:

> That reminds me of another pleasing example of diversity: some peoples like to uncover the end of the penis, circumcising the foreskin like Jews or Moslems, whereas others have such conscientious objections to ever uncovering it that, lest the top of it should ever see the light of day, they scrupulously stretch the foreskin right over it and tie it together with little cords.[7]

In another essay of the same period he writes:

> In their religions all peoples have several similarities which coincide, such as sacrifices, lights, incense, fastings, offertories and, among others, the condemnation of this act [that is, the act of sexual intercourse]. All their opinions come to it, not to mention the widespread practice of cutting off the foreskin which is a punishment for it.[8]

In these passages Montaigne adumbrates the crucial point: even if circumcision marks Jews as different vis-à-vis Christians, it does not mark

Jews as distinctive within the cultures of the world. On the contrary, many other cultures practice circumcision, despite never having had any contact with Jews. In this perspective, circumcision and, for that matter, the absence of circumcision, are just two of the many habits and customs that characterize human societies around the world. What then, if anything, is special about Jewish circumcision? Why did the Lord choose circumcision as the vehicle for his covenant with the people of Israel? Why do other peoples practice circumcision? These questions emerge implicitly but unmistakably from Montaigne's brief references to circumcision in the *Essays*.

From Montaigne's time to our own, numerous scholars, theologians, missionaries, philosophers, anthropologists, sociologists, psychologists, psychiatrists, physicians, and historians have advanced a bewildering variety of explanations for this powerful human impulse to cut away a piece of the penis.[9] There is little unanimity on the subject. Quite the contrary:

> An unwieldy array of functions, features, causes, and effects has been attributed to circumcision and associated rites: age-grade bonding and generation dividing; social exchange and rivalry; spilling blood, inflicting ordeals, remaindering prepuces, occasioning stoicism . . . ; making boys into men, ordinary men into prophets, a people into chosen or condemned, men into women ("symbolic wounds"), phalluses into vaginas, human penises into marsupial-like ones (Australia) or rhinoceros-like ones (Borneo); to enhance or diminish virility, fertility, sacrality, holiness, or other kind of potency, either to augment or to limit population growth, and thereby curing or causing disease.[10]

Circumcision has been understood to mean almost anything—and its opposite.

I am not going to enter the fray. I do not pretend that I have found the "real" meaning of circumcision or that I can answer the questions implicitly posed by Montaigne. My goals here are more modest. The central chapters of this book are devoted to a selection of texts written by rabbinic Jews in Europe between ca. 1100 and ca. 1400. In this chapter, I survey the meanings that are attributed to circumcision in the sources that these rabbinic Jews regarded as canonical, that is, the Bible, the Mishnah and Talmud, and later rabbinic works. These are the texts that medieval Jews knew and revered, and these are the texts whose teachings about circumcision are of concern to us.[11]

I begin at the beginning, the book of Genesis.

Genesis 17: The Covenant and the Sign of the Covenant

The longest and richest biblical account of circumcision is Genesis 17, the chapter in which God instructs Abraham to circumcise himself and all the males of his household. The chapter consists of four paragraphs. The opening sentences of the first paragraph establish the theme: God tells Abram *Walk in my ways and be blameless. I will establish my covenant between me and you, and I will make you exceedingly numerous* (Genesis 17:1–2). The theme is covenant and fertility. In the remaining verses of the paragraph (Genesis 17:3–8), God promises no fewer than four times that Abram shall be the father of many nations and changes Abram's name to Abraham, "father of a multitude." God also promises to give the land of Canaan to Abraham's descendants as an everlasting possession. The first paragraph, then, details God's obligation under the covenant (fertility, land); the second paragraph (Genesis 17:9–14) details Abraham's part:

> (9) God further said to Abraham: As for you, you and your offspring to come throughout the ages shall keep my covenant. (10) Such shall be the covenant between me and you and your offspring to follow which you shall keep: every male among you shall be circumcised. (11) You shall circumcise the flesh of your foreskin, and that shall be the sign of the covenant between me and you. (12) And throughout the generations, every male among you shall be circumcised at the age of eight days. As for the home-born slave and the one bought from an outsider who is not of your offspring, (13) they must be circumcised, home-born and purchased alike. Thus shall my covenant be marked in your flesh as an everlasting pact. (14) And if any male who is foreskinned fails to circumcise the flesh of his foreskin, that person shall be cut off from his kin; he has broken my covenant.

In return for the gifts of fertility and land promised in the first paragraph, in this second paragraph God demands circumcision, not just of Abraham himself but of all the males in the household.

The third paragraph (Genesis 17:15–22) concerns Sarai and Ishmael:

> (15) And God said to Abraham, "As for your wife Sarai, you shall not call her Sarai, but her name shall be Sarah. (16) I will bless her; indeed, I will give you a son by her. I will bless her so that she shall give rise to nations."

Abraham is incredulous that he and Sarah will yet have a son; he thanks God for the birth of Ishmael, born to Abraham from his concubine Hagar. God replies that he shall bless Ishmael too:

(21) But my covenant I will maintain with Isaac, whom Sarah shall bear
to you at this season next year.

Ishmael has God's blessing, but it is Isaac, to be born to Abraham from
Sarah, who is the bearer of the covenant, the subject of the first two
paragraphs.

The fourth and final paragraph (Genesis 17:23–27) is a narrative describing how Abraham fulfilled God's instructions. He circumcised himself, Ishmael, all his home-born slaves, and all his purchased slaves.
Later, when Isaac is born, we are told that Abraham circumcised him on
the eighth day, as the Lord had commanded him (Genesis 21:4). Abraham lived up to his part of the covenant.

Modern scholars agree that Genesis 17 is composite, the product of a
long history of transmission and edition. The second and fourth paragraphs, which speak about circumcision, appear to have no organic
connection with the first and third paragraphs, which speak about
covenant and name change. Each of the paragraphs contains its share of
repetitions and infelicitous transitions. Modern scholars also agree that
Genesis 17 is a product of the Priestly school of Pentateuchal writers
(known as the Priestly source or "P"), even if there is strong disagree-
ment on the setting and dating of this source. According to the once-
regnant scholarly view, P is a product of the sixth or fifth century BCE—
a response to the destruction of the Jerusalem temple in 587. According
to other scholarly views, however, which have been in the ascendant for
the last twenty years or so, P is the product not of the sixth or fifth century BCE but of the seventh or eighth century BCE, not of the exile but of
the period long before it. This scholarly debate is important, of course,
but ultimately irrelevant for my purposes.[12] I am interested here in the
canonical history of ideas; the Jews of antiquity and the Middle Ages
read Genesis 17 as a seamless whole and as integral part of the five
books of Moses, and in their wake I am doing so as well. Taken as it
stands, what does Genesis 17 say about the circumcision of men and the
non-circumcision of women?

The theme of the chapter is covenant, *berit* in Hebrew (also translit-
erated as *brith* or *bris*). The word "covenant," *berit*, appears four times
in the first paragraph, six times in the second, and three times in the
third. A *berit* is a covenant, alliance, or treaty between two parties,
whether of equal or unequal status, that spells out the obligations incumbent on each.[13] Genesis 17 depicts a covenant between unequal parties, God and Abraham. In the first paragraph God promises Abraham

fertility and land; in the second paragraph God demands circumcision. This covenant is similar, as many scholars have noted, to the covenant depicted in Genesis 15. In that chapter too, God promises Abraham progeny and land, but instead of having him circumcise himself, God has Abraham march through the carcasses of some animals that had been dismembered for the purpose (hence the rabbinic name for that covenant, "the covenant between the sections"). Circumcision here corresponds to the severed animals there; both are covenantal rituals.

The connection between circumcision and covenant in Genesis 17 is explicit, but the chapter seems to present three different formulations of the idea. First, as the logic of the chapter dictates, circumcision is an obligation incumbent on the Israelites under the terms of the covenant between Abraham and God. God will make Abraham's descendants a mighty nation and give them the land of Canaan, and in return they must circumcise all their males. Second, in a somewhat puzzling formulation, circumcision is said to be the covenant itself: *Such shall be the covenant between me and you and your offspring to follow which you shall keep: every male among you shall be circumcised* (Genesis 17:10). In other words, circumcision *is* the covenant, and the covenant *is* circumcision. What this might mean, I cannot rightly say.[14] Verse 11 advances yet a third view: *You shall circumcise the flesh of your foreskin, and that shall be the sign of the covenant between me and you.* Here circumcision is understood as *the* (or, in an alternative translation, *a*) *sign of the covenant* (in Hebrew, *ot berit*). In context this means that circumcision is a visible reminder to God of the covenant he has made with Abraham and Abraham's descendants. Similarly, the priestly writer also depicts the rainbow that appeared in the sky after the flood as a "sign of the covenant" between God and Noah (Genesis 9:12–17):

> This is the sign that I set for the covenant between me and you, and every living creature with you, for all ages to come. I have set my bow in the clouds, and it shall serve as a sign of the covenant between me and the earth. When I bring clouds over the earth, and the bow appears in the clouds, I will remember my covenant between me and you and every living creature among all flesh, so that the waters shall never again become a flood to destroy all flesh. When the bow is in the clouds, I will see it and remember the everlasting covenant between God and all living creatures, all flesh that is on earth. That . . . shall be the sign of the covenant that I have established. . . .

Like circumcision, the rainbow is an *ot berit*, a sign of the covenant. By looking at the rainbow, God is reminded of his covenant with Noah not to destroy the world in another flood. By looking at Abraham's circumcision, God is reminded of his covenant with Abraham to make him fertile and to give his descendants the land of Canaan.[15]

As we shall see, later Jews and Christians had a completely different understanding of circumcision's status as a sign of the covenant. Both Jews and Christians understood circumcision as a sign of Jewish difference from gentiles. Circumcision, like the fringes *(tzitzit)* on garments, the one a hidden sign and the other an overt sign, marked Jews as distinct.[16] For Jews, of course, this difference was a good thing, a function of virtue and piety and a manifestation of the divine election of Israel. In Christian exegesis, the mark of circumcision came to be understood as a stigma, a sign of rejection, punishment, and humiliation, a "mark of Cain."[17] Needless to say, both of these readings discover meanings not in the text.

Why is the covenant associated with circumcision? Why is circumcision presented as the chief obligation under the covenant, the very covenant itself, and the sign of the covenant? The parallel with Genesis 15 suggests that confirming a covenant in ancient Israel requires a "cutting": one "cuts a covenant," just as in English one can "cut a deal." In Genesis 15 animals are cut; in Genesis 17 the foreskin is cut.[18] And why, of all parts of the body, should the penis be cut? Why not the earlobe, the toe, the nose? The answer is obvious: circumcision, like the covenant itself, is about procreation and fertility. Circumcision has a beneficial effect on Abraham's fecundity. God promises Abraham a mighty progeny on condition that Abraham circumcise himself. The promise is kept. Abraham is nearly one hundred years old, has long been married to his wife, but does not yet have a true heir. Immediately after being circumcised, that is, in the next chapter, God announces to Abraham that Sarah will conceive. She does, and the chosen son, the son of the covenant, is born. Philo offers a medical explanation for the beneficial effects of circumcision: it promotes fertility by giving semen an unobstructed path.[19]

In numerous cultures circumcision is connected with marriage. There may be some memory of this practice behind the story in Genesis 34 (treated more fully below), in which the sons of Jacob tell Hamor, the chieftain of Shechem, that if his son wishes to marry their sister Dinah, he must first be circumcised. Similarly, Zipporah's mysterious utterance *A bridegroom of blood you are to me* (Exodus 4:25) might suggest a connection between circumcision and marriage. In his commentary on this verse, R. Abraham ibn Ezra (1089–1164) notes that "the women call a child a bridegroom *[hatan]* when he enters the covenant."[20] Islamic culture, too, preserved the memory of the connection between circumcision and marriage. On the day of the circumcision, the boy, who is typically six to eight years old, as well as the celebrants, dress up as if for a wedding; the boy is marched in procession as if he were a bridegroom (or a bride!); and a meal rivaling a wedding feast is served.[21] The Arabic name for circumcision, *khitan,* has sometimes been connected with the Semitic root meaning "to establish a family relationship by marriage" (cf. Hebrew *hatan,* "groom"; *hôtên,* "father-in-law").

From fertility to land is not a big step. If circumcision helps guarantee the birth of sons, surely the sons need a patrimony to inherit. God promises Abraham a mighty brood and a land : the land of Canaan. In the book of Joshua (5:2–12), just after crossing the Jordan and just before celebrating the Passover and eating of the produce of the holy land for the first time, the Israelites are circumcised by Joshua. (The text explains that the Israelites, while wandering in the desert for forty years, had not been circumcised.) The story marks the connection not only between circumcision and Passover, a connection that I will discuss in a moment, but also between circumcision and the possession of the land. Circumcision prepares the Israelites for their conquest and possession of the land promised by God to Abraham.

Circumcision, then, guarantees male fertility and the gift of the land. But fecund males cannot accomplish much without fecund females. What of Sarah? Genesis 17 sends out decidedly mixed signals regarding Sarah and her status. On the one hand, Sarah's non-circumcision seems to betoken her adjunctive quality among the covenantal people. Her motherhood is not celebrated the way Abraham's fatherhood is celebrated. Abraham will be *the father of a multitude of nations* (Genesis 17:4–5), but Sarah is not given the title "mother of nations." The Torah declares, *She shall give rise to nations; rulers of peoples shall issue from her* (Genesis 17:16), but the nations and peoples that she is to bear are Abraham's. He is the father and she is his reproductive agent; Sarah is not a covenantal person in her own right. The word *berit* appears thirteen times in Genesis 17, but not once is the word or concept associated with Sarah. Her son Isaac is to be the bearer of the covenant: *Sarah your wife shall bear you a son . . . and I will maintain my covenant with him as an everlasting covenant. . . . But my covenant I will maintain with Isaac, whom Sarah shall bear to you* (Genesis 17:19, 21). Sarah's husband and son are to be the bearers of the covenant, not she. Sarah has no mark on her flesh to indicate her subservience to the covenant, to embody the covenant, and to remind God of the covenant. Various scholars have argued that circumcision in Genesis 17 functions as a counterbalance to maternity. Circumcision is a hallmark of paternity, patriliny, and patriarchy. Abraham is circumcised; Sarah gives birth. Circumcision trumps birth, since paternal filiation outweighs the maternal.[22]

All of this is on the one hand. On the other hand, maternal filiation is essential to the covenantal process. Abraham circumcises Ishmael, but that circumcision does not give Ishmael covenantal status. He is the son of the maidservant Hagar; circumcision does not trump his birth. Isaac, the son who will be circumcised on the eighth day, will be the bearer of the covenant because he is the son of Sarah. Hence, while it is certainly correct to say that in Genesis 17 circumcision is a celebration of maleness and fatherhood, it is certainly incorrect to say that in Genesis 17 circumcision is *only* or even *primarily* a celebration of maleness and fatherhood.[23]

The status of Sarah mirrors the status of Ishmael. Sarah does not bear the mark of the covenant on her body, but she is nonetheless essential to the perpetuation of the covenant and is part of the covenantal people. In contrast, Ishmael is circumcised, as are slaves, both home-born and purchased, but neither his circumcision nor theirs gives any of them special status in the divine order. Hence a double paradox: a Sarah paradox and an Ishmael paradox. *The Sarah paradox:* if the covenant is circumcision, then Sarah, and by extension all Israelite and Jewish women, who are not circumcised, must be excluded, but they are not excluded. On the contrary: motherhood matters. (Indeed, with the emergence of the matrilineal principle in rabbinic Judaism, motherhood matters a great deal, since the religious status of the offspring of intermarriage follows that of the mother.)[24] *The Ishmael paradox:* if circumcision is the covenant, then Ishmael, and by extension all circumcised gentiles, should be part of the covenantal people, but they are not. The non-circumcision of Sarah and of all Jewish women, and the circumcision of Ishmael and of many other non-Israelite groups, provided fodder to later Christians who sought to impugn the covenantal value of circumcision, as we shall see in chapter 3. The Sarah paradox is the subject of this book.

Genesis 34: Tribal Mark

Genesis 34 is one of the most troubling chapters in the book of Genesis—perhaps in the Bible as a whole. The story is as follows: Dinah,

daughter of Jacob, is carried off and raped by Shechem, the eponymous
magnate of the town of Shechem. Now deeply in love with his victim,
the rapist becomes a suitor; his father approaches Jacob to request the
girl's hand in marriage. The father proposes to Jacob a series of marital
alliances between the two groups; Shechem himself offers to pay Jacob
any bride price he demands, no matter how high. Jacob says nothing.
His sons, Dinah's brothers, make a counter-offer:

> We cannot do this thing, to give our sister to a man who has a foreskin,
> for that is a disgrace among us. Only on this condition will we agree with
> you: that you will become like us in that every male among you is cir-
> cumcised. Then will we give our daughters to you and take your daugh-
> ters to ourselves; and we will dwell among you and become as one kin-
> dred. But if you will not listen to us and become circumcised, we will take
> our daughter and go [Genesis 34:14–17].

The narrator comments that the brothers spoke *with deceit* because
Shechem *had defiled* their sister (Genesis 34:13). The story now proceeds to its operatic conclusion. The Shechemites accept the proposal of
the sons of Israel and circumcise themselves en masse. On the third day,
when they were all in great pain from the procedure, Simeon and Levi,
two of Dinah's brothers, raided the city and killed all the males, including Shechem himself and his father. They took Dinah and left. The other
brothers plundered the town, because *they* [why the plural?] *had defiled
their sister* (Genesis 34:27). Jacob condemns Simeon and Levi, arguing
that the attack will cause the remaining peoples of Canaan to loathe the
sons of Israel and perhaps to attack them. Simeon and Levi reply, *shall
he treat our sister as a whore?* Here the story ends.

This tale of rustic chivalry has long troubled readers. The punishment inflicted by Simeon and Levi is far more severe than the crime
would justify. According to Deuteronomy 22:28–29 the rapist of an
unmarried virgin is to be punished by being forced to marry his victim
and to indemnify her father for his loss of the bride price. This is precisely the punishment that Shechem proposed for himself; in fact he offered far more than the fifty pieces of silver required by Deuteronomy.
Why then should he have been killed? And why were all the towns-
people killed—what evil did *they* commit? Furthermore, when Jacob
learns of what Simeon and Levi had done, his sole concern is that his
reputation may suffer; he seems oblivious to the evil that they committed.[25] Feminist scholars have observed that Dinah is silent throughout the story; she is acted upon but does not act. First she is acted

upon by Shechem, her raptor, and is then acted upon by Simeon and Levi, her rescuers. Was she really raped? Was she really rescued? Perhaps Dinah's dalliance with Shechem was entirely volitional, but the brothers—and the narrator—could not abide it because it flouted convention and therefore defined it as "rape." And having been "raped," perhaps Dinah would have preferred to remain where she was, rather than be "rescued."[26] She is not given the opportunity to speak or express her opinion.

The references to circumcision in Genesis 34 also trouble and puzzle. If we are meant to read Genesis 34 in the light of Genesis 17, that is, if we are meant to understand that circumcision is a covenantal mark that binds Israel to God, then we are puzzled how Simeon and Levi could offer circumcision to people whom they intend to kill. Later readers felt a need to rewrite the story radically.[27] And there is something of a puzzle in the brothers' offer of intermarriage with the Shechemites. We know that they were speaking with deceit, but what exactly constitutes their deceit? May we conclude from the story that in ancient Israel a foreign male normally would be allowed to marry a native Israelite woman provided that he first was circumcised? If so, the brothers' deceit lay in the insincerity of their offer: they pretended that the normal procedure would be followed here too. Or perhaps the brothers' deceit was even more thorough-going: the entire offer was a sham and a farce, since foreign males, circumcised or not, were never welcomed as marriage partners for Israelite women. The text can be construed either way, and both options have been defended by the commentators.

A few things nonetheless seem certain. The text associates the foreskin with *shame* (Genesis 34:14), thus anticipating the rabbinic texts that declare the foreskin to be "disgusting" or "loathsome."[28] The text also associates the foreskin with "impurity" or "defilement" (Genesis 34:13 and 27), thus anticipating the rabbinic texts that ascribe ritual impurity to foreskinned men.[29] Most important, Genesis 34, when read on its own, seems to understand circumcision not in terms of covenant but in terms of a tribal mark, an ethnic habit. Circumcision is one of the things that we do. If you wish to join us, then be like us and do as we do: circumcise your males. God, covenant, sign of the covenant, paternity, the land, fertility—all of these have no bearing on the text. The circumcision of the Israelite foreskin is a sign of difference vis-à-vis the Shechemites, but that difference is not invested here with any theological or covenantal meaning.

Exodus 4 and the Passover

A remarkable and remarkably obscure story is told in Exodus 4:24–26. After being commissioned by God to redeem the Israelites, Moses took his wife Zipporah and sons and set out for Egypt from Midian:

> (24) At a night encampment on the way, the Lord encountered him and sought to kill him. (25) So Zipporah took a flint and cut off her son's fore-skin, and touched his legs with it, saying "You are truly a bridegroom of blood to me." (26) And when he let him alone, she added, "A bridegroom of blood because of the circumcision."

These mysterious lines have puzzled commentators, ancient, medieval, and modern.[30] First is the problem with the pronouns. Whom did the Lord seek to kill—Moses? Moses's son? Whose legs did Zipporah touch with her son's foreskin—her son's? Moses's? the Lord's? Who is the "you" who is said to be a "bridegroom of blood"—Moses? Moses's son? Next are problems of meaning: Why did the Lord seek to kill him? What is the connection between circumcision and the cessation of the attack? What do Zipporah's two utterances mean? All is dark and mysterious. Perhaps the only point that is clear in this story is the apotropaic power of circumcision: circumcision wards away death.[31]

This point also emerges from the Passover narrative that unfolds in the following chapters. The Lord lets loose the Destroyer—the tenth and last plague before the exodus (Exodus 12:13, 23)—upon the houses of the Egyptians, killing every first born, both human and animal. The Israelites, however, are spared, protected by the blood of the Paschal sacrifice that they have daubed on the lintels and doorposts of their houses (Exodus 12:21–23). Like the circumcision performed by Zipporah, the Paschal sacrifice performed by the Israelites was apotropaic, warding away death. The two apotropaic rituals are brought together in the instructions for the Paschal sacrifice, which state that no man with a foreskin may eat of it (Exodus 12:48), as circumcision is a prerequisite for partaking of the sacrifice (Exodus 12:43–49). At the beginning of the Exodus narrative, God threatened Moses's son (or Moses himself) with death, but death was averted by circumcision. At the first climax of the Exodus narrative, God kills the first-born sons of the Egyptians but saves the sons of the Israelites through the Passover sacrifice, for which circumcision is a prerequisite. Perhaps we are meant to understand that what links circumcision to the Paschal sacrifice is blood: Zipporah's exclamation, *You are truly a bridegroom of blood to me*, suggests that circumcision blood, just like Paschal blood, is the stuff that keeps away the Destroyer. Similarly, perhaps by associating circumcision with the Paschal sacrifice, we are meant to consider circumcision as a type of sacrifice.[32] Both of these ideas, the power of circumcision blood and circumcision as sacrifice, are developed substantially in early medieval Judaism, as we shall see.

Another set of biblical passages suggests the complementary idea. If circumcision saves from death and destruction, as Exodus 4 and 12 imply, then the absence of circumcision should somehow be associated with death and destruction. This point appears explicitly in Ezekiel. In a series of visions, the prophet sees various kings and armies consigned to Sheol, the mysterious zone to which the shades of the dead go and which in some contexts is identified by later Jewish exegesis with Gehenna, what westerners call "hell." These kings and armies, the prophet says, are foreskinned; the connection between their intact genitals and their fate in the underworld is not explained by the prophet, but the connection is clear.[33]

Numerous rabbinic texts allude to the salvific, apotropaic power of circumcision, specifically, the power of circumcision to protect its bearer from punishment in the afterlife. The third of the three benedictions prescribed by the Talmud for recitation at the circumcision ritual, and still recited today, asks God that the just-circumcised baby be saved "from destruction," that is, from Gehenna.[34] The Midrash on Genesis recounts:

> R. Levi said: in the future to come, Abraham will sit at the entrance to Gehenna and will not permit any circumcised man of Israel to descend to its midst. And those that have sinned too much—what does He [God] do to them? He removes the foreskin from infants that died before they were circumcised, puts it on them, and brings them down to Gehenna. . . .[35]

Or, in another formulation:

> Circumcision is precious [before the Holy one, blessed be He, as is clear from the fact] that the Holy one, blessed be He, promised to Abraham that anyone who is circumcised will not descend to Gehenna . . . but the deniers and the sinners of Israel, who have denied the Holy one, blessed be He, and have followed the customs of the gentiles, even though they are circumcised, the Holy one, blessed be He, draws down their foreskin and they fall into Gehenna. . . .[36]

These texts carry forward the idea that circumcision protects its bearer from Gehenna and address two paradoxes connected with that idea.

First, what of the wicked? Are there not wicked Jews who on account of their heinous sins deserve to be punished in Gehenna, in spite of the fact that they are circumcised? Second, what of innocent babies who died before their eighth day—would they suffer torments of Gehenna because they happened to die before the arrival of the day appointed for their circumcision? Both texts answer the first question: in the case of sinners who "have sinned too much" or who deny God and follow the customs of the gentiles, their circumcision does not protect them at all, because God converts their circumcision into uncircumcision. How does He do that? In the second text God "draws down" the remains of the foreskin so as to conceal the circumcision. (As we shall see below, the rabbis themselves reformed the circumcision procedure so as to make such a drawing down difficult, if not impossible. But what is impossible for humans is not impossible for God.) The first text adopts a different strategy and thereby solves both logical problems at once. God removes the foreskin from dead infants, thereby rendering them circumcised and protected from the ravages of Gehenna, and affixes it to the membrum of the wicked, thus rendering them uncircumcised and unprotected. I shall return to this below.

Leviticus 12: Purification and Sacrifice

> (1) The Lord spoke to Moses saying: (2) Speak to the Israelite people thus: When a woman at childbirth bears a male, she shall be impure seven days; she shall be impure as at the time of her menstrual infirmity. (3) On the eighth day the flesh of his foreskin shall be circumcised. (4) She shall remain in a state of blood purification for thirty-three days: she shall not touch any consecrated thing, nor enter the sanctuary until her period of purification is completed. (5) If she bears a female, she shall be impure two weeks as during her menstruation, and she shall remain in a state of blood purification for sixty-six days. (6) On the completion of her period of purification, for either son or daughter, she shall bring to the priest, at the entrance of the Tent of Meeting, a lamb in its first year for a burnt offering, and a pigeon or a turtledove for a sin offering. (7) He shall offer it before the Lord and make expiation on her behalf; she shall then be pure from her flow of blood.

In this text circumcision is associated not with covenant but with purification. For the first seven days after giving birth to a son, a woman has the status of a menstruant (the rules governing menstrual impurity are spelled out in Leviticus 15). On the eighth day her impurity diminishes, and for the next thirty-three days she remains in a state of "blood purification." The meaning of this term and the conditions regulating this period are obscure, but the text clearly implies that it was a time of diminished impurity. She may not enter the sanctuary or touch any consecrated thing but otherwise is not as impure as a menstruant. Thus, the first seven days after giving birth to a son a woman is most impure, like a menstruant; for the next thirty-three days she is still impure, but to a lesser degree; finally, after forty days, she is to bring a sin offering and lose her impure status altogether. (In the case of a birth of a girl, these numbers are doubled: fourteen days of menstrual impurity, sixty-six days of intermediate impurity, for a total of eighty.)

Surely it is no coincidence that the eighth day after birth, the first day of diminished impurity for the mother, is also the day of circumcision for the infant. Before that point, the text suggests, the mother's impurity would have made the boy too impure for the ritual; after that point the mother's own purification is accomplished through waiting and through a sacrifice, while the boy's purification is accomplished through circumcision. The association of circumcision with purification is, I admit, at best implicit. Indeed, classical rabbinic exegesis denied that the infant boy was impure; according to the rabbis only the mother is impure, and only the mother requires purification. But at least one medieval rabbinic exegete saw that the implicit meaning of the passage is that the boy, at least for the first seven days, partakes of the impurity of his mother.[37] Furthermore, any number of biblical and rabbinic passages ascribe impurity to the foreskin, or speak of foreskinned men as impure, so it is not a stretch at all to see circumcision, the removal of the impure foreskin, as a kind of purification.[38]

The association of circumcision with purification is clear in other cultures too. Herodotus remarks that the Egyptians "practice circumcision for the sake of purity; for they prefer to be pure rather than handsome."[39] The association of circumcision with purification is evident also in one of the Arabic names for circumcision, *tuhr*, which means "purification" (cf. Hebrew *toharah*). For Muslims, circumcision renders the body pure (or clean) and thus fit for prayer.

The language of Leviticus 12 closely parallels the language of Leviticus 22:27 (and Exodus 22:29), thus suggesting yet another association by which circumcision might be interpreted. Leviticus 22:27 reads, *When an ox or a sheep or a goat is born, it shall stay seven days with its mother, and from the eighth day on it shall be acceptable as an offering by fire to the Lord.* Notions of impurity and purification are irrelevant in this context, since a mother ox is not menstrually impure and does not need purification. There is some other logic at work which declares that for seven days a newborn belongs with its mother and that on the eighth day *it shall be acceptable as an offering . . . to the Lord.* What that logic is, we can only speculate, but the conclusion is clear: eight-day-old animals are sacrificed, eight-day-old boys are circumcised. Circumcision is analogous to, and a surrogate for, sacrifice. Even without the parallel of Leviticus 22:27 (and Exodus 22:29), Leviticus 12 by itself suggests the association of circumcision with sacrifice, since the mother is purified by a sin offering, and the baby is purified—if my interpretation is correct—by his circumcision. The association of circumcision with sacrifice, implicit in Leviticus 12, especially in comparison with Leviticus 22, becomes explicit in later Jewish tradition and has often been commented upon by anthropologists. I shall return to this below.

Leviticus 12, then, implicitly sees circumcision as purification and sacrifice. What is striking is that Leviticus 12 says nothing about circumcision as covenant. Perhaps the authors of Leviticus 12 knew Genesis 17, and presumed that the reader would too, and therefore thought that a simple reminder such as *On the eighth day the flesh of his foreskin shall be circumcised* would suffice to evoke the covenantal theology of the earlier chapter. Perhaps. But taken by itself, Leviticus 12 omits any reference to covenant. Some medieval Jewish thinkers preferred to see Leviticus 12, rather than Genesis 17, as the scriptural warrant for the commandment of circumcision, because Leviticus 12 is part of the divine revelation of the Torah to Moses and the people of Israel, whereas Genesis 17 is pre-Sinaitic, the private revelation of God to Abraham.[40] This approach will allow Maimonides and some other thinkers to decovenantalize circumcision, as we shall see. Furthermore by omitting the covenantal theology of Genesis, Leviticus 12 also avoids the paradoxical exclusion of Sarah (and all women) from the covenant. Infant boys are to be circumcised, parturient women are to be purified; neither ritual, at least as presented by Leviticus 12, is any more covenantal than the other. When read in conjunction with Genesis 17, Leviticus 12 will suggest to other Jewish thinkers that if circumcision is the covenantal ritual for the infant boy, then the purification ritual must be the covenantal ritual for his mother. By properly observing the restrictions associated with the impurity caused by menstruation and parturition, and by properly purifying themselves afterwards, Jewish women are not simply observing a divine requirement; they are embodying the covenant between God and Israel. I shall return to this idea in chapter 7.

Circumcision in Classical Rabbinic Literature

Classical rabbinic literature, that is, the Mishnah, the Yerushalmi (the Talmud of the land of Israel), the Bavli (the Talmud of Babylonia), and related works redacted between ca. 200 CE and 600 CE, carries forward much of the biblical legacy concerning circumcision, as we have already seen. It also attests or presumes many new practices and conceptions. I treat five of these briefly.[41]

1. Covenantal Circumcision and Non-covenantal Circumcision

During the last centuries BCE and the first century CE, circumcision was deemed efficacious no matter how, under what circumstances, or by whom it was performed. It was a surgical procedure, a physical operation on a piece of skin. The circumciser did not even have to be a Jew, let alone a priest or a sage.[42] Intention was irrelevant; involuntary circumcision was fine, too.[43] As long as his foreskin was removed, a man could present himself as a convert—or as a Jew. This view persists in the Mishnah and in rabbinic Judaism generally. Thus rabbinic law permits the conversion of children and the circumcision of slaves even against their will.[44] This position is well articulated by R. Yosi in a statement that is transmitted in three different versions: "Where have we seen circumcision that is not for the sake of the covenant?" "Where have we seen that the Torah requires circumcision to be for the sake [of the covenant]?" or "Where have we found in the Torah that circumcision requires [proper] intent?"[45]

By R. Yosi's time (mid-second century), however, a contrary position was emerging. Some rabbis distinguished non-covenantal circumcision, the removal of a piece of skin, from covenantal circumcision or *berit*, the removal of that same piece of skin but under religious auspices and for religious purposes. For a circumcision to be covenantal, it must be performed by a Jew and with the intent of denoting subservience to the God of the Jews and His commandments. R. Judah, a contemporary of R. Yosi, seems to be the primary authority behind this view. He argues against R. Yosi that neither a gentile nor a Samaritan may circumcise a Jew, the former because he is not part of the covenant, the latter because he will not perform the ritual with the proper intent.[46] R. Judah's view, which accords remarkably with that of the church father Origen,[47] gradually became normative in rabbinic law in the following generations. Under its influence, the circumcision of infants, and soon of converts as well, took on a "religious" character, accompanied by benedictions and prayers. As we shall see in a moment, the sacralization of infant circumcision continued apace in the post-talmudic period.

2. Covenantal Circumcision and Conversion to Judaism

The association of circumcision with conversion to Judaism is well attested in the first century CE in the works of Philo, Paul, and Josephus. The rabbis make the requirement explicit and put circumcision in the context of a formal conversion ritual. That ritual, in turn, presumes the view of R. Judah: circumcision changes a gentile into a Jew if it is performed in the proper context with the proper intent.[48]

The circumcision of an eight-day-old male infant is surgically identical with the circumcision of a male convert to Judaism of whatever age: the same piece of skin is removed in the same way. Surgical parity, however, does not necessarily imply ideological parity, and indeed there cannot be ideological parity between the two. Male and female offspring of a Jewish mother are Jewish by birth under Jewish law; the male offspring are Jewish by birth even if they are left uncircumcised. But a gentile male cannot convert to Judaism unless he is circumcised; without circumcision he remains a gentile. The circumcision of an eight-day old Jewish boy must have a different function, therefore, than the circumcision of a male convert to Judaism. This distinction would appear to be obvious and compelling, but no classic rabbinic text advances this argument, leaving room for medieval and modern jurists to debate the matter.[49]

3. Circumcision Sometimes Can Be Postponed or Omitted

The rabbis also discuss the practicality of circumcision on the eighth day if the baby is too weak or sick to withstand the procedure. Some Jews argued that the commandment of circumcision on the eighth day is an absolute requirement that trumps every other consideration—even the life of the child.[50] This is not the rabbinic position, as the following story shows:

> R. Nathan said:
>
> When I was in Mazaca of Cappadocia [the following incident oc-
> curred]: a woman there would give birth to boys, but when they were cir-
> cumcised they would die. She circumcised the first and he died, the second
> and he died. The third she brought before me. I saw that he was green.[51]
> I examined him and did not find the blood of the covenant [or: blood suf-
> ficient for the circumcision] in him.
>
> They said to me: Should we circumcise him?
>
> I said to them: Wait until blood enters into him.
>
> They waited [for the blood to enter him], and they circumcised him,
> and he lived. And they called him "Nathan the Babylonian" after me.[52]

R. Nathan's view became normative in rabbinic law. Better that a baby
be circumcised after the eighth day and live, than be circumcised on the
eighth day and die. If there is any doubt, the circumcision is postponed
until the baby is well.

But what if the baby is never well enough to withstand a circumcision? The classic illustration of this question is the case in which a
baby's older brothers had died as a result of their circumcision. In the
case analyzed by R. Nathan, perhaps a case of jaundice, the newborn
baby ultimately can be circumcised with no risk. But in the case of hemophilia, for example, a baby will never be able to be circumcised.[53] If
a baby suffers from a chronic infirmity that renders circumcision dangerous, he is left uncircumcised and may indeed grow into adulthood,
be a member of the Jewish community, and marry a Jewish wife. This
uncircumcised Jew suffers a few minor disabilities in rabbinic law, but
he is otherwise no less a Jew than his circumcised peers.[54] In rabbinic
law, circumcision is not always essential to Jewishness; a man can be a
Jew in good standing, under certain circumstances, even if he is foreskinned. I return to this in chapter 7.

The rabbis also discuss the paired cases of a baby born without a
foreskin and an already circumcised gentile converting to Judaism. In
each case there is no foreskin to cut—what to do? In a rather confusing
passage, the House of Hillel and the House of Shammai are said to
agree that in at least one of these two cases, if not both, "the dripping of
covenantal blood" would be required, that is, some blood would be ex-
tracted from that place on the body to which the foreskin had previously been attached.[55]

The boy born circumcised, that is, born without a foreskin, also
makes an appearance in rabbinic lore. According to one list-maker, the
following biblical worthies emerged into the world already circumcised:

Job, Adam, Seth, Noah, Shem (identified with Melchizedek), Jacob, Joseph, Moses, Balaam, Samuel, David, Jeremiah, and Zerubavel.[56] It is likely that this list is a compilation of various sublists, each with its own purpose and setting. That Moses was born circumcised was a widespread midrashic motif, attested even in pre-rabbinic texts.[57] The claim that Adam was created circumcised may have been intended to respond to those heretics (Christians, for example) who argued the contrary.[58] The claim that various biblical worthies were born circumcised is based on the idea that such a birth is a sign of special status and favor; the same claim appears in various Muslim traditions about Muhammed.[59] What Balaam the wicked is doing here, I do not know.

4. Surgical Details

The rabbis spell out the surgical details of the circumcision ritual.[60] The context of this discussion is the observance of the Sabbath. All actions "necessary for a circumcision" override the Sabbath; actions that are not necessary for a circumcision do not. And which actions, essential for a circumcision, are performed even on the Sabbath? There are four:[61]

> circumcision
>
> uncovering [the corona]
>
> suctioning
>
> placing a bandage and cumin.

These are the same steps that are inventoried by Montaigne in his description of the circumcision ritual. First is the circumcision itself, in Hebrew called *milah:* the foreskin is cut off. Second is the uncovering (in Hebrew, *peri'ah*) of the corona, the "crown" or tip of the penis; the corona is completely bared by the removal of the membrane that adheres to it even after the foreskin has been removed. The circumcision removes the foreskin; the uncovering removes the membrane. The Mishnah states that if a circumcision does not remove the shreds that cover the corona, the circumcision is invalid; "if [the circumciser] circumcised but did not uncover the circumcision, it is as if he had not circumcised at all."[62] Next is the suctioning of the wound, in Hebrew called *metzitzah.* Last, the wound is bandaged and receives an application of cumin.

These mishnaic requirements have three sources: the Torah, which requires circumcision *(milah)*; the rabbis themselves, who added the requirement of completely uncovering the corona *(peri'ah)*; and ancient medical beliefs about the treatment of wounds (suctioning, bandaging, cumin). The Torah demands circumcision but does not specify exactly what should be cut or how much. Not all circumcisions are the same; the foreskin can be cut or cut off in any number of different ways.[63] When Jeremiah states that the peoples of Egypt, Edom, Ammon, and Moab are *circumcised in the foreskin* and yet are *foreskinned*, it is possible, so one scholar has recently argued, that the prophet means that these peoples are partially circumcised, because they do not remove as much of the foreskin as do the Judaeans.[64] In the middle of the second century BCE, the author of the book of Jubilees complained that some of his fellow Jews were not performing circumcision correctly. The angel, who is the narrator of the book, "predicts" the following to Moses

> I am now telling you that the Israelites will prove false to this ordinance. They will not circumcise their sons in accord with this entire law because they will leave some of the flesh of their circumcision when they circumcise their sons. All the people of Belial will leave their sons uncircumcised just as they were born.[65]

If this translation is correct,[66] the author of Jubilees is upset by the behavior of two separate groups: people who do not cut off all of the foreskin as they should, and the people of Belial, who do not circumcise their sons at all. The second group is well attested in other sources of the Hasmonean period; these are the "hellenizers," sometimes called the "extreme hellenizers," whose ambition it was to remove the marks of Jewish distinctiveness and to "make a covenant with the gentiles around us."[67] The first group, however, is not attested or attacked in any other document, so the details of the controversy are elusive.

Whatever the outcome of these prior debates and whatever the precise intent of the passages in Jeremiah and Jubilees, the rabbis are the first to demand explicitly both *milah*, the excision of the foreskin, as well as *peri'ah*, the full "uncovering" of the corona. Talmud in its own way acknowledges the novelty of *peri'ah* when it states that *"peri'ah* was not given to Abraham" but was introduced later by Moses or Joshua.[68] Several modern scholars have suggested that this severe regimen, *milah* and *peri'ah*, was introduced in order to prevent epispasm, the procedure by which the remains of the foreskin are "drawn" or "pulled" down upon the corona, so as to give the circumcised organ the appearance of not being circumcised. Epispasm is described in some detail in a Roman medical writer of the first century CE, and it was practiced at various intervals in the Hellenistic and Roman periods by Jews eager to conceal their circumcision and their Jewishness. Rabbinic circumcision, which removes all shreds of the foreskin and the membrane underneath, renders epispasm difficult, if not impossible.[69]

Suctioning the wound, bandaging it, and applying cumin to it, share the common purpose, at least in the rabbinic mind, of hastening the healing process. The Talmud explains that the wound is suctioned in order to promote healing,[70] but does not explain how the suctioning is to be performed; medieval Jewish authorities unanimously assume that the suctioning is to be done by the circumciser by mouth, and the procedure was thus performed until the middle of the nineteenth century, when alternative procedures were propounded. Suctioning was a bloody affair, as Montaigne's account emphasizes, but in the talmudic period the blood that was suctioned out was not yet ideologically significant, nor was its treatment the subject of custom (see below). In any case, we may safely assume that the one doing the suctioning did not swallow; he must have spit out the blood somewhere somehow. Cumin was applied to the wound because it was believed to staunch the flow of blood.[71] By Montaigne's time, cumin had been replaced by "red powder, which they say is dragon's blood."[72] The Mishnah states that the child should be washed in warm water on the third day following the circumcision (according to R. Eleazar b. Azariah, even if the third day be the Sabbath), probably because such washing was believed to promote healing.[73]

5. Praise of Circumcision

Rabbinic texts laud circumcision. Jubilees had elaborated on its importance, Philo had explained it at length, Josephus promised to devote a treatise to it.[74] But the praise that circumcision receives in rabbinic literature is entirely unprecedented and extraordinary. Here is the Mishnah:

> R. Ishmael said: great is circumcision, since thirteen covenants were made [lit. "cut'] on its account.
> R. Yosi[75] said: great is circumcision, since it supersedes the Sabbath the severe.
> R. Joshua b. Korha said: great is circumcision, for Moses the righteous was not given a reprieve [from punishment] for [even] one full hour on its account.[76]
> R. Nehemiah said: great is circumcision, since it supersedes skin afflictions.

> Rabbi [Judah the Patriarch][77] said: great is circumcision, for [notwith-standing] all the commandments that Abraham performed he was not called complete until he circumcised himself, as it is written, *walk before me, and be perfect* [Genesis 17:1].[78]

The Tosefta, a collection of materials that supplements and parallels the Mishnah, quotes the statement of Rabbi and continues in the same vein:

> Another statement: Great is circumcision, for it equals in value all the [other] commandments of the Torah, as it is written, *This is the blood of the covenant which the Lord [now makes with you concerning all these commands]* [Exodus 24:8].
> Another statement: Great is circumcision, since but for it heavens and earth would not endure, as it is written, *but for my covenant* [that is, circumcision, which persists] *by day and night, I would not have appointed the ordinances of Heaven and earth* [Jeremiah 33:25].[79]

Some of this material is already familiar to us: the word *berit* appears thirteen times in Genesis 17; circumcision supersedes the Sabbath; the failure to observe circumcision put Moses's life in jeopardy. I cannot fully unpack the remainder of this material here. What is important for our purposes is not only that circumcision elicits such praise but also that such praise is extraordinary. Nowhere else do the Mishnah and Tosefta proclaim a given commandment to be "great." In the repertoire of rabbinic homiletics not many commandments are said to equal in value the entire Torah or all the rest of the commandments.[80] Praise of circumcision continues in the Bavli and Yerushalmi.[81] In these rabbinic texts circumcision is special; but for it heaven and earth would not endure.

What prompted such an outpouring of praise? Many scholars have conjectured that the mishnaic rabbis are here engaged in anti-Christian polemic, specifically anti-Pauline polemic. As I shall discuss in chapter 3, Paul uses the figure of Abraham to prove that God does *not* demand physical circumcision of his devotees. The proof is that God deemed Abraham worthy even before he was circumcised; Abraham's faith, not his circumcision, made him righteous before God.[82] Later Christian writers on circumcision basically followed Paul, as we shall see. In response, at least according to this interpretation, the rabbis extolled circumcision, emphasizing how important it is in God's eyes. In particular Rabbi (Judah the Patriarch) responds directly to the Pauline argument: even if Abraham was righteous before his circumcision, he was "complete" or "perfect" only after it.[83] There is another possible target of the

rabbinic praise of circumcision: "hellenized" Jews. In the middle of the
second century BCE, the Hasmoneans fought against Jews who, in order
to efface signs of Jewish difference, tried to hide their circumcision.
During the Bar Kokhba War also (132–35 CE), some Jews tried to hide
their circumcision through epispasm, leading one scholar to conjecture
that the Bar Kokhba war was to some extent a reprise of the Hasmonean rebellion. Both were primarily civil wars between religious traditionalists and "hellenizers," in which the observance of circumcision
was one of the main points of contention.[84] In the wake of the Hasmonean wars, the book of Jubilees enlarged upon circumcision's importance; in the wake of the Bar Kokhba War, so did the rabbis. Perhaps,
then, the target of the polemical praise of circumcision in the Mishnah
is not nascent Christianity but hellenized Judaism.

Early Medieval Rabbinic Judaism (ca. 600–ca. 1050 CE)

The centuries following the close of the Talmud in the history of rabbinic Judaism are generally called the "geonic period," named for the
heads of the talmudic academies of Babylonia who bore the title *gaon*
(sing.; pl: *geonim*). During this period (ca. 600–ca. 1050 CE), the ideology and ritual of circumcision develop significantly. I shall survey some
of these developments.

Circumcision Blood as Efficacious Blood

Blood is the inevitable by-product of any surgical procedure, and circumcision is no exception. Biblical and rabbinic texts, however, seldom
mention the blood of circumcision. In the Bible the blood of circumcision is alluded to only in the mysterious bloody bridegroom story of Exodus 4. Jewish texts between the Bible and the Mishnah never mention
the blood of circumcision.[85] The Mishnah has two extended discussions
of circumcision, as well as several stray references to circumcision, but
none of them even mentions blood. The Talmudim and other ancient
post-mishnaic works mention circumcision blood from time to time, either in the context of discussing the baby's health or in the context of
"dripping covenantal blood" when circumcision is not practical. Nowhere in these discussions is any significance or power attributed to the
circumcision blood itself. The benediction to be recited at an infant's

circumcision does not mention blood; the paeans of praise lavished on circumcision do not mention blood; even the rabbinic discussions of the mysterious story in Exodus 4 do not mention blood.[86] If the talmudic rabbis subscribed to a theology of circumcision blood, our corpora have failed to record it.[87]

In contrast with this silence, rabbinic texts of about 800 CE and later explicitly acknowledge the potency of the blood of circumcision. Our main evidence in this regard is the *Pirqei de Rabbi Eliezer*, "The Chapters [or: Sayings] of Rabbi Eliezer," a Midrash that retells biblical history from the creation of the world until the wanderings of the children of Israel in the desert. The work frequently digresses from its story line, is filled with numerous fanciful elaborations of the biblical original, and seems to have been based, in part, on the "rewritten bible" of the Second Temple Period. The work is extant in numerous manuscripts, each one, it seems, providing its own version of the text, and probably derives from the land of Israel in the eighth century.[88] In this work, the blood of circumcision is endowed with new significance, as is evident in its retelling of a rabbinic Midrash linking Ezekiel 16 with circumcision and the Paschal sacrifice:

> On the day when the children of Israel went forth from Egypt all the people were circumcised, both young and old, as it says *For all the people that came out were circumcised* [Joshua 5:5]. The Israelites took the blood of the covenant of circumcision and put it upon the lintel of their houses, and when the Holy one, blessed be He, passed over to plague the Egyptians, he saw upon the lintel of their houses the blood of the covenant of circumcision and the blood of the Paschal lamb, and was filled with compassion on Israel, as it is said *When I passed by you and saw you wallowing in your blood, I said to you: In your blood live. I said to you: In your blood live* [Ezekiel 16:6]. *In your blood* [sing.] is not written here, but *in your blood* [pl.], in twofold blood, the blood of the covenant of circumcision and the blood of the Paschal lamb.[89]

I cannot treat here the entire tradition history of this Midrash. The important point is that in this extraordinary version, the blood of circumcision—not the observance of the commandment but the blood itself—moves God to pity the enslaved Israelites. The Israelites daub the blood of their circumcision on the lintels, alongside the blood of the Paschal sacrifice. The blood of circumcision was no less effective than the blood of the sacrifice in protecting the Israelites from the Destroyer of the first-born. Following Exodus 12:13, in which God declares *when I see the blood, I will have pity on you,* our author does not ascribe "magical" power to the blood; that is, the blood itself does not ward off evil. Rather, the sight of the circumcision blood and the Paschal blood, mixed together on the lintel, moved God to compassion.[90] The blood of circumcision, like the blood of the Passover, is protective, salvific, and apotropaic.

The linkage between circumcision and the Paschal sacrifice is, of course, established by Exodus itself, which requires circumcision of all males that would eat of the sacrifice (Exodus 12:43–49). The importance of circumcision blood may well have been deduced from the mysterious story in Exodus 4. Many modern scholars have suggested that the function of Exodus 4:24–26 within its redactional context is to have the redemption of Zipporah's first born adumbrate the redemption of the Israelite first-borns, and indeed of Israel itself, God's first born (Exodus 4:22). Zipporah's first born is redeemed from death through the blood of circumcision; the Israelite first-borns are redeemed from death through the blood of the Paschal sacrifice.[91] Unfortunately, the extant texts of *Pirqei de Rabbi Eliezer* do not include any paraphrase of, or allusion to, the story in Exodus 4:24–26, but the Targumim, the Aramaic translations of Scripture, give us a sense of how these verses were construed. Targum Jonathan paraphrases Exodus 4:26 as follows: "How precious is the blood of this circumcision that saved the bridegroom from the hands of the Destroying Angel."[92] Here the exegete does not need to buffer the magical potency of the blood with references to God's compassion, since the verse has no such references. The blood of circumcision saves. This reading of the Zipporah story no doubt is behind the reevaluation of the blood of the Passover circumcision in *Pirqei de Rabbi Eliezer.* This exegetical reevaluation is not attested in any source prior to *Pirqei de Rabbi Eliezer,* approximately 800 CE.[93]

After *Pirqei de Rabbi Eliezer,* and under the influence of that book, circumcision blood attains real significance in Jewish liturgy, custom, and thought. The medium by which *Pirqei de Rabbi Eliezer* exerted its greatest influence was the *Zohar,* the central book of Jewish mysticism. This work, written in northern Spain in the thirteenth century, drew heavily on the *Pirqei de Rabbi Eliezer* and in turn, became the object of intense study and meditation. As we shall see below, the Zohar propounds a new theology of circumcision. It also, under the direct influence of *Pirqei de Rabbi Eliezer,* ascribes much significance to circumcision blood.[94]

Circumcision as Sacrifice

The importance of circumcision blood in *Pirqei de Rabbi Eliezer* is connected with another idea: circumcision is a sacrifice, and circumcision blood consequently ranks as sacrificial blood.[95] After seeing all the miracles that God had done for Jonah, the sailors cast away their idols "and went up to Jerusalem and circumcised the flesh of their foreskins, as it is said *And the men feared the Lord exceedingly; and they offered a sacrifice unto the Lord* [Jonah 1:16]. Did they offer a sacrifice? [No, they did not.] This [sacrifice] refers to the blood of the covenant of circumcision, which is like the blood of a sacrifice."[96] Even more striking is the following passage:

> Know then that on the Day of Atonement Abraham our father was circumcised. Every year the Holy one, blessed be He, sees the blood of our father Abraham's circumcision, and He forgives all the sins of Israel, as it is said, *For on this day shall atonement be made for you to cleanse you* [Leviticus 16:30]. On the very place where Abraham was circumcised and his blood remained, there the altar was built, and therefore it is written *And all the blood thereof shall he pour out at the base of the altar* [Leviticus 4:30]. [Scripture also says] *I said unto thee, in thy blood live; I said unto thee, in thy blood live* [Ezekiel 16:6].[97]

Once again the author of *Pirqei de Rabbi Eliezer* avoids attributing "magical" power to the blood; rather God is so moved by the sight of Abraham's blood that he forgives the sins of Abraham's descendants, just as God is moved by the sight of the circumcision blood of the Israelites in Egypt. In this passage Abraham's circumcision blood mingles with the blood of the sin offerings, just as in the earlier passage the blood of the Israelites' circumcision mingles with the blood of the Paschal sacrifice. Abraham's circumcision blood flowed into the ground on the very spot at which the altar would later be built and the blood of sin offerings would be poured. These two bloods, the blood of Abraham's circumcision and the blood of the sin offerings, are understood as the twin bloods celebrated by Ezekiel.

The equation of circumcision with sacrifice is not a complete innovation of *Pirqei de Rabbi Eliezer,* since the idea appears in inchoate form in Leviticus 12, as I argued above, and in earlier midrashic collections.[98] But this idea became a major ingredient in rabbinic reflection on circumcision only after the *Pirqei de Rabbi Eliezer.* The idea was even given concrete expression in liturgy and custom. R. Jacob b. Asher (ca. 1270–1340) writes as follows in his law code:

> It is a custom that the father of the boy stands next to the circumciser in order to make known to him that he [the circumciser] is his [the father's] agent. As we say [in the Talmud] concerning a sacrifice:[99] is it possible that a person's sacrifice should be offered [on the altar] when he is not standing next to it? [Of course not; his presence is required.][100]

Circumcision is a sacrifice. A father must stand next to the circumciser just as a person must stand next to, or at least close by, the sacrifice that he (or she) has brought to the temple. Even today many circumcision manuals prescribe the following prayers to be recited before the actual event. The father says, ". . . may [the fulfillment of] this commandment be reckoned before You as the delightful fragrance [of a sacrifice]." The circumciser says, ". . . may the Holy one, blessed be He, find favor with this sacrificial offering . . . May it be Your will to reckon the blood of this circumcision as if I had built an altar and brought on it whole burnt offerings and sacrifices." The *sandaq* (the person upon whose lap the circumcision is performed; see below) says, ". . . May it be your will, O God . . . that [my lap] become an altar of atonement."[101] These prayers, which became part of the circumcision ritual in the sixteenth and seventeenth centuries, give liturgical expression to ideas that were elaborated in the *Pirqei de Rabbi Eliezer*.

Ritual Disposal of Blood and Foreskin

The blood of circumcision having become significant, its disposal now became an issue of importance and the subject of a wide variety of customs. *Pirqei de Rabbi Eliezer* itself endorses the custom of burying the severed foreskin and the blood. This custom perhaps reflects the equation of circumcision with sacrifice, since, as we have seen, the blood of Abraham's circumcision entered the ground precisely where the blood of the atonement sacrifices would later be poured. Circumcision blood, like sacrificial blood, is to return to the earth.[102] The Jews of medieval Babylonia, however, had a different custom. They allowed the circumcision blood to drip into a cup of water, and the resulting mixture was applied to the hands (in some versions, the faces as well) of those assembled for the event.[103] In Germany during the high Middle Ages, additional customs arose concerning the blood: after suctioning the wound, the circumciser would spit the blood from his mouth into a cup of wine from which the baby would then be given a few drops to drink;[104] the circumciser would use a cloth to wipe the blood off his hands and mouth, and this cloth would be spread over the synagogue entrance;[105] the blood would be collected in a cup and poured out on the ground in front of the Torah ark;[106] some blood would be allowed to drip onto the baby's swaddling clothes, from which a Torah binder (a *wimpel*) would later be made and presented to the synagogue.[107] Montaigne, alas, does not tell us what became of the severed foreskin or of the wine-blood mixture at the circumcision that he witnessed in 1581.

Montaigne is struck by the fact that the circumciser allows his mouth to remain bloody while he recites the benedictions. Even at the end of the ceremony, after everyone has had the opportunity to inhale the fragrance from the spice container, "he meanwhile still has his mouth all bloody." A circumciser writing in Modena, ca. 1805, says that the circumciser should recite the benedictions after the circumcision "with the blood of the suction *(metzitzah)* still on his mouth"; such is the custom in Modena, he says, which follows the custom of Saloniki (Salonica).[108] This is the very custom that Montaigne witnessed in Rome two and a quarter centuries earlier. Similarly, R. David ben Samuel Halevi of Poland (1586–1667) reports that Rabbi Feibush of Krakow would not wipe his mouth after performing a circumcision on Rosh HaShanah, the Jewish new year, so that he could blow the *shofar* with a mouth "dirtied by the blood of circumcision." His goal was to mix the fulfillment of the commandment of circumcision with the commandment of *shofar.*[109] In contrast, R. David Abudarham (fourteenth century), also known as Abudraham, whom we will meet again in chapter 5, says that a circumciser must wash his hands and mouth before reciting the benedictions, so that he may utter the prayers "in cleanliness."[110]

Montaigne also reports that the Jews told him "that he who has circumcised up to a certain number, which they know, when he is dead has this privilege, that the parts of his mouth are never eaten by worms." This is a striking statement, and I leave it for others to elucidate. The mouth of the circumciser is spared from post-mortem corruption because the mouth has come into direct contact with the circumcision and the blood. If circumcision and/or circumcision blood can ward away death and protect one from the torments of Gehenna, surely they can also ward away the corruption of the body. The emphasis on the mouth suggests that the organ that performs the *metzitzah* (suctioning) enjoys the greatest boon in the hereafter.[111]

The Ceremony

The Talmud prescribes three benedictions that are to be recited at a circumcision, as well as a response to be proclaimed by "the bystanders."[112] In the post-talmudic centuries the ritual was much expanded. It now became a formal ceremony, a sacred celebration, and a communal event, as is evident from the following innovations.

NAMING THE CHILD   The earliest evidence associating circumcision with the bestowal of a name is the New Testament. John the Baptist is named at his circumcision (Luke 1:59–63) as is Jesus (Luke 2:21). Genesis 17, of course, might itself suggest such an association, since the divine command to circumcise is accompanied by the bestowal of new names on Abram (who becomes Abraham) and Sarai (who becomes Sarah), but no Jewish text before the New Testament even suggests that the bestowal of a name was part of the circumcision ceremony. After the New Testament, the custom is not attested until the *Pirqei de Rabbi Eliezer,* which mentions casually that Moses's parents named him at his circumcision.[113] Other sources of the same period also state that a boy is named at his circumcision.[114] I do not know how to explain the gap in our documentation between the Gospel of Luke and the *Pirqei de Rabbi Eliezer.*

WINE   As Montaigne observed, a cup of wine is blessed and drunk at a circumcision celebration. This practice is an innovation of the early medieval period. R. Yaakov haGozer ("R. Jacob the circumciser"), author of the first circumcision manual (Germany, ca. 1230), writes as follows:

> Why do we make a benediction over [a cup of] wine on the day of a circumcision, when it is not mentioned at all in the Talmud? But [the source for the benediction is that] the *geonim* R.Yehudai and R. Sherira and other *geonim* introduced it, parallel to the cup [of wine] of the groom at the [recitation of the] seven wedding benedictions. In the book *The Legal Precedents of the Geonim,* I have found that R. Zadoq Gaon said that the one who recites the benediction at a betrothal or a wedding or a circumcision or the sanctification [*qiddush,* the prayer recited over a cup of wine marking the inception of a Sabbath or festival], and drinks an amount equal to the capacity of his cheek, [either directly by mouth] or by [dipping his] hand [in the cup and sucking the wine from his fingers], and afterwards gives the cup to the groom and bride to drink, or, in the case of the cup of circumcision, sends it to the mother of the child, since praise of God was recited over the cup, or, in the case of sanctification [*qiddush*] and of separation [*havdalah,* the ceremony marking the end of the Sab-

bath or of a festival], gives it to the people of his household—[if he has acted thus, he has acted properly].[115]

R. Jacob makes three important points: first, that the cup of wine at a circumcision is nowhere mentioned in the Talmud but is an innovation of the *geonim*, the sages of the talmudic academies of medieval Babylonia; second, that the cup of wine at a circumcision parallels the cup of wine at a wedding; and third, that there was some dispute among the *geonim* as to who actually drank the wine of circumcision.

According to R. Jacob, the presence of a cup of wine at a circumcision ceremony is an innovation of the *geonim*, specifically R. Yehudai (ca. 757), R. Zadoq (ca. 820), and R. Sherira (ca. 968). Other sources of the ninth and tenth centuries confirm the presence of a cup of wine at a circumcision.[116] The introduction of a cup of wine into the circumcision ceremony precisely parallels its introduction into the wedding ceremony. The Talmud prescribes a series of benedictions for a wedding, but the blessing over wine was not among them, apparently because wine did not yet have a place in the ceremony. In the post-talmudic period, wine became a fixture at weddings and circumcisions alike.[117] Wine in rabbinic liturgy represents joy, since wine gladdens the heart, and sanctity, since wine was a regular accompaniment to the temple sacrifices.[118] The Mishnah and Talmud ordain that the Sabbath and festivals be marked upon their arrival by the ceremony of "sanctification" or *qiddush*, a prayer recited over a cup of wine that thanks God for the gift of sacred time.[119] By introducing a blessing over a cup of wine at weddings and circumcisions, the post-talmudic sages were stating that these liminal moments were imbued not only with joy but also with sanctity, akin to the Sabbath.[120]

The cup of wine, symbol of sanctity and joy, is a perfect complement to weddings and circumcisions, but it is also the source of a legal paradox. In normal rabbinic usage, a person who recites a blessing over food (a cup of wine, a slice of bread, a piece of fruit, etc.) immediately partakes of the food after completing the blessing. So, for example, on Friday night, at the beginning of the Sabbath, immediately after reciting the *qiddush* over a cup of wine we drink from the cup; immediately after blessing God "who brings forth bread from the earth," we eat some bread. But at weddings and circumcisions something strange happens, since the one who recites the blessing over the cup of wine is not the one who drinks the wine. At weddings the wedding performer recites the blessing but the groom and bride drink; at circumcisions the circumciser recites the blessing but the mother of the baby drinks—or, at least, such is the custom that is attested in all the earliest references to wine at a circumcision. Hence a problem: is it acceptable that he who blesses is not he who drinks? This question much exercised many of the *geonim*. In the excerpt translated above, R. Zadoq is quoted as saying that the one who recites the blessing must at least take a sip of wine before sending the cup on to those who will actually drink it. Many *geonim* agreed with this opinion, but some did not.[121]

At some point in the geonic period the custom arose to give a few drops of wine to the just-circumcised baby. The logic that is given is that the cup of wine is a cup of blessing ("praise of God is recited over the cup," as R. Zadoq put it), and both mother and baby need divine blessing to recover from their respective ordeals. So now we have three people drinking from the cup: the one who recites the blessing, who must take a sip (at least according to R. Zadoq and his supporters); the baby, who gets a few drops; and the mother who drinks the cup. This is precisely the practice as observed by Montaigne. In the centuries that followed R. Zadoq additional customs arose: the cup would be drunk by the circumciser, the godfather (the *sandaq*, see below), or the children present, either instead of, or in addition to, the mother. The one custom that would become almost universal in the Jewish world was to give the baby a few drops of wine to drink, although there was no universal agreement on precisely when in the ceremony this was to happen. The custom of giving the baby some drops of wine during the recitation of *I said to you: In your blood live. I said to you: In your blood live* from Ezekiel 16:6, a verse that was interpolated into a prayer for the welfare of the baby, is attested for the first time in the twelfth century in Europe. The midrashic background to this practice, we have seen above.[122]

MINYAN AND SYNAGOGUE   The introduction of the cup of wine implies that the circumcision celebration was now endowed with sanctity. Two other innovations of the geonic period are further evidence of this development: the circumcision began to be celebrated in the synagogue, and in the presence of a prayer quorum (a *minyan*). These innovations are also evidence for the revaluation of circumcision as a community ritual and not just a home or family ritual.

The Talmud nowhere states the proper venue of a circumcision ceremony. The first clear evidence that a circumcision should take place in a synagogue is provided by a gaon of the ninth or tenth century: "As to what you asked, whether . . . an infant should be brought to the synagogue [for circumcision], [our reply is that] it doesn't matter and there is no prohibition one way or another that would impel us to order you to change your customs."[123] Synagogal circumcision became the norm for most Ashkenazic communities (the Jewish communities of northern and eastern Europe).[124] Precisely where in the synagogue the circumcision was to occur, whether in front of the ark or near the door, was the subject of diverse customs.[125] In contrast, home circumcision remained the norm in the communities of southern Europe and the east. The circumcision witnessed by Montaigne, for example, was celebrated in the home.[126]

Circumcision in the synagogue is not only a sacred act but also a communal act. The community joins the family in welcoming the newborn into its midst. Therefore it is probably not a coincidence that the preference for the presence of a *minyan*, a prayer quorum of ten men, is attested at the same time as circumcision in the synagogue. A *minyan* does not so much represent a community as constitute it: a quorum of ten men *is* a community, and their presence at a circumcision testifies at once to the event's sacred and communal character. The Talmud is silent on the subject of a *minyan* in connection with a circumcision; the first attestation of this preference is in the *Pirqei de Rabbi Eliezer,* with some geonic material close behind.[127]

Four Additional Novelties: Godparents, the Chair of Elijah, Food, and Fragrance

Four additional novelties are first attested in the early medieval period (ca. 600–1050); three of them may well be connected with the emergence of the synagogue as a (or the) locus for the circumcision ritual. First, the person upon whose lap the circumcision was performed emerges from obscurity into importance. The Talmud paid this person no heed, but during the centuries under review here he became known as the *sandaq* (from the Greek *sunteknos,* "the one with the child") or the *ba'al berit,* "the lord of the covenant." His wife was known as the *sandaqit* or the *ba'alat berit,* and her task, as Montaigne witnessed, was to take the baby from the mother and bring him to her husband, upon whose lap he would be circumcised. (In some instances a woman would provide the lap for the circumcision; see below.) For a couple to be named a *ba'al berit* and a *ba'alat berit* was a great honor, and they in effect were the godparents to the child. Indeed, many scholars have argued that the emergence of this office is the product of the influence of

Christianity on Judaism, first of Greek Christianity and later of Latin Christianity. Greek Christianity gave the Jews not only the title *sandaq* but also the concept: Christian "godparents" sponsor a baby at a baptism in the church, Jewish "godparents" sponsor a baby boy at a circumcision in the synagogue. Latin Christianity taught the Jews the social utility of the institution: since a baby's circumcision, like a baby's baptism, was a public, communal ritual, celebrated in the sacred building of the community, it afforded the parents an opportunity to forge a link with a couple who might be socially useful to them and to the child. The institution of godparents allowed both Jews and Christians to create and maintain advantageous social connections.[128]

In time the office of the *sandaq* became invested not only with social importance but also religious importance. Recall the idea that circumcision is a sacrifice, and that a father bringing his son to be circumcised is akin to a man bringing an animal to be sacrificed. If circumcision is a sacrifice, then the lap on which the circumcision takes place must be an altar. Here is a report concerning R. Jacob Molin (ca. 1360–1427), known as the Maharil:

> The Maharil, when he was made a *ba'al berit,* what is called a *sandiq* in the language of the sages, would follow the custom of washing and immersing himself [first] so as to bring the infant into the covenant in purity. He said: greater is the commandment of the *ba'al berit* than the commandment of the circumciser, because his legs [upon which the circumcision takes place] resemble the altar, as if he were offering up incense to heaven.[129]

Since circumcision is sacrifice, the provider of the lap is fulfilling an even more important commandment than the circumciser: the latter, if we follow the logic of the analogy, resembles a priest, but the former resembles an altar.[130] This statement of the Maharil shaped future Jewish thinking , at least in Christian Europe, about the significance of the *sandaq;* for example, the contemporary prayer of the *sandaq* that I quoted above is inspired directly by the Maharil.

The *Pirqei de Rabbi Eliezer,* which, as we have seen above, is the first to attest so many ideas and customs regarding circumcision, is also the first with two more: the chair of Elijah, and a festive meal. Regarding the chair of Elijah, *Pirqei de Rabbi Eliezer* writes as follows:

> The sages have instituted [the custom] that there should be [at every circumcision] a seat of honor for the Messenger of the Covenant; for Elijah is called the Messenger of the Covenant, as it is said, [*I am sending my*

messenger to clear the way before me . . .] the messenger of the covenant, whom you desire, he is coming [Malachi 3:1].[131]

The exact function of this "chair of Elijah" is the subject of numerous conflicting customs. In some communities, the chair on which the *sandaq* sits and on which the circumcision takes place is said to be the chair of Elijah, but in most communities the Elijah chair is set aside and left unoccupied, just as at the Passover seder table a glass of wine is filled and left untouched, having been declared to be "for Elijah." Some communities had special "Elijah" chairs reserved for this purpose alone; such chairs, which were decorated and outfitted with appropriate biblical and rabbinic citations, were kept in the synagogue and can now be found in many Jewish museums around the world.[132]

Montaigne does not mention a chair of Elijah, and I am not sure why. Perhaps the Jews of Rome did not have the custom of an Elijah chair. Or, perhaps they observed the custom by temporarily designating a regular household chair as a place for Elijah, and since no one explained this point to Montaigne he missed it. In any event, if a special chair of Elijah had been brought from the synagogue to the home for the ceremony witnessed by Montaigne, surely he would have noted it and commented on it.

When circumcision became a communal event, it very naturally, like a wedding, would be celebrated by large and festive meal. The Talmud contains various hints that opulent parties may have been part of the circumcision celebration,[133] but we have to wait until the *Pirqei de Rabbi Eliezer* to be told that a banquet is an "obligation": "Hence the sages have said: A man is obligated to make festivities and a banquet on that day when he has the merit of having his son circumcised, like Abraham our father."[134] Circumcision was an event not just for the household but for the entire community of Israel.

A fourth novelty first attested in this period is the presence of fragrance at the ceremony. Montaigne remarked with approval that at the conclusion of the circumcision ceremony "another person takes a silver instrument, round as a tennis ball, held by a long handle (which instrument is pierced with little holes, like our perfuming pans), and carries it to the nose, first of the minister, and then of the infant, and then of the godfather." The sniffing of fragrant herbs, contained in a "spice box," is a familiar part of Jewish ritual, especially at the *havdalah* ("separation") service that marks the conclusion of the Sabbath. The presence of fragrant herbs at a circumcision is first attested, I believe, in a responsum of a gaon of the ninth or tenth century. I mentioned this responsum above, since it also attests the custom of having the circumcision blood drip into a cup of water. What I did not mention is that this source also says that the water is to be "warm, and in it are myrtle and various fragrant herbs, whose odor wafts thoroughly."[135] R. Tzidqiyah b. Avraham the Physician, who lived in Rome ca. 1240, endorses the custom of sniffing fragrant herbs at a circumcision, but concedes that he is at a loss to explain it.[136] The most likely explanation is that fragrant herbs, myrtle in particular, were widely regarded as effective agents in warding away demons. Hence many communities had the custom of sniffing fragrant herbs, especially myrtle, at weddings, since a bride and groom, no less than a newborn, are favorite targets of noxious powers. Fragrant herbs, like wine, are another link between weddings and circumcisions.[137]

The Circumcision of Dead Infants

As we saw above, the rabbis believed that circumcision had the power to protect its bearer from death and from Gehenna (hell). At the same time the rabbis were aware of two logical problems that emerged from this belief: first, some Jews are so sinful that, even though circumcised, they do not deserve to be saved from the torments of Gehenna; second, infants who die before the eighth day should not be consigned to Gehenna, even though not circumcised. As we have already seen, the Midrash solves these two problems by arguing that God removes the foreskin from infants who died before they were circumcised, thus allowing them to escape Gehenna, and affixes it to those Jews who sinned "too much," thus causing them to lose the protection that their circumcision had afforded and to descend to Gehenna.[138] Problems solved.

What perhaps was metaphor for the Midrash became reality in the early medieval period. Some Jews concluded that the foreskin of a dead infant should be removed before burial. Our earliest source for this custom is the following:

> R. Nahshon Gaon [ca. 865] has written: an infant [boy] who was born and was three or four days old at his death—thus is our custom and our tradition, that we circumcise him at the grave but we do not recite the blessing over the circumcision. We bestow a name upon him so that, when mercy is shown him from heaven and the dead are resurrected, there will be knowledge in that child and he will discern his father.[139]

This circumcision is not a "real" circumcision, says the gaon, hence no blessing is recited, but it has the same effect as a real one: it guarantees that the infant will participate in the resurrection of the dead and, we may presume, in the interim it protects the infant from the torments of Gehenna. We circumcise the baby beside the grave, because as we bury him we assure him—and ourselves—that he will share in the resurrection of the righteous. We also bestow a name on the child so that at the resurrection "there will be knowledge in that child and he will discern his father," meaning that at the resurrection, when he regains consciousness ("knowledge"), he will be able to find his father because he has a name.[140] The reference to recognition in the second sentence suggests that recognition is germane in the first as well. This circumcision "works" because, by removing the infant's foreskin, our forefather Abraham will recognize him to be a Jew and will not allow him to descend to Gehenna.

By the eleventh century this custom, and opposition to it, reached the Jews of northern Europe. R. Solomon b. Isaac (1040–1105), better known by his acronym Rashi, arguably the greatest scholar produced by European Jewry in the high Middle Ages, turned to various sages in Rome with the question "whether it is necessary to cut the foreskin of an infant who died before reaching the eighth day, or not." He received this reply:

> Certainly our women have the custom of cutting it [the foreskin] with a sliver of reed, but it is not a commandment, for we have received in tradition that it is [merely] a cutting of the flesh, and nothing is accomplished, and it is prohibited. The Torah says *at the age of eight days* [Genesis 17:12], and he is not eight [days] old. When the Holy one, blessed be He, gave the commandments, He gave them to the living, and not to the dead; when a person dies he is freed of the commandments.[141]

I am not sure what to do with the words "and it is prohibited" (in the original these four English words are expressed by one Hebrew word, *ve'asur*). If we set these words aside, the responsum is clear and consistent: post-mortem removal of the foreskin is permissible but not necessary ("nothing is accomplished"), because the commandment of circumcision becomes operative only on the eighth day of life, not before. In the following paragraphs, not translated here, the respondents cite various rabbinic passages to prove that even uncircumcised babies have a share in the world to come. Among these proofs is the midrashic passage, which has God remove the foreskin from the prematurely dead. If God does it, we do not. The respondents also cite R. Hayya Gaon (usually pronounced "Hai," d. 1038) for support for the view that "we do not cut." The writer who has cited and thereby preserved this responsum comments at the end that "my teacher has ruled that it is not a Torah custom to remove the foreskin of dead infants."[142] These rabbis did not approve of post-mortem circumcision and, if asked before the fact whether it should be done, they would have replied in the negative. This moderate condemnation of the practice was not sufficient for some later reader who thought that the practice was not only unnecessary but also prohibited. This reader, I suggest, added the words "and it is prohibited" to the first sentence.

The custom of post-mortem circumcision is endorsed by R. Nahshon Gaon in the ninth century, but is opposed by R. Hayya Gaon in the eleventh, and by a host of European rabbis from the eleventh to the thirteenth century. By then, the custom had become "popular" (it was performed by "our women")[143] and had acquired greater metaphysical force. R. Nahshon thought, as we have seen, that the beneficial result of post-mortem circumcision is knowledge and recognition. In contrast, by the twelfth century the beneficial result of post-mortem circumcision is salvation. The famous biblical commentator Abraham ibn Ezra (1089–1164) opposes the custom but reveals the argument of those who support it:

> Mistaken are they who think that a dead child who is not circumcised has no share [in the world to come]. The meaning of the word *nefesh* [in Genesis 17:14] is not as they think; *nefesh*, rather, is synonymous with "person," and its meaning is "a body that has a soul."[144]

In biblical Hebrew, the word *nefesh* sometimes means "soul," sometimes "a person," that is, as ibn Ezra puts it, "a body with a soul." The proponents of post-mortem circumcision argued that in Genesis 17:14 the word *nefesh* means "soul," so that the verse should be understood to mean "And if any male who is foreskinned fails to circumcise the flesh of his foreskin, that soul shall be cut off from his kin." Does not the verse state, so they argued, that if the body is not circumcised the soul is cut off? Ibn Ezra rejects this interpretation, arguing that in this verse *nefesh* means "person," nothing more; we may presume that ibn Ezra would have added, "and a person who is less than eight days old is not bound by the law of circumcision and cannot be punished for violating it." For its proponents, post-mortem circumcision is necessary to save souls. Circumcision of the body guarantees salvation of the soul.

Circumcision has now become, in the popular imagination, almost completely analogous to Christian baptism.[145] In the fifth century, Augustine had said that unbaptized infants were consigned to hell: punish-

ment for original sin. Medieval scholastics argued instead that such infants were consigned to "limbo," a category outside heaven but not
quite hell.[146] In the Jewish legal tradition, circumcision does not play
the same role as Christian baptism, so that the question of the "salvation" of uncircumcised infants did not arise. An uncircumcised Jew is
an uncircumcised Jew. But among the Jewish masses ("our women")
many apparently believed that the absence of circumcision meant for
Jews what the absence of baptism meant for Christians, namely, exclusion from heaven. This popular tradition gradually prevailed. When the
great medieval law codes were written, post-mortem circumcision of infants was endorsed as a licit custom.[147] The popular tradition was soon
supported by the mystic. When the mystics of the thirteenth century began to see circumcision not merely as a warden against the torments of
Gehenna and a ticket to heaven but also as an agent of spiritual transformation, the analogy of Jewish circumcision with Christian baptism
will be complete, as we shall now see.

Circumcision Becomes a Sacrament: The Zohar

What is a sacrament? The core meaning of this Latin word is "obligation, oath," but in Christian theology the term has come to designate
any of seven rituals that were thought to confer "grace" on its participants. The classic definition is given in a bull issued by Pope Eugenius
IV on November 22, 1439. The issue at hand was the prospect of the
unification of the Roman Church with that of the Armenians. As part of
these ecumenical efforts, which ultimately came to naught, the pope set
out to explain to his brethren in the East the essentials of Christianity as
they were understood in the West:

> There are seven sacraments of the new law, namely, baptism, confir-
> mation, eucharist, penance, extreme unction, orders, and matrimony . . .
> [all of these] both contain grace and bestow it on those who worthily re-
> ceive them. . . .
> Three of the sacraments, namely baptism, confirmation and orders,
> imprint indelibly on the soul a character, that is, a kind of spiritual stamp
> which distinguishes it from the rest. Hence they are not repeated in the
> same person. The other four, however, do not imprint a character and can
> be repeated.[148]

All seven sacraments "contain and confer grace"; they affect the
soul. All seven are transformative; their recipients are no longer the

same people they had been before. The trio of baptism, confirmation, and ordination also imprint on the soul an "indelible character," "a kind of spiritual stamp [or: sign]." This special quality makes these three sacraments un-repeatable; they are once-in-a-lifetime experiences.

With these ideas in mind, let us turn to the Zohar, the classic text of Jewish mysticism. Written in northern Spain in the thirteenth century by Moses de Leon, the Zohar sets out a new theology of Judaism and a new rationale for the observance of the commandments. Maimonides and the Jewish philosophers spoke of God's absolute unity, but the Zohar conceived of God as manifesting himself through numerous emanations and potencies, each endowed with its own name, identity, and purpose. Maimonides and the Jewish philosophers conceived of the observance of the commandments as the path to perfection; living a life in accord with the dictates of the Torah enables a person to achieve a state of holiness that fosters contemplation of God and, as a result, brings about proximity to God. According to the Zohar, the observance of the commandments by humans below mirrors and influences the actions and passions of the Divine emanations above, so that the very foundations of the cosmos are affected by whether, and how, Jews observe the dictates of the Torah. Within this structure, the commandment of circumcision plays a particularly significant role.

The Zohar depicts circumcision as a ritual that imprints an indelible "character" on the soul. This is new; prior Jewish texts had extolled circumcision, as we have seen, but had not seen it as transformative.[149] The practice of the post-mortem circumcision of dead infants seems to be based on an inchoate version of the idea that first achieves full expression in the Zohar. According to the Zohar, circumcision changes its bearer from "closed" to "open," hence able to "see God" and participate in the mysteries of the Godhead. A profound interpreter of this difficult material puts the case as follows, "Circumcision [in the Zohar and related texts] effects a change in the very substance of the individual— and not only in his ethicoreligious stature—which prepares him for the visionary experience."[150] Circumcision brings its bearer into union with the Holy Name of God. The Zohar explains, "Before one is circumcised one is not united to the name of the Holy one, blessed be He; when one is circumcised one enters the name and is united to it."[151] And further: circumcision represents an "imprinting" or "inscribing" of a letter (the Hebrew word *ot*, "sign," here understood as "letter") of the divine name on the body, perhaps the divine name itself.[152] Circumcision makes Israel God's people, the bearers of his holy Torah, and the earthly embodiments of the supernal emanations; gentiles—that is, Christians—because they are not circumcised, are excluded from the study of the Torah and from contact with God. The foreskin is the corporeal manifestation of the evil inclination, and through its excision the Jewish male is saved from the dominion of sin; gentiles,—that is, Christians—belong to the forces of "the other side."[153] Circumcision, then, is not simply a commandment of the Torah, nor is it merely the covenant or the sign of the covenant. Circumcision makes a (male) Jew a Jew. Hence circumcision in Zoharic mysticism is entirely analogous to Christian baptism: a physical operation with metaphysical results, performed once only, an imprinting of a special character on the soul. In the *halakhic* or legal tradition, circumcision was never understood as the sine qua non of Jewishness or as a transformation of the soul, but in the mystical tradition it was.[154]

The Exclusion of Women from the Circumcision Ceremony

The last innovation to be considered here is the exclusion of women from the circumcision ceremony. This exclusion is the work of R. Meir b. Barukh of Rothenburg (d. 1293), known as the Maharam, the leading sage of German Jewry in the second half of the thirteenth century. Here is his ruling:

> In my opinion the custom that is followed in many places, that a woman sits in the synagogue among the men, and the infant is circumcised on her lap [lit.: bosom], this is not a proper custom, even if her husband or her father or her son is the circumciser. Because it is not proper that a decorated woman enter [a synagogue] among the men and before the divine presence . . . And furthermore, she is not bound by the commandment of circumcision at all, even to circumcise her own son . . . therefore why should we go so far so as to have a circumcision in her lap [lit.: bosom] and to [have her] snatch the commandment from men? Whoever is able to protest [this improper custom], let him protest, and may blessings come upon him who is strict [in this matter]. Peace. Meir b. Barukh.[155]

From this responsum we learn that in the Jewish communities of Germany, and perhaps elsewhere in Europe, the role of the *sandaq* was sometimes taken by a woman. Since the circumcision was customarily done in the synagogue, as we have seen, this meant that a woman would enter the synagogue and sit among the men in the "men's section," that is, in the main part of the synagogue in which women would not normally be present when liturgical activities were taking place. The woman is not the mother of the infant but a "godparent" of the child whom the parents wished to honor.[156] Her husband or father or son might be the circumciser, and she would provide the lap on which the circumcision would take place. The Maharam is shocked and offended by this custom; his opposition to it is based on two grounds. First: it is not proper that a dressed-up ("decorated") woman enter the synagogue among the men, and that a man, even a close relative, have his hands in her "bosom." Second: a woman, who is not bound by the commandment of circumcision, ought not to take the place of a man, who is bound by the commandment.

Although the two arguments are presented cumulatively ("not only . . . but also. . ."), it is clear that the Maharam thinks that the first is the main one, or, at least, that later tradition remembers the Maharam as thinking of the first argument as the main one. Thus, an alternate version of this responsum presents only the first argument, completely omitting the second.[157] Similarly R. Jacob Molin (ca. 1360–1427), known as the Maharil, whom we met briefly above and whom we will meet again in chapter 6 below, notices only the first argument. The Maharil's endorsement of the Maharam's responsum was decisive in the adoption of this ruling as the norm among Ashkenazic Jewry; this is how the Maharil reports it:

> The Maharil said: the Maharam has written that a woman who is a *ba'alat berit* [that is, a godparent at a circumcision]—[her responsibility is] to take the baby from his mother and bring him to the synagogue in order to be circumcised. She may bring him up to the entrance of the synagogue but she may not, entering within, also be the *sandak* so that the child would be circumcised on her knees. [She may not do this] because it is sexual license that a woman go among men.[158]

A woman can be honored with the title and function of *ba'alat berit*, but that does not mean that she should provide the sacred lap—the lap that resembles an altar—on which the circumcision would take place. No; a female godparent brings the baby from the mother to the doorway of the synagogue, no further. Her job is done. In the circumcision ceremony witnessed by Montaigne, even though it was celebrated in a home, this ruling was carefully followed. As the Maharil puts it, for a woman to enter the arena of men when men are present is "licentious" behavior, especially when that male space is the sacred space of the synagogue.

The second reason advanced by the Maharam, even if it gradually disappears from the later tradition, is also significant. Here the Maharam has made explicit, perhaps for the first time in rabbinic culture, that circumcision is a celebration of maleness and manhood, observed in a male space (the synagogue), from which women should absent themselves. Any number of ancient and medieval rabbinic texts had commented on the fact that circumcision applies only to men; some had argued, for example, that for this reason a woman should not serve as a circumciser.[159] But the Maharam is perhaps the first rabbi to say explicitly that women do not belong at a circumcision ceremony because the presence of a woman at a male ritual is inappropriate.

Three Eighteenth-Century Views

I began this chapter with a sixteenth-century Christian description of the Jewish circumcision ceremony and end it with three eighteenth-century Christian descriptions. These descriptions are not literary but artistic, engravings that illustrate some themes discussed in this chapter.

The first (fig. 1) is *La circoncision des juifs portugais* (The Circumcision of Portuguese Jews) by the well-known artist and engraver Bernard Picart (1673–1733). The circumcision takes place in the well-appointed home of a Sephardic family in Amsterdam. The engraving, dated 1722, depicts the moment before the actual circumcision; the *mohel* (the circumciser) has his instruments in his hands, the *sandaq* (the godfather) holds the baby, a vacant chair next to the *sandaq* is reserved for Elijah, and the baby has soiled his diaper (a touch of burlesque). The father of the baby stands to the left behind the *sandaq* and holds a glass of wine; another figure, identified in the caption as "the rabbi, a relative, or a friend" and standing in the center, holds another glass of wine. One glass provides wine for the circumciser to use while suctioning the wound (*metzitzah*); this wine is not actually drunk. The other glass contains the wine that will be drunk after the recitation of the benedictions. The mirror at the upper right reflects an image of the mother, the godmother, and a third woman. They wait in an adjacent room because, as the caption explains, "Jewish women are not present at this ceremony." Montaigne, too, had commented that during the ceremony "the women are in some other part of the house." The caption also explains that "the women who are seen here are Christian," not only she in the foreground with the cross around her neck but all the other women as well. The large and active crowd, then, consists of Jewish men, Christian men, and Christian women. We may safely assume that R. Meir of Rothenburg, who enacted the decree prohibiting a woman from being a *sandaq*, thereby launching the process that would remove women alto-

FIGURE 1. *La circoncision des juifs portugais* (The Circumcision of Portuguese Jews), by Bernard Picart (1673–1733), dated 1722, from volume 1 of his *Cérémonies et coutumes religieuses de tous les peuples du monde* (Amsterdam, 1723)

gether from the circumcision ceremony, would have disapproved of the presence of all these Christian women, at least two of whom are showing quite a bit of décolletage. We may imagine that when Montaigne witnessed a circumcision in Rome in 1581 he struck a pose much like that of the Christian man kneeling next to the *sandaq*, hat under his arm, and staring intensely at the action.

Our second engraving (fig. 2) illustrates a scene from the New Testament but reflects Jewish practice. Entitled *The Circumcision of Christ*, drawn by Bernard Picart and engraved by G. de Broen (1658–1740), it is a naturalistic depiction of the scene described by Luke 2:21. Were it not for the title (given in Greek, English, German, Latin, French, and Dutch) there would be no way to know that the baby is meant to be Christ, that the baby's father, who is standing left of center with his hands clasped and looking intently at the child, is meant to be Joseph, and that the mother, seated in the background with the other women, is meant to be Mary. The setting is rustic ("a manger"), as evidenced by

FIGURE 2. *The Circumcision of Christ*, drawn by Bernard Picart (1673–1733) and engraved by G. de Broen (1658–1740), from *Figures de la Bible* by Pieter de Hondt (The Hague, 1728)

the exposed beams, the sheaf of wheat on the shelf, and the basket on the wall. The engraving depicts the actual moment of the circumcision; a young man holds a tray with the circumcision implements at the ready while the circumciser does his work. A Torah scroll on the shelf is open to Genesis 17:12, *Throughout your generations every male among you shall be circumcised at the age of eight days.* The presence of ten men, the *sandaq* holding the baby on his lap, the cup of wine, the tray of implements, and the separation of the women from the men—these elements were taken by Picart and de Broen from contemporary Jewish practice.

Our first two engravings depict the circumcision ceremony in a domestic setting; our third (fig. 3), entitled *Cérémonies de la circoncision des juifs* (The Circumcision Ceremonies of the Jews), depicts a circumcision inside the sparsely furnished interior of a synagogue. There are three groups of people. Those on the left are involved in the actual circumcision. The *sandaq* holds the baby while the circumciser, knife in hand, gets ready to make the incision. Nearby a youth holds a tray with the circumcision implements. (But where is the cup of wine?) A chair stands empty, reserved for Elijah who, as the caption explains, according to Jewish belief "is invisibly present at all circumcisions." A bareheaded man—a Christian, we may presume—leans over the *sandaq* in order to get a good look at the proceedings (cf. the Christian observer in fig. 1), while another man (the father?) stands a little further off. In the right foreground is a cluster of six men who seem to have no interest in what is going on; one wonders if they are present merely to fill out the quorum for a *minyan*. (Alternative explanation: they are about as close as most men want to be at a circumcision.) The godmother, probably the wife of the *sandaq*, stands outside the synagogue door with some other women because, as the caption explains, "they are not permitted to enter the synagogue." The mother of the baby is not to be seen; she is at home in bed.

Conclusions

Our survey of the canonical history of Jewish circumcision confirms Montaigne's reputation as an acute observer of human society and its rituals. It also shows that Jewish circumcision, "the most ancient religious ceremony there is among men," changed dramatically over time. The surgical aspect changed; the attendant ceremonial changed; the

T.1.P.433.

CÉRÉMONIES DE LA CIRCONCISION DES JUIFS.

a. Le Parain qui tient l'enfant pendant la
   circoncision.
b. le Mohel, ou circonciseur
c. Enfant qui tient le plat ou sont toutes les choses
   nécessaires pour l'opération.

d. Siege vuide pour Elie qu'ils croyent assister
   invisiblement a toutes les circoncisions.
e. La Mareine accompagnée de quelques femmes
   a qui il n'est pas permis d'entrer dans la
   Synagogue.

FIGURE 3. *Cérémonies de la circoncision des juifs* (The Circumcision Ceremonies of the Jews), an anonymous engraving from Augustin Calmet, *Dictionnaire historique . . . de la Bible enrichi de plus de trois cent figures . . . qui representent les antiquitez judaïques* (Paris, 1730; original ed. 1722)

meanings changed. The ritual as delineated in the Bible is at once the same as, and yet very different from, the ritual as practiced and understood by the Jews of Europe in the high Middle Ages. I would like to summarize these changes by grouping them under four trajectories. These trajectories are, of course, artificial constructs that I am imposing on the material, but they help to provide a picture of the whole. Since the trajectories also overlap somewhat, some ideas may be mentioned more than once. The four trajectories are: from purity to sanctity; from foreskin to blood; from protection to salvation; from covenant to sacrament.

Purity to Sanctity

Leviticus 12 implicitly equates circumcision with purification: the circumcision of the infant boy parallels the purification sacrifice of the mother. Many biblical and rabbinic passages see the foreskin as a source of impurity, and consequently the foreskinned as impure. If the foreskin is impure, then its removal is purification. In the talmudic and post-talmudic periods, circumcision became associated not only with purification but also sanctification, that is, it became one of the "matters of holiness."[160] It was celebrated publicly, preferably in the presence of a prayer quorum, and, in some communities, preferably in a synagogue. It was marked by the recitation of benedictions, including a benediction over a cup of wine. To be effective, it required proper intent by the one performing it; it was declared to be similar to a sacrifice. Perhaps the institution of the chair of Elijah has its place along this trajectory as well.

Foreskin to Blood

Originally circumcision meant simply the removal of the foreskin. The sages of the Talmud insisted that both the foreskin and the membrane under the foreskin be completely removed, but this surgical innovation, whose purpose was to inhibit the possibility of epispasm, did not change the focus of the ritual. Nor did the institution of the ritualized sucking of the wound; circumcision was a bloody affair, but the blood did not yet have any ideological significance. Circumcision blood began its rise to ideological prominence in various post-talmudic texts, notably the midrashic work known as "The Chapters of Rabbi Eliezer." In this remarkable book, the blood of circumcision, not just the blood of the aboriginal circumcision of Abraham but the blood of the circumci-

sion of every Jewish infant, is powerful and salvific. It atones for sin, moves God to mercy, and protects against death. These conceptions, advanced so powerfully in the Chapters of Rabbi Eliezer, entered the mystical tradition of the high Middle Ages; that tradition, in turn, greatly influenced the liturgy and customary of the circumcision ceremony.

Protection to Salvation

Circumcision's power to protect from death is adumbrated already in the Bible. Zipporah saves the life of Moses, her husband, by circumcising her son. Circumcision is a prerequisite of the Paschal sacrifice, perhaps because both are apotropaic rituals that protect against the angel of death. The foreskinned kings of the enemies of Israel are consigned to Sheol, according to a vision of Ezekiel, thus suggesting an association between foreskin and a spectral hereafter. In rabbinic legend, Abraham sits at the entrance to Gehenna and bars the way for all those who have been circumcised. In post-talmudic times, some Jews would perform a post-mortem circumcision on an infant who had died before the eighth day in order to make sure that Abraham would recognize the boy as a Jew and save him from Gehenna. In the mystic world of the Zohar, the salvation afforded by circumcision is both physical and metaphysical. Through the excision of the foreskin, the Jewish male is saved from both Gehenna and sin, from both death and evil.

Covenant to Sacrament

In Genesis 17 circumcision is the physical embodiment of the covenant between God and Israel as well as the "sign" of that covenant. The two essential parts of that covenant are fertility and land: God promises Abraham that he will have a mighty progeny who one day will inherit the land of Canaan. Other passages highlight the distinctiveness conferred by circumcision even if they do not speak of its covenantal value. In Genesis 34 it is a tribal mark, something that Israelites do, apparently in connection with marriage, in contrast with the Shechemites who do not. Many passages speak of the "foreskinned" Philistines. In rabbinic texts "the foreskinned ones" is a standard expression for "the gentiles." In the Middle Ages "a foreskinned man" is a common Jewish way of referring to a Christian; a Christian woman is occasionally referred to as "a foreskinned woman."[161] The Bible also associates circumcision with the Paschal sacrifice, the celebration of which marks the exodus from

Egypt and the formation of the people of Israel. Some medieval Jewish thinkers emphasize circumcision's unique status as the embodiment of the covenant, others deemphasize it, but all alike see circumcision as a hallmark of Jewishness. It is just another of the 613 commandments, and yet it is not just another of the 613 commandments. It is not only done *by* the body but, unlike any other commandment, it is done *to* the body and done only once, never to be repeated. Medieval mystics concluded that circumcision had a power akin to that of the Christian sacraments. The special status of Israel in God's eyes, the special status of both collective Israel and the individual Jew, was a function of circumcision, for it is circumcision that gives Israel the ability to see God and to penetrate the mysteries of God's Torah. Baptism makes a Christian a Christian; circumcision, according to the mystics, makes a Jew a Jew.

And so, at long last, we have reached our theme. If circumcision is indeed analogous to baptism, and if indeed circumcision makes the Jew, what then is the status of that half of the Jewish people that lacks a male organ and consequently is not circumcised? Or, in an alternative formulation, a logical conundrum results from the collocation of two facts: first, circumcision has been practiced by Jews since time immemorial, and is widely seen, by Jews and non-Jews alike, as a distinctive, if not essential, marker of Jewishness; second, at any given time approximately one half of the Jewish people, namely the female half, lacks circumcision and, it would seem, any functional equivalent. If circumcision is such an important factor in Jewish identity, are women Jews? If women are Jews even without circumcision, what exactly is circumcision? This is the gender paradox raised implicitly by Genesis 17, and this is the paradox that is at the heart of this book.

CHAPTER 2

Were Jewish Women Ever Circumcised?

Ancient Hebrewism was a sacramental association of men,
characterized by the circumcision of the male member. . . .
there is no comparable sacrament for newborn girls, which
points to the fundamentally patriarchal character of Judaism.

Schalom Ben-Chorin

Having treated male circumcision in the previous chapter, I turn now to
female circumcision. Lest I be misunderstood, I would like to repeat a
sentiment that I first expressed in the preface. Not for a moment in this
book am I suggesting or implying that Jewish women *should* be circumcised. The subject of this book is not female circumcision but the absence of circumcision, or any equivalent covenantal mark, from the
bodies of Jewish women. What does the absence of circumcision from
Jewish women tell us about the meaning of circumcision and the meaning of Jewishness? These are the questions that drive this book. Nonetheless one cannot talk about the gender implications of circumcision
without taking about female circumcision. What will be important for
us is a passage of Philo, the earliest Jewish reflection on the absence of
female circumcision from Judaism.

Female Circumcision

In contemporary times circumcision (excision) of women is practiced
primarily across northern and central Africa (from Mauritania, Senegal,
Guinea in the west, to Sudan, Ethiopia, and Somalia in the east, and vir-
tually everywhere in between, from Egypt in the north to Kenya and
Tanzania in the south), on the perimeter of the Arabian Peninsula
(Yemen, Oman, the United Arab Emirates, and Bahrain), and among

various Muslim groups in Pakistan, Malaysia, Indonesia, and the Philippines.[1] The operation is not the same everywhere. In some societies the surgery is minimal. Jomo Kenyatta, who later in life would go on to become the first president of independent Kenya, claimed that the Gikuyu of Kenya cut off only the skin covering the clitoris, not the clitoris itself. Hence, he argued, the practice did not deserve the condemnation of censorious and pale-skinned English missionaries. Kenyatta was probably being disingenuous.[2] In most societies that practice female circumcision, the clitoris and portions of the labia are cut off. In the most extreme form of the procedure, observed in some societies and known as "pharaonic circumcision" or "infibulation," all of the external genitalia are cut off. Scar tissue covers the wound except for openings that are allowed to remain for the excretion of urine and menstrual fluid. On her wedding night an infibulated girl needs to be ripped open by her husband in order to facilitate sexual intercourse.[3] In spite of these substantial variations in practice, for the sake of convenience I will lump them all together and refer to them collectively as female circumcision or the circumcision of women.[4]

The circumcision of women is first attested in Egypt in the Hellenistic period. The earliest evidence is a papyrus document from 163 BCE, a petition written in Greek by an Egyptian monk at the temple of Serapis in Memphis.[5] In it an Egyptian woman claims that her daughter "is of the age to be circumcised" since she is about to be married; the monk in turn explains to the Greek governor that such circumcision "is the custom among the Egyptians." The verb used is *peritemnein,* the standard Greek verb for the circumcision of men, here applied to the circumcision of a woman. This document shows that the circumcision of women just before marriage was an established custom, at least in Memphis (middle Egypt), not later than the middle of the second century BCE. The absence of any reference to female circumcision in any Egyptian document of the preceding two thousand years suggests that this practice was a relatively recent importation into Egypt, even if we cannot be sure when it was imported, why, or whence (Ethiopia? Arabia?).[6] By the first century of our era, the Egyptian practice was well known. The geographer Strabo and the philosopher Philo mention it, as we shall see in a moment. Various medical writers of the Roman and Byzantine periods, not to mention the physicians of nineteenth-century Europe and America, recommended clitoridectomy if a woman's clitoris grew too large, thereby constituting "a deformity" and leading "to a feeling of shame" or causing too much sexual stimulation. These writers cite the Egyptians as wise precedents for this surgery.[7]

Female circumcision, like male circumcision, is not mentioned anywhere in the Qur'an, but it has come to be associated with Islam. One medieval Islamic jurist claims that the practice was commonly observed by pre-Islamic Arabs. Whether or not this is true, we do not know. There are several early Islamic traditions, however, that show that the practice was widely observed in early Islamic society. In some legal texts sexual intercourse is described as "when the circumcision touches the circumcision" or "when the two circumcisions meet." In one early tradition about Muhammad, the prophet is reported to have told a female circumciser in Medina "do not destroy it completely [that is, do not cut away too much], for that is more favorable for the woman and preferable for the husband." In another early tradition, the prophet describes circumcision as a proper or obligatory practice for men and a "noble deed" or "honor" for women. Medieval Islamic jurists debated whether circumcision of women was simply permitted or whether it was recommended or even required by Islam. This debate probably reflects variations in local practice.[8] In modern times, although the circumcision of women is practiced by Christians in Egypt and Ethiopia, and by various non-Christian, non-Islamic peoples elsewhere in Africa, the practice is most conspicuously Islamic. The spread of Islam in Africa has strengthened the observance of this practice in societies in which it had previously been observed and has led to the introduction of this practice into societies from which it had previously been absent. In particular, the most extreme form of female circumcision is practiced today only among Moslems.[9]

One common denominator of virtually all the societies that circumcise women is that they also circumcise men. Any number of societies, Jewish society for example, circumcise men but not women, but few if any circumcise women but not men. This suggests that the circumcision of women may have originated in imitation of the circumcision of men. The assimilation of the two practices to each other extends also to language and rationale. The Greek papyrus that provides our earliest attestation for the circumcision of women uses a verb that more appropriately refers to the circumcision of men than that of women. Similarly in Arabic the same terms can designate equally the circumcision of either sex.[10] The rationale offered in Islamic sources for the two rituals is often the same: to enhance fertility, to prepare for marriage, to remove impurity, and to enhance beauty. One Islamic explanation sees the two rituals as complementary: the male foreskin is a "female" part, just as the female clitoris is a "male" part. The removal of the foreskin from men and the clitoris from women removes residual bisexuality from both sexes, thereby promoting the masculinity of men and the femininity of women.[11]

The assimilation of the two rituals to each other should not be construed as a function of gender equality. The social setting of each shows that the opposite is the case. The circumcision of boys is a public event, celebrated by an entire clan or village, marked by processions and parades, finery and feasting. In opulence and display the celebration rivals that of a wedding; indeed anthropologists have frequently noted connections between circumcision celebrations and wedding celebrations in Islamic society.[12] Circumcision marks the emergence of a boy from the world of women to the world of men; even if after the surgery the boy returns to his mother for comfort and sustenance—after all, he is only six or seven years old—the ritual marks the entrance of a new male into the corporate body of the family, the clan, the age cohort, the village, and/or Islam in general.[13] In contrast the circumcision of girls is private, almost secret. Performed by women and attended only by women, with no public celebration whatever, it belongs to the female sphere and the female sphere alone. Male circumcision confirms that public space is male space and that the circumcised boy will someday take his place alongside other men in positions of power, authority, and prestige. Female circumcision confirms that private space is female space and that the circumcised girl will someday take her place alongside other women in positions of subordination to men. The dominant explanation for the circumcision of women, from medieval to modern times, is that women's sexuality needs to be controlled. The assumption is that women possess an extraordinary sexual appetite but lack the means to control it. By diminishing desire for and pleasure in sexual intercourse, female circumcision helps to ensure a woman's virtue. Women's passions, like women themselves, need to be controlled. This rhetoric is occasionally found also in Islamic discussions of the circumcision of men, but the social consequences of the rhetoric in each case are very different. Circumcision is a sign of enfranchisement for men, subjugation for women.[14]

Were Jewish Women Ever Circumcised?

Were Jewish women ever circumcised? The answer is no. Female circumcision was unknown in the ancient Near East in general and unknown to ancient Israel in particular. In Genesis 17 God enjoins circumcision upon Abraham and his male descendants, but neither the writer nor the earliest readers of the text seem to have been aware of the possibility that women too could be circumcised.[15] Rabbinic texts, both ancient and medieval, also do not mention the practice. The talmudic rabbis state explicitly that "it is not possible" to circumcise a woman, because a woman does not have a foreskin.[16] Aside from the Beta Israel of Ethiopia (the so-called Falashas), to whom I shall return in a moment, no Jewish community, in either ancient, medieval, or modern times, is known to have practiced female circumcision.[17] We may conclude with some certainty that within the Israelite and Jewish communities that have given us the Tanakh and rabbinic literature, women were not circumcised.

Strabo and the Black Jews of Ethiopia

There are two exceptions to this pattern, two pieces of evidence that female circumcision was practiced by at least some Jews. The first is provided by Strabo, a Greek geographer of the last part of the first century BCE, who writes as follows:

> One of the customs most zealously observed among the Egyptians is this, that they rear every child that is born, and circumcise the males, and excise the females, as is also customary among the Jews, who are also Egyptian in origin, as I have already stated in my account of them.[18]

Strabo comments on three remarkable characteristics of the Egyptians: they rear all their children, they circumcise the males (the verb is *peritemnein*), and they excise the females (the verb is *ektemnein*). Strabo notes that the same three remarkable characteristics can be found among the Jews (the word can also be translated "Judaeans") "who are Egyptian in origin." In another passage Strabo remarks that the successors of Moses instituted the practice of "circumcisions and excisions."[19] In yet a third passage, part of his description of Ethiopia, Strabo mentions the excision of Jewish women:

> They [the Creophagi, lit.: "meat-eaters", of Ethiopia] are mutilated in their sexual organs and the women are excised in the Jewish manner.[20]

Two points are striking about this passage: first, the excision of the women (the verb again is *ektemnein*) is said to be done "Jewishly" or "in the Jewish manner"; second, the mutilation of the male genitals is not said to be done in the Jewish manner. The males are not "circumcised" but "mutilated" (the Greek noun is *koloboi*). Elsewhere, when describing another Ethiopian tribe, Strabo explains that "not only are they mutilated in their sexual organs, but some of them are also circumcised, just as the Egyptians."[21] Whatever it is that one has to cut or cut off in order to become "mutilated" *(kolobos)* clearly is less, in Strabo's opinion, than whatever it is that one has to cut or cut off in order to be "circumcised" (from the verb *peritemnein*).[22] Egyptians, like Jews, are circumcised; the Meat-Eaters of Ethiopia are not. But their women are excised in the Jewish manner.

What are we to make of Strabo's thrice-told statement that Jewish women are excised? We have two possibilities: either Strabo is correct or he is not. If he is correct, this will mean that some Jewish community somewhere in the ancient world practiced female circumcision and that Strabo somehow discovered this fact, which otherwise is completely hidden from us. There is nothing implausible about this scenario; given the great diversity of ancient Judaism, it is hard to identify a practice that some Jews might not have observed, and given the paucity of our historical documentation, it is not impossible that a stray document (Strabo, for example) may preserve information not found anywhere else. We might perhaps seek to confirm Strabo's statement by appeal to the Beta Israel, the "black Jews" of Ethiopia, the so-called Falashas, who practice female circumcision, but this will not work, because surely the practice of the Beta Israel is to be explained as a manifestation of their Ethiopianness, and not of their Jewishness. (The Beta Israel today are Jews, having been brought to Israel in large numbers in 1984 and 1991, but their origins are most obscure and the degree of their connection with Judaism in pre-modern times is disputed; it is most unlikely that a "Jewish" Beta Israel community existed in the time of Strabo.)[23] The practice of the Beta Israel is simply part of general Ethiopian culture, in which female circumcision is widely practiced, and is not a relic of some long-lost Jewish tradition. A distinguished scholar of Ethiopian culture writes, "Falasha circumcision takes place on the eighth day, and since the Falashas also practise female excision it is virtually certain that their circumcision rites are part of the general Ethiopian heritage and not the result of any separate Jewish inspiration."[24] The Beta Israel are irrelevant to Strabo and offer scant proof that Jews ever practiced female circumcision; even if Strabo is correct, his statement remains uncorroborated.

The alternative possibility seems far more likely: Strabo simply is wrong.[25] The source of Strabo's error is easy to see. Strabo, a geographer, historian, and anthropologist, believed that the Jews were originally and "really" Egyptians,[26] and since he knew that Egyptians circumcised both males and females, he naturally concluded that the Jews did the same. Strabo was the victim of his own anthropological theory.

Philo

The best evidence against Strabo is provided by Philo of Alexandria, a Jewish philosopher, exegete, and apologist, who flourished in the first half of the first century CE. The fundamental point of his numerous works is that the Torah, the five books of Moses, is not a collection of inconsequential stories and recondite laws, but rather a book suffused with divine wisdom and penetrating insights on the relationship of God to the cosmos. Philo devotes two long passages to circumcision. The first is the introduction to his *On the Special Laws,* a book that discusses the meaning of the commandments of the Torah.[27] Philo concedes that circumcision is an object of ridicule among some people, but replies that the custom is observed by many nations, "particularly by the Egyptians, a nation regarded as the most populous, the most ancient, and the most philosophical." Philo, like Strabo, associates the Jewish practice with the Egyptian, but Philo's motive is to make the Jewish practice seem respectable and rational. He lists six reasons for the practice:

1. Circumcision affords protection against disease of the foreskin;
2. Circumcision, like the shaving of the body by Egyptian priests, promotes the purity[28] of the body;
3. Circumcision causes the reproductive organ, the generator of bodies and things seen, to resemble the heart, the generator of thought and things unseen;
4. Circumcision promotes fertility by giving semen an unobstructed path.

Philo claims these four explanations to be traditional, handed down "from the old-time studies of divinely gifted men." To these Philo adds two other explanations for which he claims credit; each of these interprets circumcision as a "symbol" of some moral quality "necessary to our well-being":

5. Circumcision represents "the excision of excessive and superfluous pleasure";

6. Circumcision represents the banishment of conceit, the removal of the evil belief that humans alone cause the creation of life.

Philo sees circumcision as efficacious on two levels, the physical and the metaphysical. On the physical level, the removal of the foreskin prevents disease (1) and promotes fertility (4) and purity (2). I am not entirely sure how to understand Philo's third argument. He is clearly connecting the circumcision of the body (penis) with the circumcision of the mind (heart) and no doubt is inspired to do so by passages like Deuteronomy 10:16, *You shall circumcise the foreskin of your heart.*[29] Perhaps Philo is advancing the argument so frequently raised in Christian and Jewish polemics (see chapter 3), that the circumcision of the body is meant to strengthen or represent the circumcision of the heart. However, since the other three arguments in this group of four are operating on the physical level, this one should as well. Perhaps, then, Philo is saying that the circumcised penis more closely resembles the heart than the uncircumcised penis. Is this what Philo means? I am not sure.[30] What is clear is that Philo's last two explanations, which he claims to be his own inventions, are metaphysical. Circumcision represents the excision of excessive pleasure (5) and the banishment of the arrogant belief that we humans alone can create life, even without divine assistance (6). The physical cutting away represents a moral cutting away.

These six arguments recur in different order and in slightly different formulation in Philo's other long passage about circumcision, the commentary on Genesis 17 in his *Questions and Answers on Genesis*.[31] The last two arguments, that is, the "symbolic" arguments for which Philo himself takes credit, are here applied to the question of the non-circumcision of women. Philo writes:

Why does He [God] command that only the males be circumcised?

In the first place, the Egyptians by the custom of their country circumcise the marriageable youth and maid in the fourteenth year of their age, when the male begins to get seed, and the female to have a menstrual flow. But the divine legislator ordained circumcision for males alone for many reasons.

The first of these is that the male has more pleasure in, and desire for, mating than does the female, and he is more ready for it. Therefore He rightly leaves out the female and suppresses the undue impulses of the male by the sign of circumcision.

> The second is that the matter of the female in the remains of the menstrual fluids produces the fetus. But the male provides the skill and the cause. And so, since the male provides the greater and more necessary part in the process of generation, it was proper that his pride should be checked by the sign of circumcision, but the material element, being inanimate, does not admit of arrogance. . . . [32]

While in the *Special Laws* Philo was eager to associate Jewish practice with the Egyptian, here he is eager to dissociate them. Jews circumcise only the males, while Egyptians circumcise both males and females. Jews circumcise boys at the age of eight days, Egyptians at the age of fourteen years.[33] Philo thus confirms the joint testimony of Strabo and the Greek papyrus that Egyptian women were circumcised but refutes Strabo's claim that Jewish women were too.

This Philonic passage is the earliest evidence for Jewish concern about the disparity between the circumcision of men and the noncircumcision of women. Why do Jews circumcise only the males? Philo gives two answers. The first, an elaboration of argument 5, maintains that circumcision serves to check male lust, which is much stronger than the female's—in fact, a little too strong. The second, an elaboration of argument 6 above, maintains that circumcision serves to check male pride, which has its origin in the fact that males contribute the more important part in the process of generation.[34] Since males have more pleasure than females in intercourse, their lust needs to be checked, but not the lust of women; since males have greater pride than females for their role in procreation, their pride needs to be checked, but not the pride of women. I shall return to these answers in chapter 6.

Undoubtedly Philo would have argued that Jewish women, no less than Jewish men, need to suppress their lust and their pride, and that this suppression is an essential ingredient in righteousness for both sexes alike. Females, for Philo, are inferior to males, but even they, within their limited abilities, are capable of righteousness.[35] Only males need physical circumcision, while both males and females need the lesson taught by circumcision (what Christians would call spiritual circumcision). Since Philo nowhere says that circumcision is an essential criterion for membership in the people of Israel—in only one exceptional passage does Philo even mention the "covenantal" value of circumcision—for him the status of women within Israel is not affected by the absence of circumcision. Circumcision does not determine status.[36]

"Why does he [God] command that only the males be circumcised?" was only one of a series of questions about circumcision that Philo an-

swered. In the first century of our era, the practice of circumcision
seems to have been widely debated by Greek-speaking Jews.[37] The historian Josephus promised to write an essay on the subject but apparently did not succeed in fulfilling his promise (or, if he did, his work is
lost).[38] Some Jews attempted to conceal their circumcision through epispasm, the drawing down or stretching of penile skin so as to give the appearance of a foreskin.[39] Some Jews argued that circumcision was not
necessary. If we excise excess pleasure and suppress the impious conceit
of believing that we are capable of creating without divine assistance,
why do we need the circumcision of the body? This argument much
troubled Philo, who insists that the circumcision of the body was as necessary as the circumcision of the heart.[40] Our passage in the *Questions
and Answers on Genesis* suggests that these Jewish opponents of circumcision may also have appealed to the non-circumcision of Jewish
women to buttress their case.[41] As we shall see in our next chapter, these
arguments of the Jewish opponents of circumcision found a receptive
audience in early Christianity.

Conclusions

Female circumcision is first attested in Hellenistic Egypt. In contemporary times the practice has become associated with Islam and is observed in many regions of Africa, the Near East, and Asia. Aside from
some statements of the geographer Strabo, there is no evidence that any
Jewish community—aside from the Beta Israel of Ethiopia—has ever
practiced female circumcision. If we reject Strabo's testimony on the
grounds that he has incorrectly conflated the Jews with the Egyptians,
who did in fact practice female circumcision, and if we set aside the
customs of the Beta Israel, on the grounds that their observance of female circumcision is more a function of their Ethiopianness than of
their Jewishness, we may restate the sentence more simply: there is no
evidence anywhere that any Jewish community has ever practiced female circumcision.

   Philo, the Alexandrian Jewish philosopher of the first century, says
explicitly that Egyptians circumcise women but that Jews do not. Philo
is also the first Jewish author to deal with the question that animates
this book: why did God command only Jewish men to be circumcised
and not Jewish women? He replies that men need to be circumcised because men need to have both their lust checked and their pride dimin-

ished, and these desirable goals are achieved through circumcision. I shall return to this idea in chapter 6. Philo also implies that Jewish critics of circumcision had used the non-circumcision of women as one of their arguments. We shall see this argument more clearly and fully expressed in Christian polemic, to which I now turn.

Appendix: Richard Francis Burton on the Circumcision of Jewish Women

In his translation of *The Book of the Thousand Nights and a Night*, Richard Francis Burton (1821–1890) inserts a long note on female circumcision that includes the following:

> As regards the popular idea that Jewish women were circumcised till the days of Rabbi Gershom (A.D. 1000) who denounced it as a scandal to the Gentiles, the learned Prof. H. Graetz informs me, with some indignation, that the rite was never practiced and that the great Rabbi contended only against polygamy. Female circumcision, however, is I believe the rule amongst some outlying tribes of Jews. The rite is the proper complement of male circumcision, evening the sensitiveness of the genitories by reducing it equally in both sexes: an uncircumcised woman has the venereal orgasm much sooner and oftener than a circumcised man, and frequent coitus would injure her health; hence, I believe, despite the learned historian, that it is practised by some Eastern Jews. [42]

This paragraph, grounded in Burton's sexual fantasies, contains no reliable information about Jews, Judaism, circumcision, or sex. He does not reveal the source of his statement "that Jewish women were circumcised till the days of Rabbi Gershom." The "learned Prof. H. Graetz" is the well-known Jewish historian Heinrich Graetz (1817–1891), who has correctly informed Burton that Rabbenu Gershom of Mayence (Mainz), "the Light of the Exile" (ca. 1000 CE), issued an edict prohibiting polygamy. Graetz also correctly informed Burton that there is no evidence linking R. Gershom with female circumcision or attesting to the practice of female circumcision among medieval Jews. [43]

   As for the rest, Burton conjectures that some eastern or "outlying" Jews practice female circumcision because it is good for a woman's sex life. Burton asserts that "an uncircumcised woman has the venereal orgasm much sooner and oftener than a circumcised man, and frequent coitus would injure her health." Whence Burton derived this fantastic information, he does not say. Elsewhere he has a far more realistic assessment of the horrific effects that female circumcision might have on a woman's sexuality.[44] Nor does he explain how "outlying" Jews—that is, Jews whom he has never seen and about whom he knows nothing— came to be privy to this sexual secret and not, say, the Jews of England or Poland. Perhaps Burton has the Beta Israel of Ethiopia in mind, but he does not mention them, and surely he would have done so had he known anything about them.

In sum, the paragraph is valueless except as a window into the sexual imagination of Richard Francis Burton. Some writers have accepted Burton's assertions, not realizing that he knows nothing about Jewish practice.[45]

CHAPTER 3

Christian Questions, Christian Responses

He, who with all Heav'n's heraldry whilere
Enter'd the world, now bleeds to give us ease;
Alas, how soon our sin
Sore doth begin
His Infancy to seize!

　　　　　　John Milton, *Upon the Circumcision*

At the end of the previous chapter, I discussed the evidence of Philo, which shows that the Jews did not practice female circumcision, that the Egyptians did, and that some Jews were opposed to the Jewish circumcision of males. One of the arguments advanced by these opponents may have been based on the non-circumcision of women: why did God command the circumcision of males but not of females? Exactly how these opponents of circumcision developed this line of thought, we do not know. Christian opponents of Jewish circumcision also hit upon this argument, perhaps having learned it from their Jewish predecessors, and in this chapter we shall see how they developed it. I begin with Paul, not only because Paul in one passage appeals to the non-circumcision of women as an argument against Jewish circumcision, but because Paul's legacy determines the contours of all subsequent Christian reflection on "the Law" and circumcision. From Paul I move on to the Christian writers of antiquity and the high Middle Ages who advance one or another version of the argument drawn from the non-circumcision of women. Finally, in the last part of the chapter, I discuss the Christian responses to their own question, for even Christians had to explain why God in Genesis 17 gave the sign of the old covenant only to men.

Paul

Philo's opponents were not the only Jewish critics of circumcision in the first century of our era. Among these critics certainly the best known is the apostle Paul, a younger contemporary of Philo. Paul was a Jew and always thought of himself as a Jew, but he believed that Judaism had been forever changed by the death and resurrection of Jesus. The relationship between God and the Jews, and between God and the gentiles, was no longer what it once had been. Ethnic Israel was replaced as God's chosen people by the non-ethnic community of believers in Jesus Christ. These believers would soon be called "Christians," and their belief system would soon be called "Christianity," but Paul was still unaware of these developments; for him the belief in Christ was the heart of the new Judaism. The old covenant between God and Israel, what Paul frequently calls "the Law," had been replaced by a new and much better one. Of all the requirements of "the Law," the one that elicited more criticism from Paul than any other was the requirement of circumcision. Paul was the most outspoken Jewish critic of Jewish circumcision in the first century. According to him, circumcision was unnecessary, even dangerous, in the new dispensation. Gentiles who believe in Jesus Christ, Paul argued, should pay no attention to the rantings of those who insist that salvation is unattainable without circumcision. On the contrary: if gentile Christians become circumcised, they run the risk of losing everything they have gained by believing in Christ. *Now I, Paul, say to you that if you receive circumcision, Christ will be of no advantage to you* (Galatians 5:2). Justification before God is through faith, not works of the law; in other words, ultimate salvation is to be attained only by faith in Jesus, not by circumcision and the other observances of the Torah.

Paul's main objections to circumcision are spelled out over and over again in his letters to the Romans and the Galatians. In addition, the letters to the Ephesians and Colossians, which, most modern scholars agree, were written not by Paul himself but by members of his school, further develop some of Paul's ideas. In the following paragraphs I shall cite four of the most significant Pauline passages about circumcision and discuss them briefly. My goal is to explain in the briefest possible terms what Paul and his disciples thought about Jewish circumcision, and what the Christian tradition in subsequent centuries learned about circumcision from each passage. Needless to say, almost every detail in the interpretation of these passages has been disputed by scholars, and if I were so inclined, the following paragraphs could easily become pages, and the pages could easily become chapters. But to avoid straying from my theme, I will tread lightly and quickly through some dangerous and highly contested terrain.[1]

First passage:

> For he is not a real Jew who is one outwardly, nor is true circumcision something external and physical. He is a Jew who is one inwardly, and real circumcision is a matter of the heart, spiritual and not literal. His praise is not from men but from God [Romans 2:28–29].

God wants not the circumcision of the flesh but the circumcision of the heart; *real circumcision is a matter of the heart, spiritual and not literal.* True Jewishness—what later Christians would call the true Israel—is an inward or spiritual state, not an external mark on the body. This argument will recur again and again in virtually all subsequent Christian thinking about the biblical requirement of circumcision. Numerous Christian writers expatiate upon the virtues of "spiritual" circumcision.[2] By abstaining from sinful words, Christians circumcise their lips; by abstaining from sinful thoughts Christians circumcise their hearts; and by abstaining from sinful lusts and passions Christians circumcise their flesh. These writers routinely adduce for support biblical passages that speak of the "circumcision" of the heart, such as *Then the Lord your God will circumcise your heart and the hearts of your offspring to love the Lord your God with all your heart and soul, in order that you may live* (Deuteronomy 30:4), and *Circumcise your hearts to the Lord, remove the foreskins of your hearts, O men of Judah and inhabitants of Jerusalem* (Jeremiah 4:4). This, the spiritual circumcision of the heart, is the true circumcision that God really wants, as Paul explains, *For we are the true circumcision, who worship God in spirit . . . and put no confidence in the flesh* (Philippians 3:3).[3]

Second passage:

> He [Abraham] received the sign of circumcision as a seal of the righteousness which he had by faith while he was still uncircumcised. The purpose was to make him the father of all who believe without being circumcised and who thus have righteousness reckoned to them, and likewise the father of the circumcised who are not merely circumcised but also follow the example of the faith which our father Abraham had before he was circumcised [Romans 4:11–12].

Abraham and his descendants occupy a special place in the unfolding of sacred history not because of their circumcision but because of their faith. Even before he was circumcised, Abraham was just in God's eyes because of his faith. Through his faith in God, Abraham is the father to all those who similarly have faith in God, whether or not they are circumcised. Virtually all subsequent Christian writers on circumcision follow Paul in citing Abraham as proof that physical circumcision is not necessary to find favor in God's eyes. Not only Abraham, of course: Enoch, too, *walked with God* (Genesis 5:24) even though uncircumcised. Noah was *a righteous man, blameless in his generations* (Genesis 6:9). Job (Job 1:1), and Melchizedeq (Genesis 14:18), too, were righteous. None of these biblical worthies was circumcised. If circumcision were an essential element of righteousness, why was Adam not created circumcised? And so on.[4] These further illustrations merely expand upon Paul's point: the stories about biblical heroes show that one can be righteous and just before God even without circumcision.

A serious problem rises naturally from this mode of reading. If Abraham's righteousness is proof that God wanted and wants spiritual circumcision and not physical circumcision, why did he command Abraham to circumcise his foreskin? Paul responds that Abraham *received the sign of circumcision as a seal of the righteousness which he had by faith while he was still uncircumcised.* The meaning of this is not at all clear, and later exegetes, ancient and modern, had to work hard to make sense of it. I shall return to the idea of circumcision as a "sign" below.

Third passage:

> Therefore remember that at one time you Gentiles in the flesh, called "the foreskin" by what is called "the circumcision"—which is made in the flesh by hands—remember that you were at that time separated from Christ, alienated from the commonwealth of Israel, and strangers to the covenants of promise, having no hope and without God in the world. But now in Christ Jesus you who once were far off have been brought near in the blood of Christ [Ephesians 2:11–13].

Jewish circumcision divides humanity into two camps, Jews and gentiles. Jews call gentiles *"the foreskin"* or "the foreskinned," and gentiles reciprocate by calling Jews *"the circumcision"* or "those of the circumcision." In various passages Paul uses "the circumcision" as a metonym for "Judaism" or "the collectivity of Jews," in contrast with "the foreskin," which is a metonym for "the beliefs and practices of non-Jews" or "the collectivity of non-Jews."[5]

According to Paul, circumcision has separated Jews from gentiles and gentiles from God; now, however, through *the blood of Christ,* gentiles *who once were far off have been brought near.* This is the language of religious conversion, and surely we have here an allusion to circumcision as the Jewish conversion ritual par excellence. Formerly a gentile had to be circumcised in order to draw near to God, but most gentiles did not become circumcised and did not draw near to God. On the contrary, circumcision served as a barrier. Therefore God has allowed the gentiles to draw near through *the blood of Christ,* which clearly will be a more effective agent of salvation than circumcision ever was. Circumcision divides humanity; the blood of Christ unites it. As we shall see, later Christian writers routinely see Christianity's superiority to Judaism, and baptism's superiority to circumcision, precisely in the fact that the former are more universal than the latter.

Fourth passage:

> In him [Christ] also you were circumcised with a circumcision made without hands, by putting off the body of flesh in the circumcision of Christ; and you were buried with him in baptism, in which you were also raised with him through faith in the working of God [Colossians 2:11–12].

Christians participate in the circumcision of Jesus through their own spiritual circumcision, "a circumcision made without hands." Later exegetes explain that Christians need only spiritual circumcision, because the physical circumcision of Christ (Luke 2:21) exempts them from the necessity for physical circumcision. Christians participate in the life of Christ in another way too: through baptism they experience Christ's death and rebirth. The juxtaposition of these two sentiments suggested to later readers the idea that baptism replaced circumcision. No other verse in the New Testament makes this association, and one might argue that even this verse does not intend to equate the two, but Christian thinkers regularly cited Colossians 2 to support their assertion that circumcision had been replaced by baptism, just as Judaism had been replaced by Christianity.[6]

Having surveyed the Pauline foundations of all subsequent Christian reflection about circumcision, I return to our theme. In a well-known passage, Paul proclaims, *There is neither Jew nor Greek, there is neither slave nor free, there is neither male nor female; for you are all one in Christ Jesus* (Galatians 3:28). Paul implicitly contrasts the community of "the Law," as represented by circumcision, with the community of faith in Christ, as represented by baptism. Circumcision discriminates, baptism does not. Circumcision marks the Jew, not the gentile; the slave owned by a Jew, not the free gentile; the male, not the female. In contrast, baptism knows none of these distinctions.[7] The ritual marker of the community of faith in Christ, baptism, unifies humanity, whereas the ritual marker of the community of the Law, circumcision, separates humanity. Here, then, Paul implicitly adumbrates the gender argument: circumcision discriminates on the basis of gender; baptism does not. What is only implicit in Paul will become explicit in later Christian thinkers and polemicists.

Is Paul in fact arguing that men and women are the same, equal, in Christ? Does the replacement of the gendered ritual of circumcision with the gender-neutral ritual of baptism betoken the removal of all gender boundaries within the community of faith? This question has been much debated, with no consensus on the matter. I think that Paul indeed intended to abolish, or at least to radically reconceive, the social boundary between Jew and gentile,[8] but had no intention whatever to abolish the social boundaries between male and female. Paul believed that men and women had separate functions in the new order, as in the old, and that the place of women was decidedly below that of men. He writes *Man is the image and reflection of God; but woman is the reflection of man* (1 Corinthians 11:7), and *Women should be silent in the churches. For they are not permitted to speak, but they should be subordinate. . . . If there is anything they desire to know, let them ask their husbands at home* (1 Corinthians 14:34–35). In the same spirit the author of Colossians writes *Wives, be subject to your husbands, as is fitting in the Lord* (Colossians 3:18), and the author of First Timothy writes *I permit no woman to teach or to have authority over men; she is to keep silent* (1 Timothy 2:12). This attitude probably explains the fact, noted by many commentators,[9] that when Paul refers to those who witnessed the appearance of the risen Jesus (1 Corinthians 15:4–8), he omits the female witnesses who play a prominent role in the gospels' accounts of the same events. Paul did not want women to serve as guarantors of Christian truth.

Indeed, the resounding proclamation *there is no longer Jew or Greek, there is no longer slave or free, there is no longer male and female* (Galatians 3:28) recurs in somewhat different form in three other Pauline passages. Only the passage from Galatians includes *there is no longer male and female*. The other versions read *there is no distinction between Jew and Greek* (Romans 10:12) and *for in the one spirit we were all baptized into one body—Jews or Greeks, slaves or free* (1 Corinthians 12:13), and *there is no longer Greek and Jew, circumcised and uncircumcised, barbarian, Scythian, slave and free* (Colossians

3:11). I conclude that *There is no longer male and female*, which appears only in Galatians 3:28, does not mean that men and women are "the same" according to Paul; even baptized women are to keep their separate—and inferior—position. Unity in Christ does not obliterate social distinctions; unity is not uniformity.[10] Some contemporary Christians would like to see Paul as a proponent of women's "liberation," but in this respect, as in so many others, Paul does not always say what his later interpreters want him to say.[11]

Against the Jews

In the following pages I shall cite various Christian works, most of them written in Latin, which use the non-circumcision of women as an anti-Jewish argument. Most of these works have as their explicit goal the demonstration of the error of Judaism and the truth of Christianity. In terms of their content, they belong to a single category, often called by modern scholars "*adversus Judaeos* literature," that is, literature directed against Jews and Judaism.

From its inception, Christianity defined itself simultaneously against paganism and against Judaism. Paganism was the belief in many Gods, Judaism was the belief in only one God. Christianity defined itself as the belief in one God who nevertheless was three, a triune God. Paganism was the worship of the emperor, which both Judaism and Christianity rejected. Paganism was the belief in the Greek and Roman myths, which both Judaism and Christianity ridiculed. Paganism and Judaism worshipped the divinity through animal sacrifices and other offerings, which Christianity rejected. Judaism, like Christianity and unlike paganism, was based on the divine revelation contained in the Bible, but the Jews, like the pagans, refused to accept the subsequent revelation contained in the words and life of Jesus, which the Christians accepted. And so on. Christians needed to wage an intellectual and spiritual war on two fronts, and as a result, ancient Christian literature contains numerous works entitled *Against the Greeks*, designed to justify Christianity's departure from paganism, and numerous works entitled *Against the Jews*, designed to justify Christianity's departure from Judaism. This literature begins in the second century and played an important role in Christian self-definition.

Christian anti-Jewish literature constitutes a single category only in terms of its intent to prove the error of Jews and Judaism. Otherwise it is a disparate collection, varying by date, genre, language, mode of argumentation, audience, and setting. The collection ranges in date from the second century to modern times. It varies by genre. Some of the oldest works are dialogues between a Jew and a Christian, but other genres were common too: sermon, essay, commentary, epistle, and, in the Middle Ages, poetry and drama. The literature varies by language: first Greek, then Latin, and then a wide range of languages. It varies in mode of argumentation. Some works are content merely to paraphrase the letters of Paul or the stories of the gospels in order to highlight Jewish error and evil. Others collect biblical verses, either from the Old Testament alone or from both testaments, to prove that the Jews misunderstand their own scriptures. Biblical exegesis is a central theme, since both Jews and Christians claim the same scriptures and the same sacred history. This literature also varies in audience. Some of the works entitled *Against the Jews* were not intended to be read by Jews; their intended audience was Christian, and these works sought to strengthen faith, to quell doubts, and to answer questions. These works were not "missionary" at all. Other works, in contrast, seem to have had a proselytizing intent. The author hoped either that Jews would read the work and convert, or that Christians might arm themselves with the author's arguments, venture forth to encounter Jews, and return home victorious, having won over some Jewish souls. Works written under the Roman empire do not have the same setting as those written, say, in Spain during the seventh century or in France during the twelfth. This literature is not only varied but also extensive. A comprehensive survey consists of three hefty volumes, requiring over fourteen hundred pages to survey the literature from the second century to the thirteenth.[12]

Christian anti-Jewish literature is enormously rich and varied, and I cannot claim to have read it all, let alone to have mastered it all. In my pursuit of Christian reflection on the non-circumcision of women I have uncovered a fair number of relevant passages, but I have no doubt that many others remain to be identified. I can only hope that the basic outlines of my survey will not be much affected by additional references.[13]

Justin Martyr

The *Dialogue with Trypho the Jew,* written in Greek by Justin Martyr, a Christian apologist of the middle of the second century, is one of the earliest extant specimens of Christian anti-Jewish literature. It depicts a dialogue between Justin himself and a Jew named Trypho. Whether the dialogue was real or imagined is an open question, but the answer does not much matter for our purposes. Justin, of course, represents the Christians, the winners of the debate, and Trypho represents the Jews, the losers. One of the central concerns of the work is the interpretation of the Hebrew Bible; Justin is determined to show that Christians, who accept Jesus as God and Christ but ignore many of the laws of the Torah, interpret the Bible correctly, while the Jews, who deny Christ but observe the laws, do not. Thus Justin devotes a good many paragraphs to the ritual observances of the law, especially circumcision. His fundamental thesis is that the ritual requirements in general, and circumcision in particular, are not universal timeless commandments, but were intended for a specific people (the Jews) for a specific time and for a specific reason. God never intended them to be observed by his true worshippers, the Christians. Justin argues in the Pauline manner (but without citing Paul) that circumcision cannot be a requirement for salvation:

> The Scriptures and the facts of the case force us to admit that Abraham received circumcision for a sign, not for justification itself. Thus was it justly said of your people, *That soul which shall not be circumcised on the eighth day shall be destroyed out of his people* [Genesis 17:14]. Moreover, the fact that females cannot receive circumcision of the flesh shows that circumcision was given as a sign, not as an act of justification. For God also bestowed upon women the capability of performing every good and virtuous act. We see that the physical formation of male and female is different, but it is equally evident that the bodily form is not what makes either of them good or evil, but rather their piety and justice.[14]

That Abraham's circumcision is a "sign," and not a function, of righteousness is an argument with which Paul would certainly have agreed; Paul himself makes the same point in the second Pauline passage cited above. No doubt Justin, like Paul, has Genesis in mind: *And Abraham believed in the Lord; and the Lord reckoned it to him as righteousness* (Genesis 15:6). The verse demonstrates that Abraham was righteous even without circumcision. After this Pauline beginning, Justin goes his own way. Since Genesis also says that he who is not circumcised is to be cut off from his people, Justin argues that circumcision is just a "sign," that is, a sign of belonging to the people. Earlier in his argument, Justin had asserted that circumcision was to serve as a "sign" that would separate the Jews from other nations by making them conspicuous and identifiable.[15] Circumcision, then, is just a sign. As further proof that circumcision cannot have anything to do with righteousness, Justin adduces women. Like men, women are deemed righteous or wicked by their actions; their circumcision—or lack of it—is irrelevant. Since women's non-circumcision is not a function of their righteousness, the same must be true for men.

Justin probably derived the basis of this argument from Jewish circles of the sort combated by Philo. Scholars have long argued that much of the early Christian polemic against Jewish law derives from "radical" or "radically hellenized" Jewish groups; similarly, scholars have long argued that Justin is much indebted to Hellenistic Judaism, perhaps even to Philo directly. It is reasonable to suggest, therefore, that Justin, in arguing that the non-circumcision of women demonstrates that God does not demand the circumcision of men, may be echoing the arguments of Jewish opponents of circumcision whom Philo had combated a century earlier.[16]

Cyprian of Carthage and Zeno of Verona

Many of Justin's anti-circumcision arguments became commonplace in subsequent Christian polemic in both Greek and Latin, but the argument that interests us, the argument derived from the non-circumcision of women, did not. As far as I have been able to determine, this argument nowhere recurs in the subsequent anti-Jewish literature written in Greek. There are numerous polemics against Judaism, numerous attacks on Jewish circumcision, but the argument drawn from the non-circumcision of women does not recur again—or, if it does, I have not found it, and the standard handbooks do not record it.[17]

On the Latin side, the argument makes a few significant appearances in antiquity, not enough to call the argument a commonplace but enough to say that the argument took root. I do not know whether any of these authors read Justin, but each, perhaps independently, has hit upon Justin's argument and developed it further than Justin had himself. Cyprian, a bishop in Carthage in the mid-third century, gathered a collection of biblical citations to prove the truth of Christianity, by showing (among other things) the concordance of the Old Testament with the New. Under the heading "That the first circumcision, the carnal, has been made void, and that a second, a spiritual, has been promised instead," Cyprian briefly marshals some verses demonstrating the Christian position, already familiar to us from Justin, and then tacks on at the end the following line: "That sign [circumcision] is of no use to women, while all [Christians] are signed with the sign of the Lord." The superiority of baptism to circumcision consists, in part, in the fact that the former is performed on all adherents of the faith community, men and women alike, while the latter is performed only on men.[18]

This argument is developed by Zeno of Verona, who flourished about a century after Cyprian (second half of the fourth century). He is the author of ninety-two brief but highly rhetorical essays (or "tractates") on a variety of themes. The essay on circumcision is dedicated to proving the error of the Jews:

> The Jew is accustomed to boast, often and with much clamor, that circumcision is the nobility of his people, that it is the power of a heavenly sign, that it is the true bearer of eternal life, that it is the perpetual consort of the future kingdom, without which no one is able to come to the notice of God at all.[19]

Behind these rather high-blown and almost untranslatable phrases—in particular I am not sure what Zeno means by the word *sacramentum,* which I have translated "sign" both here and in the following excerpt—we recognize that Zeno's Jew magnifies the importance of circumcision no less than the rabbis do.[20] In response, Zeno gives a medical definition of circumcision. It is merely "a circular scar, made by a knife, at the place where the skin has suffered a round injury."[21] The Jew contends that circumcision is the remedy against Adam's sin and the guarantor of eternal life, but how can that be, Zeno asks, when this remedy is available only to one sex? Perhaps it cured Adam, but it certainly did not cure Eve.[22] The true circumcision that God wants is not the carnal circumcision of the Jews but the spiritual circumcision of the Christians.

> With this sign [spiritual circumcision] we are circumcised, both men and women. . . . The prior circumcision cuts away flesh, the second cuts away the vices of the soul; the former with a knife, the latter by the spirit; the former a part, the latter the entire human being; the former the male alone, the latter both sexes; the former the foreskin of a small piece of flesh, the latter the foreskin of all worldly desire. . . . The former rejoices in blood, the latter in grace.[23]

The gender equality of Christian spiritual circumcision is evident from the fact that it even began with a woman, Mary, all of whose sins of the heart were "cut off" when she received Christ "through her ear."[24] By obeying God, Mary circumcised her heart—a true spiritual circumcision. In sum, the spiritual circumcision of Christianity, which is available to both men and women and which receives ritual expression in Christian baptism, is superior to the physical circumcision of Judaism, which is available only to men. This argument, first shaped by Cyprian and Zeno, recurs in other Latin Christian writers of Late Antiquity.[25]

The Dispute between the Church and the Synagogue: A Dialogue

Our next text is even richer and more interesting. *The Dispute between the Church and the Synagogue: A Dialogue* is an anonymous work, probably written in the fifth century, perhaps in Spain.[26] It contains one of the earliest, if not the earliest, representation of the conflict between Judaism and Christianity as a debate between two women, Lady Synagogue *(Synagoga)* and Lady Church *(Ecclesia)*, a conceit that would become popular in medieval Christian art and drama.[27] The two women argue in court, each disputing the claims of the other. In large part, the ground covered in this dispute is familiar, even if the literary form is novel. After Lady Synagogue has boasted of her possession of the Law and circumcision, what she calls her "sign," Lady Church responds:

> For if you say that your people is to be saved through the sign of your passion—what shall your virgins do, what shall your widows do, what shall even the Mothers of the Synagogue do, if you testify that the sign of circumcision gives to the people the benefit of eternal life? Therefore it is fair to conclude that you do not have Jewish women: men are circumcised; women, however, cannot have a foreskin; therefore they are not able to be saved, if you are saved by circumcision. You see, therefore, that you are able to have men, that is, the circumcised, as Jews. Women, however, who are not able to be circumcised, I declare are neither Jews nor Christians, but pagans.[28]

The argument of the first sentence is fundamentally the same as Justin's. Circumcision cannot be an agent or "sign" of salvation, because in that case women would be excluded from salvation. The author calls circumcision a "passion," that is, a suffering, because from the Christian perspective the blood of Christ has replaced the blood of circumcision; as Justin says, "the blood of that [carnal] circumcision has been nullified, and we trust [instead] in the blood of salvation," namely, the blood shed by Christ on the cross.[29] The author highlights three categories of women who would not be saved if circumcision were an agent of salvation: virgins, widows, and Mothers of the Synagogue. Jewish inscriptions from Italy commemorate three women, each of whom was a "Mother of the Synagogue." Whether the title was merely honorific, or whether it also brought with it communal responsibility and leadership, is unknown.[30] In any case, I am not sure how to interpret this list of three. Perhaps the author simply means "all Jewish women": from the young and undistinguished (virgins), to the old (widows) and the distinguished (Mothers of the Synagogue). Or perhaps the author is deliberately choosing as his examples women who are not married: virgins, widows, and Mothers of the Synagogue (a title that seems to have been bestowed most often on elderly widows; not one of the three attested "Mothers of the Synagogue" had a husband at the time of her death). We shall see below that one possible Jewish response to the Christian argument is that Jewish women do not need circumcision because they fulfill their Judaism by facilitating the Jewish observances of their husbands and sons. Perhaps to forestall this response, the author chose to highlight women who do not have husbands. The question must remain open.

If the first sentence is still within Justin's framework, the following sentences go well beyond it. Justin had argued that circumcision was a sign of membership in the people, not a sign of righteousness, and therefore of no consequence to Christians, who, like women, could be righteous even without circumcision. The author of this text takes this argument and develops it brilliantly. If circumcision is a sign of membership in the people, then Jewish women are excluded not only from salvation but even from the name "Jew" altogether. If Jewish men are Jews by virtue of their circumcision, then Jewish women cannot be Jews. Not circumcised, they are not Jews. Not baptized, they are not Christians. Therefore, concludes the author in a wonderful *reductio ad absurdum,* they must be pagans.

This argument is especially effective in its literary context. There is something odd about having a woman, in this case Lady Synagogue, defend the importance of circumcision, when women are excluded from membership in the synagogue because of their lack of circumcision. Similarly, in the following sentences the author goes on to mock circumcision as an agent of salvation, and again adduces women as proof. Jewish women who have committed adultery, he says, ought not to be punished or condemned, since their only sin is to have played with the circumcised male organ, the sign of salvation. The organ on which circumcision is performed is normally kept hidden and private, to be seen only by a wife. Circumcision is thus a sign not of salvation but of sin, shame, and lust.[31] In contrast, the Christian sign is borne publicly on the forehead (the author seems to be referring to the chrism that is applied right after baptism) by men and women alike.

Medieval Christian Writers

So far we have seen that the non-circumcision of Jewish women provided three arguments to Christian anti-Jewish writers in Late Antiquity. First, Justin's argument: the non-circumcision of women proves the superfluity of circumcision, since women can be righteous before God just as men can. Second, Cyprian's and Zeno's argument: the non-circumcision of Jewish women proves the inferiority of Judaism to Christianity, since Judaism circumcises only men, whereas Christianity baptizes men and women alike. Third, the argument of *The Dispute between the Church and the Synagogue*: the non-circumcision of Jewish women proves their anomalous character within Judaism, since circumcision is essential to Jewishness, but Jewish women are not circumcised.

After about 600 CE, these arguments seem not to recur in Christian Latin literature until the twelfth and thirteenth centuries, when they become commonplace in Christian anti-Jewish polemic and are to be found in the mouths and pens not only of learned clerics but also of mystics and merchants.[32] The battleground of the Christian-Jewish debate in these centuries was not only the church and the royal court, but also the marketplace, the village square, and country taverns. The debate was not only public but also private.[33]

A good example of this "democratization" is the disputation of Ceuta (in Morocco on the straits of Gibraltar) that took place in 1179 between William Alfachinus of Genoa, the protagonist and author of the written account of the proceedings, and a Jew named Abraham. Neither William nor his disputant was a scholar; both were merchants who were loyal to their respective religious traditions and were prepared to defend them. The first topic of the disputation was circumcision:

> The Jew said: You say that the messiah has come and was circumcised. Why then are Christians not circumcised?
> William Alfachinus of Genoa responded: Tell me first if you accept as true all the things that the prophets have said, and then I shall respond to you.
> The Jew said: If I did not accept as true those things that the prophets have prophesied, I would not claim that I am a Jew.

> William replied: I say truly that the Messiah has come, was born under the law, and was circumcised because he wished to fulfill the law. He was the end of circumcision, as the prophet testifies, who said that circumcision in the time of the Messiah would necessarily change into holy water and hyssop.[34] And you know that women were not circumcised, and therefore it was necessary that in the course of history there should be and appear something by which humankind of each sex would be able to be saved in common. [William continues by citing various passages from the prophets to prove that God desires the circumcision of the heart.][35]

Here the non-circumcision of women proves the theological inevitability of spiritual circumcision and Christianity. The Jewish disputant has no reply. Indeed, in another literary dialogue, this one written by a Jewish convert to Christianity, the Jewish disputant does not know how to refute the anti-circumcision argument based on the non-circumcision of women; he is forced to admit, "About this I certainly do not know any reply to give you, because none has been shown to me."[36] From the Christian perspective, the non-circumcision of Jewish women provided a crushing anti-Jewish argument.

Christian Views of Biblical Circumcision

From the Christian perspective, at least the Western Christian perspective, the non-circumcision of women had two contradictory implications: it provided several arguments against Judaism, as we have just seen, and it also posed a problem for the Christians themselves: why did God impose circumcision only upon the male descendants of Abraham? True enough, circumcision was theologically obsolete, having been superseded by Christian baptism, but even so, the old covenant would appear to have been faulty since it made no provision for one half of God's chosen people. This small problem required attention because it was part of a large problem.

The large problem was circumcision itself.[37] If, as Paul says and all later Christians repeat, physical circumcision has no value in God's eyes because God wants spiritual circumcision, why did God demand physical circumcision of the Israelites? If, however, physical circumcision once had value in God's eyes, why did he abrogate it and replace it with baptism? The God of the Christians thus appeared to be either malevolent or capricious: malevolent, because he once demanded a painful and dangerous procedure that had no purpose, or capricious, because he first demanded one ritual of his followers and then substituted another in its place. Bad enough that pagan critics of Christianity advanced such arguments; even worse, Christian heretics used such arguments to support their notion that the God of the Old Testament was distinct from the God of the New Testament. The God of the Old Testament, they said, was an evil God who wanted to harm human beings and prevent them from attaining knowledge and eternal life; the God of the New Testament, in contrast, was the true God, the God of truth and light, in whom alone all true Christians should believe and from whom alone all true Christians should expect salvation. One of the arguments for the perversity and malevolence of the God of the Old Testament was the requirement of circumcision. Upholders of Christian orthodoxy, or, to speak more accurately of the early centuries when this debate first broke out, upholders of what would *become* Christian orthodoxy, were shocked by the prospect of a Christianity without the Old Testament. They did all they could to prove the conformity of the Old Testament with the New and the inherent reasonableness of the requirements of the Torah. Already in the second century, we can witness the surprising phenomenon of Christian writers defending the Old Testament in general, and the requirement of circumcision in particular—all from a Christian perspective of course. The phenomenon continued until early modern times.[38]

Why, then, did God command the Israelites to be circumcised? The classic Christian answer, found all over Christian literature from ancient to modern times, is that circumcision was a "sign." The idea that circumcision is a "sign" derives from the Pauline verse that I cited above, *[Abraham] received the sign of circumcision as a seal of righteousness* (Romans 4:11), which in turn alludes to a verse of Genesis, *You shall circumcise the flesh of your foreskin, and that shall be the sign of the covenant between me and you* (Genesis 17:11). In Genesis circumcision is a "sign" by which God remembers his covenant with Abraham's offspring, as I explained in chapter 1; in the Christian reading of the verse, however, circumcision becomes a sign by which Israelites are recognized, either by one another or by non-Israelites. It is a sign of Israelite difference. And why did the Israelites need a sign of their distinctiveness? Here are some of the reasons that were suggested: to separate them from pagans, especially the Egyptians and the Canaanites; to inhibit intermarriage; to provide Abraham's children with a sign "by which they would know if they were living in accordance with the zeal of their ancestors or were falling short in their virtue"; to make it easier to prove that Jesus Christ was one of them; to facilitate the recognition of Israelite corpses on the battlefield.[39] And if one should object that circumcision cannot function as a sign of Israelite distinctiveness since other nations, too, practice circumcision, the answer is simple: the other nations adopted the practice in imitation of the Israelites![40]

Some Christian thinkers suggested that circumcision of the flesh had never been the divine will because God had always and only wanted spiritual circumcision. Circumcision of the flesh was instituted by the foolish Jews, who misunderstood the divine mandate, or it was instituted by God for the Jews alone in order to punish them.[41] These explanations, which stripped circumcision of its positive place in Christian sacred history, were too radical to be adopted by emergent Christian orthodoxy, and these suggestions went nowhere. It was the explanation of circumcision as a sign that allowed Christian theology to come to terms with the Old Testament's requirement of carnal circumcision. The Israelites were God's special people; God gave the Israelites a sign of their distinctiveness; Christ, too, was signed by circumcision, in order to indicate that he was a scion of God's holy people. With the death and resurrection of Christ, however, the old Israel was replaced by the new Israel, the old covenant by the new covenant. Jewish particularity no longer had any reason to continue, since all of God's children were now to be brought into the universal church. Ethnic Israel, Jewish particularity, and Jewish circumcision were all supposed to come to an end. Baptism replaced circumcision, and Christianity replaced Judaism. If carnal circumcision continued to be a sign, it was a sign of Jewish obduracy and sinfulness. For some Latin fathers of the church, Jewish circumcision became the mark of Cain, marking out Jews as murderers condemned to eternal exile.[42]

Christian Explanations of the Non-circumcision of Women

I return now to the non-circumcision of women. If circumcision were merely a sign of Jewish nationhood and distinctiveness, then Scripture's failure to impose it upon women was not a problem, because everyone in antiquity and the Middle Ages, Jews and Christians alike, knew that a nation's citizens were its men; women are not citizens. The Israelites who constituted the people of Israel and who needed to be marked as distinctive were the males. Cornelius à Lapide (1567–1637), a Flemish commentator on the Bible, expresses this idea very well: "Circumcision was given specifically for this purpose, so that the Abrahamitic people might be distinguished by it, as if by a mark, from the other nations; this mark of a people is required of men, not women."[43] Hence we understand why Justin saw the non-circumcision of women as only a Jewish problem and not a Christian one. Justin the Christian believes that God gave circumcision to Abraham to be a sign for his descendants, and it was obvious to him that only males needed to be so signed. But Trypho the Jew believes (or, at least, Justin would have the reader believe that Trypho the Jew believes) that circumcision is not only a sign of membership and descent but also a sign of righteousness; hence, Justin asks, surely women too can be righteous before God even though they are not circumcised. For Justin, God's imposition of carnal circumcision on men, and non-imposition of carnal circumcision on women, were perfectly explicable in Christian terms. Later Christian thinkers who wrote in Greek followed Justin's lead. As far as I have been able to determine, Greek Christian writers routinely understood biblical circumcision as a sign, nothing more. For them, as for Justin, the biblical requirement of circumcision and the non-circumcision of women were not problems that needed solution or discussion.[44]

Latin Christian writers, however, found themselves in a different situation. Everyone knew Colossians 2:11–12, the last of the four Pauline passages that I cited above, which states that circumcision foreshadowed baptism and was replaced by baptism. But Augustine (354–430), the most important and influential Latin theologian of Late Antiquity, added an important point: circumcision also anticipated baptism in the sense that it too was instituted by God to signify purification from the effects of original sin.[45] Circumcision was indeed a sign, as Genesis and Paul had said; but for Augustine it was not just a sign of the distinctiveness of Israel; it was a sign of the faith that enables humanity to be purified of sin. Augustine writes:

> From the time that circumcision was instituted for the people of God, because it was then a sign of the justification by faith, it had the effect of signifying the purgation of the original and ancient sin, even for children, just as baptism, from the time when it was instituted, began to have the effect of the renewal of humanity. This does not imply that before circumcision there was no justification by faith—for Abraham himself, the father of nations who were to follow his faith, was justified by faith while he was still in his foreskin—but in earlier times the sacrament of the justification by faith lay entirely hidden. Nevertheless, the same faith in the mediator saved the just of ancient times, both children and adults . . . be-

cause just as we believe that Christ has come in the flesh, they believed
that he would come; just as we believe that he has died, they believed that
he would die; just as we believe that he rose from the dead, they believed
that he would rise from the dead; both we and they believe that he will
come for the judgment of the dead and the living.[46]

A careful reading of this and related passages shows that Augustine did
not believe that circumcision itself saved humanity from the effects of
original sin. Rather, he believed that circumcision was a sign of the faith
that saved humanity, and still saves humanity, from original sin.[47] Augustine has introduced the notion of original sin, which was not known
to Paul, and he has emphasized the circumcision-baptism parallel far
more than Paul or his immediate followers had done, but otherwise Augustine is still within Paul's universe of discourse: like Paul, Augustine
sees circumcision as a sign of faith, not as a ritual that confers spiritual
benefit in and of itself.

This subtle point, however, was lost on most of Augustine's readers,
who believed that just as baptism in and of itself saves from sin, so too
circumcision in and of itself once saved from sin. The shift is well un-
derway by the time of Gregory the Great, who was pope from 590 until
his death in 604. Gregory writes:

What is accomplished for us by the water of baptism, was accomplished
for the ancients either by faith alone, in the case of children, or by the act
of sacrifice, in the case of adults, or by the mystery of circumcision, in the
case of those who issued from the line of Abraham.[48]

Note that circumcision here has been promoted to a "mystery," akin to
baptism, and that circumcision is construed as an alternative to faith.
The pagans of antiquity were saved either by faith or sacrifices; the
Jews, by circumcision.

The equivalence of circumcision and baptism having been established by Augustine via Gregory, the scholars of the church began to debate whether circumcision in its time bestowed sanctifying grace, just as
baptism did. Thomas Aquinas (ca. 1225–1274), the great systematizer
of medieval Latin theology, summarizes the debate:

Some have maintained that no grace was conferred [by circumcision] but
that sin alone was remitted. . . . Others have said that grace was conferred by circumcision only to the extent that it effected the remission of
sin but not in its positive effects. . . . Certain others have said that grace
was conferred in circumcision even with the positive effect of making a
person worthy of eternal life, but it did not extend to all the effects. . . .[49]

In contrast with all these views, which he finds unsatisfactory, Thomas gives his own:

> We must say that in circumcision grace is bestowed and with all the effects of grace, but not in the same way as in baptism. In baptism grace is conferred by the power of the sacrament itself which it has in so far as it is an instrument of the already realized passion of Christ. Circumcision, on the other hand, conferred grace in so far as it was a sign of faith in the coming passion of Christ in such a way that a man who accepted circumcision made profession of such a faith, an adult for himself, someone else for an infant.

The three positions that Thomas rejects, each of them maintained by distinguished medieval theologians, show how far circumcision has come in Latin Christianity. Its effect was deemed to be almost, but not quite, identical with the effect of baptism. Thomas's own position is that the effect of circumcision is identical with the effect of baptism, even if the effect is achieved by different means: in the case of baptism, by the power of the ritual itself; in the case of circumcision, by the underlying faith of the participant (or, in the case of an infant, his parent). This marks a partial retreat to the position of Augustine.

What we have, then, in the Latin West, and what we do not have in the Greek East, is the effort, inspired by a creative misreading of Augustine, to invest circumcision with theological value, to see it not merely as an ethnic marker but also as a sign of the faith that remits sin, hence as part of the sacred prehistory of the church. Do not, however, mistake this theology as "pro-Jewish" in any way. These Christian thinkers are speaking about the Old Testament and the circumcision observed by Abraham and the Israelites of old, not about Judaism and the circumcision observed by contemporary Jews. All Latin Christian writers, no less than their Greek counterparts, knew that Jewish circumcision no longer effected remission of sin, because circumcision had been superseded by the Passion of Christ and the rite of baptism. After the advent of Christ, circumcision by Jews was proof of obduracy, and circumcision by Christians was proof of heresy.[50]

If circumcision was instituted by God to be, like baptism, an agent for the remission of sin, why then did God not institute a ritual that could also be observed by women? It would appear that God made a serious omission in the salvation history of humanity. Christian women, like Christian men, are saved from sin through baptism; how were Israelite women of the Old Testament saved from sin? This problem perplexed thinkers in the Latin West, but not thinkers in the Greek East. I am not sure when this question first erupted in Latin theology;[51] perhaps it was not until the twelfth century, when the rise of the Scholastic movement produced a generation of scholars who demanded consistency in their theology and systemic cogency in their thinking. Perhaps this development was abetted by the fact that Jewish anti-Christian polemicists had begun to use the non-circumcision of women as an anti-Christian argument: if God really wants spiritual circumcision, why did not God demand the circumcision of women as well as that of men? I shall return to this in chapter 4. In any case, many Christian writers of the twelfth and thirteenth centuries attempt to explain the non-circumcision of women.[52] Here are the responses of three prominent twelfth-century thinkers.

Perhaps the least interesting and least effective answer is that given by Peter Lombard (1100–1160), author of the *Book of Sentences (Sententiarum Liber),* a work that became the standard textbook of Christian theology in the Middle Ages and the object of numerous learned commentaries. In his discussion of sacraments and sacramental signs, Peter devotes a few paragraphs to circumcision, including the following:

> The question is asked about men who lived before circumcision and about women who lived before it and after it: what remedy did they have against sin? Some say that sacrifices and offerings accomplished for them the remission of sin. But it is better to say that those who issued from Abraham were justified by circumcision, and that the women were justified by faith and good works, either their own if they were adult, or, if they were children, of their parents. As for those who lived before circumcision, the children were justified by the faith of their parents, and the parents were justified by the power of their sacrifices, or, more precisely, by the power that they spiritually perceived to be in those sacrifices.[53]

Peter clearly is developing the ideas of Gregory the Great, whom he cites in his next sentence. Gregory had not considered the problem posed by the non-circumcision of women, but Peter has. His answer is that women are justified by faith and good works, their own if they are adult, their parents' if they are children.[54] This is an excellent answer; it is so excellent that it immediately causes a problem. If the women of old were justified by their faith and good works, why not the men too? Why did they need circumcision? In his next paragraph Peter explains further:

> Circumcision was commanded to be performed on the flesh of the foreskin because it was instituted as a remedy for original sin, which we bear from our parents through carnal lust, which much dominates in that part.

> And because in that part the first man experienced the guilt of disobedi-
> ence, it was fitting that he accept there a sign of obedience.[55]

Circumcision is a remedy for original sin, which is transmitted through
sexual union, which is occasioned by lust, which dominates the penis. It
is not entirely clear why women too should not be circumcised, since
they also share in the transmission of original sin—note that Peter says
"parents"—and they also experience carnal lust. Perhaps they cannot
be circumcised because they lack "that part," or perhaps because Peter,
like Philo, thinks that lust is primarily a male problem. Peter's explanation would have been cleaner and clearer had he adopted the view that
original sin is transmitted through the male, because this view would
have explained easily the absence of circumcision from women. Thus,
as the second of his three explanations for the institution of circumcision for males only, Thomas Aquinas writes: "Circumcision was ordered in a special way as a remedy for original sin which is contracted
from the father and not the mother."[56] But Peter clearly was one of
those who thought that original sin is transmitted through both parents,
and therefore his explanation does not quite work.

A more original set of propositions is advanced by Peter Abelard
(1079–ca. 1142), another first-rate thinker. In his commentary on Paul's
letter to the Romans, he devotes three paragraphs, one right after the
other, to our theme. Here is the first:

> Circumcision of the flesh is a sign of the circumcision of the soul within,
> just as the external ablution of baptism is a sign of the cleansing of the
> soul within through the remission of sins. It was necessary that this sacra-
> ment be performed especially on the genital member, by which, through
> carnal lust, the sin of original guilt is propagated together with offspring.
> The result is that the very member by which sin itself is transmitted to
> posterity is rightly punished. Woman, to whom it was said *In pain you
> shall bring forth children* [Genesis 3:16], was not to be affected by a pun-
> ishment of this sort. For her the most grievous pain of childbirth, which
> she endures, was necessarily sufficient punishment for her genitals, by
> which sin is similarly transmitted. For her sex, unless I am mistaken, the
> sacrifice offered for childbirth suffices for indulgence and for the remedy
> of original sin.[57]

The novelty here is the conception of circumcision as punishment, not,
as some ancient church fathers had said, as punishment for the rebellious and wayward Israelites, but punishment for the sinful state of humanity. Original sin began with carnal lust, and therefore the organ of
carnal lust, through which original sin is transmitted, was to be pun-

ished. Men were punished by circumcision; women were punished by painful childbirth.[58]

Abelard anticipates an objection: circumcision is not only a punishment, it also is, like baptism, a sacrament that removes sin, but childbirth is not a sacrament and does not remove sin.[59] How then did Israelite women remove the original sin that they too transmit to their offspring? By the sin offering prescribed by Leviticus 12 for women after childbirth, is Abelard's reply. This answer, like Peter Lombard's, would have been neater and smoother had Abelard adopted the position that original sin is transmitted through the father and not the mother; this would have allowed him to say that only the males needed to be punished by circumcision because only the males transmit original sin. But at least Abelard is able to achieve theological parity for men and women: men are punished and atoned through circumcision: women are punished through childbirth and atoned through sacrifices.

Abelard continues:

> In addition, it seems to us that the genital of the male specifically was to be circumcised, rather than that of the female, for the following reason. The circumcision of the male signaled to everyone in that people, all of whom were produced through that member, that the remedy of this sacrament was necessary for their expiation from the contagion of the old man [Adam]. But this is not so for the female, since the Lord Jesus was born from a woman without any sin.[60]

If I understand this correctly, propagation through the male necessarily involves original sin, the sin of Adam, and circumcision was instituted to teach the Israelites this important lesson. But propagation through the female does not necessarily involve original sin, since Jesus, the new Adam, was born immaculately. Therefore women were not circumcised.

In the third paragraph, the connection between circumcision and Christ is even more striking:

> The circumcision of a man can designate spiritually that same blessed man who alone was conceived without lust and who received pure flesh without the foreskin of impurity anywhere. The type of this was the "thigh" of Abraham which, having been the first to be circumcised, was held by his servant during his oath [Genesis 24:1, 9], as if he were swearing by the one who had been promised to be born to him first from his seed, that is, by Christ.[61]

Here the circumcised member itself, or at least the circumcised member of Abraham, is understood as the "type," or symbolic model, of Jesus. The circumcision of Abraham prefigures the birth of Jesus, who was conceived without lust and without impurity, that is, without "foreskin." Since both the "type" and the fulfillment are male (Abraham, Jesus), circumcision applies only to males.[62] This spiritual and typological exegesis completely abandons the literal commandment of circumcision.

The last of our three twelfth-century authors is Hildegard of Bingen (1098–1179), the famous mystic, composer, and teacher. In the course of explaining the significance of one of her visions, she turns to Abraham and addresses him:

> Those of your people who in the time of circumcision were not circumcised . . . *have transgressed the pact of my covenant* [Genesis 17:14], except for woman, who is not to be circumcised, because a maternal tabernacle lies hidden in her body and may not be touched except as flesh binds flesh, and because she is under the power of a husband, like a servant under his master.[63]

Hildegard's explanation is based on her sense of a woman's passivity. As she elaborates in her next paragraph, in propagation the female is entirely passive; she is merely fertile and humid earth. Since she is the passive partner, her genitals are to be left untouched, except for the sexual act.[64] In contrast, men are the active partners in creation, and therefore males are circumcised. (And therefore too, Hildegard argues in another passage, women cannot serve as priests, since they are incapable of "creating" or "consecrating" on their own.)[65] A woman's passivity is evident as well, says Hildegard, in the fact that a woman is under the power of her husband, like a servant under his master. Hildegard certainly knows that women are baptized, that baptism has replaced circumcision, and that circumcision was once a remedy for original sin.[66] Nevertheless, God saw no reason to demand the circumcision of women, because circumcision is a sign of independent personhood and women are not independent persons.

Conclusions

The non-circumcision of women was a two-edged sword for Christian thinkers: it was an effective argument against Jewish circumcision, but it was also the source of an exegetical problem.

The anti-Jewish argument was expressed in three classic forms. First, the non-circumcision of women proves that God does not really require circumcision from his devotees, since women, too, can be right-eous before God. Second, the non-circumcision of women proves the inferiority of Judaism to Christianity, since Jews circumcise only men whereas Christians baptize men and women alike. Third, the non-circumcision of women proves that women are anomalous within Judaism, since circumcision is essential to Jewishness, but Jewish women are not circumcised.

This argument, especially in its second and third forms, is predicated on the equation of circumcision with baptism: circumcision accomplishes for Jews what baptism accomplishes for Christians.[67] Indeed, on the Christian side, virtually all thinkers in the West, from antiquity through the high Middle Ages, knew not only that circumcision was replaced by baptism but also that the two were functionally equivalent. However, as we have already seen in chapter 1, on the Jewish side the equation was neither ancient nor straightforward; the equation is not securely attested in Jewish sources before the high Middle Ages and at no point was it universally accepted or given the force of law. As we shall see in chapter 7, a Jewish respondent says explicitly that circumcision is not equivalent to baptism: perhaps baptism makes one a Christian, but circumcision does not make one a Jew.

The Christian equation of circumcision with baptism led to a Christian problem (and this is the other edge of the two-edged sword): why did God in Genesis 17 give the sign of circumcision only to men? Why should God have given a covenantal ritual to only half of the covenantal people? If circumcision were merely a sign of Israelite distinctiveness, or a punishment for Israelite sins, then the omission of circumcision from Israelite women would have been perfectly unproblematic. But for church writers in the Latin West, circumcision prefigured baptism, and thus they were faced with a problem: baptism is available to all Christians, so why wasn't circumcision available to all Israelites of the Old Testament? This problem exercised some of the great minds of the high Middle Ages in the West, who tried to explain exactly what Old Testament circumcision meant in Christian terms.

When we moderns ask about the ritual imparity between Jewish men and women, we are asking a question about rights, equality, and equity. Our modern sensitivities are aroused, perhaps offended, by the fact that so much public ritualized fuss is made at the birth of a Jewish boy and so little at the birth of a Jewish girl. I shall discuss this in the concluding chapter. However, when the ancients and the medievals asked about the ritual imparity between Jewish men and women, they were not asking a question about gender discrimination and women's rights. Jews and Christians (and Muslims too, for that matter), in both ancient and medieval times, differed on many things, but they agreed that women were, and should be, subordinate to their fathers and husbands. Hildegard says explicitly that a woman "is under the power of a husband, like a servant under his master," a position that would have found favor with many Jewish thinkers, as we shall see in chapter 5. When Christians turned the non-circumcision of Jewish women into an anti-Jewish argument, they did so not because they were advocates of women's rights but because they were eager to score points against their theological opponents. All is fair in love and polemics. They were willing to use an argument whose implications they themselves would have rejected. We shall see in chapter 7 that Jewish polemicists were not necessarily motivated any differently.

In this chapter I have surveyed the Christian arguments based on the non-circumcision of women. In the next, I turn to the Jewish responses.

CHAPTER 4

From Reticence to Polemic

In chapter 3 I surveyed the three anti-Jewish arguments that Christians derived from the non-circumcision of Jewish women. First, God does not require circumcision from his devotees, since women too can be righteous before God even though they are not circumcised. Second, Judaism is inferior to Christianity, since Jews circumcise only men, whereas Christians baptize men and women alike. Third, women are anomalous within Judaism, since circumcision is essential to Jewishness, but Jewish women are not circumcised. As we shall see in the following chapters, Jewish thinkers of the high Middle Ages advanced at least four different explanations for the non-circumcision of Jewish women. In contrast, the rabbis of the Mishnah, the Talmud, and the Midrash are completely unperturbed by the non-circumcision of women. They know that Jewish circumcision is performed only on men, not women, but do not think that the imparity requires discussion or explanation. The goal of this chapter is to explain why the rabbis of antiquity ignore the Christian arguments based on the non-circumcision of women, while their medieval continuators saw fit to respond to them.

Jewish Men Are Circumcised, Jewish Women Are Not

The rabbis of antiquity noticed that circumcision was performed on the sexual organ of males, and not on the sexual organ (or any other part!) of females. Let us begin with a passage from the Tosefta:

> R. Yosi said: Whence [do we know] that circumcision is to be [per-
> formed] at the place of [the body that produces] fruit? As it says. [*When
> you enter the land and plant any tree for food*], *you shall regard its fruit
> as foreskin* [; *for three years it is to be foreskinned for you, not to be
> eaten*] [Leviticus 19:23].
>
> And it is written, *And if any male who is foreskinned fails to circum-
> cise the flesh of his foreskin*[, *that person shall be cut off from his kin*]
> [Genesis 17:14]. At the place [on the body] by which it is recognized
> whether the child be male or female—at that place do [we] circumcise
> him.[1]

These two paragraphs are separate bits of scriptural exegesis that arrive
at the same conclusion via different routes. The first, attributed here to
R. Yosi, argues that circumcision is to be performed at the place of the
body that produces fruit. This conclusion is supported by the fact that
the Torah uses the striking locution *foreskin* to refer to the forbidden
fruit of newly planted fruit trees. Just as foreskin-fruit is prohibited, so
too the human foreskin is prohibited. Just as foreskin-fruit is prohibited
in order to prepare the way for fruit, so too human foreskin is removed
in order to prepare the way for "fruit."[2] In other words, circumcision is
about procreation, a motif that we have already seen in chapter 1. But if
circumcision is about procreation, is it not possible that women should
be circumcised since they, too, participate (classic understatement) in
procreation? The anonymous exegete in the second paragraph responds
by citing the scriptural phrase *a male who is foreskinned*. Does a female
have a foreskin?[3] Of course not; women cannot be circumcised. Why
then does Scripture refer to *a male* with a foreskin? In order to teach us
that circumcision is to be performed at the place of the body where the
distinction between male and female is evident. In other words, circumcision is about maleness.

I turn next to a fascinating Mishnah from tractate Nedarim:

> [If a man swore,] "May any benefit that I derive from the foreskinned
> be as forbidden to me as a sacrificial offering," he is permitted to have
> benefit from the foreskinned of Israel, but is forbidden to have benefit
> from the circumcised of the nations.
>
> [If a man swore,] "May any benefit that I derive from the circumcised
> be as forbidden to me as a sacrificial offering," he is forbidden to have
> benefit from the foreskinned of Israel, but he is permitted to have benefit
> from the circumcised of the nations, since "foreskin" is but another name
> for "gentiles."[4]

When a Jew swears an oath referring to "the foreskinned" and "the circumcised," he means, says the Mishnah, "gentiles" and "Jews." He is

not referring to the physical state of individuals, but to the physical and metaphysical states of the groups to which individuals belong. The vast majority of gentile men are foreskinned; hence gentiles in popular discourse can be called "the foreskinned." The vast majority of Jewish men are circumcised; hence Jews in popular discourse can be called "the circumcised." The presence or absence of a prepuce does not determine whether an individual man belongs to "foreskin" or "circumcision." The category "circumcision" includes even those Jewish men who for whatever reason are not circumcised (for example, a Jewish man left uncircumcised because his older brothers had died from complications following their circumcision),[5] and the category "foreskinned" includes even those gentile men who for whatever reason are circumcised (for example, a circumcised Arab). "Circumcision" is Jewishness, and "the circumcised" are Jews; "foreskin" is gentileness, and "the foreskinned" are gentiles.

This Mishnah reminds us of Paul (or the disciple of Paul) who wrote an epistle addressed to the *Gentiles in the flesh, called "the foreskin" by what is called "the circumcision"* (Ephesians 2:11, the third Pauline passage cited in chapter 3). According to both Paul and this Mishnah, gentiles call Jews and Judaism "the circumcision," and Jews call gentiles and gentileness "the foreskin." The Mishnah would also seem to agree with Paul, at least to some degree, that "true circumcision" is not "something external and physical" but rather "a matter of the heart, spiritual and not literal" (Romans 2:28–29, the first Pauline passage cited above), so that according to the Mishnah an uncircumcised Jew nevertheless belongs to "the circumcision," because "circumcision" is synonymous with "Israel." The Mishnah and Paul disagree, however, on the implications of these facts. For the Mishnah, as for rabbinic tradition as a whole, the metaphoric usage of "circumcision" does not obviate or diminish the literal requirement. On the contrary: the fact that most Jewish men are circumcised allows the Jews to be called, and to call themselves, "the circumcised," even though not every male individual is circumcised. Letter trumps metaphor. For Paul, the logic is the opposite: metaphor trumps letter. Physical circumcision separates Jews from gentiles and gentiles from God; belief in Christ, or "spiritual circumcision," unites Jews to gentiles, and gentiles to God.

This Mishnah does not address the status of Jewish women. Surely they do not belong to "the foreskinned," for they have no foreskin, but do they belong to "the circumcised"? If a man swore, "May any benefit that I derive from the circumcised be as forbidden to me as a sacrificial offering," is he forbidden to derive benefit from a Jewish woman? Neither the Bavli nor the Yerushalmi addresses the question here. In another tractate and in another context, however, the Bavli does address this question, albeit implicitly. The discussion is long and somewhat complicated, but full of interest. I present it here with the addition of a good deal of explanatory material in brackets:

> It has been stated:
>
> What is the scriptural basis for the ruling that circumcision performed by a gentile is invalid?
>
> Daru b. Papa said in the name of Rav: *You shall keep my covenant* [Genesis 17:9]. [Therefore gentiles, who are not obligated to keep the covenant of circumcision, do not perform a valid circumcision.]
>
> R. Yohanan said: *Circumcised he shall be circumcised* [Genesis 17:13] [which means *he shall certainly be circumcised,* but which can be construed to mean] he who is circumcised shall circumcise[; since gentiles are not circumcised they do not perform a valid circumcision].
>
> What [practical difference] is there between these [two positions]?
>
> [First suggestion:] [The case of] a circumcised Arab or a circumcised Gibeonite is [a point of disagreement] between them.
>
> [Explanation:] [For] the one who says *Circumcised he shall be circumcised*—[the criterion] is [satisfied, because an Arab or Gibeonite is circumcised]. [For] the one who says *You shall keep my covenant*—[the criterion] is not [satisfied, because an Arab or Gibeonite is not obligated to keep the covenant of circumcision].
>
> [Objection:] And for the one who says *Circumcised he shall be circumcised*—is [the criterion satisfied]? But we have learned in a Mishnah:
>
> [If a man swore,] "May any benefit that I derive from the foreskinned be as forbidden to me as a sacrificial offering," he is permitted to have benefit from the foreskinned of Israel, but is forbidden to have benefit from the circumcised of the nations of the world.
>
> Hence even though they [Arabs and Gibeonites] are circumcised, they resemble those who are not circumcised [and therefore Rav and R. Yohanan would not disagree in this case, for both would say that a circumcised Arab or Gibeonite may not perform a valid circumcision on an Israelite].
>
> [Second suggestion:] Rather, an Israelite who was not circumcised because his brothers died in consequence of circumcision—[this case] is [a point of disagreement] between them.
>
> [Explanation:] For the one who says *You shall keep my covenant*—[the criterion] is [satisfied, because an uncircumcised Israelite is still liable to the commandment of circumcision even if he has not fulfilled it]. For the one who says *Circumcised he shall be circumcised*—[the criterion] is not [satisfied, because he is not circumcised].

[Objection:] And for the one who says *Circumcised he shall be circumcised*—is [the criterion] not [satisfied]? But we have learned in a Mishnah:

[If a man swore,] "May any benefit that I derive from the circumcised be as forbidden to me as a sacrificial offering," he is forbidden to have benefit from the foreskinned of Israel, but he is permitted to have benefit from the circumcised of the nations of the world.

Hence even though they [Israelites left uncircumcised because of their brothers' deaths] are not circumcised, they resemble those who are circumcised [and therefore Rav and R. Yohanan would not disagree in this case, for both would say that an Israelite left uncircumcised because of the deaths of his brothers may perform a valid circumcision on an Israelite].

[Third and final suggestion:] Rather, a woman is [a point of disagreement] between them.

[Explanation:] For the one who says *You shall keep my covenant*—[the criterion] is [not satisfied], because a woman is not susceptible to circumcision [and therefore a woman may not perform a valid circumcision]. For the one who says *Circumcised he shall be circumcised*—[the criterion] is [satisfied], because a woman resembles one who has been circumcised [and therefore a woman may perform a valid circumcision].[6]

All the sages here agree that a circumcision performed on a Jewish infant by a gentile is not a valid circumcision, but debate the origin of the ruling. Is it because gentiles are not commanded to be circumcised, or is it because gentiles are themselves not circumcised? This is the debate between (Daru b. Pappa in the name of) Rav and R. Yohanan, each of whom adduces a scriptural proof text. The verse *You shall keep my covenant*, when read rabbinically, suggests that only those who are obligated to follow the commandment of circumcision, may perform a circumcision. The verse *circumcised he shall be circumcised*, when read rabbinically, suggests that only he who is circumcised may circumcise others. The proof texts do not "prove" anything, but simply provide a scriptural "hook" on which the debate may hang.

The anonymous voice of the Talmud is not content to let the matter stand here; surely Rav and R. Yohanan must be debating a practical point of law, the Talmud assumes, for otherwise their debate is rather pointless. The task the Talmud sets itself is to find a case in which the different approaches of Rav and R. Yohanan would yield contrasting conclusions. The Talmud at first pursues the obvious strategy of suggesting that Rav and R. Yohanan would disagree on the validity of a circumcision performed by someone who is circumcised but not obligated or by someone who is obligated but not circumcised. The former is the circumcised Arab or Gibeonite, the latter is the Jewish man who is left uncircumcised because his older brothers had died from complications following their circumcision. In each case, the criterion of one position is met but not the criterion of the other.

The Talmud, however, rejects both of these suggestions on the grounds that neither of them is ground for debate between Rav and R. Yohanan. Both sages hold, the Talmud says, that a circumcised gentile, because of his gentileness, is to be regarded as foreskinned and consequently unable to perform a valid circumcision on a Jew; and conversely, the Talmud says, both sages hold that a foreksinned Jew, because of his Jewishness, is to be regarded as circumcised and consequently able to perform a valid circumcision on a Jew. This by no means is the simple or obvious way to construe the debate between the two sages, but this is the way that the Talmud has chosen. In support of this construction of the debate, the Talmud adduces the Mishnah from Nedarim that I presented above. This Mishnah proves that, in some contexts at least, the language of "circumcision" and "foreskin" is metaphoric, not literal, referring more to the presence and absence of Jewishness than to the presence or absence of the foreskin. Therefore, it is obvious, the Talmud says, that a foreskinned Jew is "really" circumcised, that is, Jewish, and that a circumcised gentile is "really" foreskinned, that is, gentile.

Finally the Talmud comes to its third and final suggestion: women. Unlike the first two suggestions, which are rejected on the basis of the Mishnah in Nedarim, this suggestion is allowed to stand: Rav and R. Yohanan debate whether or not a Jewish woman may perform a valid circumcision.[7] Apparently it is obvious to the Talmud that a foreskinned Jewish man is included among "the circumcised," but it is not obvious that a Jewish woman is included as well. If it were obvious, this suggestion would have been rejected on the same basis as the first two. No, it is not obvious; a woman's inclusion among "the circumcised" is the core of the debate between Rav and R. Yohanan. According to R. Yohanan, a woman resembles a man who has been circumcised; consequently she may take her place among "the circumcised" and she is able to perform a valid circumcision. According to Rav, however, a woman is not said to resemble a circumcised man. She does not have a place among "the circumcised," and she is not able to perform a valid circumcision.[8]

In what sense can a woman be said to resemble a circumcised man?[9] Perhaps the resemblance is based on the fact that both a woman and a circumcised man are "missing something." The woman lacks a penis completely, the circumcised man lacks it partly, but both alike are "maimed" or "wounded." This Freudian interpretation was advanced by at least one medieval scholar.[10] Alternatively, and perhaps more simply, we might suggest that both a woman and a circumcised man lack a foreskin. The most elegant interpretation, however, which is advanced by several medieval scholars,[11] has nothing to do with the genitals and everything to do with religious status. A Jewish woman resembles a circumcised Jewish man in that both are Israel, part of the holy people, sanctified by the Torah and the commandments. Even if women cannot be numbered among "the circumcised" physically speaking, they certainly can be numbered among "the circumcised" metaphorically. Even though a woman has no part in the covenant of circumcision, she is part of the covenant between God and the people of Israel. In this sense she resembles a Jewish man, who is brought into the covenant through circumcision.

In sum, if a man swore, "May any benefit that I derive from the circumcised be as forbidden to me as a sacrificial offering," is he forbidden to derive benefit from a Jewish woman? According to R. Yohanan he is, because a Jewish woman resembles a circumcised Jewish man, consequently the category of "the circumcised" includes her as well. According to Rav, however, he is not, because a woman is not said to resemble a circumcised man. Whether or not "the circumcised" is a metaphoric expression, it does not include women.

According to R. Yohanan, a woman resembles a circumcised Jewish man, but, of course, she is not actually circumcised. A Jewish man enters the covenant through circumcision; how does a Jewish woman enter the covenant? The rabbis notice this problem:

> Our rabbis taught:
> A convert [to Judaism] who was circumcised but did not immerse—
> R. Eliezer says: such a man is indeed a convert, for we find in connection with our forefathers that they were circumcised but did not immerse.
> [A convert to Judaism who] immersed but was not circumcised—
> R. Joshua says: such a man is indeed a convert, for we find in connection with the foremothers that they immersed but were not circumcised.
> But the sages say:
> [If he] immerses but is not circumcised, [or if he] circumcises but does not immerse—he is not a convert until he is circumcised and immerses.[12]

The two standard rituals of conversion to Judaism in rabbinic law are circumcision, whose connection with conversion I discussed briefly in chapter 1, and immersion in water, usually in a special pool known as a *miqvah*. This passage, which inquires as to the status of a convert who has performed only one of the two required rituals, and which seems to suggest that for some rabbis at least, circumcision was not an essential part of conversion to Judaism, has provoked much scholarly discussion, which is not our concern here.[13] I am interested rather in the parallel between the circumcision of the forefathers and the immersion of the foremothers.

"Our forefathers were circumcised but did not immerse." As all the commentators explain, this refers to the Israelites who left Egypt and received the Torah at Mount Sinai, thereby "converting" to Judaism. These men had been circumcised in Egypt before partaking of the Paschal sacrifice,[14] but Scripture nowhere says or implies that they had also immersed in water. Hence, says R. Eliezer, our forefathers are paradigms of converts to Judaism who have been circumcised but who have not immersed. In contrast are the foremothers "who immersed but were not circumcised." The commentators debate the identity of these foremothers; the simplest explanation is that they are Israelite women who along with their men folk ("our forefathers") left Egypt and received the Torah at Mount Sinai.[15] On the next page the Talmud asks how R. Joshua knows that the foremothers immersed, since such immersion is nowhere mentioned in Scripture. "Logic," is the reply, "for otherwise by what means did they come under the wings of the divine presence?"[16] Circumcision was the ritual act that prepared the men to come under the wings of the divine presence, that is, to accept the Torah. What ritual act prepared the women for accepting the Torah? Surely they too received the Torah just as the men did.[17] Logic dictates that it must have been immersion—this is not the monthly immersion for purification after menstruation, which I shall discuss in chapter 8, but rather the immersion that is part of the conversion ritual.

The Talmud posits a parallel between circumcision for men and immersion for women. But, we might object, the parallel is not a parallel, because all Jewish men throughout the generations are circumcised, while the immersion of women at Mount Sinai was a one-time event. Perhaps the Talmud assumes that the circumcision of conversion does not have the same function as the circumcision of a native-born Jewish boy. The circumcision of conversion, it can be argued, actually brings its recipient under the wings of the divine presence (or prepares the way for its recipient to come under the wings of the divine presence). It is "sacra-mental" in that it is a physical operation that has metaphysical effects. But the circumcision of a newborn does not have the same effect, at least in the halakhic tradition, since a native-born Jewish boy is Jewish even if he is not circumcised. If so, the circumcision of the Israelite men in antic-ipation of accepting the Torah was indeed just like the immersion of the Israelite women. Both were one-time events, like the circumcision of male converts and the immersion of female converts.[18]

In sum, what can we glean from all these rabbinic passages? Circum-cision is to be performed at the place of the body where the distinction between male and female is evident. A woman is said to resemble a cir-cumcised man; therefore, at least according to one opinion, she is in-cluded in vows that refer to "the circumcised." A woman is also said to resemble an uncircumcised man; therefore, at least according to one opinion, just as our foremothers at Mount Sinai were immersed but not circumcised in anticipation of the receipt of the Torah, an uncircum-cised male too can be converted through immersion alone. These pas-sages prove, in case evidence were needed, that the rabbis noticed that circumcision was performed only on men, not women. What is striking here is what the rabbis do *not* say. The rabbis ignore the Christian argu-ments that I surveyed in the previous chapter, the arguments that use the non-circumcision of women as evidence against Jewish law and Jewish circumcision.[19] The rabbis know that Jewish women lack the mark of circumcision or anything functionally equivalent, yet they seem com-pletely undisturbed by this fact. When medieval Jewish thinkers came to answer the Christian arguments, they had no canonical answer on which to rely.

Why Did Ancient Rabbis Ignore the Christian Arguments?

Why did the rabbis of antiquity ignore the questions raised by Justin, Cyprian, Zeno, and the *Dispute between the Church and the Syna-gogue?* The simplest answer is that the talmudic sages knew little and cared less about what Christians were saying and doing. This answer, however, brings us into the center of large debate. Some scholars, whom we may call "minimalists," argue that rabbinic Judaism took shape in antiquity in isolation from Christians and Christianity; aside from a story here or a stray passage there, the sages fundamentally ignored Christianity, not perceiving it as a problem that concerned them. Other scholars, whom we may call "maximalists," have argued that ancient rabbinic literature is filled with anti-Christian polemics and responses to Christian theology; indeed some have even said that the development of "Christianity" was an essential catalyst in the development of rabbinic "Judaism."[20] And of course all sorts of intermediate positions are possible. In chapter 1 I suggested that the extravagant praise heaped upon circumcision by the Mishnah and other early rabbinic documents may have been intended as a response to Paul and his successors; the maximalists would certainly be comfortable with this interpretation, the minimalists probably not.[21] No matter which stance we adopt, we should like to find some specific values or concepts within ancient rabbinic culture that would explain the rabbinic indifference to the absence of female circumcision. Perhaps in the rabbinic reflections about the primacy of men, the ethnicity of Israel, and the meaning of circumcision, we will find such an explanation.

As I shall discuss in my next chapter, classical rabbinic Judaism has always been, and in many circles still is, a male-dominated culture, whose virtuosi and authorities are males, whose paragon of normality in all legal discussions is the adult Jewish male, whose legal rulings in many areas of life (notably marriage and ritual observance) accord men greater privilege than women, and whose values define public communal space as male space. These cultural norms explain why the absence of circumcision from women was not problematic for rabbinic Judaism; on the contrary, it would have confirmed for the rabbis their deeply held conviction that only men were the "real" Jews, and that while women certainly were part of the Jewish people, their Jewishness was inferior to that of males, the real Jews. This explanation for the non-circumcision of women was so obvious, so inevitable, and so pedestrian, that it did not need to be articulated. Virtually all cultures of antiquity, Jewish, Christian, and pagan, if we leave aside a few small but highly interesting exceptions, believed that women were physically, morally, and intellectually inferior to men. What was obvious to the rabbis was no less obvious to the Christians.[22]

This explanation places the rabbis and the early Christians on the same cultural continuum. The non-circumcision of women was rendered non-problematic for the rabbis by two further ideas that, in contrast to our first explanation, distinguish rabbinic Judaism from Christianity. Both Judaism and Christianity claim to be "Israel," but in Judaism Israel is an ethnic community, while in Christianity it is a faith community. "Christians are made, not born." That is, the status of being a Christian

("Christianness") needs to be achieved by an individual, whether by faith, baptism, or some combination of the two, while Jewishness, in contrast, is automatically ascribed to an individual through birth. As a church writer of the late fourth century correctly says, "from a Jew a Jew is born."[23] The Mishnah, the core document of the canon of rabbinic writings, conceives of Jews ("Israel") primarily in genealogical terms: they are the lineal descendants of Abraham, Isaac, and Jacob. Within the people of Israel, one's status, especially one's marriageability, is determined largely by birth. The Mishnah does permit gentiles to convert to Judaism and thereby to become part of the people of Israel, but they remain anomalous and unequal, precisely because their fathers are not "our" fathers. Post-mishnaic documents partly redress this imbalance, improving the lot of converts and emphasizing Judaism's "religious" character, but the fundamental point remains. Israel is primarily a descent group that one joins at birth.[24] If so, Jewish women, like Jewish men, are Jewish by virtue of their birth. In contrast, Christian women, like Christian men, need to be baptized in order to become Christian.

This leads to the next point. In Christianity, almost from its inception, baptism is a distinctive and essential ritual. Baptism makes one a Christian. In Christian eyes, baptism replaces circumcision, and baptism's role in Christianity is conceived as analogous to circumcision's role in Judaism. Christians assume that without circumcision there is no Judaism, just as without baptism there is no Christianity.[25] But the rabbis of the Talmud do not make these assumptions. They magnify the importance of circumcision and invest it with cosmic significance, but they do not see it as synonymous with Judaism. As we have seen in this chapter, they admit the Jewishness of a born Jew who, for health reasons, is unable to be circumcised; according to one opinion, at least in theory, a conversion is valid even without circumcision. Thus, for the rabbis of antiquity, circumcision is an important and distinctive part of Jewishness, but it does not, in and of itself, confer or embody Jewishness. For the rabbis, Jewish women, like Jewish men, were Jewish by virtue of their birth. The non-circumcision of women was a non-issue.

Why Did Medieval Rabbis Respond
to the Christian Arguments?

In the high Middle Ages in Europe (ca. 1100–1400), Jewish thinkers and writers at last turned to the questions that had been posed by

Justin, Cyprian, Zeno, and the *Dispute between the Church and the Synagogue,* and that were being posed again by contemporary Christian polemicists. Questions once ignored as insignificant, and answers hitherto considered obvious, now became worthy of discussion, no doubt because social conditions dictated that Christian polemic could not be ignored. But, as before, we should like to find some specific values or concepts within medieval rabbinic culture that would explain the end of rabbinic indifference to the absence of female circumcision. If we look at medieval rabbinic reflections on the primacy of men, the ethnicity of Israel, and the meaning of circumcision, we shall understand why the non-circumcision of women now elicited some attention.

Medieval Judaism was no less patriarchal and male-dominated than ancient Judaism had been, but the status of women, at least in Western Europe, the area of concern to us, underwent a perceptible change. From our perspective this change was a decided improvement. In marriage law, monogamy was now the norm, and for a period of time women even had a limited right to initiate divorce. Many women owned property in their own name and were active in commerce. The educational attainments of women also improved substantially, and female virtuosi, who observed modes of behavior normally associated with men, were not rare. Women even participated actively in non-liturgical public rituals of the community, including the circumcision ceremony.[26] As a result of these developments, perhaps, it was no longer as obvious as it once had been that women, the chattel of men, did not need their own sign of circumcision. This position could still be maintained, but because it could no longer be assumed, it had to be articulated explicitly. This is the theme of my next chapter.

Medieval Judaism was no less an ethnic community than ancient Judaism had been, but the growth of Jewish philosophy, which first emerged in Islamic lands in the tenth century and gradually made its way westward and northward, meant that a religious or philosophical definition became more pronounced during these centuries. If Jews were Jews not only, or not primarily, through birth, but through belief and practice, as most medieval Jews believed ("Our nation, the children of Israel, is a nation only by virtue of its laws," one philosopher remarked),[27] then the place of women within the religious system of Judaism was more problematic than ever, because women were excluded from so many of the delights of the Torah. If Jewishness itself was no longer primarily a function of birth but a function of piety, then the Jewishness of women was anomalous and decidedly different from that of men.

Further, as I discussed in my brief history of Jewish circumcision in chapter 1, during the last centuries of the first millennium many Jews began to see circumcision as analogous to Christian baptism, a sacrament conferring spiritual gifts, a physical procedure with metaphysical results. It was circumcision that protected a (male) Jew from the fires of Gehenna; Jewish women would circumcise their babies who had died before the eighth day so that the infant could partake of eternal life. In mystical circles an entire theology of circumcision was elaborated, which explained how circumcision allowed a (male) Jew to penetrate the inner mysteries of the Torah.[28] In sum, in Christian countries circumcision became identified with Judaism itself. As a result, the questions posed by the Christians gained force, because the exclusion of women from circumcision now seemed to bespeak their exclusion from Judaism itself.

If I am right, these internal developments within medieval rabbinic culture in Europe[29] facilitated the awareness of the problematic exclusion of women from circumcision. Still, I do not wish to exaggerate. We may be sure that without the external stimulus of Christian polemic, which forced Jewish thinkers to contemplate Jewish history, theology, laws, and texts in new ways, medieval rabbinic Judaism would never have been troubled by the non-circumcision of women. The explanation assumed and left unstated by the rabbis of old would have sufficed. Surely it is no accident that all the medieval rabbinic texts that deal explicitly with our question were written by authors who were actively involved in anti-Christian polemics and the defense of Judaism.

Against the Christians

Jewish anti-Christian literature in the Middle Ages was not as abundant and luxuriant as the Christian anti-Jewish literature that I surveyed briefly in chapter 3, but it was rich enough. From 1170 to 1400, the heyday of this literature, dozens of works were written whose explicit aim was to defend Jewish theology, the Jewish interpretation of Scripture, and the Jewish way of life. Some works went on the offensive; not content with defending Judaism, they attacked Christianity. Just as Christian polemicists quarried the Talmud and rabbinic literature for proof that rabbinic Judaism was false to its own origins, so too Jewish polemicists quarried the New Testament for proof that Christianity was false to its origins. Some of these polemics are philosophical in charac-

ter and concern themselves with the nature of creation, sin, free will, in-
carnation, redemption, and the like. Other polemical works are decidedly not philosophical in character. The most prominent of these are
those that rebut Christian interpretations of the Bible. In addition to
these explicitly anti-Christian works, numerous medieval works, especially philosophical tracts and commentaries on Scripture, respond to
Christianity implicitly. These works, too, can be deemed to be anti-
Christian literature.[30]

In the following chapters I present four medieval Jewish responses to
the Christian arguments derived from the non-circumcision of women.
Three of these responses are explicit, one is implicit. The explicit responses are all to be found either in anti-Christian tracts with a strong
scriptural orientation or in scriptural commentaries that have as one of
their purposes the refutation of Christianity. The philosophical anti-
Christian polemicists were not much interested in circumcision, either
of men or women; the non-circumcision of women seems to have been
primarily a question for the scriptural exegetes. Although the responses
are few, their variety is impressive; since the ancient rabbinic texts did
not provide these apologists with ready-made answers, they were free to
invent new ones.

A Rabbinic Argument Based on
the Non-circumcision of Women

The non-circumcision of women was used by Christians as an anti-
Jewish argument, as we have seen. It was also used by Jews as an anti-
Christian argument. Our source for the Jewish argument is R. Joseph b.
Nathan Official.

The Official family in Sens, southeast of Paris, provided French
Jewry with several champions in the struggle against Christianity, the
most prominent being R. Nathan and his sons R. Joseph and R. Asher.
These scholars debated bishops and priests, in public and private, and
even used the New Testament in their attacks on Christianity. The family's polemical activity is best known to us through the *Sefer Yosef
HaMeqanne,* "The Book of Joseph the Zealot," which was completed
about 1260 by R. Joseph b. Nathan. This book opens with a series of
137 brief notes defending the Jewish interpretation, or attacking the
Christian interpretation, of various biblical passages, and closes with a

critique of various gospel passages and Christian beliefs about Jesus.[31] In his notes on the book of Ezekiel, R. Joseph writes the following:

> [The Christians] rant and say that circumcision is an allegory whose intent is the circumcision of the heart. But they have covered their eyes with plaster and cannot see.[32] First, it says *every male among you shall be circumcised* [Genesis 17:10]. Does Scripture mean that only males need to circumcise their heart and that females do not need to circumcise their heart? Another difficulty: at the end of Ezekiel it is written *Let no alien, foreskinned in spirit and flesh, enter my sanctuary* [Ezekiel 44:9], and Scripture testifies[33] about them that they are foreskinned, for it is written *all the nations are foreskinned, but all the house of Israel are foreskinned in the heart* [Jeremiah 9:25].[34]

R. Joseph Official knows that Christians understand circumcision "spiritually," and he responds with two arguments. First, if God, as the Christians say, really wants spiritual circumcision and not physical circumcision, why did he not command women too to be circumcised? Women are capable of spiritual circumcision no less than men. Why then does Genesis 17 omit women? Second, Ezekiel 44:9 shows that God does not want Christians to enter his sanctuary, for even if Christians are circumcised in spirit, they certainly are *foreskinned in . . . flesh.* And if Christians should retort that they are circumcised in the heart and therefore not foreskinned in either spirit or flesh, the prophet Jeremiah puts them in their place by declaring that *"the nations are foreskinned."* Their alleged circumcision counts for nothing. I am not sure that I have parsed the second argument correctly; surely it would have been simpler to argue that Ezekiel 44:9 proves that God wants the circumcision of both the spirit and the flesh.[35] In any case, R. Joseph's first argument turns the non-circumcision of women from a Jewish problem into a Christian one.

Conclusions

This brief chapter requires only brief conclusions. The rabbis of the Mishnah, the Talmud, and the Midrash were well aware of the gender implications of circumcision but were not bothered by them. No rabbinic passage of antiquity explains why Jewish women are not circumcised. The rabbinic silence on this matter is all the more remarkable given the fact that ancient Christian polemicists used the non-circumcision of women as an anti-Jewish argument. But the rabbis paid these Christians no heed. In this chapter I speculated as to the reasons for this rabbinic silence, but I forebear to repeat these speculations here. What matters is that the rabbis said nothing on the subject.

As a result, when the rabbis of the high Middle Ages in Europe began to respond to Christian polemics, they had no classical or canonical text that they could cite in order to rebut the Christian argument drawn from the non-circumcision of women. The Jewish respondents were left to their own devices and were free to invent any answer they could. As we shall see in the coming chapters, they advanced a variety of explanations. Some said that the non-circumcision of Jewish women betokens their second-tier status within Judaism (chapter 5); others argued, or implied, that the absence of circumcision from women was not a defect but an asset, since only men suffered from the problem for which circumcision was a cure (chapter 6); others argued that Jewish women are Jewish the same way that Jewish men are Jewish, since Jewishness is a function of faith and not of circumcision (chapter 7); others argued that Jewish women have a uniquely feminine analogue to the uniquely masculine ritual of circumcision (chapter 8).

These respondents disagree among themselves as to the place of women in the Jewish order and the place of circumcision in the hierarchy of Jewish rituals. Some assume that Jewish women are equal to Jewish men (chapters 7 and 8), if not superior to them (chapter 6); in contrast, others state explicitly that women are inferior to men (chapter 5). Some respondents agree with the Christian assumption that circumcision confers Jewishness or is somehow to be connected with membership in the people of Israel (chapters 5 and 8), even if they disagree among themselves whether women do (chapter 8) or do not (chapter 5) have a ritual of their own that is functionally equivalent to the circumcision of men. Others argue that circumcision, unlike Christian baptism, has no connection with membership or status within the religious community, because it is simply a commandment like any other commandment (chapter 7) or because its intended effect is to remove a moral blemish affecting men (chapter 6). Hence the non-circumcision of women has no bearing on the place of women within the social order of Judaism. The Christian arguments derived from the non-circumcision of Jewish women prompted Jewish reflection on the Jewishness of women and the meaning of circumcision.

PART TWO

Why Aren't Jewish Women Circumcised?

Four Responses

CHAPTER 5

The Celebration of Manhood

The only question left to be settled, now, is: Are women
persons? And I hardly believe any of our opponents will
have the hardihood to say they are not. Being persons,
then, women are citizens.

Susan B. Anthony (1872)

Why do Jewish men bear a covenantal mark on their bodies but not
Jewish women? The fundamental answer to be developed in this chapter is that the Jewishness of women is different from the Jewishness of
men, or, to be more blunt, the Jewishness of women is of a lesser kind
than the Jewishness of men. The absence of circumcision bespeaks their
second-tier status. This is the answer that I have been calling the implicit answer of rabbinic Judaism, the answer that the rabbis of the Talmud would have given had they bothered to answer this question. What
was implicit for them became explicit in the thirteenth century.

Jacob Anatoli

Two texts form the centerpiece of our discussion. The first is by Jacob
ben Abba Mari Anatoli, who was born and educated in southern France
but spent a good part of his life in Naples at the court of Frederick II,
who had become Holy Roman Emperor in 1215. Anatoli, one of several
scholars, Jewish and Christian, who graced the court of this liberal
monarch, is best known as the translator of philosophical works from
Arabic into Hebrew, especially Averroes's commentary on the *Logic* of
Aristotle. Anatoli was also the author of *Malmad Hatalmidim*, "The Instruction of Students" (or "The Goad of Students"), a collection of sermons apparently completed around 1236–40 when the author was al-

ready in Naples. In these sermons, Anatoli, deeply influenced by Maimonides, attempts to demonstrate the rationality and reasonableness of the commandments of the Torah; as part of this enterprise, he attempts to demonstrate that Judaism is more rational and reasonable than Christianity and also to respond to Christian critiques of Judaism.[1] His anti-Christian orientation is evident in a sermon that speaks about the commandment of circumcision.

Anatoli explains that the purpose of circumcision is to reduce lust, and, by doing so, to teach us to moderate our desires and pursue the golden mean. The circumcision of the body is the physical expression of the "spiritual" circumcision of the ear, the lips, and the heart that is also necessary if we are to attain moral perfection.[2] All of this is an expansion of Maimonides' explanation for circumcision, to which I shall return in the following two chapters. Anatoli also notes two areas where the Christians err: they valorize celibacy, thus deviating from the golden mean, and they replace circumcision with baptism, although "their sign [baptism] is transient, while our sign [circumcision] is on the body itself and permanent."[3] Anatoli continues:

> It is sufficient that the sign of the covenant be on the males, because the female was created to be a *helper* [Genesis 2:18] for the male, [as Scripture says] *her urge shall be for her husband and he shall rule over her* [cf. Genesis 3:16] to lead her, to instruct her in his ways, and to have her act according to his dictates. For the same reason a woman is exempted from all the positive commandments that must be observed at a specific time. If she were burdened with the observance of such commandments at their proper time, at those times the husband would be without a helper, and strife would come between them, and the dominion [of husband over wife], which was intended to benefit him as well as her, would be diminished. In accordance with this reason it was sufficient that this sign [of circumcision] be only on the males.[4]

Anatoli argues that the complete subjugation of wife to husband renders otiose any covenantal sign for women. If, as a result of his circumcision, a man is moderate in his desires and proper in his behavior, he will inevitably instruct his wife to follow the same path, and she, dutiful creature that she is, will obey. Therefore she does not require any circumcision of her own. Anatoli argues that a woman's subjugation to her husband will also explain why she is exempt from positive commandments that must be observed at a specific time.[5] This is a significant point to which I will return below.

In his next paragraph, Anatoli, once again in a Maimonidean mode, says that circumcision has the additional benefit of being an ethnic marker that preserves Jewish existence. The gentiles lack such a mark and therefore fight each other constantly, but Jews stick together, says Anatoli, because their solidarity is strengthened by the common mark of circumcision:

> Even though our sins have caused us to be driven from one end of the earth to the other,[6] and all the nations in whose midst we are scattered *have sought to wipe us out as a people, so that the name of 'Israel' should no longer be remembered* [cf. Psalms 83:5], nevertheless we are still called by the name of Jacob on account of the sign [of circumcision] that was given our patriarchs.[7]

This argument anticipates Spinoza's famous quip that the mark of circumcision alone would have sufficed to preserve the Jewish people during its long stay in the diaspora.[8] Needless to say, for both Anatoli and Spinoza a nation is marked and preserved through its menfolk.

Menahem

Women's subservience to men explains their lack of a covenantal mark. The same argument, but in a very different formulation, is advanced by our second respondent, a polemicist named Menahem. Virtually nothing is known of this man except for what can be inferred from the sole manuscript that cites him, an anthology of Jewish anti-Christian polemics. He seems to have moved in the circles of R. Joseph ben Nathan Official and his brother R. Asher, whom we met briefly in the previous chapter. This would place him in northern France, perhaps in Sens, the seat of the Official family, in the middle of the thirteenth century. In 1269 Menahem debated the apostate Pablo Christiani, whose earlier and more famous Jewish opponent had been R. Moses ben Nahman in the disputation of Barcelona in 1263.[9] In an anonymous critique of the New Testament and Christianity, Menahem is cited as the source for the following:

> With regard to what they ask: how do women enter into Judaism, since they are not subject to circumcision? The answer is: their husbands render them exempt. A parable: it is just like two partners who are liable to a tax. The one exempts the other. Thus when a man is circumcised, his entire body is exempted, and a woman comes from his rib. And thus we find

in the Psalms that David called his wife his "rib," as it says *and upon my rib they have rejoiced and gathered* [Psalms 35:15]. This is a good argument in the case of married women, but what of unmarried women? The answer is: her father exempts her, just as we find that a daughter, for as long as she is not married, is under the authority and control of her father, whether in vows, in financial liabilities, or anything else. And even something that is prohibited to other Israelites, like the heave-offering given to the priest, whose prohibition is stated in the verse *No lay person shall eat of the sacred donations* [Leviticus 22:10], as long as the daughter of a priest is not married she may eat of it, but when she is married [to a non-priest], she may not eat of it again. The words of Menahem.[10]

According to Menahem, a woman does not need her own circumcision because she is always the "junior partner" to a man: a wife to her husband, a daughter to her father. Circumcision is a tax that must be paid, and a man's circumcision exempts from payment the woman who is part of him.[11] That a wife is a man's rib, hence part of her husband, is demonstrated not only by the Genesis creation story but also by a verse from the Psalms. In this verse, as paraphrased by the Talmud, David says that "the sages have gathered together to mock me for the sin that I committed with Bathsheva, my rib."[12] Hence a wife is a man's rib. That a daughter is dependent on her father is demonstrated by the legal control that a father wields over his unmarried daughter. Menahem envisions only two situations for women, wifehood and daughterhood. We may presume that he would have applied the same logic to situations that he does not explicitly consider. What of a daughter whose father has died? Probable answer: she is subordinate to her brother. What of a widow or divorced woman? Probable answer: she is once again subordinate to her father. At some point, of course, Menahem's answer will break down, but what matters is the principle. The normal situation of a woman is to be subordinate to a man, and a man's circumcision exempts his womenfolk.

For both Anatoli and Menahem, the non-circumcision of women is explicable on the basis of women's subordination to men. Both use the story of Genesis to justify that subordination: Anatoli cites Eve's status as "helper" to Adam and Adam's dominion over Eve, Menahem cites Eve's creation from Adam's rib. Perhaps we might conclude that in Anatoli's universe women rank lower than in Menahem's, since Anatoli grants husbands complete dominion over wives, while Menahem sees wives as junior partners to their husbands, which sounds much better. In consonance with his low estimation of women, Anatoli states explicitly that only males were created in the image of God, not females.[13]

This difference between Anatoli and Menahem is important for a history of medieval Jewish conceptions of women, but is not important for our purposes, because both agree that the non-circumcision of women bespeaks their subordinate status. According to both authors a woman, whether as "rib" or as helper and servant, expresses her Jewishness by assisting a man.

The Exemption of Women from Some of the Commandments

The responsibility of women to assist their menfolk in performing acts of piety is stated in the Talmud. "How do women attain merit?" Rav asks R. Hiyya. The point of Rav's question is that women are exempt from the observance of many of the commandments and, as a result, have many fewer opportunities than men for demonstrating obedience to God's will. But women need merit in God's eyes no less than men, because such merit has two beneficial effects: it affords protection from the consequences of sin in this world, and it enhances one's share in the next world. What, then, can women do in order to enhance their merit in God's eyes? R. Hiyya replies: "[They attain merit] by making their sons go to the synagogue to learn Scripture and their husbands to the academy to learn Mishnah, and by waiting for their husbands till they return from the academy."[14] Women's piety is facilitative, enabling, perhaps, we might even say, vicarious. By facilitating the Torah study of her sons and husband, a woman attains merit even though she herself is exempt from the obligation to study Torah. Only men partake fully of the delights of the Torah; by aiding the men in their sacred tasks, a woman attains her reward.

Anatoli argues that the domination of a wife by her husband will explain both the non-circumcision of women and the exemption of women from commandments that must be observed at a specific time. This argument is an innovation, because earlier sources had not explained the exemption on this basis. The classic text on the exemption of women from some of the commandments is the following Mishnah:

A. Every commandment that a father must fulfill for his son—men are obligated but women are exempt; but every commandment that a son must fulfill for his father—men and women are equally obligated.

B. Every positive commandment that must be observed at a spe-
    cific time—men are obligated but women are exempt; but every
    positive commandment that does not need to be observed at a
    specific time—men and women are equally obligated.

C. Every negative commandment, whether it needs to be observed
    at a specific time or not—men and women are equally obligated,
    except *You shall not round off [the side-growth of your head]*
    [Leviticus 19:27], and *[you shall not] destroy the side growth of
    your beard* [Leviticus 19:27], and *you shall not impurify your-
    self [by contact] with corpses* [cf. Leviticus 21:1]. [Women are
    exempt from these three negative commandments.][15]

Before I discuss this Mishnah, I need to provide a little background information.

The rabbis understood the Torah to contain a series of commandments, obligations imposed by God on the people of Israel. The commandments are of two sorts, positive and negative. A positive commandment is an injunction to do something (or, in the language of the
King James Bible, a *thou shalt*), a negative commandment is a prohibition from doing something (a *thou shalt not*). The Ten Commandments,
for example, contain both positive commandments *(Remember the Sabbath day, Honor your father and mother)* and negative commandments
(You shall not murder, You shall not commit adultery). A "positive
commandment that must be observed at a specific time" is a commandment that can be put into effect only on a specific day or days, or only
on a specific part of a day, or only on specific occasions.[16] In contrast, a
"positive commandment that does not need to be observed at a specific
time" can or must be observed on any time of any day, perhaps even all
day every day.

Let us now look at the Mishnah. Paragraph A discusses the mutual
obligations of parents ("father") and children ("son"). Obligations of
parent to son are incumbent only on the father, not the mother. The Talmud explains: "The father is obligated vis-à-vis his son to circumcise
him, to redeem him [if the son is a first-born], to teach him Torah, to
marry him a wife, and teach him a craft."[17] In other words, a mother is
not obligated to see to it that her son is circumcised, redeemed, taught
Torah, married, or taught a craft. In contrast, the Mishnah says, obligations of a child to a parent are incumbent on both the male and female
offspring. In other words, a daughter is obligated to treat her parent the
same way that a son is obligated. Even though the Mishnah says "fa-

ther," we may presume that both fathers and mothers are intended, because the Torah says explicitly that one is obligated to *honor one's father and mother* (Exodus 20:12) as well as *fear one's mother and father*
(Leviticus 19:2). What is *honor* and what is *fear*? The Talmud explains:
" '*Fear*' means that one must not stand in their place, sit in their place,
or contradict their words. . . . '*Honor*' means that one must feed them,
provide them with drink, clothe them and cover them, and lead them in
and out."[18] Thus the obligation of fear entails actions that we must
avoid, while *honor* entails actions that we must do. Or, formulated differently, "*fear*" entails proper attitude, but "*honor*" entails outlay of
money and time as well. Although the obligations of "*fear*" and
"*honor*" are incumbent on both sons and daughters, the Talmud adds
an important qualification regarding "*honor*": "Both men and women
are equally obligated, but the man has it in his power to act, while a
woman does not have it in her power to act, because the authority of
others is upon her."[19] A woman who is married is under the authority of
her husband. Consequently she may well lack the time and money
needed to honor her parents properly—time, because she must do what
her husband bids; money, because whatever money she earns belongs to
her husband. Thus in principle, but not in practice, a married woman is
obligated to honor her parents. Once she is widowed or divorced, or if
her husband does not object, we may presume that her exemption
lapses and that her theoretical obligation becomes real.[20]

Paragraphs B and C deal with the exemption of women from commandments that need to be observed at a specific time. According to
paragraph B, women are exempt from such commandments if they are
positive (that is, injunctions to do something), but, according to paragraph C, are not exempt from such commandments if they are negative
(that is, prohibitions from doing something). The Talmud explains:[21]

> What is an example of a positive commandment [from which women
> are exempt because] it needs to be observed at a specific time?
> The obligation to dwell in booths during the holiday of *Sukkot*, the
> obligation to carry a palm-branch during the holiday of *Sukkot,* the obli-
> gation of hearing the sound of a ram's horn on the holiday of *Rosh
> Hashanah*, the obligation of wearing fringes, and the obligation of wear-
> ing phylacteries.[22]
> What is an example of a positive commandment [from which women
> are not exempt because] it does not need to be observed at a specific time?
> The obligation to affix a *mezuzah* on the doorpost, the obligation to
> erect a fence on a roof, the obligation to return a lost object, and the ob-
> ligation to send a mother bird from the nest before taking the chicks.[23]

The Talmud adduces these principles in its discussion of yet another Mishnah: "Women, slaves, and minors are exempt from the recitation of the *Shema* and the wearing of phylacteries, but are obligated [by the commandments of] prayer, *mezuzah*, and Grace after Meals."[24]

The exemption of women from the recitation of the *Shema* and the wearing of phylacteries is consistent, the Talmud tells us, with the principle that women are exempt from commandments that need to be observed at a specific time. In contrast, prayer, *mezuzah*, and Grace after Meals are commandments that can be observed at any time.[25] I shall return below to women's obligation to recite the Grace after Meals.

The Yerushalmi, the Talmud of the land of Israel, and the Bavli, the Talmud of Babylonia, differ somewhat in their strategies in their discussions of these and related rulings.[26] The Bavli seems more interested than the Yerushalmi in applying wherever possible the principle that women are exempt from positive commandments that need to be observed at a specific time. The Bavli, as usual, is far longer and more rhetorically developed than the Yerushalmi. But the two Talmudic discussions share two fundamental assumptions. First, they assume that each and every exemption of women can be derived exegetically from the Torah, and, second, they assume that the exemption of women from commandments that must be observed at a specific time cannot be explained on the basis of a single all-encompassing explanation. Both Talmudim adduce strings of biblical citations in order to justify each and every exemption separately. Thus, the exemption from the obligation of *Sukkah* is said to derive from one verse, the exemption from fringes is said to derive from another, and the exemption from phylacteries is said to derive from yet another. Neither Talmud explains why women should be exempt from positive commandments that need to be observed at a specific time.

What makes the absence of an explanation particularly puzzling is the presence of numerous exceptions that seem not so much to "prove" the rule as to call its utility into question. The Bavli itself notes the existence of positive commandments that are incumbent upon women even though they need to be observed at a specific time (for example, the obligation to eat *matzah* on Passover, the obligation to rejoice during the festivals), as well as the existence of positive commandments that are *not* incumbent upon women even though they do *not* need to be observed at a specific time (for example, the obligation to study Torah, the obligation to procreate). Medieval commentators on the Talmud had no trouble identifying numerous additional exceptions. The Bavli quotes

R. Yohanan as saying that "we cannot draw specific conclusions from general principles."[27] If, then, the principle has no prescriptive value, a point that has convinced all modern scholars,[28] what, then, is its status and what does it mean?

Jacob Anatoli is one of the first scholars to attempt to make sense of the mishnaic principle.[29] The principle is perfectly reasonable and rational, he says, because a woman, who spends most of her life in a married state, is subservient to her husband, and must be able to help him and support him at all times. Consequently, she cannot be expected to serve both her lord and the Lord at the same time. Since God gave dominion over her to her husband, let her first serve him and then, during those moments when she is not so occupied, she can observe some positive commandments. The source for Anatoli's explanation is in the Talmud's statement that women are bound in principle by the obligation of honoring their parents but are exempt in practice "because the authority of others is upon her." Anatoli has taken this statement, moved it to a new context, and substantially broadened its application; it now explains the exemption of women not only from commandments that require an outlay of money but also from commandments that require an outlay of specific time. No doubt Anatoli will have derived further support for his explanation from the common Talmudic juxtaposition of the woman and the slave. "Whatever commandment is incumbent on a woman is also incumbent on a slave; whatever commandment is not incumbent on a woman is not incumbent on a slave." And why is a slave exempt from some of the commandments? Because "he has a master other than God."[30] The same logic applies to women.

It is unfortunate for us that Anatoli did not work out his explanation in detail, treating both the principle and its exceptions, but his fundamental insight—given the social and ideological realities of rabbinic culture—is cogent. Anatoli's successors, from the fourteenth century to the twenty first, have not been able to improve much on his explanation. One medieval work even argues that the rulings governing the exemption of women from the commandments make no sense unless they are treated mystically or allegorically.[31] One modern rabbi has suggested that the rabbinic laws of menstrual purity and impurity "invest women's natural cycle with an awareness of sanctity of time which makes other time-bound commandments unnecessary."[32] Unless we are prepared to adopt an explanation based on the place of the female principle in the cosmos or on a woman's essence or nature, Anatoli has done about as well as anyone in making sense of the talmudic exemption of women from positive commandments that need to be observed at a specific time.[33]

Are Women Israel?

The exemption of women from some of the commandments expresses the fundamental rabbinic perception of woman as Other, as Not One of Us. Throughout the Torah, the Us of the text—the people to whom the text is addressed and about whom the text speaks—is the Israelite male. At the great scene of the revelation of the Ten Commandments, God commands Moses *Go to the people and warn them to stay pure today and tomorrow . . . for on the third day the Lord will come down, in the sight of all the people, on Mount Sinai* (Exodus 19:10–11). Moses did as he was instructed. *Moses came down from the mountain to the people and warned the people to stay pure . . . And he said to the people, "Be ready for the third day: do not go near a woman"* (Exodus 19:14–15). Apparently the phrases *the people* and *all the people* do not include women. Were they present at the revelation at Mount Sinai? Did women receive the commandments? A contemporary Jewish feminist theologian entitles her book *Standing Again at Mount Sinai* because in her estimation that is what the Jewish people needs to do, and this time it needs to include women.[34]

A text that places men at the center, that speaks to and about men, that presumes men to be the paragons of normality—such texts are *androcentric* and their world view is *androcentrism*. Rabbinic texts are no less androcentric than the Torah. They specify in great detail who is the Us: the Us is the free adult competent Israelite male. The Mishnah and virtually all pre-modern rabbinic texts imagine this person as their audience and reader; the free adult competent Israelite male is the paragon of normality. Rabbinic law was written by, for, and about such men. In contrast, slaves, minors, the incompetent ("deaf-mutes and the insane"), gentiles, and females are not Us; they are Other. All these Others are not the same, of course. Gentiles and slaves are not of Israelite birth, whereas minors, the incompetent, and women may be. Women always remain women, the incompetent usually remain incompetent, but minors usually grow up, slaves can be emancipated, and gentiles can convert. Slaves, minors, and women are always under the authority of one of Us, but the incompetent not always, and gentiles never. Minors and the incompetent cannot be held responsible for their actions, but slaves, women, and gentiles can. These Others appear on the pages of the Talmud in various combinations, depending on the specific law under discussion and the principle that is at issue. What all these Others have in common—indeed what makes them Other to begin with—is their exemption from some or all of the commandments of the Torah. "We" are characterized and sanctified by the commandments, the Others are not.

Between the free adult competent Israelite male and his Opposite, the Mishnah and Talmudim frequently interpose a series of Ambiguous creatures who are both Us and not Us at the same time. Between the free and the slave is the one who is half-slave and half-free. Between the adult and the minor is the minor on the verge of adulthood, or, in the case of women, the girl who is between the ages of twelve years and twelve years and six months. Between the competent and the incompetent are the half-competent, for example, one who can hear but cannot speak or one who can speak but cannot hear. Between the Israelite and the gentile is the convert (one of Them who has become one of Us) or the apostate (one of Us who has become one of Them). Between male and female is the hermaphrodite, who is both male and female, and the one whose genitals are undeveloped and therefore is neither male nor female. Rabbinic legal texts devote enormous intellectual energies to elucidating the status of the Other and the Ambiguous: wherein are they like Us and wherein are they not? Which commandments are incumbent upon them and which not? In innumerable lists and statements, the Other and the Ambiguous, either in standardized clusters or in eccentric variations, are said to be bound by this commandment or exempt from that, either included or excluded.

We have already seen some of this classificatory activity above. "Women, slaves, and minors are exempt from the recitation of the *Shema* and the wearing of phylacteries." In this Mishnah three Others are grouped together, a very common grouping. Here is another Mishnah: "All are obligated to bring the pilgrimage sacrifice except a deaf person, an incompetent person, and a minor; a person whose genitals are undeveloped and a hermaphrodite; women and unemancipated slaves."[35] The list goes on, but we can see that the opening word "all" really means Us, free adult competent Israelite males. The Other are excluded, as are some of the Ambiguous. In its discussion of this Mishnah, the Bavli argues that the half-free and half-slave, as well as the one who cannot hear but can speak, or who cannot speak but can hear, are in-

cluded in the word "All." At least with respect to the obligation of
bringing pilgrimage sacrifices, these Ambiguous creatures are like Us.[36]

The classification schemes of the early rabbinic commentaries on the
Torah are particularly striking and reveal a great deal about rabbinic
conceptions of self and Other. The laws of the Torah are usually addressed to *the people of Israel* (in some translations *the children of Israel*), but often additional phrases are used: *anyone, a person, a man,
one of your brethren, a native,*[37] and so on. Who exactly is included by
these expressions and who excluded? The status of women is particularly ambiguous because the Torah sometimes specifies that a given law
is to apply to *man or woman* or to *son or daughter.*[38] An exegete may legitimately ask about the status of women in those laws that do not
specifically include them. In one verse (Deuteronomy 23:18) the Torah
even contrasts *daughters of Israel* with *sons of Israel;* since the phrase
sons of Israel in this verse is exactly the same as that translated everywhere else *people of Israel* or *children of Israel*, an exegete may legitimately ask whether *people of Israel* includes women. On almost every
page, the rabbinic commentaries on the Torah ask whether the law under discussion applies only to Us or also to the Other (especially
women, slaves, or gentiles) and the Ambiguous (especially converts).
These questions and answers are highly rhetorical in character, leaving
the distinct impression that the exegete knows in advance exactly what
conclusion needs to be reached, even if some modern scholars have tried
hard to prove that legitimate and real exegetical activity is taking place.
Thus in many passages the exegetes argue that when the Torah uses the
word *ish*, usually translated "man", it intends to exclude women, but
this reading does not stop the same exegetes from stating that "in all
laws regarding damages the Torah has equated women with men"—
and this in spite of the fact that many of those laws utilize the same
word *ish*.[39]

I would like to return to our theme by looking briefly at the treatment of the terms *"Israel"* and *"native"* (*ezrah* in Hebrew) in these
commentaries. When confronted by the phrase *Israel* or *people of Israel*, the exegete commonly argues that these words exclude women but
that their exclusion is offset by some other locution in the verse that
shows that they are meant to be included. A verse in Leviticus reads
*And the Lord spoke to Moses: Say further to the people of Israel: Any
man of the people of Israel or any alien who resides in Israel who gives
any of his offspring to Molech, shall be put to death* (Leviticus 20:1–2).
The Sifra, the earliest rabbinic commentary on Leviticus, explains:

> *Say further to the people of Israel, speak further to the people of Israel, say to the people of Israel, speak to the people of Israel, command the people of Israel, you shall further command the people of Israel –*
>   R. Yosi the Galilean says:
>   The Torah has spoken in many different forms of expression, and all of them should be interpreted [as follows]:
>   *Israel*—these are [male)]Israel[ites].
>   *An alien*—these are converts [to Judaism].
>   *Who resides*—to include the wives of converts.
>   *In Israel*—to include women and slaves.[40]

The details of this exegesis need not detain us. The fundamental point advocated here by R. Yosi the Galilean is that in all locutions such as *speak to the people of Israel* the word *Israel* excludes women and slaves, who are Other, and converts, who are Ambiguous, except that inevitably the Torah's language indicates that the law applies to them as well. Women and converts are not *Israel* but are bound by the law. Exegesis of this sort appears in at least six other passages in close proximity in the Sifra, four of them focusing on the term *Israel,* two of them focusing on the word *native.*[41] Women, slaves and converts are no more *natives* than they are *Israel.*

A slightly different pattern appears in the Sifrei, the earliest rabbinic commentary on Numbers and Deuteronomy. On the verse *The Lord spoke to Moses: Speak to Aaron and his sons: Thus shall you bless the people of Israel* (Numbers 5:22–23), the Sifrei comments:

> I might deduce from the verse that the blessing applies only to Israel. Whence do I know that the blessing applies also to converts, women, and slaves? Scripture says *and I shall bless them* [Numbers 6:27, implying a blessing beyond that given to Israel].[42]

Similarly, in two other passages the Sifrei assumes that women would be excluded by the terms *the congregation* and *the community,* except that some other phrase demonstrates that the law applies to them as well.[43]

Sometimes, however, the exegete is unable to convince himself that some other locution cancels the exclusionary effect of *Israel* or *native.* Commenting on the opening verses of the book of Leviticus, the Sifra states:

> The *people of Israel* press [their hands on the sacrificial animal before it is offered], but gentiles do not. . . .
>   The *people of Israel* press [their hands on the sacrificial animal before it is offered], but women do not. . . . [44]

A little further along, the Sifra says:

> The *people of Israel* wave [the breast and thigh of the sacrificial meat before presenting it to the priest], but gentiles do not. . . .
> The *people of Israel* wave [the breast and thigh of the sacrificial meat before presenting it to the priest], but women do not. . . .[45]

Gentiles and women, both of them Other, are excluded by the phrase *people of Israel* and consequently do not perform two of the sacrificial procedures observed by Israelite men. Similarly, in one verse the word *native* was taken to exclude women definitively. Women are not obligated to dwell in a *sukkah* during the holiday because Scripture obligates *every native in Israel,* but not women.[46]

What are we to make of the exclusion of women from the categories of *Israel* and *native*? We must bear in mind that the setting of these statements is the exegesis of Scripture, not a tract on the status of women in Judaism. It would be unfair to make a blanket statement like "In the eyes of the rabbis women were no more part of the people of Israel than were gentiles" and to adduce our midrashic exegesis as support. These texts are speaking about women's obligation to observe the commandments, and within this context the rabbis assume that women are not "Israel," because Israel is obligated to observe all the commandments, but women are not. Insofar as gentiles too are not obligated to observe the commandments, they can be grouped together with Women as Other and as not-Israel, but women and gentiles are not the same. Gentiles are entirely outside the category of Israel, while women are outside it only partially. After all, women *are* obligated to observe *some* of the commandments, and the bulk of these midrashic comments conclude that the law under discussion does apply to women, in spite of their exclusion from the notion "Israel." In other contexts surely the rabbis would concede to women the status of Israel and would deny their otherness. Does not the mishnaic statement "All Israel have a share in the world to come" include women?[47] I offer this explanation not to apologize for these rabbinic texts—if I were to begin engaging in apologetics, this chapter would have to be twice as long as it is—but to make sure that we pay attention to what they are saying. The exemption of women from many of the commandments is a cause and a consequence of their status as Other, as not-entirely-Israel. This is the exemption that Jacob Anatoli has tried to explain.

"Who Has Not Made Me a Woman"

Certainly the best-known and most offensive expression of the rabbinic othering of women is the series of three benedictions that are to be recited daily by every Jewish man:

> Blessed are you, Lord our God, king of the universe, who has not made me a gentile.
> Blessed are you, Lord our God, king of the universe, who has not made me a slave.
> Blessed are you, Lord our God, king of the universe, who has not made me a woman.

These benedictions have had a long and tortuous history, which I cannot pursue here.[48] They have often been cited as evidence for rabbinic disdain, if not hatred, toward gentiles and women. An immensely learned, but immensely nasty, anti-Jewish writer of the seventeenth century, Johann Christopher Wagenseil, writes:

> You Jewish men are great haters of women, and you give thanks to God everyday publicly in synagogues that he did not make you women—as if women were abortions of nature, horrifying monsters, ill-formed, from whom the light of the divine image has been entirely removed. In contrast, we Christians, even if we hardly disagree that the female sex is the lesser, nevertheless, do not extol the male sex to such a degree that we should attribute to it alone the dignity of the divine image, and that we should think it alone to be worthy of that which pertains to the special indulgence of the divine presence.[49]

According to Wagenseil, Jewish men thank God for not creating them female because women were not created in the image of God. Wagenseil conveniently omits the fact that some Christian thinkers, too, believed that women were not created in the image of God, but on the Jewish side we must admit that Wagenseil's claim is not baseless. Some medieval Jewish thinkers, Jacob Anatoli for example, believed that women were not created in the image of God, and a few passages in ancient rabbinic literature seem to reflect the same belief.[50] For example, one midrash states, perhaps in response to the Christian argument that Adam should have been created circumcised, that "Adam, the first man, was created circumcised." How do we know? "As Scripture says, *God created Adam in his image.*" If Adam was created in the image of God, and if Adam was created circumcised, we may deduce that God, too, is circumcised, that God too is male, and that women are not in the image of God.[51]

Although Wagenseil has given us a possible interpretation of the benediction, an interpretation that may well have been maintained by *some* Jews who recited this benediction, this interpretation is not necessarily the only, the best, or the original one. In fact, our earliest source for these benedictions provides a different explanation entirely:

> R. Judah says:
> A person is obligated to recite the [following] three benedictions every day:
> Blessed [is God] who has not made me a gentile, Blessed [is God] who has not made me a boor, Blessed [is God] who has not made me a woman.
> [Who has not made me] a gentile, because Scripture says, *All nations are as naught in his sight; he accounts them as less than nothing* [Isaiah 40:17].
> [Who has not made me] a boor, because a boor is not a fearer of sin.
> [Who has not made me] a woman, because women are not obligated in the commandments.[52]

R. Judah states that these benedictions are to be recited daily by "a person," *adam* in Hebrew, but it is clear that he means one of Us, the Israelite male. According to R. Judah, the trio of Others is gentile-boor-woman.[53] The trio of Others in Jewish Orthodox prayer books today is gentile-slave-woman, reflecting the emendation suggested by the Bavli that "slave" replace "boor." Even though a slave resembles a woman, the blessings are not redundant, the Talmud says, because one of them is lower than the other. Who is lower than whom varies according to the manuscript or edition of the Talmud; some versions have the Talmud say that a slave is lower than a woman, others that a woman is lower than a slave.[54]

According to R. Judah, the Otherness of the gentile differs from the Otherness of the woman. The gentile is Other by his (or her) very essence. Between Us and Them there is an existential divide: the gentiles are as nothing in God's eyes, but we are God's holy people. Does R. Judah conceive of gentiles as created in the image of God? Rabbinic opinion, most of it expressed implicitly and ambiguously, was divided in the matter.[55] In contrast, the Otherness of Woman is a function of her exemption from the commandments. R. Judah says that "women are not obligated in the commandments"; I assume he means that "women are not obligated, as men are, to observe *all* the commandments, even if they are obligated to observe *some*."[56] The contrast between Jewish men and women is not one of essence but of function. Men are obligated to observe all the commandments; women are not. Men are to thank God every day for their multiple opportunities to serve him.

This explanation for the Otherness of women becomes canonical in rabbinic Judaism. In his comprehensive commentary on the prayer book, R. David b. Joseph Abudraham, a Spanish scholar of the mid-fourteenth century, embellishes R. Judah's explanation of this benediction:

> [We say] "who has not made me a woman" because [a woman] is not obligated to observe positive commandments that need to be observed at a specific time. . . . A man resembles a laborer who enters someone's field and plants it with permission, but a woman resembles one who enters [and plants it]without permission. Furthermore, the fear of her husband is upon her, and she is unable to observe even [the commandments] that she has been commanded. Instead of "who has not made me a woman," women have the custom of saying "who has made me according to his will," like someone justifying an evil decree that has come upon him.[57]

A man resembles a laborer who enters someone's field and plants it with the owner's permission, because a man, like an authorized laborer, will receive full compensation for his efforts. But a woman resembles one who enters a field and plants it without the owner's permission, because a woman, like an unauthorized laborer, will not receive compensation. Abudraham is alluding to the rabbinic principle that one who performs a religious act because he is obligated to do so receives greater reward than one who performs it voluntarily. When women voluntarily observe commandments that need to be observed at a specific time, they do not receive reward from God for their efforts (or perhaps they receive a lesser reward), because only men are obligated and women are not.

Abudraham is among our earliest sources (perhaps the earliest) for the custom of women to recite the benediction "who has made me according to his will." This custom is still widely observed in traditional Jewish circles. Abudraham gives a male's interpretation of the female substitute. When a woman blesses God for creating her according to his will, perhaps she is being truly grateful and thankful, happy with her lot in life. But Abudraham cannot conceive of this possibility and assumes that her tone must be that of resignation and acceptance, "like someone justifying an evil decree that has come upon him."[58] In other times and places, Jewish women elaborated other substitutes for the benediction "who has not made me a woman." In fifteenth-century Austria women blessed God "who has not made me an animal." Some women's prayer

books from Provence and Italy even have the blessing "who has made
me a woman."[59]

"The Covenant You Have Sealed in Our Flesh"

There are only two passages in the rabbinic prayer book whose language prevents, or has been thought to prevent, their recitation by
women. The first is the benediction "who has not made me a woman,"
which I have just discussed. The second is the benediction in the Grace
after Meals which thanks God for "your covenant that you have sealed
in our flesh," that is, circumcision. As we shall see, in medieval Europe
some women omitted this phrase in their recitation of the Grace after
Meals because the covenant of circumcision does not apply to women.
Hence the question: can women thank God for the covenant sealed in
their flesh when they are not circumcised?[60]

Pelimo and Rav

The core of the rabbinic Grace after Meals consists of three paragraphs,
each of them phrased as a blessing. The first thanks God for the gift of
sustenance; the second thanks God for the gift of the land of Israel; the
third is a prayer for the restoration of Jerusalem. The Talmud discusses
the precise wording of the second benediction:

> R. Eliezer says: whoever does not [thank God for] "a desirable, good,
> and spacious land" in the blessing concerning the land, and [whoever
> does not pray for the restoration of] "the kingdom of the house of David"
> in the blessing concerning the building of Jerusalem, has not fulfilled his
> obligation [of reciting the Grace after Meals].
> Nahum the Elder says: one must [also] include in it "covenant."
> R. Yosi says: one must [also] include in it "Torah."
> Pelimo says: "covenant" must precede "Torah," because the latter
> ["Torah"] was given in three covenants but the former ["covenant"] was
> given in thirteen covenants.[61]

The blessing for the land must contain appropriate praises of the land;
we thank God for a "desirable, good, and spacious land." We must also
thank God for covenant and Torah, because the gift of the land is inti-
mately linked with these other gifts. Pelimo, an obscure figure whose
name is transmitted in various forms and who is known only from several citations in the Bavli,[62] says that the mention of "covenant" must

precede the mention of "Torah," because the Torah was given in three covenants, but the covenant—that is, the covenant of circumcision—was given in thirteen covenants. Numerous rabbinic texts state or assume that the Torah was given to Israel in three covenantal ceremonies, the precise identification of which was the subject of abundant discussion by the medieval commentators.[63] Numerous other passages state or assume that the covenant of circumcision has the force of thirteen covenants, since the word *berit* appears thirteen times in Genesis 17, the chapter in which God enjoins the observance of circumcision upon Abraham.[64] Pelimo has juxtaposed these discrete bits of information and drawn a novel conclusion: since thirteen is greater than three, the covenant of circumcision should precede Torah in the second paragraph of the Grace after Meals.

For our purposes, the intellectual cogency of Pelimo's exegesis is not important. What is important is Pelimo's assumption that "covenant" in the Grace after Meals means "the covenant of circumcision," an interpretation that is by no means obvious or inevitable. The same assumption appears on the next page of the Talmud in an interesting story:

> R. Zeira said to R. Hisda: let the master come and teach us [how to recite the Grace after Meals].
> [R. Hisda] replied: the Grace after Meals I have myself not learned [correctly], and shall I teach it?
> [R. Zeira] said to him: what is this? [What do you mean?]
> [R. Hisda] said to him: once I was at the house of the Exilarch, and I recited the Grace after Meals. R. Sheshet [was so amazed that he] stretched out his neck at me like a serpent. Why? Because I said neither "covenant" nor "Torah" nor "kingdom [of David]."
> [R. Zeira said:] and why did you not say them?
> [R. Hisda said: because I followed the view] of R. Hannanel in the name of Rav.
> For R. Hannanel said: Rav did not say[65] "covenant," "Torah," and "kingdom" [when reciting the Grace after Meals]. "Covenant," because it does not apply to women. "Torah" and "kingdom," because they apply to neither women nor slaves.
> [R. Zeira said:] you abandoned all of these Tannaim and Amoraim [who require the recitation of "covenant," "Torah," and "kingdom"] and you followed Rav?![66]

This wonderful story reveals a great deal about the history of the Grace after Meals, about the relations between the rabbis of Babylonia and the Exilarch (the leader of the Jewish community of Babylonia), about the interrelationship of various Babylonian rabbis, and about the authority of Rav versus the authority of other sages. All of this is fascinating and important, but none of this is important for our purposes. What is germane for us is R. Hannanel's report of Rav's behavior.

When reciting Grace after Meals, Rav did not thank God for covenant and Torah in the second benediction and did not pray in the third for the restoration of the Davidic kingdom. Why not? The Talmud supplies an explanation, but it is impossible to be sure whether the explanation is Rav's own, R. Hannanel's (who reported Rav's behavior), R. Hisda's (who is adducing Rav as the model of his own behavior), or the editor's (who helpfully supplied an explanation where none had existed). In any case, we are told that Rav did not say "covenant" because "it does not apply to women," and did not say "Torah" and "kingdom" because "they apply to neither women nor slaves." "Covenant," that is, the covenant of circumcision, does not apply to women.[67] "Torah" and "kingdom" apply neither to women nor to slaves. Torah, because women and slaves are exempt from the obligation to study Torah. Kingdom, because women and slaves will be subordinate to their husbands and masters even after the restoration of the Davidic monarchy. The lot of Jewish men will be much altered—improved—by the messianic restoration, but the lot of women and slaves will remain the same, forever servile.

The logic of Rav's argument is the following:[68] women and slaves are obligated to recite the Grace after Meals;[69] the terms "covenant," "Torah," and "kingdom" do not apply to women; the phrases "Torah" and "kingdom" do not apply to slaves; therefore, if these terms are to be retained in the Grace after Meals, women and slaves will be required either to omit them or to recite something else in their stead; but the sages made no provision either for the omission of these phrases or their emendation by women and slaves; therefore, Rav concludes, the phrases should not be said at all by anyone in the Grace after Meals. Rav's solicitous concern for the feelings of the Other, women and slaves, is remarkable. We are curious to know what Rav thought about the recitation of the benedictions "who has not made me a gentile, who has not made me a slave/boor, who has not made me a woman." Too bad that his opinion is nowhere recorded.

Rav lost. In the liturgical tradition of Babylonia, shaped by the Bavli's citation of Pelimo, the word "covenant" was retained in the second paragraph of the Grace after Meals and the allusion to circumcision was made clear and unmistakable. A medieval Babylonian version reads:

> We give thanks to you, Lord our God, [for] the desirable, good, and spacious land that you willed to inherit to our forefathers, for your covenant that you have placed in our flesh, and for the Torah that you have given us, and for life and favor, grace and sustenance.[70]

"The covenant that you have placed [in other versions: sealed] in our flesh" is an indubitable reference to circumcision. This Babylonian version forms the basis for the version that would become normative for the Jews of Ashkenaz (northern and eastern Europe) and their descendants in the United States.[71]

The Tosafot

Rav realized that if the word "covenant" means "the covenant of circumcision," women would have difficulty in reciting the second paragraph of the Grace after Meals, and he therefore omitted the word. R. Hisda followed suit. Their position is rejected by R. Sheshet, R. Zeira and apparently by the Bavli itself. The question that Rav raised is a real one, however: can women thank God for the gift of circumcision? The question is ignored by the Talmud but reasserts itself in the Middle Ages.

The Mishnah states that women are obligated to recite the Grace after Meals. The Bavli asks: is this obligation a function of Torah law or rabbinic law? In other words, does the Torah itself (as construed by the rabbis) require women to recite the Grace after Meals or was this requirement instituted by the rabbis? After some give-and-take, the Talmud concludes that the obligation derives from the Torah itself. The medieval commentators object: why was the Talmud uncertain? Isn't it obvious that the verse *When you have eaten your fill, give thanks to the Lord your God* (Deuteronomy 8:10) applies to women too?[72] Rashi (1040–1105) explains that the doubt was caused by the last part of the verse, *give thanks to the Lord your God for the good land which he has given you.* Since the land was distributed only to the males and not the females,[73] perhaps the phrase *the good land which he has given you* implies that women are to be excluded from the obligation of giving thanks. This is how Rashi explains the Talmud's question. The Tosafot—glosses on the Talmud written by Rashi's school in the twelfth and thirteenth centuries—suggest a different interpretation:

> The reason [for the Talmud's doubt] is that it is written [in the Grace after Meals] "[We give thanks to you, our God] for your covenant that you have sealed in our flesh, and for your Torah that you have taught us." But

neither covenant nor Torah applies to women, and the Talmud says further along[74] "whoever does not [in the second paragraph of the Grace after Meals thank God] for the covenant and the Torah has not fulfilled his
obligation."[75]

Since circumcision and Torah do not apply to her, a woman cannot say
"[We give thanks to you, our God] for your covenant that you have
sealed in our flesh, and for your Torah that you have taught us." Her inability to recite these words led the Talmud to suggest that perhaps her
level of obligation was a function only of rabbinic law, not Torah law.
Thus the Tosafot.[76] Various other sources confirm that medieval Jewish
women, in those areas that followed the liturgical custom of the Babylonian Talmud, either did not, or were not supposed to, include these
words in their recitation of the Grace after Meals.[77]

    The Tosafot's explanation eloquently attests two important but con-
tradictory strands of medieval Jewish piety in Christian Europe: the increased participation of women in the sacred and the increased effort by
rabbis to minimize or circumscribe that participation.[78] In the high
Middle Ages women did recite the Grace after Meals, but by omitting
(or being required to omit) "your covenant that you have sealed in our
flesh" and "your Torah that you have taught us," they were reminded
of their womanly status. Even when observing a commandment that is
incumbent upon them, they are not equal with men.

Does "Covenant" in the Grace after Meals Mean Circumcision?

All of this is only half the story. Rav, following Pelomi, assumes that the
word "covenant" in the second paragraph of the Grace after Meals
means "the covenant of circumcision." This is what the Bavli assumes,
and this is what the word means in the liturgical traditions based on the
Bavli, as we have just seen. But there was and is an alternative. The
Yerushalmi, the Talmud of the land of Israel, does not know the comment of Pelomi or the story of Rav. The Yerushalmi contains not a hint
that "covenant" means "circumcision."[79] In these texts the word "covenant" refers to the general covenant between God and the Patriarchs,
and between God and Israel. This covenant is spelled out in many passages of the Torah: the covenant between the sections (Genesis 15); the
covenant of circumcision (Genesis 17); God's repeated promises to
Abraham, Isaac, and Jacob to multiply their progeny and give them the
land of Israel as an inheritance; God's repeated promises to Moses and
Israel in Egypt and in the desert; etc. Under the terms of this covenant,

God promises to give the people of Israel the land of Israel, and a reference to this covenant makes perfect sense in a benediction thanking God for the gift of the land. The covenant of circumcision is part of the general covenant, to be sure, but the latter is broader and more inclusive than the former.

In prayer books that follow the rite of the land of Israel, the word "covenant" in the second paragraph of the Grace after Meals refers to the general covenant, not circumcision. Thus one such text reads, "We give thanks to you, Lord our God, that you have given to us to inherit a desirable, good, and spacious land, [that you have given us] covenant and Torah, life and sustenance."[80] Surely the plain meaning of the word "covenant" here is "the covenant between God and Israel" or "the covenant between God and the patriarchs," not "the covenant of circumcision." This interpretation of the word is the only possible one in the following version:

> Hear our request, and in our land may there not be want. We thank you for the land and for sustenance when we eat our fill from your sustenance, as it is written, *When you have eaten your fill, give thanks to the Lord your God for the good land which he has given you.* Remember for us speedily the covenant of our fathers. Blessed are you, Lord, for the land and for sustenance.[81]

"Covenant" here must mean "the covenant with the patriarchs."

Elsewhere, too, rabbinic liturgy uses the unmodified word "covenant" to refer to the general covenant between God and Israel. Perhaps the best example is the *zikhronot* ("memorials," "remembrances") section of the Rosh HaShanah liturgy, which almost certainly dates from talmudic times. This section refers several times to "the covenant" and concludes with a benediction of God who "remembers the covenant." Surely the covenant that God remembers is not (only) the covenant of circumcision but (also) the general covenant between God and the Patriarchs, between God and Israel.

Does "the Covenant" Include Women?

Does the covenant between God and Israel include Jewish women? As far as I have been able to determine, among the relatively few rabbinic texts touching on this question, not a single one implicitly or explicitly excludes women from the covenant, and several explicitly include them. On the verse *Then will I remember my covenant with Jacob; I will remember also my covenant with Isaac, and also my covenant with Abra-*

ham (Leviticus 26:42), the midrash comments: "The verse mentions only the patriarchs; how do I know that the matriarchs are included too? Scripture says *et* [The Hebrew word indicates the direct object and is often construed expansively]."[82]

God remembers the covenant with the matriarchs as well as the covenant with the patriarchs. Male slaves who have been circumcised in accordance with the requirement of Genesis 17 have become *bene berit,* "sons of the covenant" or "people of the covenant"; according to at least one rabbinic passage, female slaves too become *bene berit,* presumably through immersion.[83] If female slaves can be thought to belong to the "people of the covenant," we may assume that the same would be true of native women. In fact, various passages demonstrate that the phrase *bene berit* includes women.[84]

The midrash emphasizes that women were present at the revelation at Mount Sinai and are indeed partners to the covenant between God and Israel. In its paraphrase of Exodus 19, the chapter that describes the revelation at Mount Sinai, the midrash consistently finds a way to include women, who are otherwise missing from the text or excluded.[85] On the phrase *Thus shall you say to the house of Jacob and declare to the children of Israel* (Exodus 19:3), the midrash comments "*the house of Jacob*—these are the women, *the children of Israel*—these are the men."[86] Moses warns the Israelites *do not go near a woman* (Exodus 19:15). The midrash understands this phrase as evidence not for the exclusion of women but rather for their inclusion: Moses wanted to ensure the ritual purity of the *women,* and therefore ordered that *they* abstain from sexual intercourse.[87] At Mount Sinai the women, too, no less than the men, "came under the wings of the divine presence."[88]

If "covenant" in the second paragraph of the Grace after Meals means the general covenant between God and Israel, Rav's problem, the exclusion of women, was not a problem at all. Women are members of the people of Israel, and are part of the covenant between God and Israel. In the Grace after Meals, all Jews, men and women alike, thank God for the gift of the covenant, because the covenant embraces all Jews, men and women alike. Perhaps "Torah" and "kingdom" exclude women and slaves, but "covenant" does not.

Victor of Karben, a fifteenth-century convert from Judaism to Christianity, argued that Jewish women were more passionately committed to Judaism and more ready to be martyred for it than were Jewish men. The explanation for this phenomenon, he said, lay in the women's sense of their own inferiority. Not circumcised, they saw themselves as excluded from the blessings of the world to come unless they could remedy their defect through supererogatory devotion such as martyrdom. Circumcised Jewish men had less soteriological need for martyrdom than uncircumcised Jewish women. Thus Victor of Karben.[89] I cannot here comment on Victor's striking claim that Jewish women were more devoted to Judaism than were Jewish men, but surely his explanation for this alleged phenomenon is a decidedly Christian reading of Judaism. Victor assumes that circumcision occupies a position in Judaism akin to that of baptism in Christianity, so that an uncircumcised Jew (a woman, for example) is as anomalous as an unbaptized Christian. Victor cannot distinguish between the covenant of circumcision and the general covenant between God and Israel; exclusion from the one betokens exclusion from the other. In contrast, rabbinic texts, at least in the legal tradition, do not understand circumcision as a sacrament and do not understand exclusion from circumcision as tantamount to exclusion from the covenant of God with Israel. In eyes of the sages Jewish, women are included in the general covenant between God and Israel, even if they are excluded from, and by, the covenant of circumcision.

First Conclusions: Real Jews Are Men

Circumcision celebrates the birth of a male, marking him as a member of the covenant, as a member of his people, as his father's son, as a future citizen. Circumcision excludes women; by investing circumcision with covenantal value, both the Bible and the talmudic sages declare that Judaism, or at least Jewishness, is in the first instance synonymous with maleness.[90]

Classical rabbinic Judaism has always been, and in many circles still is, a male-dominated culture, whose virtuosi and authorities are males, whose paragon of normality in all legal discussions is the adult Jewish male, whose legal rulings in many areas of life (notably marriage and ritual observance) accord men greater privilege than women, and whose values define public communal space as male space. Within this culture, women are unable to initiate a marriage or a divorce, are obligated to dress modestly in public and to segregate themselves behind a partition in synagogue, and are excluded from the regimen of prayer and Torah study that characterizes, and in the rabbinic perspective sanctifies, the life of Jewish men. Numerous rabbinic texts, whether legal or homiletical, philosophical or mystical, ancient, medieval, or modern, assume that men are the norm and that women are anomalies, whose existence must be explained and whose status must be determined.

In this culture, women are socially and legally inferior to men. A woman's role is to enable acts of piety by her husband and sons, acts from which she herself is excluded. Hers is the classic role of the enabler or facilitator. I am speaking now, of course, of values and ideology. How real women lived their lives across the centuries in all the varied locales of the Jewish experience is not my concern here. From the point of view of realia, we should not confuse antiquity with the Middle Ages, Germany with Poland, Italy with Morocco, France with Yemen, Israel with Babylonia, or the seventeenth century with the nineteenth. Nor am I speaking here of the social prestige, economic power, or political influence of individual women. Nor do I deny, of course, that rabbinic texts are polyphonic and multivalent. One can find passages that are not androcentric; for example, as we have already seen, the rabbis went out of their way to ensure the inclusion of women in the revelation at Mount Sinai. In subsequent chapters I shall try to show that some rabbis explained the non-circumcision of women in decidedly non-androcentric ways, some of which could actually be called "feminist." I am aware of all this, but I stand firm. If we ask rabbinic culture across time and space to tell us what is the proper role for a woman, the answer that we will receive will be that a woman's role is to be a wife and mother and thus enable her menfolk to perform acts of piety. The constancy and relative univocality of this culture in this matter are quite remarkable.[91]

These cultural norms explain why the absence of circumcision from women was not a problem for classical rabbinic Judaism; on the contrary, the absence of circumcision from women will have confirmed for the rabbis their deeply held conviction that only men were the "real" Jews and that, while women certainly were "Israel" and part of the Jewish people, their Jewishness was inferior to that of males, the real Jews. This explanation for the non-circumcision of women was so obvious, so inevitable, and so pedestrian that it did not need to be articulated for a long time.[92]

The pressure of medieval Christian anti-Jewish polemics forced some Jewish thinkers to articulate explicitly what until then had only been implicit. In Menahem's formulation, a Jewish woman does not need to be circumcised because her husband fulfills that obligation for her. In Jacob Anatoli's formulation, a Jewish woman does not need circumcision because she is entirely subject to her husband. *The Dispute between the Church and the Synagogue* and its medieval continuators ask whether

Jewish women are Jews, since they are not circumcised; in response Anatoli and Menahem say that Jewish women are Jews, but that theirs is a lesser Jewishness, because real Jews are men. For Menahem, Jacob Anatoli, and virtually all pre-modern Jews, this truth was not only a social fact; it was also a divinely ordained and legally sanctioned fact.

Anatoli argues further that the non-circumcision of women and the subjugation of women to their husbands are to be connected with the exemption of women from positive commandments that need to be observed at a specific time. In this chapter I have tried to show how right Anatoli was. The exemption of women from the commandment of circumcision is not just an exemption from a positive commandment that needs to be observed at a specific time,[93] it also presages a more fundamental exclusion, the exclusion from the covenantal obligation to observe all the commandments. The history of the second paragraph of the Grace after Meals shows the thinness of the distinction between "covenant" and "covenant of circumcision." Neither circumcised nor obligated to observe all the commandments, Jewish women are Israel yet not quite Israel. Not Us, they are Other. Like slaves, they are subject to us, live with us, and are obligated to observe some of the commandments, but they are not Us. Every day we thank God that we are not one of Them.

Second Conclusions: Comparisons and Contexts

Rabbinic androcentrism and patriarchy might disappoint us but should not surprise us. Virtually all pre-modern cultures were androcentric and patriarchal, and many modern cultures still are; in the words of Sherry Ortner, "everywhere, in every known culture, women are considered in some degree inferior to men."[94] Only in the most recent times has western culture entered into a self-conscious and often painful process of reducing male dominance and control. To expect the rabbis of pre-modern times (or Paul for that matter) to have done the same is entirely unreasonable. In the following paragraphs I highlight some striking parallels between the androcentrism of the rabbis and that of other ancient cultures and medieval Christianity. I do not much care here whether these parallels are representative of these other cultures, although I believe that they are. My point simply is that the rabbis of antiquity and the Middle Ages must be judged by the canons of their time and place, not ours.

Much of rabbinic androcentrism is simply a continuation of the Torah's. We have already seen several examples in this chapter. A good example of the Torah's androcentrism, which is germane to my previous discussion about women's inclusion in the covenant, is Deuteronomy 29:9–11:

> You stand this day, all of you, before the Lord your God—your tribal heads, your elders and your officials, all the men of Israel, your children, your wives, even the stranger within your camp, from woodchopper to waterdrawer—to enter into the covenant of the Lord your God.

At first glance, this text would appear to assume equality of status between men and women in the covenant: all are included in the covenant, men and women alike. However, the androcentric perspective of the text is clear: *you* (second-person plural) means *all the men of Israel.* You, the men of Israel, are accompanied by your leaders, who are *your tribal heads, your elders and your officials,* and by your retainers, your chattel, your dependents, who are *your children, your wives, even the stranger within your camp.* Wives are not *you;* they are *yours*—a big difference. They are included in the covenant because they are *yours.* If I may skip ahead a millennium or two, the same perspective is canonized in the prayer for the congregation that is still recited in traditional synagogues every Shabbat:

> May he [God] who blessed our fathers, Abraham, Isaac, and Jacob, bless this entire congregation and all other congregations—them, their wives, their sons and daughters, and all that belongs to them.[95]

In this prayer, *them* is the membership of the congregation, which, of course, consists of men. Women are not members of the congregation in this rabbinic prayer any more than they are in the book of Deuteronomy.

Rabbinic androcentrism is of a piece with the androcentrism of Greeks, Romans, and Christians.[96] In classical Athens, as in classical Judaism, women of citizen status could not participate in the activities of the public sphere. As we have seen, the term "Israel" sometimes includes, sometimes excludes, women. In classical Athens the linguistic situation is much simpler: the term "Athenians" excludes women. "Athenians" are those who vote and participate in the Athenian democracy, that is, male citizens; Athenian women were not "Athenians."[97] The story is told of Thales the sage—although some tell the story of Socrates: "He used to say there were three blessings for which he was grateful to fortune: 'that I was born a human being and not a

beast, a man and not a woman, a Greek and not a barbarian.'"[98]
There clearly is some relationship between this Greek tradition, the
rabbinic prayer that I discussed above, and the Pauline utterance *there
is neither Jew nor Greek, there is neither slave nor free, there is neither
male nor female, for you are all one in Christ Jesus* (Galatians 3:28),
but what that relationship might be is the subject of scholarly speculation.[99] As I remarked in chapter 3, Paul's denial of the distinction between male and female in Christ hardly means that Paul rejected the
androcentric norms of ancient culture. His statement that *the head of
every man is Christ, the head of a woman is her man, and the head of
Christ is God* (1 Corinthians 11:3), part of a long paragraph whose
point is to ensure that women know their place, seems to say that a
man relates to God as a woman (wife) relates to a man (husband).[100] I
think that both Menahem and Jacob Anatoli would have had no difficulty with this formulation.

A Christian writer of a martyr text describes the crowd that gathered
to witness the trial of the hero; the crowd consisted of "Greeks, Jews,
and women." Apparently women are neither Greeks nor Jews; they are
women.[101] A Greek anti-Christian writer of the second century contends that Christianity has drawn most of its converts from "the foolish, dishonorable, stupid. . . slaves, women, and little children."[102] The
juxtaposition of "women" to slaves, children, and the incompetent
would have sounded quite natural to the rabbis. The legal inferiority of
women to men was also a given of ancient culture. A Roman jurist remarked that "In many articles of our law the condition of women is inferior to that of men."[103]

Medieval Christianity provides many illustrations of our theme. At
a church council in Mâcon in 585, it is reported that: "At this synod
one of the bishops arose and said that a woman is not able to be called
'a human.' But, after accepting the argumentation of the other bishops,
he was quiet."[104] This free-thinking anonymous bishop went even further than any rabbinic exegete. For the rabbis, women are, or might be
thought to be, excluded from the scriptural categories of *Israel, native,*
and *man,* but not *person* or *human* (in Hebrew *adam*). In no ancient
rabbinic text known to me is the word *adam* adduced as excluding
women.[105] In contrast, this bishop in Mâcon argued that the category
"human" *(homo)* did exclude women. The other bishops, however,
won the day, by arguing that the verse *Male and female He created
them; and when they were created, He blessed them and called them
Adam* (Genesis 5:2) clearly implies that both male and female are

deemed to be Adam, that is, *homo*. Further, they argued, the savior, whose human parent was his mother, is called "son of man" (or, more literally, "son of human"); how could that be unless woman too was included in the category *homo?* This excellent argument ended the matter.[106] In the late sixteenth century, one Valens Acidalius published a treatise entitled *A New Argument against Women, in Which It Is Proven That They Are Not Humans.* The treatise was an exercise in irony and sarcasm, an implicit polemic against the Anabaptists, one of the main Protestant heresies of the period. Acidalius intended to demonstrate that by the Anabaptist method of reading Scripture, one could conclude that women were not humans! This was meant to be a *reductio ad absurdum.* Alas, sarcasm is not always easy to catch, and not all scholars, then or now, are endowed with a sense of humor. Thirty years after Acidalius, one Simon Geddick, in all seriousness, wrote a learned rebuttal, proving that indeed women were humans.[107]

Behind this debate—if I may call it that—is the more serious and better-documented debate about the creation of women in the image of God. As we have seen above, Jacob Anatoli was hardly the first or the only Jewish thinker to have believed that Adam, but not Eve, was created in the image of God. Within Christianity the argument begins with Paul, who says that a man *is the image and glory of God, but woman is the glory of man* (1 Corinthians 11:7). This suggests that according to Paul men were created in the image of God, and women were created in the image of men. At most theirs is a derivative, not a direct, image of God. One line of interpretation, from antiquity to the Middle Ages, understood Paul in this way; we may presume that the bishop who argued that woman was not included under the category "human" would have subscribed to this reading of Paul. The most prominent opponent of this reading was Augustine, who had to labor long and hard to avoid the plain implication of the verse. The debate persisted for centuries, and in some circles persists still.[108]

Christian androcentrism is well attested. Among the medieval Christian explanations for the non-circumcision of women that I cited in the previous chapter is the explanation of Hildegard of Bingen. She says that God did not impose circumcision on women because a woman "is under the power of a husband, like a servant under his master." Jacob Anatoli would have agreed with this formulation. An English divine of the early seventeenth century writes: "the priviledge and benefit of circumcision was extended also unto the females, which were counted with the men, the unmarried with their fathers, the married with their husbands."[109] Menahem would have agreed.

Final Conclusions: Why, Then, the Matrilineal Principle?

I anticipate an objection. If women in rabbinic culture are ancillary and dependent; if, at some level, only men constitute Israel and only men are Jews; if a woman's Jewishness in the first instance is vicarious, experienced through her husband and her other menfolk—if all this be so, why did the rabbis institute the matrilineal principle? According to the rabbinic matrilineal principle, the offspring of a gentile mother and a Jewish father is a gentile by birth, while the offspring of a Jewish mother and a gentile father is a Jew by birth. If woman is secondary to man, and wife secondary to husband, why did rabbinic law choose the mother as the determinative parent in cases of intermarriage?

In an earlier study, I suggested that the rabbinic matrilineal principle, which is not attested in any pre-rabbinic source and seems to be a creation of the rabbis themselves, is a reflection of the Roman matrilineal principle, which, at least in theory, determined the status of the offspring of unions between Roman citizens and non-citizens; I also suggested that the rabbinic matrilineal principle should be understood as an expression of rabbinic thinking about mixed breeding, because the status of the offspring of mixed breeding (for example, a mule, the offspring of a horse and a donkey) was determined matrilineally by some rabbis. The arguments in favor of these suggestions are technical and not entirely convincing, and I do not wish them to rehearse them here.[110]

Historically considered, the rabbinic matrilineal principle is the result of its own logic and has no connection with the "citizenship" (or lack of citizenship) or "equality" (or lack of equality) of women. Teleologically considered, however, the matrilineal principle can be seen as systemic compensation to women for their secondary status in rabbinic culture as a whole. In return for not being considered fully as "citizens" and "Israel," women are given the essential task of producing citizens and Israel. If a Jewish man strays and fathers a child by a non-Jewish woman, that offspring is a gentile, neither citizen nor Israel, because without Jewish motherhood there is no Jewish fatherhood. This point has its mythic origins in Genesis 17: Isaac, son of Sarah and Abraham, is the child of the covenant, whereas Ishmael, son of Hagar and Abraham, is not. Motherhood matters.[111] The non-circumcision of women bespeaks their exclusion and subordination, the matrilineal principle bespeaks their inclusion and equality. The one is compensation for the other.

CHAPTER 6

The Reduction of Lust
and the Unmanning of Men

The mark of circumcision, too, I consider to be such an
important factor in this matter that I am convinced that
this by itself will preserve their nation forever. Indeed,
were it not that the fundamental principles of their religion
discourage manliness, I would not hesitate to believe that
they will one day, given the opportunity—such is the
mutability of human affairs—establish once more their
independent state, and that God will again choose them.

Benedict Spinoza

In chapter 5 I discussed the question "what does the absence of circumcision from Jewish women tell us about Jewish women?" In this chapter
I discuss the question "what does the absence of circumcision from Jewish women tell us about Jewish men?" In chapter 5 I argued that circumcision celebrates manhood and masculinity. It marks Jews as men
and men as Jews; its absence from Jewish women implies that they are
Jews of a lesser sort. Their Jewishness derives from, or is subordinate to,
the Jewishness of their menfolk. Men are the norm, women are Other.
In this chapter I argue the opposite. Jewish men need to be circumcised
in order to remedy some defect that inheres in Jewish men; Jewish
women do not need to be circumcised because this defect does not in-
here in them. Men suffer from a defect whose remedy is circumcision.
Women are fine just as they are.

What is this defect that inheres in Jewish men? According to Philo
and Maimonides it is an excess of lust (and pride as well, according to
Philo). Philo explains that the purpose of circumcision is to teach men
to moderate their lust. Maimonides explains that the purpose of circumcision is to weaken the male organ, thereby in fact reducing lust and

diminishing performance. Christians used this same idea to support the conclusion that circumcision makes Jewish men "unmanly," because it reduces their virility. Some Christians went even further, claiming that Jewish men were not only "unmanly" but also effeminate, this also being, at least in part, the result of circumcision. These Christian arguments are not to be found in any pre-modern Jewish sources, even if some Jewish men in the Middle Ages explicitly acknowledged that foreskinned Christian men were better able to please their sexual partners than were circumcised Jewish men. In modern times some Jewish men, conflicted about their Jewishness and their sexuality, have adopted the Christian argument that the regimen of Judaism, circumcision in particular, effeminates Jewish men. In contrast, some apologists for traditional Judaism have argued that the absence of circumcision from women implies that women are naturally on a higher spiritual plane than men and that circumcision allows men to attain the spiritual level that women naturally have. These arguments, both the Christian and the Jewish, begin with a position consonant with that of Maimonides (circumcision reduces male lust) but reach conclusions (circumcision effeminates men; women are spiritually superior to men) that Maimonides himself would almost certainly have rejected.

The theme of this chapter, then, is that Jewish women do not need to be circumcised because only men need to reduce their lust.

Philo

As I discussed in chapter 2, Philo, a Jewish philosopher of the first century CE, attempted to explain why Jews circumcise only the males. For the convenience of the reader, I excerpt here the key paragraphs of Philo's text:

> Why does He [God] command that only the males be circumcised? . . . The divine legislator ordained circumcision for males alone for many reasons.
>
> The first of these is that the male has more pleasure in, and desire for, mating than does the female, and he is more ready for it. Therefore He rightly leaves out the female and suppresses the undue impulses of the male by the sign of circumcision.
>
> The second is that the matter of the female in the remains of the menstrual fluids produces the fetus. But the male provides the skill and the cause. And so, since the male provides the greater and more necessary part in the process of generation, it was proper that his pride should be

checked by the sign of circumcision, but the material element, being inanimate, does not admit of arrogance. . . . [1]

According to Philo, circumcision addresses two moral defects found in men but not in women. First, men have more lust than women because men enjoy sex more than women. Second, men have more pride in their procreative role than do women, because men contribute the active principle ("skill and cause") and women the passive ("matter"). Circumcision teaches men to check their lust and their pride; women do not need this lesson and therefore do not need circumcision.

In many passages Philo assumes that men are superior to women in all things, especially the all-important virtue of self-control. Men can use their natural faculties to control their passions; women need the assistance of men (e.g. their husbands) and social constraints (e.g. sexual segregation) to achieve the same degree of self-control. Philo believed that his opinions in these matters were consonant with the teachings of the Torah, but Torah or no Torah, these opinions are substantially identical with those of the Greek and Roman philosophers of his time, not to mention his Jewish contemporary Paul, as well as the rabbinic sages of later generations.[2] Hence it is remarkable that in his first explanation for the non-circumcision of women Philo concedes that women have at least one advantage over men: they do not suffer from an excess of lust and passion. Civilized, enlightened, and virtuous men are able to control their excess lust, especially if they heed the lesson that circumcision provides, but the challenge that faces them is greater than the challenge that faces women. Philo here reverses the paradigm that dominates premodern western discourse about sexuality, namely, that women are more sexual, and less self-controlled and morally centered, than men. Philo never attributes to women uncontrollable sexuality.[3] On the contrary; it is men who suffer from an excess in this area.

In his first explanation, then, Philo acknowledges that in the matter of sexual self-control men are disadvantaged and women advantaged. In his second explanation, however, Philo does not ascribe any advantage to women. The fact that only men suffer from an excess of pride for their role in procreation does not redound to the moral benefit of women, because a woman's absence of pride is a function of her inferiority. Philo associates the masculine with activity, completeness and rationality, and the feminine with passivity, incompleteness, and irrationality.[4] A woman's role in procreation is entirely passive: she provides the matter, but the male provides the form (the skill and cause).

Since the active principle is superior to the passive principle, it is no wonder that a woman's pride does not need to be checked: she has no pride.[5] The male needs to be reminded by circumcision to curb his pride. So the implications of Philo's second explanation, which sees women as inferior to men, are at odds with the implications of the first explanation, which sees women as enjoying an advantage over men. Philo was not one to be troubled by such inconsistencies.

Philo's influence on subsequent Jewish thought was nil. The Greek Jewish culture of Alexandria that he represented so brilliantly disappeared a century or so after his death. Jews stopped writing literature in Greek and stopped expounding the scriptures philosophically. Rabbinic culture, which would come to dominate the Jewish world, spoke not Greek but Hebrew, Aramaic, and, after the Islamic conquests, Arabic. The works of Philo, like all of the abundant literature in Greek produced by the Jews of antiquity, were ignored by the rabbis. Some Greco-Jewish works were reclaimed by rabbinic culture during the last centuries of the first millennium and translated into Hebrew, but Philo was not among them. Since his works, unlike those of other Greek philosophers, were never translated into Arabic, they remained unknown to the Jews for the duration of the Middle Ages. From the second century CE until the sixteenth, Philo's readers were not Jews but Christians. Some of Philo's reflections on the meanings of circumcision are quite similar to those of Maimonides, as we shall now see, but the coincidence is the result of two philosophical minds treating the same questions and working within the same Greek philosophical tradition. Philo did not influence Maimonides—or any other medieval Jewish thinker.

Maimonides

Rabbi Moses ben Maimon, known in Hebrew as Rambam and in western languages as Maimonides (1135 or 1138–1204) was born in Cordoba. When he was thirteen years old, he and his family fled Spain, eventually reaching Cairo, where he spent most of his life. There he achieved distinction not only as court physician to the vizier but also as jurist, philosopher, and community leader. He is best known for two monumental works, the *Mishneh Torah,* an encyclopedic summary of all of Jewish law, written in Hebrew and completed in 1180, and the *Guide of the Perplexed,* the zenith of medieval Jewish philosophy, com-

pleted in 1190 and written in Arabic. Maimonides' Judaism is a philosophical Judaism, a religion that, like Christianity and Islam, can be defined dogmatically. Maimonides is the first Jewish philosopher to argue
that Judaism can be apprehended as a series of "I believe's," that is, a series of truth claims. In the *Guide* Maimonides labored to reconcile the
truths of philosophy with the truths of Judaism. The God of the Torah
and the rabbis was no less respectable and believable, he argued, than
the God of Aristotle and his medieval continuators. The commandments of the Torah, Maimonides further argued, are not arbitrary but
serve a higher purpose: to bring a Jew closer to God, to nurture contemplation of God, to purify the intellect, and to achieve an elevated
morality. The commandments were not ends in themselves but rather
the means to an end, and that end is intellectual and spiritual communion with God.

Within this sustained program of elaborating the reasons for the commandments, Maimonides' devotes two long pages to circumcision. I
quote the masterful English translation of Shlomo Pines:

> Similarly with regard to circumcision, one of the reasons for it is, in
> my opinion, the wish to bring about a decrease in sexual intercourse and
> a weakening of the organ in question, so that this activity be diminished
> and the organ be in as quiet a state as possible.
>
> It has been thought that circumcision perfects what is defective con-
> genitally. This gave the possibility to everyone to raise an objection and to
> say: How can natural things be defective so that they need to be perfected
> from outside, all the more because we know how useful the foreskin is for
> that member? In fact this commandment has not been prescribed with a
> view to perfecting what is defective congenitally, but to perfecting what is
> defective morally.
>
> The bodily pain caused to that member is the real purpose of circum-
> cision. None of the activities necessary for the preservation of the individ-
> ual is harmed thereby, nor is procreation rendered impossible, but violent
> concupiscence and lust that goes beyond what is needed are diminished.
>
> The fact that circumcision weakens the faculty of sexual excitement
> and sometimes perhaps diminishes the pleasure is indubitable. For if at
> birth this member has been made to bleed and has had its covering taken
> away from it, it must indubitably be weakened. The Sages, may their
> memory be blessed, have explicitly stated: It is hard for a woman with
> whom an uncircumcised man has had sexual intercourse to separate from
> him. In my opinion this is the strongest of the reasons for circumcision.
> Who first began to perform this act, if not Abraham who was celebrated
> for his chastity—as has been mentioned by the Sages, may their memory
> be blessed, with reference to his dictum: *Behold now, I know that thou
> art a fair woman to look upon* [Genesis 12:11].[6]

In order to facilitate discussion, I interrupt Maimonides here. I continue the citation below.

The context of these paragraphs is a discussion of the commandments of the Torah that prohibit certain sexual unions (for example, adultery, incest, intercourse with a menstruant). The purpose of these prohibitions is "to make sexual intercourse rarer and to instill disgust for it so that it should be sought only very seldom," or, in a somewhat less extreme formulation, "to bring about a decrease of sexual intercourse and to diminish the desire for mating as far as possible."[7] Circumcision belongs to this class, as the first paragraph states, since it too aims "to bring about a decrease in sexual intercourse and a weakening of the organ in question." This point is restated in the third paragraph. Circumcision does not remove sexual desire or interfere with the ability to procreate, but it does diminish concupiscence and lust so that only "what is needed" remains. This explanation, of course, is similar to Philo's, but for Philo circumcision is symbolic and for Maimonides it is not. According to Philo, the cutting away of the foreskin represents or symbolizes the cutting away of excess lust and pleasure. According to this first explanation of Maimonides, however, circumcision does not represent or symbolize anything. The physical act of cutting away the foreskin brings about a moral improvement in the individual by weakening the organ and thereby reducing the need for, and the pleasure in, sexual intercourse.[8] In numerous passages throughout his many works, Maimonides emphasizes that bodily pleasure in general, and sexual pleasure in particular, need to be limited and controlled. Excessive sexual indulgence is bad for the body and bad for the soul:

> To the totality of purposes of the perfect Law there belong the abandonment, depreciation, and restraint of desires in so far as possible, so that these should be satisfied only in so far as this is necessary. You know already that most of the lusts and licentiousness of the multitude consist in an appetite for eating, drinking, and sexual intercourse. . . . The ignoramus regards pleasure alone as the end to be sought for its own sake. Therefore God, may his name be held sublime, employed a gracious ruse through giving us certain laws that destroy this end and turn thought away from it in every way. He forbids everything that leads to lusts and to mere pleasure.[9]

The purpose of circumcision too is to limit lust and pleasure.

In the second paragraph, Maimonides argues that circumcision corrects not a physical ("congenital") defect but a moral defect. The foreskin is not a physical blemish—how could it be when it was created by

God? As part of the divine creation it is even "useful." The foreskin, rather, needs to be removed because it is the source of a moral blemish; its continued presence renders sexual self-control difficult. Maimonides acknowledges that rabbinic tradition ("it has been thought") opposes him on this point.[10] The Midrash on Genesis explicitly refers to the foreskin as a "sore" or a "boil" that needs to be removed from the body.[11] A midrashic parable compares the foreskinned penis to a fingernail in need of a manicure, or to a fig whose stalk needs to be removed. No moral blemish here.[12] In another midrashic story, when a philosopher asked "If circumcision is so precious [before God], why was it not given to Adam?," a sage replied "Whatever was created in the first six days requires further preparation, for example, mustard needs sweetening, vetches need sweetening, wheat needs grinding, and man too needs improvement."[13] These are not isolated passages, since they are repeated in one form or another in many midrashic collections. R. Saadya Gaon (882–942), the first rabbinic philosopher of note, also explained the commandment of circumcision in terms of physical amelioration. In a departure from earlier tradition he sees the foreskin not as a blemish but as something useless. "The creator created this part of the body [the foreskin] with a redundancy, with the result that when it is cut off, the redundancy is removed; what is left is in a state of perfection."[14] Maimonides argues that these views cannot be correct, first, because the foreskin is "useful," and, second, because all of God's creations "are most perfect, that no deficiency at all is commingled with them, that there is no superfluity in them and nothing that is not needed."[15]

In the last paragraph of the excerpt Maimonides adduces three proofs that circumcision diminishes sexual desire and pleasure. The first proof is based on logic, "For if at birth this member has been made to bleed and has had its covering taken away from it, it must indubitably be weakened."[16] In the second paragraph Maimonides comments that the foreskin is "useful"; hence its removal must indubitably impair the function of the organ to which it had been attached. The third proof is based on the rabbinic traditions about the chastity of Abraham; until the moment that he descended to Egypt with his wife, Abraham had no idea that Sarah was beautiful.[17] Maimonides argues that the fact of Abraham's chastity is to be connected with his status as the first man to be circumcised. The second proof is the most interesting and problematic. Maimonides cites the following Midrash on Genesis 34:26, *they took Dinah out of Shechem's house and went away:*

R. Judah said: They dragged her out and departed.

R. Hunia said: When a woman has sexual intercourse with a foreskinned man, it is difficult for her to separate from him.[18]

This Midrash argues that Dinah did not want to be "rescued" by her
brothers; she would have preferred to remain with Shechem. Why? Because, as R. Hunia explains, once a woman has had sexual intercourse
with a foreskinned man, she does not want to leave him: a foreskinned
man affords his sexual partner greater pleasure than does a circumcised
man. This passage reveals a great deal about the sexual self-perception
of rabbinic males, a topic that I shall discuss in the next section.[19] Maimonides cites this Midrash to prove that circumcision diminishes pleasure and lust—surely Maimonides means the pleasure and lust of the
man[20]—but it is not clear how this Midrash proves his point, since it
implies that circumcision diminishes the pleasure of the *woman*. Perhaps Maimonides simply assumes that if circumcision diminishes the
pleasure of the woman, it must have the same effect on the man. Or, an
explanation that I think is more likely, perhaps Maimonides means that
a woman whose sexual partner is circumcised will importune him for
sex less frequently than would a woman whose sexual partner is foreskinned. This is the effect of circumcision that Maimonides is seeking:
to reduce the frequency of, and need for, sexual intercourse. I shall consider this explanation further below.

I return now to Maimonides and his second explanation for the commandment of circumcision.

According to me circumcision has another very important meaning,
namely, that all people professing this opinion—that is, those who believe
in the unity of God—should have a bodily sign uniting them so that one
who does not belong to them should not be able to claim that he was one
of them, while being a stranger. For he would do this in order to profit by
them or to deceive the people who profess this religion. Now a man does
not perform this act [circumcision] upon himself or upon a son of his unless it be in consequence of a genuine belief. For it is not like an incision in
the leg or a burn in the arm, but is a very, very hard thing.

It is also well known what degree of mutual love and mutual help ex-
ists between people who all bear the same sign, which forms for them a
sort of covenant and alliance. Circumcision is a covenant made by Abraham our father with a view to the belief in the unity of God. Thus everyone who is circumcised joins Abraham's covenant. This covenant imposes
the obligation to believe in the unity of God: *to be God to you and to
your offspring after you* [Genesis 17:7]. This is also a strong reason, as
strong as the first, which may be adduced to account for circumcision;
perhaps it is even stronger than the first.[21]

In this explanation Maimonides turns from the individual to the community, and from moral perfection to intellectual perfection.

Circumcision is a sign that unites all those "who believe in the unity of God," that is, Jews and Muslims. In various passages Maimonides affirms that the monotheism of Islam is no less pure than the monotheism of Judaism, in contrast with the purported monotheism of Christianity, which was no monotheism at all.[22] Jews and Muslims have two important traits in common: both circumcise, and both believe in the unity of God. Maimonides even argues that Muslims are obligated to circumcise themselves, no less than Jews![23] As a result, Muslims, descendants of Abraham through Ishmael, as well as Jews, descendants of Abraham through Isaac, are part of Abraham's "covenant." Membership in the covenant, as represented by circumcision, imposes the obligation to believe in the unity of God. Neither circumcised nor believing in the unity of God, Christians are excluded from Abraham's covenant. Presumably any kind of bodily sign could have served the purpose of marking and uniting all those who truly believe in God; in this explanation Maimonides does not allege anything special about the foreskin that would have singled it out rather than some other body part for excision.[24] The advantage of circumcision is that it is "a very, very hard thing," hence something that would be observed only by those who are genuine and sincere in their belief in the unity of God. For Christian thinkers, as we saw repeatedly in chapter 3 above, circumcision is a sign of Jewish difference, but for Maimonides, who spent his entire life among Muslims, circumcision is a sign of Jewish commonality with their God-fearing neighbors. Christians by their uncircumcision show their estrangement from God and from the covenant of those who believe in God.

What does Maimonides mean by the phrase "covenant of Abraham"? Josef Stern explains:

> [N]owhere does Maimonides describe Abraham's covenant as a covenant *with* God or *between* humans (or a nation) and God. Instead he says that the "mutual love and mutual help [which] exists *between people* who all bear the same sign . . . forms *for them* a sort of covenant and alliance." . . . In other words, the covenant is a relation entirely among humans. . . . [T]he Abrahamic covenant is an entirely natural, human relation constituted by the sentiments of mutual love and mutual help that exist among all the people who bear the sign of circumcision.[25]

"Covenant," then, is a synonym for "alliance" or "league." Circumcision does not establish a relationship between God and the individual

Jew or between God and the people of Israel. Circumcision is not even a "sign" of that relationship. In fact, in this entire discussion Maimonides has not a single reference to a special relationship between God and the people of Israel. Rather, circumcision is a sign of membership in the covenant of Abraham, the league of those who believe in the unity of God. The covenant is the bond between one believer and the next, and circumcision is the sign of that community.[26] According to Maimonides, circumcision is not the bond between the believer and God, and certainly not the distinctive bond between the people of Israel and God.

Nowhere in his voluminous writings does Maimonides see circumcision as a bond between God and Jew or between God and Israel, or as any more of a bond than any other commandment. In his *Book of the Commandments,* completed about 1170, a decade before the *Mishneh Torah,* Maimonides gives a thematically arranged list of all 613 commandments of the Torah. On the list of the 248 positive commandments, circumcision is placed at number 215, in the context of commandments regulating sexual relations. By placing circumcision in this context, Maimonides seems to presume the first explanation that he would develop later in the *Guide,* namely that the purpose of circumcision is to restrain lust and diminish sexual pleasure. Circumcision is not called *berit,* "covenant." The *Mishneh Torah,* Maimonides' encyclopedic law code, completed about 1180, retains this contextualization but also develops a new one. The list of commandments from the *Book of the Commandments* is incorporated in its entirety in the introduction.[27] We might have thought, then, that Maimonides would have included "The Laws of Circumcision" in "The Book of Women" or "The Book of Holiness," the two books of the *Mishneh Torah* that regulate sexual relations, but he does not. Instead he includes "The Laws of Circumcision" in "The Book of the Love [of God]," the book that contains the laws regulating prayers, blessings, phylacteries, fringes, and the like. In the introduction he explains that "circumcision is included here because it is a sign in our flesh, serving as a constant reminder [of our obligation to love God], even when phylacteries and fringes, etc. are absent."[28] This explanation resembles the second explanation that he would develop later in the *Guide,* namely that the purpose of circumcision is to be a sign for all those who believe in the unity of God.

Within the Laws of Circumcision, Maimonides does not connect circumcision with the chosenness of Israel, does not assign circumcision any special position within the system of the commandments, and does not use the phrase *berit milah*, "the covenant of circumcision."[29] He refers to circumcision as a "covenant" only in liturgical and legal phrases that are taken directly from the Talmud. The Talmud claims that "the commandment of circumcision was given in thirteen covenants," that is, that circumcision has the value of thirteen covenants. The retelling by Maimonides is more specific, "in connection with circumcision, thirteen covenants were made with our ancestor Abraham."[30] Maimonides apparently thinks that circumcision established a covenantal relationship between God and Abraham, just as it establishes a covenantal relationship between God and converts to Judaism, but it does not establish a covenantal relationship between God and the native-born Jew who is circumcised at the age of eight days. For the native born, circumcision is a sign of membership in the Abrahamic league of believers, no more.[31]

Maimonides' minimization of the significance of circumcision becomes conspicuous when we compare the praise of circumcision found in other medieval law codes and lists of the 613 commandments. A contemporary of Maimonides in Germany opens his discussion of the laws of circumcision with the words, "Let us fear and worship the Lord our God who has cherished us and placed his covenant in our flesh."[32] A widely read enumeration of the 613 commandments, written by a Spanish scholar ca. 1300 and otherwise much indebted to Maimonides, expatiates on the function of circumcision: "The Lord, may he be blessed, wished to affix in the people that he set apart to be called by his name, a permanent sign in their bodies to differentiate them from the other nations in their bodily form, just as they are differentiated in their spiritual form."[33] The *Shulhan Arukh*, the law code written by R. Joseph Karo in the sixteenth century that would become normative for all traditionally observant Jews, opens its account of the laws of circumcision with the simple phrase "This commandment is greater than [all the] other positive commandments."[34] Maimonides has none of this.

In sum, Maimonides gives two different explanations for circumcision and seems unable to decide between them. According to the *Guide*'s first explanation, which is presumed by *The Book of the Commandments*, the purpose of circumcision is to diminish sexual pleasure and lust. Maimonides says "In my opinion this is the strongest of the reasons for circumcision." According to the *Guide*'s second explanation, the purpose of circumcision is to signal membership in the covenant of Abraham, a pact of all those who believe in the unity of God. (A slightly different version of this argument appears in the *Mish-*

neh Torah to explain why circumcision was placed in the context of commandments that evince our love of God.) Of this explanation Maimonides says "This is also a strong reason, as strong as the first, which may be adduced to account for circumcision; perhaps it is even stronger than the first." I do not know how to explain this ambiguous utterance, especially in light of the fact that the *Guide* puts circumcision back into the context of sex laws and explicitly rejects the classification scheme defended in the *Mishneh Torah*.[35] Maimonides seems to have been undecided about the relative priority of the two explanations.[36] In any case, neither explanation sees circumcision as the covenant between God and Jew or between God and Israel, and neither sees circumcision as better or more important than any other commandment. Later in this chapter and in the next, we shall see how these two Maimonidean explanations can be applied to the question of the non-circumcision of Jewish women.

Envy of the Gentile Foreskin

Maimonides argues that the purpose of circumcision is to weaken a man's sexual desire and pleasure. Maimonides cites the Midrash on Genesis 34 to prove his case, but, as I already noted, the Midrash does not say precisely what Maimonides wants it to say. Maimonides adduces it to prove that circumcision reduces male desire and pleasure, but the Midrash actually says that a foreskinned man can pleasure a woman more than a circumcised man can. Maimonides probably interpreted the midrashic passage as follows: a woman whose sexual partner is circumcised derives less pleasure from sexual intercourse than a woman whose sexual partner is foreskinned, and the former woman will as a result importune her partner for sex less frequently than the latter. The net effect of circumcision, then, is to reduce the frequency of, and need for, sexual intercourse. In his legal writings Maimonides acknowledges the sexual obligation that a husband has to his wife. A husband must have intercourse with his wife at regular intervals, and a husband who is unable to fulfill this obligation must divorce his wife and pay her the marriage settlement *(ketuvah)* to which she is entitled. But for Maimonides the obligation incumbent on the husband is only to have sex with his wife; nowhere does Maimonides extend the obligation to include sexual satisfaction. Maimonides knows that sexual intercourse can afford pleasure to a woman, but he always describes intercourse from the perspective of the man and never obligates a husband to pleasure or satisfy his wife. According to Maimonides, a man needs to engage in sex for his own health and for the sake of offspring. His wife, apparently, will have to content herself with whatever her husband gives her. The theory that circumcision of a man reduces his lust and pleasure as well as his ability to pleasure his sexual partner fits well within an ideological framework that minimizes a husband's obligation to satisfy his wife's sexual needs.[37]

All of this is developed in a remarkable way by R. Isaac ben Yedaiah, an obscure scholar who seems to have lived in southern France in the middle of the thirteenth century. Heavily indebted to Maimonides, R. Isaac develops the theory that the goal of circumcision was to reduce a man's sexual desire and pleasure. And, following the hint of the Midrash on Genesis 34 that Maimonides had cited, R. Isaac contrasts the sexual prowess of the circumcised man with that of the foreskinned:

> A man foreskinned in the flesh desires to lie with a beautiful-looking woman. . . . She too will court the man who is foreskinned in the flesh and lie against his breast with great passion, for he thrusts inside her a long time because of the foreskin, which is a barrier against ejaculation in intercourse. Thus she feels pleasure and reaches an orgasm first. When a foreskinned man sleeps with her and then resolves to return to his home, she brazenly grasps him, holding on to his genitals, and says to him, "Come back, make love to me." This is because of the pleasure that she finds in intercourse with him. . . .
>
> But when a circumcised man desires the beauty of a woman, and cleaves to his wife or to another woman comely in appearance, he will find himself performing his task quickly, emitting his seed as soon as he inserts the crown. . . . This is the way the circumcised man acts time after time with the woman he loves. He has an orgasm first; he does not hold back his strength. As soon as he begins intercourse with her, he immediately comes to a climax.
>
> She has no pleasure from him when she lies down or when she arises, and it would be better for her if he had not known her and not drawn near to her, for he arouses her passion to no avail, and she remains in a state of desire for her husband, ashamed and confounded. . . . She does not have an orgasm [even] once a year, except on rare occasions, because of the great heat and the fire burning within her. . . .
>
> In this manner a woman has greater pleasure from a foreskinned man than from a circumcised man.[38]

According to R. Isaac, circumcision weakens not only desire and pleasure, but also performance, or, in a different formulation, by weakening performance, circumcision also weakens desire and pleasure. A circum-

cised man is unable to pleasure his woman, since he suffers from pre-
mature ejaculation (as we would call it). As a result the woman will become sexually frustrated and will lose interest in sex, allowing the man
to devote his spiritual and physical energies to the contemplation of
God and other noble pursuits. A foreskinned man, in contrast, affords
his partner so much pleasure that she is unable to leave him alone, as
the Midrash says, with the result that a foreskinned man will not have
energy for anything other than sex. And this, for R. Isaac, is a bad thing.

The indifference to a woman's sexual pleasure that is implicit in Maimonides becomes explicit in R. Isaac.[39] The sexual inadequacy of the
circumcised man, implicit in the Midrash on Genesis and in Maimonides, becomes explicit in R. Isaac. Maimonides' implicit contrast of
the circumcised man with the foreskinned, the former sexually re-
strained and therefore devoted to God, the latter sexually unrestrained
and therefore estranged from God, becomes explicit in R. Isaac. The
crucial difference between them is that Maimonides lived in a Muslim
environment in which virtually all men were circumcised, while R. Isaac
lived in a Christian environment in which virtually all non-Jewish men
were foreskinned. In R. Isaac's eyes, Christian men were sexual super-
men, who could pleasure their women to a degree far beyond the ca-
pacities of Jewish men, and who could do so far more often. If virility
were to be defined in terms of sexual prowess, Jewish men would fail
miserably, because their circumcision has rendered them incapable of
pleasuring their women. But for R. Isaac, of course, virility is a function
not of sexual prowess but of intellectual and spiritual capacity, and by
this criterion circumcised Jewish men are manly indeed, while foreskinned Christian men are impotent.[40]

It is difficult to know how much of R. Isaac's construction is the idio-
syncratic product of his own soul, perhaps tormented by feelings of sexual inadequacy, and how much represents views that were widespread
among the Jews of Christian Europe.[41] A Jewish text from Germany ca.
1400 shows that approximately one hundred and fifty years after R.
Isaac, other Jews, too, conceded that circumcision made Jewish men
sexually inadequate compared with Christian men.

Before we turn to that source, I must first present the talmudic text to
which it refers. In the middle of a discussion about punishments of sinners in the hereafter, the Babylonian Talmud comments that "our father
Abraham comes, brings sinners up from Gehenna, and receives them,
except for the Israelite who has had intercourse with a gentile woman,
since his foreskin has been stretched and so [Abraham] does not dis-

cover him [to be circumcised]."[42] The idea that our father Abraham prevents the circumcised from entering Gehenna, permitting entrance only to the uncircumcised, recurs in various midrashic passages, and well illustrates the salvific or saving function of circumcision that I discussed at some length in chapter 1.[43] The idea that the wicked of Israel "stretch" or "draw down" the remnants of their foreskin in order to hide their circumcision and appear foreskinned, also recurs in various rabbinic passages.[44] But this is the only rabbinic passage that combines these motifs in this way: circumcision guards against the fires of Gehenna, but it does not rescue the man who has had intercourse with a gentile woman. The foreskin of this man has been drawn down, so that Abraham does not recognize him to be circumcised and he is left to endure his punishment.

This passage is discussed by R. Jacob ben Moses ha Levi Molin (or Moellin), known as the Maharil, one of the leading rabbis of Germany in the early fifteenth century. He spent most of his life in Mainz and died in 1427. His disciples recorded their master's memorable actions and rulings, as well as some of his stray teachings. Among these is the following:

> It says [in the Talmud] at the end of the first chapter of tractate Eruvin that in the hereafter Abraham our father will sit at the entrance to Gehenna[45] and raise up from there all those who are circumcised, except for the man who has had intercourse with a gentile woman [and] has closed up his circumcision with a foreskin. Since he is not recognized, he is not raised up but remains there with all the other sinners who do not ascend.
>
> On this the sinners sneer: why is this sin greater than the other categories of sins whose violators [nevertheless] ascend [from Gehenna]? The Maharil reports that he heard from R. Isaac [of] Weida an explanation [fitting] for the common folk.
>
> Everyone knows [the facts of] nature, as it says [in the Midrash on Genesis], "it is difficult [for a woman] to separate from the foreskin," that is, a woman derives more pleasure from intercourse with a foreskinned man than from intercourse with a circumcised man. And now, when the circumcised man who is having sex with a gentile woman senses that she does not desire him as she does a gentile man and he is overcome with desire to endear himself to her just like a foreskinned man, he imagines himself at the moment of intercourse, in order to endear her to him, as if he were a complete foreskinned man. Therefore his punishment is magnified to the ultimate, because he imagined himself to be a complete gentile.[46]

Another remarkable text! Here we see clearly Jewish envy of the gentile foreskin. A Jewish man having an affair with a Christian woman senses that he cannot compete with the woman's Christian lovers, because his equipment cannot compare with theirs. At that moment he wishes for nothing more than a foreskin. Circumcision unmans Jewish men, if manhood or manliness be defined in terms of sexual prowess. In the male Jewish imagination, sexual virility requires a foreskin. The Maharil attributes this insight to his contemporary R. Isaac (of) Weida.[47] How the good rabbi knew the secret fantasies of Jewish men who were having sex with Christian women, he does not reveal. But the fact that the Maharil considers R. Isaac's explanation to be appropriate for the common folk (lit:, "the masses of the people") would suggest that such self-perception was common among male Jews of medieval Germany.

I am unable to explain what role this fantasy played in medieval Jewish culture. Sexual self-control is a quality that many cultures ascribe to themselves and deny to others. Rabbinic culture, for example, sees sexual self-control as a virtue cultivated by Jewish men, in contrast with gentiles, both men and women, who are promiscuous and unrestrained.[48] Greeks and Romans thought of barbarians (including Jews) as lusty and uncontrolled, and medieval Christians thought of Jews and Muslims in the same way. American whites thought of American blacks as oversexed. Therefore there is nothing particularly surprising in the Jewish belief that Jewish men, in part because of their circumcision, are able to exercise sexual self-control and restraint to an extent beyond the capacity of uncircumcised gentiles.

What is surprising, however, is that this cultural construction in praise of the Self and in denigration of the Other included, for at least some Jews of Christian Europe, self-denigration as well. What did these Jews gain by believing that in the realm of sex Jewish men were far less proficient than Christian men? I cannot imagine that the rabbis adopted this rhetoric in order to excuse sexual liaisons of Jewish women with Christian men. Were they engaging in psychological warfare to discourage Jewish men from having affairs with Christian women? No doubt Jewish society had an interest in discouraging such affairs, but surely this belief is an odd way of accomplishing this goal. Perhaps we see here an attitude akin to the "inferiority complex" that colonialized peoples often feel vis-à-vis their colonizers. This attitude, then, anticipates the self-denigration and self-hatred that would characterize so many segments of modern Jewry in the late nineteenth century and beyond.[49] Perhaps the self-portrait of Jewish men as sexual incompetents is a reflection of Jewish powerlessness vis-à-vis the gentiles. In the realm of the physical, Christians were more powerful—more "masculine"—than

Jews, and this political fact came to be represented in sexual terms. The logical end-point of this construction is the perception of circumcision as castration, and of Jewish men as effeminate or feminized. I shall return to this below.

Christian writers of the sixteenth and seventeenth centuries regularly assume that circumcision of the man diminishes the sexual pleasure of the woman and claim that Jewish women are aware of this fact. A collection of humorous anecdotes by the German writer Heinrich Bebel, first published in 1508 in Latin and soon translated into German and Italian, contains the following joke:

> Once I was in the little town of Hechingen, which is in the domain of the Count von Zollern. There I met a Jewess who was of beautiful form, and very clever besides. When I tried to persuade her to accept the Christian faith, she replied in a not unseemly manner. Inasmuch as she believed that circumcision was of the same worth as baptism, she asked me how great a value did we Christians assign to baptism.
>
> I answered, "Much indeed, for without it the gates of the kingdom of heaven are closed."
>
> She responded, "But we Jewish women value circumcision much less."
>
> When I asked her why, she said, "Because we would prefer that a piece be added to the male parts of our men rather than taken away."[50]

Sir Thomas Browne (1605–1682) writes that Jewish "women desire copulation with them [Christian men], rather than their owne nation, and affect [i.e., prefer] Christian carnality above circumcised venery," a statement that is cited with approval by his contemporary John Bulwer and others.[51] A medical writer of the seventeenth century writes that "Jewish women even today declare that the pleasure is greater if they lie with a man whose foreskin has never been removed or has been skillfully reconstituted."[52] Within Christian culture, this argument makes sense, and clearly is connected with the myth of the beautiful Jewess. In this view of the world, Christian men are real men, able to satisfy not only their own women but also the women of the Jews. Jewish men are weak and ugly, but Jewish women are beautiful, alluring, exotic. From Jessica in *The Merchant of Venice* to Rebecca in *Ivanhoe*, European literature is full of Jewish heroines who are too beautiful, too noble, and too attractive to remain within the Jewish fold. And why should such a woman be satisfied with a Jewish man when she deserves better, a real man—a Christian?

Sebastian Münster (1488–1552), an accomplished Hebraist, prolific author, and a supporter of Martin Luther, wrote a tract in 1539 to promote the conversion of Jews to Christianity. The work is in the form of a dialogue, a literary form that goes back to Justin Martyr in the second century CE, as we saw in chapter 3. What is unusual about this dialogue is that Münster wrote it in two languages, Latin and Hebrew, so that it could be read by both Christians and Jews. A hundred years later, one Paul Isaiah, "A Jew born, but now a converted and baptized Christian," translated the dialogue into English, and it is this version that I cite. The dialogue begins with a Christian, who clearly represents Münster himself, hailing a Jew on the street and addressing him in Hebrew. The Jew asks how the Christian recognized him to be a Jew. The Christian responds:

> *Christian:* From the form of your face I knew you to be a Jew: For you Jewes have a peculiar colour of face, different from the form and figure of other men; which thing hath often fill'd me with admiration [i.e., astonishment], for you are black and uncomely, and not white as other men.
> *Jew:* It is a wonder, if wee be uncomely, why you Christians doe so love our women, and they seem to you more beautifull than your owne.
> *Christian:* Your women indeed are more comely than your men. . . .[53]

The dialogue turns for a few pages to the subject of the blackness and ugliness of Jewish men, and then returns to the subject of Jewish women:

> *Christian:* You have not yet told me, why the women amongst you are more beautifull than the men, and are not so easily known [i.e., recognized] as the men.
> *Jew:* Because you Christians doe not so much reproach them, as the men; moreover wee adorne them with excellent apparell, that they may find favour in your eies, and we by them obtaine what we desire, and it may bee well with us by reason of them, and our soules may live for their sakes among the Gentiles; as it is written, *and they intreated* [i.e., treated] *Abraham well for Sarahs sake, because she was a woman of a comely countenance, Gen.* 12.16.[54]

The theme of the ugliness and blackness of Jewish men has a long history, which ascends to the high Middle Ages and reaches down to the twentieth century (during which the Ku Klux Klan, the Nazis, and others argued that the Jews were not white but black), but this is not our concern.[55] The novelty here is the point that is asserted by the Jew and conceded by the Christian, that Christian men find Jewish women beautiful and attractive, even more beautiful and attractive than Christian women. More astonishing is the assertion that Jewish men consciously and deliberately exploit the attractiveness of Jewish women. Just as

Abraham displayed Sarah before Pharaoh, so, too, do contemporary Jews display their women before the Christians, in order to obtain favorable terms from the ruling society.

In Christian sexual fantasy of the early modern period, Jews occupied a place akin to that of blacks in American sexual fantasy. Jewish men, like black men, were regarded either as sexual predators or as sexual weaklings, either as oversexed and lascivious or as weak and unmanly. Only the latter conception is of concern to me here. The men are seen as contemptible but the women are seen as beautiful, attractive, and desirable. The myth of the beautiful Jewess who converts to Christianity and marries a Christian hero allows the fantasy to reach its full development: a Christian man may not marry a Jewish woman, but through her conversion to Christianity, the illicit becomes licit, and the woman previously forbidden can unite with a man who deserves her. There may well have been an analogous fantasy in rabbinic society, which forbade marriage, indeed all sexual unions, between Jewish men and non-Jewish women. But once a gentile woman has converted to Judaism, she immediately becomes a legitimate marriage partner who nonetheless retains something of her foreign allure and exotic charm. "Why is everyone eager to marry a female convert?" the Talmud asks.[56] Perhaps rabbinic culture once developed a theory of the gentile sexual mystique, akin to the Christian theory of the Jewish sexual mystique.

I return, then, to my puzzle. Within the context of European Christian culture of the early modern period, this fantasy, the fantasy that circumcision renders Jewish men inferior to Christian men in affording sexual pleasure to women, makes sense. It fits well into a larger pattern of Christian perceptions of Jewish men and Jewish women, and into the larger pattern of abuse directed against out-groups by dominant societies. Jewish men, or at least some Jewish men, also subscribed to this same fantasy, thereby belittling themselves and their sexual prowess. I do not know why they did, but they did.

Does Circumcision Effeminate Jewish Men?

Howard Eilberg-Schwartz argues that Jewish culture understood circumcision not just as an "unmanning," that is, a reduction of male sexual power, but also as a feminization, that is, an act that turns men into women, culturally speaking.[57] I am not convinced. No rabbinic passage explicitly connects circumcision with feminization, and all the passages that in Eilberg-Schwartz's eyes connect them implicitly are susceptible to other interpretations. As far as I can discover, when Freud and other modern secular Jews interpret circumcision as feminization or emasculation, they are saying something that Jewish tradition had previously not said. On the contrary, the equation of circumcision with feminization or emasculation was often for Christians and for self-hating modern Jews an expression of anti-Jewish fantasy.

In order to show the ambiguities of the rabbinic evidence I would like to consider one text adduced by Eilberg-Schwartz, a parable cited by R. Levi to illustrate the verse *Walk in my ways and be perfect* (Genesis. 17:1). How does circumcision render the body *perfect?*

> R. Levi said:
>   This [verse may be illustrated by the following parable]:
>   [Abraham] resembles a noble lady whom the king commanded, "Walk before me." She walked before him and her face went pale.
>   She said, "Perhaps he will find some blemish in me?"
>   The king said to her, "You have no blemish, except that the nail of your little finger is slightly too long; pare it and the defect will be gone."
>   Similarly, God said to Abraham, "You have no other blemish except this foreskin: remove it and the defect will be gone."[58]

The foreskin is a minor imperfection in the body, the removal of which makes the body perfect. This is one of the rabbinic texts cited by Eilberg-Schwartz to show that circumcision "feminizes" its subject. Eilberg-Schwartz argues that R. Levi's parable imagines circumcision to be "a detail of proper female adornment," that it "depicts circumcision as the final touches in an elegant woman's toilette," and that it "makes an Israelite man into God's beautiful female lover."[59] This interpretation is certainly possible, but hardly necessary or even likely. It assumes a simple mechanical equivalence between the signifier and the signified, but rabbinic parables seldom imply such equivalence.[60] In biblical and rabbinic imagery, God is often represented as a husband or groom, and the people of Israel as wife or bride. A real paradox lies at the heart of this imagery, since collective Israel, which is female, consists first and foremost of individual Jews who are male. This paradox, which is the source of much gender-bending in the Midrash, most obviously in the Midrash on the Song of Songs, has nothing to do with circumcision. The attribution of feminine traits or characteristics to the Jewish people, and by extension to individual male Jews, hardly means that male Jews were understood as "feminine," let alone female. In her study of Christian spirituality of the Middle Ages, Caroline Walker Bynum has cautioned us against reading such images too literally, and the same caution is necessary in the reading of rabbinic texts.[61] I am similarly unconvinced by Eilberg-Schwartz's exegesis of other rabbinic passages.

The claim that Jewish men are effeminate, and that their effeminacy is linked to their circumcision, is of Christian, not Jewish, origin. Late medieval Christian texts regularly refer to Jewish men as effeminate: they are weak, do not carry arms or fight back when attacked, and do not engage in "manly" occupations. *Gente afeminada*, Miguel Cervantes (1547–1616) called them.[62] According to an old Christian tradition, reaching back to Late Antiquity, Jewish men regularly or constantly suffer from bleeding hemorrhoids, and in the late fifteenth century this bleeding came to be understood as male "menstruation." "Their men and their women equally suffer from menstrual flux" is how one source puts it.[63] Another Christian tradition regularly associated Jewish circumcision with castration, as if Jewish men were hardly men at all.[64] In the nineteenth century, these Christian arguments were taken up by westernized Jews, for example Sigmund Freud, who were conflicted about their Jewishness (and their masculinity). Freud argued that "for the uncircumcised Aryan, the Jew is analogous to the woman" and that the circumcised man, like the woman, arouses in the Aryan male the fear of castration, which is the source of both anti-Semitism and misogyny.[65]

What Would Maimonides Have Said about the Non-circumcision of Women?

Maimonides spent his entire life in the Islamic orbit. We may safely imagine that Maimonides knew little and cared less about Christian anti-Jewish polemic. No surprise that he does not address the question of the non-circumcision of women. Yet, if he had seen fit to address the question, what would he have said?

According to the first explanation of Maimonides, the purpose of circumcision is to diminish male sexual desire and pleasure. The physical removal of the foreskin aids in the correction of a moral defect, too much lust. The fact that women are not circumcised implies one of two things, either that women have no means by which to control their lust, or that women are not assailed by excessive lust. I believe that the second reading is more plausible than the first. True, Maimonides believes that women are less capable than men in controlling their emotions,[66] but he nowhere states that women are more lust-prone than men or that they are dominated by an uncontrollable sexuality. Hence I think that Maimonides' first explanation implicitly recognizes a slight advantage possessed by women in the battle for self-control: men in their natural state suffer from the moral defect of excessive lust, but women do not. As we saw above, Philo acknowledges this point as well. This slight advantage enjoyed by women is offset by male circumcision and does not, of course, alter the fundamentals of society. For Maimonides, no less than for Philo, the male is at the top of the social and moral hierarchy; the male is Form, the female is Matter.[67] But at least in one respect, the human proclivity to lust, women have a modest, if temporary and ultimately inconsequential, advantage.

According to the second explanation of Maimonides, circumcision is a sign of membership in the Abrahamic covenant, the league of those who believe in the unity of God. Jewish women no less than Jewish men are obligated to know God, love God, fear God, etc. Maimonides believes that exceptional women, like exceptional men, can attain the highest level of cognition of God. Average women, however, have limited intellectual capacity, akin to that of children and fools.[68] Maimonides nowhere sees the inferiority of women as a difference in ontology or essence; nowhere, for example, does he say that women were not created in the image of God, and nowhere does he imply that women constitute an order of human being different from that of men. No, the inferiority of women for Maimonides is social: the roles that they play in society—the roles that they *must* play in society, according to Maimonides—are roles that are inferior to those of men. The differences between men and women are physical and social, not physical and essential.[69] So, although Jewish women are obligated to believe in the unity of God, and although Jewish women in fact do believe in the unity of God to the best (he would argue) of their limited abilities, they are not members of the Abrahamic league in the same way that men are members. We may be sure that Maimonides would have advanced the classic rabbinic answer that I developed in chapter 5. He would have said that insofar as the Abrahamic league is a social organization, women are members only in an adjunctive way, through their menfolk. The non-circumcision of women attests to their secondary social status.

Men Need to Be Perfected; Women Do Not

Let us return to the first explanation of Maimonides and its implications. In their natural state women enjoy a modest advantage over men. The advantage they have is that they are less troubled by lust than are men; the advantage is modest because when a boy is circumcised on the eighth day of life the deficit disappears. However, the idea that women enjoy a modest advantage over men, even if only briefly and even if without long-term consequence—this idea had and has powerful appeal for modern Jews eager to find ways to make tradition appear respectable. These Jews develop this Maimonidean idea in ways that Maimonides himself would no doubt have rejected. They argue that the non-circumcision of women demonstrates the natural moral superiority of women over men. First and foremost among these defenders of tradition is Rabbi Samson Raphael Hirsch.

Samson Raphael Hirsch (1808–1888), a tireless apologist for traditional Jewish observances and beliefs, was the founder of German "Neo-Orthodoxy."[70] His movement was "Orthodox" in the sense that it opposed any changes in traditional practice and saw itself as a guardian of the faith against the depredations of the Reform movement; his movement was "neo" in the sense that it endorsed the emancipation of the Jews and their emergence from the ghetto into western society and culture. Hirsch was much influenced by Maimonides, and he may even have seen himself as a latter-day Maimonides.[71] In numerous works he tried to explain to the perplexed Jews of his time that a life lived according to the dictates of traditional Judaism was meaningful, respectable, and decorous, in conformity with all that was valued by the emerging German-Jewish bourgeoisie. German Jews did not need to turn to Reform, Hirsch argued again and again, in order to find a Judaism that would not embarrass them in front of German Christians. Hirsch's favorite mode of argumentation was "symbolism"; the commandments of the Torah represent or symbolize messages that ennoble and inspire. For Hirsch circumcision is "symbolic"; its message is as follows:

> Keep the strength of your body holy: do not squander it in vile, sensuous lust. Do not dissipate it against God's will. Expend it only as a servant of God, seeing even in the most animal-like actions but the sacred mission planned in holiness for the upbuilding of the world. Keep your strength holy for this sacred purpose; and to this divine end curb your animal passions.[72]

We recognize here, of course, the influence of Maimonides, except that for Maimonides circumcision physically removes some of the male's desire and pleasure, whereas for Hirsch (like Philo) circumcision merely represents symbolically or metaphorically the excision of improper desire and pleasure.[73]

And what of the non-circumcision of women? Hirsch addresses this question in his commentaries on the Torah. A discussion of the Sabbath and the holidays leads Hirsch to a discussion of the commandments that must be observed at a specific time, commandments from which women are exempt. As I discussed in the previous chapter, Jacob Anatoli argues that the exemption of women from these commandments and their non-circumcision betoken their ancillary status. A woman's Judaism is expressed by and through her menfolk, especially her husband. Hirsch, however, argues the opposite. Women's exemption from some of the commandments and their non-circumcision betoken their superiority to men:

> The Torah did not impose these *mitzvot* [commandments] on women *because it did not consider them necessary to be demanded from women.* All *mitzvot shehazeman gerama* [commandments that must be performed at a specific time] are meant, by symbolic procedures, to bring certain facts, principles, ideas, and resolutions, afresh to our minds from time to time to spur us on afresh and to fortify us to realize them to keep them. God's Torah takes it for granted that our women have greater fervor and more faithful enthusiasm for their God-serving calling, and that this calling runs less danger in their case than in that of men from the temptations which occur in the course of business and professional life. Accordingly it does not find it necessary to give women these repeated spurring reminders to remain true to their calling, and warnings against weaknesses in their business lives.
>
> Thus, at the very origin of the Jewish People, God's foresight did not find it necessary to ensure their bond with Him by giving women some permanent symbol in place of Mila [circumcision] for men. So, also, at the Lawgiving on Sinai, God reckoned first of all (Ex. XIX,3) on the faith and devotion of the women. So also, the Jewish Nation has established the fact—and all our generations have inherited it—that in all the sins into which our nation has sunk, it has been *bisechar nashim tzadqaniyot* [as a reward for the righteousness of women], the faithfulness of our women to their convictions and sense of duty which has preserved and nurtured the seed of revival and return.[74]

In Hirsch's worldview, a woman belongs at home, where she maintains the proper environment for the spiritual and religious nourishment of her husband and children.[75] A man, of course, is at his business during the day. Therefore, a man needs constant reminders and spurs to think about God, while a woman, safely ensconced within the home, does not. But woman and man contrast not just in function but also in essence. Women are naturally more spiritual and more religious than men. As evidence of their spiritual superiority, Hirsch cites three proofs. First, they have no need of any "permanent symbol" in place of circumcision, which is required only of men.[76] Second, at the revelation at Mount Sinai, God instructed Moses to address the women before the men. (At least this is how Hirsch, following rabbinic exegesis, understood Exodus 19:3.) Third, at various tragic moments in Jewish history, the Jewish people have been saved by God from disaster only through the merit of righteous women.[77]

Hirsch realizes that the position of women in traditional Judaism was a problem, and as a good apologist he tries to turn a deficit into an asset. Women are not *subjugated* in traditional Judaism, says Hirsch; they are *venerated*. In the spiritual sphere, they are naturally superior to men. Their exemption from some of the commandments that are incumbent on men attests not to their unworthiness and unimportance, but to the opposite: they do not need the commandments that men do. This apologetic may strike us as shallow and disingenuous, an argument based on a naïve essentialist distinction between men and women, but in some circles it found, and continues to find, a receptive audience.[78]

Hirsch's basic idea—that women enjoy spiritual and moral superiority over men—is a distant relative of Maimonides' idea that women do not need the aid that circumcision provides in controlling lust. For Hirsch, the advantage enjoyed by women is a function of their feminine nature and a key to understanding their place in the structure of rabbinic Judaism. For Maimonides, of course, the advantage enjoyed by women was implicit, temporary, and ultimately of no consequence. Although Hirsch has gone much further than Maimonides—indeed Maimonides would never have endorsed the idea that women are by their essence spiritually superior to men—nevertheless, the two explanations are akin to each other.

For some contemporary apologists, Hirsch did not go far enough. Judith S. Antonelli is a self-styled "radical feminist and religious Jew." In her Torah commentary published in 1995, she endeavors "to refute the common feminist stereotype that Judaism is a 'patriarchal religion,' and to refute the sexism in Judaism by exposing it as sociology rather than 'divine law.'"[79] For Antonelli, true authentic Judaism, which can be dis-

covered through a radical feminist reading of the Torah, is not patriarchal and does not oppress women in the slightest. If Jewish society has
oppressed women, it is only because Jews have been influenced and cor-
rupted by gentile culture.[80] We can get a sense of her enterprise from her
explanation of the commandment of circumcision:

> Circumcision does something to a boy to bring him *up to the level of
> women*. This is indicated by the fact that women are considered in Ju-
> daism to be 'already circumcised,' for one who is uncircumcised may not
> participate in eating the Pesach sacrifice, and this does not refer to women
> (Exodus 12:48). This should make it clear that any attempt to use cir-
> cumcision to exclude women or to imply that men have an exclusive
> covenant with God is a grand fallacy. Assertions by male Jews, for exam-
> ple, that "one must have a member to be a member" or have a penis to be
> a part of the covenant are absolutely invalid from an authentic Torah
> point of view and reduce circumcision to some kind of Jewish tribal phal-
> lic rite.[81]

The opening sentence of this paragraph ("Circumcision does something
to a boy to bring him *up to the level of women*") derives ultimately
from Hirsch.[82] Men need to be perfected, but women do not. Antonelli
next alludes to the talmudic utterance that I considered in chapter 4: "a
woman resembles someone who has been circumcised," in order to
prove that circumcision is not a vehicle for discrimination between men
and women in Torah-true Judaism.[83] She attributes to the statement a
global significance that is absent in its original context. Originally an
explanation for the view that a woman can perform a circumcision, the
statement for Antonelli is an assertion of the insignificance of the non-
circumcision of women in general "from an authentic Torah point of
view." The rest of the paragraph is directed against the voices and views
that I considered in the previous chapter.[84]

The richness of the Maimonidean approach can be gauged by its appeal to such diverse types as Antonelli and Hirsch. For Hirsch, a woman
belongs at home with her family; hers is a supporting role. For Antonelli,
in contrast, a woman should be able to find fulfillment as a Jew wherever
she wants. But both are working within a Maimonidean framework that
sees circumcision as remedying a defect that inheres only in men. Both
agree that men need to be perfected and women do not. And both, like
Maimonides, slight the covenantal value of circumcision.

The Maimonidean approach has even found its way into modern
biblical scholarship. A contemporary biblical scholar, in a study entitled
"The Significance of Circumcision," writes as follows: "The very fact

that it is the males who bear this sign means that it is the males who embody spiritual and mental unfitness to belong to the people of promise. . . . It [the sign of circumcision] draws attention to the fact that men in particular lack the moral and spiritual commitment and discipline that makes holiness possible."[85] Hirsch and Antonelli would certainly have approved this comment. Philo and Maimonides would have disagreed but would have understood.

Conclusion

This chapter and the previous one are an antonymous pair; the thesis of the one is directly opposed to the thesis of the other. In the previous chapter, using Jacob Anatoli and Menahem as my points of departure, I argued that in classic rabbinic culture circumcision is a sign of the covenant between God and Israel, and that the absence of this sign from women bespeaks women's lesser role in the covenantal relationship between God and Israel. Women are not obligated to study Torah or to observe all the commandments; their exclusion from circumcision represents their exclusion from many of the core aspects of rabbinic culture. In this chapter, using Maimonides as my point of departure, I have argued that circumcision is not primarily a sign of the covenant between God and Israel, and that the absence of this sign from women says nothing about their place in the covenantal relationship between God and Israel. Rather, Maimonides says, in the first of his two explanations, the purpose of circumcision is to reduce lust. Circumcision reduces male potency; if maleness be defined as sexual vigor, circumcision is an act of "unmanning."

Maimonides does not explain why women do not need to have their lust reduced. A possible inference is that women naturally occupy a higher and more spiritual plane than men, and do not need the remedy that circumcision provides. Men need circumcision in order to attain the status that women have on their own. Maimonides himself would have rejected this inference, because he believed that men were socially and emotionally superior to women, but this non-Maimonidean explanation in the spirit of Maimonides was advanced by Samson Raphael Hirsch in the nineteenth century. Hirsch was not interested in countering the arguments of Christian polemics, whose day had long since passed, but in countering the novel arguments of Reform Judaism, which I shall consider in the concluding chapter.

Many Jewish thinkers either anticipate or follow Maimonides in seeing circumcision as an effective agent for the limitation of concupiscence.[86] Medieval Christian sources go even further: Jewish men do not behave as real men do because they are not real men. They have been "effeminated" by circumcision. Some medieval Jews conceded that Christian men were more virile, and sexually more proficient, than they, but as far as I have been able to discover they never went so far as to see themselves as effeminate. That judgment belongs to Christians alone—and to Jewish men in the modern period who, like Freud, were conflicted about their masculinity, their absent foreskin, and their present Jewishness.

By minimizing the significance of circumcision, by seeing it as no more important than any other commandment, by implicitly denying that circumcision establishes a bond between God and Israel or between God and Jew, Maimonides also laid the foundation for yet another response to the Christian argument based on the non-circumcision of women. That ingenious response is the subject of my next chapter.

Appendix: Spinoza on Circumcision and the Effeminacy of Jewish Men

Benedict Spinoza (1632–1677), the famous philosopher, was a descendant of New Christians (or "Marranos") of Portugal, Jews who had lived outwardly as Christians but privately as Jews, at least to some degree. When the New Christians were allowed to leave Portugal, they congregated in Amsterdam and other cities that afforded them the freedom to reclaim their ancestral religion. Many New Christians were unaware of the borderlines between Judaism and Christianity, and some New Christians were moved by their experience to question the truth of all institutionalized religions. In response, the newly constituted Jewish communities tried to establish for their members firm guidelines to govern both behavior and thought. These processes are evident in Spinoza's case. In 1656, at the age of twenty-four, he was excommunicated by the Jewish community of Amsterdam because of his freethinking. He never returned to the Jewish community and soon changed his name from the Hebrew Baruch to the Latin Benedict. Neither a believing Jew nor a baptized Christian, Spinoza has often been seen as the first "modern" or "secular" Jew.[87]

The work that concerns us here is the *Theological-Political Tractate,* published anonymously by Spinoza in 1670. In this book, which provoked a storm of protest upon publication, Spinoza argued that the Bible was written by men, not God; that the Bible must be interpreted on its own terms, and not by appeal to Jewish or Christian tradition; that the Israelites of old were not particularly gifted or unusual, and enjoyed no special status in God's eyes; that the prophets of the Bible were simply men endowed with great imagination; that truth claims were the domain of philosophy, not religion; and that the state should not attempt to control the beliefs and thoughts of its citizens.

In the midst of debunking the election or chosenness of Israel, a belief that was central to both Jewish and Christian self-understanding, Spinoza considers various counterarguments, among them the continued existence of the people of Israel. Does not the seeming indestructibility of the Jewish people imply that they enjoy special divine favor? The answer, says Spinoza, is no. The survival of the Jews is neither miraculous nor remarkable.

> As to their continued existence for so many years when scattered and stateless, this is in no way surprising, since they have separated themselves from other nations to such a degree as to incur the hatred of all, and this not only through external rites alien to the rites of other nations but also through the mark of circumcision, which they most religiously observe.[88]

The Jews have been preserved by their self-segregation, which in turn incurred widespread, and, sometimes, deeply felt hatred. The self-segregation and the hatred, both perfectly normal historical processes, have worked together to guarantee the Jews' survival. Circumcision is a mark of Jewish separation, and is singled out by Spinoza because of its special quality.

> The mark of circumcision, too, I consider to be such an important factor in this matter that I am convinced that this by itself will preserve their nation forever. Indeed, were it not that the fundamental principles of their religion discourage manliness, I would not hesitate to believe that they will one day, given the opportunity—such is the mutability of human affairs—establish once more their independent state, and that God will again choose them.
>
> The Chinese afford us an outstanding example of such a possibility. They, too, religiously observe the custom of the pigtail which sets them apart from all other people, and they have preserved themselves as a separate people for so many thousands of years that they far surpass all other

nations in antiquity. They have not always maintained their independence, but they did regain it after losing it, and will no doubt recover it again when the spirit of the Tartars becomes enfeebled by reason of luxurious living and sloth.[89]

The mark of circumcision has functioned to preserve the Jew just as the pigtail has functioned to preserve the Chinese. Again, there is nothing miraculous or remarkable about this: circumcision, like the pigtail, is a mark that makes its bearer distinctive and different. Circumcision is the only Jewish ritual that Spinoza mentions here, clearly because he recognizes the power and importance that were traditionally ascribed to it. Spinoza concedes the power of circumcision, but contends that that power derives not from divine favor or from circumcision's mystical effects on the body and soul of Israel, but from the social separation that circumcision represents. Jewish circumcision is no more profound than the Chinese pigtail.

The analogy with the Chinese is pursued further. Just as the Chinese in the past once regained their independence after losing it, and will likely regain it again when their current conquerors the Tartars (that is, the Manchus) become "enfeebled by reason of luxurious living and sloth," similarly the Jews, who in the past once regained their independence after losing it, will likely regain it again if only they are able to abandon the principles of their religion that "discourage manliness," or literally "effeminate their minds."[90] In the case of the Chinese, the conquerors will one day become "enfeebled"; in the case of the Jews the conquered will one day be able to shake off that which makes them "effeminate."

These paragraphs have attracted a good deal of attention. Spinoza's prediction that the Jews would someday reestablish an independent state was hailed by Zionists in the nineteenth and twentieth centuries and realized in 1948. (I might add that Spinoza's prediction that the Chinese would overthrow the Manchus was realized in 1911.) Spinoza correctly intuited that if the Jews were to reestablish the state of Israel they would need to abandon their traditional religion; in fact, most of the active Zionists who established the state were non-religious, and many were anti-religious. Few Zionists adopted Spinoza's philosophy, but most agreed that traditional Judaism had to be rejected.[91] What needed to be rejected in particular was the reliance on a future God-sent messiah, which in turn bred a politics of subservience and an unassertive ("feminine") demeanor. Spinoza's idea that Jewish beliefs and attitudes "effeminated" the minds of Jews was probably inspired by Niccolo Machiavelli's critique of Christianity. Machiavelli (1469–1527) argued that Christianity was inimical to the spirit of liberty because it glorified "humble and contemplative men" and distracted men from political life and the need to be free. As a result, the world became "effeminate." Machiavelli's criticism of Christianity was carried forward by Jean-Jacques Rousseau (1712–1778), and finds its analogue in Spinoza's critique of Judaism.[92]

I have dilated upon these paragraphs of Spinoza because of their intrinsic interest and importance and because of Spinoza's juxtaposition of circumcision to effeminization. Some scholars have deduced that Spinoza implicitly equates the two, as if circumcision were one of the "fundamental principles," if not the main principle, that has effeminated Jewish minds.[93] But, if I have understood Spinoza correctly, he does not make this claim. Circumcision for Spinoza is a mark of separation from the gentiles, while the fundamental principles of the religion that effeminate Jewish minds are the belief in a messianic deliverer and deference toward authority. Spinoza does not say that circumcision has effeminated Jewish minds.

CHAPTER 7

True Faith and the Exemption of Women

Is it really conceivable that, since the sign of the covenant
was the circumcision, the covenant was not concluded with
all Israel, but only with its male members!

Eliezer Berkovits

In the previous chapter I discussed answers that Maimonides might
have given to our question. Men need circumcision, Maimonides says,
because circumcision reduces lust and sexual passion, thereby allowing
Jewish men to devote themselves more fully to God and Torah than
they otherwise would be able. And why do women not need circumcision? Apparently because they, unlike men, do not suffer from a surfeit
of lust. Maimonides does not actually say this, of course, but it is a
conclusion that logically follows from his position. Some modern Jewish thinkers have taken this Maimonidean idea and developed it in
ways that Maimonides himself would not have accepted. In this chapter I develop another response that is both non-Maimonidean and yet
very Maimonidean. For Maimonides, circumcision is not covenantal;
the relationship between the people of Israel and God, and between the
individual Jew and God, is not a function or consequence of circumcision. Therefore the exclusion of women from the commandment of circumcision does not (necessarily) betoken their inferiority or their exclusion from the covenant. By believing in God and by observing the
commandments of the Torah that are incumbent upon them, women
can find favor in God's eyes just as men do. This idea, adumbrated by
Maimonides, is developed in a remarkable way by one of his later
followers.

Maimonides, *The Book of the Commandments*

The Torah contains 613 commandments in all, of which 248 are positive commandments ("thou shalt's") and 365 are negative commandments or prohibitions ("thou shalt not's"). This fact is stated explicitly in the Babylonian Talmud, but the Talmud nowhere enumerates the commandments. Medieval jurists, poets, and philosophers took up this task. Certainly the most significant and influential such effort was that of Maimonides in his *Book of the Commandments,* completed about 1170. We met this work briefly in the previous chapter, where I noted that on the list of the 248 positive commandments, Maimonides places circumcision at number 215, in the context of commandments regulating sexual relations. In this chapter, I turn to Maimonides' analysis of the obligation to observe the positive commandments, an analysis that is appended to the list of the positive commandments. Maimonides briefly discusses the exemption of women from some of the commandments and makes an implicit statement on the absence of circumcision from women. He begins as follows:

> If you examine all the commandments thus far presented, you will find that some of them are obligatory upon the whole congregation of Israel collectively, and not upon every person individually. . . . Others are obligatory on an individual who has performed a certain act, or to whom something has happened. . . . it is possible for a man to go through life without doing or experiencing any of these things. Again, there are among these commandments, as we have explained, certain laws . . . which may never be applicable to a particular man, and which he may never be liable to carry out, throughout the whole of his life. Other commandments are binding only during the existence of the Temple. . . . Others are binding only on owners of property . . . it is possible for a man to be exempt from them because he has no property, and to go through life without being obliged to fulfill any of this class of commandments. Some commandments [, however,] are obligatory unconditionally on every man, at all times, everywhere, and in all circumstances. . . . These we call unconditional commandments, because they are unconditionally obligatory upon every adult Israelite man at all times, in all places, and in all circumstances.
>
> If you will examine these two hundred and forty-eight positive commandments, you will find that the unconditional commandments are sixty in number—provided that we assume that this man, whom we regard as bound by these sixty unconditional commandments, is living a life akin to that of the majority of men, that is, that he lives in a house in a community, eats ordinary food, namely bread and meat, pursues a nor-

mal occupation, marries a wife and has a family. These sixty commandments are the following. . . . [1]

Maimonides proceeds to list the sixty commandments that he considers
"unconditional" (the term might also be translated "of necessity," or
perhaps "inevitable"). By "unconditional" Maimonides means "not
predicated on a specific situation," or, in Aristotelian language, "not
predicated on a specific accident or set of accidents." The specific conditions that they do not require are the presence of the temple, residence
in the land of Israel, or Jewish political autonomy. Maimonides says
that these commandments are "obligatory . . . at all times, in all places,
and in all circumstances," and in fact some of them are to be observed
every moment of one's life (for example, the commandments to believe
in God, to love God, to fear God, to study Torah). But most of these
sixty commandments are conditioned upon specific times or circumstances. Some are to be observed once a day (for example, to wear phylacteries), others twice a day (for example, to recite the *Shema*), some
only one day a week (to rest on the Sabbath, to sanctify the Sabbath).
Some are to be observed a few times a year (for example, to rest on
Passover, to eat *matzah* on Passover, to hear the sound of the *shofar* on
the New Year), while others are likely to be observed only once, or only
a few times, in the course of one's life (for example, the commandment
of a bridegroom to devote himself to his wife in the first year of their
marriage, the commandment to circumcise one's sons, the commandment to write or acquire a Torah scroll). What Maimonides means,
then, by "unconditional" is not that these commandments are to be observed every minute of every day but rather that are inevitable: they will
be observed by every male Jew at some point in his life.[2]

What of women? Maimonides continues:

> Of these sixty unconditional commandments, forty-six are binding on
> women as well as on men, and fourteen are not binding on women. A
> mnemonic for the number of these unconditional commandments is
> *There are sixty queens* [Song of Songs 6:8], and a mnemonic for the re-
> duction of fourteen from women is *their might is gone* [Deuteronomy
> 32:36] [since the numerical value of the letters of the Hebrew word *yad*,
> "hand" or "might," is fourteen]. Or, [as an alternative,] a mnemonic for
> the forty-six that are binding on women is *And you, as for you, because
> of the blood of your covenant* [*I have released your prisoners from the
> pit*, Zechariah 9:11], that is, the numerical value of the word *because of
> the blood* [in Hebrew: *bedam*, the sum of whose letters is forty-six] is an
> obligation to them. These [forty-six commandments] are the uncondi-
> tional covenant especially for women.[3]

The basic math is simple: sixty unconditional commandments in all, of which fourteen are binding only on men, not on women, leaving forty-six unconditional commandments that are binding on both genders. For each of these three numbers (sixty, fourteen, forty-six), Maimonides finds a mnemonic in a biblical verse that contains a word the numerical value of whose letters equals the desired sum.

The third of these mnemonics is particularly intriguing and brings us to our theme. Zechariah 9:11 is a hopelessly difficult verse, perhaps corrupt; the first-person singular of the verse would seem to be God, and the second-person singular of the verse would seem to be the people of Israel personified, as so often in the prophets, as a woman—all the pronouns in the verse are feminine.[4] What is *the blood of the covenant,* and what is the *pit* from which the prisoners have been released by God? Rabbinic exegetes understood this verse to be referring to an episode in God's redemption of Israel from Egypt, but they disagreed on its precise identification.[5] Some said that *the covenant* was the acceptance of the Torah by the Israelites at the foot of Mount Sinai, and that *the blood of the covenant* was the blood that Moses sprinkled on the people of Israel while reciting the words *Behold the blood of the covenant* (Exodus 24:8). The waterless pit is the desert of Sinai. In this reading God tells the people of Israel that he has brought them out of the desert and into the land of Israel by the merit of their acceptance of the Torah at Mount Sinai.[6] Other exegetes, however, explained that *the covenant* was the covenant of circumcision, and that *the blood of the covenant* was the blood shed by the Israelites when they circumcised themselves in Egypt in anticipation of partaking of the first Paschal sacrifice. Moses told the Israelites that *no foreskinned man* might eat of the Paschal sacrifice (Exodus 12:48). Since immediately after announcing this requirement, the Torah says that the Israelites did exactly as God had commanded Moses and Aaron, it was a reasonable deduction that they must have circumcised themselves before partaking of the Paschal sacrifice. The *waterless pit* is Egypt, of course. In this reading, God tells the people of Israel that he has brought them out of Egypt by the merit of their circumcision.[7]

What, then, does Maimonides mean to imply by choosing Zechariah 9:11 and the word *bedam,* "because of the blood," as the mnemonic for the forty-six unconditional commandments that are incumbent upon women? If he is alluding to the covenant ceremony at the foot of Mount Sinai, he is implying that Jewish women are indeed part of the covenant. Jewish men in the here-and-now express their covenantal status by the observance of sixty unconditional commandments; Jewish women do so by the observance of forty-six unconditional commandments.[8] Men and women are not "equal" but both alike are within the covenant. If Maimonides is alluding to the circumcision that preceded the first Passover, he is implying that women, by observing those commandments that are incumbent upon them, can compensate for the absence of circumcision.

Either reading is possible, but all in all, the first is preferable, because I think it unlikely that Maimonides is here alluding to circumcision.[9] He does not attribute any special significance to circumcision, as I discussed in chapter 6 and as I shall discuss again below, and therefore he has no reason to be troubled by the non-circumcision of women. In these paragraphs, Maimonides is cataloguing the positive commandments and determining precisely the commandments that apply to women, nothing more. Perhaps in his selection of the biblical text for his third mnemonic he reveals that he is aware that the exemption of women from some of the commandments raises the difficult question of the Jewishness of Jewish women. But this is implicit at best. There is no reason to think that circumcision has suddenly become a defining ritual for Maimonides and the non-circumcision of women has become a problem. And even if circumcision has somehow magically become more important than the other commandments, there is some illogic in saying that women can compensate for the absence of circumcision by observing forty-six of the very same commandments that men observe. If men have the special commandment of circumcision, what do women have? As we shall see in the next chapter, those thinkers who ascribed special importance to circumcision—and, just to be absolutely clear, I am arguing that Maimonides was not among them—sought female analogues in rituals that only women observe or that have special significance for women. The obvious association of women with blood no doubt inspired the mnemonic *bedam*, "because of the blood," but Maimonides is not ascribing any particular significance to women's blood here. We shall see in the next chapter that other thinkers interpreted the blood of menstruation as analogous to the blood of circumcision, but I do not think that we can attribute such a view to Maimonides.

The importance of these paragraphs of *The Book of the Commandments* for our purposes is the following: Maimonides clearly demonstrates that no single Jew, either male or female, is obligated, or has ever been obligated, to observe all of the 248 positive commandments. This fact, coupled with Maimonides' decovenantalization of circumcision and emphasis on faith as the critical definer of Judaism, will lay the groundwork for some later interpreters who confront the question of the non-circumcision of women. The most important of these is R. Yom-Tov Lipmann Mühlhausen, to whom I now turn.

R. Yom-Tov Lipmann Mühlhausen

R. Yom-Tov Lipmann Mühlhausen was one of the most learned and distinguished rabbis in the Germanic lands of central Europe in the late fourteenth and early fifteenth centuries. He was active in Jewish communal affairs and lived in Krakow, Prague, and Jena before moving to Erfurt, where he died around 1421. A talmudist, philosopher, and mystic, he was also an ardent defender of Judaism. He was well equipped for the task; he knew Latin, he knew Christianity, and he knew philosophy. He composed his *Sefer HaNizzahon,* "the Book of Victory," or perhaps "The Book of Polemic," in Prague or Krakow around 1400. In this large work, divided into 354 sections, one for every day of the lunar year, Mühlhausen comments on all the passages of the Tanakh that in his opinion have been, or might be, misconstrued as inconsistent with the truths of rabbinic Judaism. Prominent among those misconstruing the Scriptures are Christians and Karaites, who share the common ground of rejecting rabbinic Oral Torah. Mühlhausen does more than just attack his opponents' reading of Scripture; he also mounts an active defense of the Bible, arguing, in the spirit of Maimonides, that the biblical portrait of God is philosophically respectable and that the commandments of the Torah serve a rational purpose. Writing in Hebrew, Mühlhausen intended his work to be an encyclopedia of arguments that pious Jews could use whenever called upon to defend the truths of rabbinic Judaism.

Mühlhausen's book had a tremendous impact and a wide following. Christian theologians came to realize that *The Book of Victory* raised the level of the Jewish side of the Jewish-Christian debate, and that if Christians were to succeed in winning over Jewish souls, they would need to find a way to rebut Mühlhausen's arguments. In the sixteenth and seventeenth centuries, many of the most distinguished Christian Hebraists, among them, Johannes Reuchlin, Sebastian Münster (whom we met briefly in chapter 6), and Johann Wagenseil (whom we met briefly in chapter 5), wrote full or partial rebuttals of Mühlhausen's book. In fact the first printed edition of *Sefer HaNizzahon* was published by the Christian Hebraist Theodor Hackspan in 1644. The first Jewish printing appeared only sixty-five years later.[10]

Mühlhausen knows the Christian argument drawn from the non-circumcision of women, and advances a thoroughly novel and ingenious answer:

> *Every male among you shall be circumcised* [Genesis 17:10]. The Christians mock us, saying, "Women, who have no circumcision, do not have the status of Jews." But they do not know that faith is dependent not on circumcision but on the heart. He who does not believe properly—his circumcision does not make him a Jew; also, he who believes properly—behold, he is a Jew even if he is not circumcised, except that he is committing a sin. The commandment of circumcision does not pertain to women; likewise they [women] have the commandment of the sacrifice after childbirth that does not pertain to men.
>
> And on these grounds I rebuked them, because they act improperly: Jews who have been condemned to death they acquit so that they can be baptized. [I rebuked them] because faith depends not on their water but on the heart. If that Jew had believed in his heart in accordance with their faith, he would have been baptized before they compelled him to be baptized. And as to what he says that he is accepting their faith, his mouth is not consonant with his heart. The result is that he is not [really] a gentile [i.e., Christian], and they have judged him falsely in that they have acquitted him. He is simply a *min* ["heretic"], which means "two-faced," as I shall explain below, with God's help, in section 348. As to his desire to accept their faith, he is acting out of duress and the fear of death, and in order to save his skin.[11]

Mühlhausen here advances three remarkable arguments: religion is a function of belief; circumcision is not essential to Jewishness; and the exemption of Jewish women from the commandment of circumcision is not significant since even Jewish men are exempt from some commandments. I shall discuss each of these in turn.

Religion Is a Function of Belief

The non-circumcision of women leads Mühlhausen to the extraordinary view that Jewish identity depends entirely on "faith." The term that he uses, *emunah*, like the English word "faith," is capable of two different meanings: either "belief," or, by extension, "religion." The simple meaning is "belief," but there are any number of passages in the *Sefer HaNizzahon* in which the meaning "religion" seems intended.[12] When Mühlhausen writes in the first paragraph that the Christians fail to understand that "[Jewish] faith is dependent not on circumcision but on the heart," he probably is using the word *emunah* in the sense "religion," so that the sentence means that one's status as an adherent of the Jewish religion depends entirely on one's beliefs, and not on the ritual of circumcision. Similarly, when he writes in the second paragraph "[Christian] faith depends not on their water but on the heart," he probably is using the word *emunah* in the sense "religion," so that the sentence means that one's status as an adherent of the Christian religion depends entirely on one's beliefs, and not on the ritual of baptism.

What is remarkable here is that Mühlhausen has reversed the classic Pauline critique of Judaism. Paul argued that God prefers "faith" to "works," "spirit" to "flesh," and "freedom" to "slavery." In the course of time, these Pauline polarities were understood to mean that God preferred "Christianity" to "Judaism," for God preferred Christian faith, a religion of the spirit, to Jewish works, a religion of the flesh. Mühlhausen accepts the validity of these Pauline polarities but reverses their application; it is Judaism that is a religion of faith, and Christianity that is a religion of works! We Jews know, says Mühlhausen, that a Jew is someone who accepts the theological tenets of Judaism, and that a Christian is someone who accepts the theological tenets of Christianity. In contrast, says Mühlhausen, Christians think that a Jew is someone who is circumcised, and that a Christian is someone who is baptized. The Christians, of course, are wrong. Judaism is a religion of faith; Christianity also ought to be a religion of faith, Mühlhausen seems to be saying, but it isn't. The similarity of Mühlhausen's formulation to Paul is striking and unmistakable. In Romans 4:11, Paul contrasts "faith" with "circumcision," arguing that Abraham's circumcision was merely the *sign or seal of the righteousness which he had by faith while he was still uncircumcised*. This Pauline argument, as we saw in chapter 3, shaped Christian thinking about circumcision. Mühlhausen deliberately appropriated the Pauline critique of Judaism and turned it into a critique of Christianity.[13]

As I have noted several times in this book, all is fair in love and polemics. We may ask whether Mühlhausen really believed that Judaism was a religion of faith and Christianity a religion of works. In one passage he explicitly acknowledges that the true answer to a question may differ from the answer that can be given to ignorant heretics.[14] In the second paragraph translated above, Mühlhausen says that Jews who convert to Christianity under duress do not really become Christians; they are no longer Jewish, but they are not quite Christian either.

Mühlhausen applies to them the talmudic term *min,* and refers the reader to section 348 for an explanation. There Mühlhausen advances a series of arguments that are so outrageous and so implausible that we may wonder how he could have expected anyone to take them or him seriously. I shall explain.

In the Talmud the word *min* (pl.: *minim*) means "heretic." In the *birkat ha minim,* "the blessing against heretics," which was included in the daily prayers by the mishnaic rabbis, we pray to God for the destruction of "the heretics." Numerous Christian writers in antiquity argued that the prayer was directed against Christianity, and a persistent tradition arose that the Jews curse Christ and Christians in their prayers.[15] Mühlhausen, too, was confronted by this complaint and came up with an ingenious apologia. When we pray "may the apostates have no hope," we are not, contrary to what Christians think, referring to Christians in general. Instead we are referring to apostates from Judaism to Christianity, and our prayer is that such apostates should have no hope of returning to Judaism; they should realize that they have left Judaism not to return. The next phrase in the prayer, "and may all the *minim* be instantly wiped out," is a prayer not against "heretics," Mühlhausen argues, but against those who are "two-faced" or "duplicitous." Those people who cannot decide between Judaism and Christianity, who rely on both but firmly believe in neither—we pray that such people should be wiped out. Mühlhausen proceeds to explain the rest of the prayer along the same lines. So, the *birkat ha minim* should not cause offense to Christians; on the contrary, it expresses hopes that Christians as well can endorse. No doubt Mühlhausen's tongue was in his cheek when he wrote these lines, since these arguments, for all of their cleverness, are close to absurd.[16] Mühlhausen himself drops his pretense elsewhere when he uses the word *minim* to mean what it does mean, "heretics," a category that for the Jews of medieval Europe included Christians.[17]

We need to ask, then, whether Mühlhausen was sincere in his presentation of Judaism as a belief system. Did he really believe that Judaism "is dependent not on circumcision but on the heart"? Did he really think that "He who does not believe properly—his circumcision does not make him a Jew"? Or was all this merely an elaborate set-up for his brilliant attack on Christianity as a works-centered religion? These questions need to be asked, but I think that the answer is clear. Mühlhausen was a follower of Maimonides and really believed that Judaism was a theology, a series of truth claims about God and the Torah. It was Maimonides who first defined Judaism thus and enumerated the philosophical/theological principles that constitute Judaism. After explaining these principles, which are thirteen in number, Maimonides concludes as follows:

> When all these foundations are perfectly understood and believed in by a person, he enters the community of Israel, and one is obligated to love and pity him and to act towards him in all the ways in which the Creator has commanded that one should act towards his brother, with love and fraternity. Even were he to commit every possible transgression, because of lust and because of being overpowered by the evil inclination, he will be punished according to his rebelliousness, but he has a portion [in the world to come]; he is one of the sinners of Israel. But if a man doubts any of these foundations, he leaves the community [of Israel], denies the fundamental, and is called a sectarian *[min]* . . . One is required to hate him and destroy him.[18]

According to Maimonides, if you believe properly, you are a Jew—a member of the community of Israel in this world and a recipient of a share in the world to come. If you do not believe properly, you are a bad Jew, perhaps not a Jew at all; you are excluded from the community of Israel in this world and denied a share in the world to come. For Maimonides, Judaism is at its heart a series of truth-claims. Later Jewish philosophers grappled with these novel assertions of Maimonides. Was Judaism really a theology (or a philosophy)? Was it based on truth-claims (or "dogmas")? If so, what were they and how many were they? Maimonides set the agenda for Jewish philosophy for centuries after his death.[19]

Mühlhausen was a Maimonidean. He cites and appeals to Maimonides throughout the *Sefer HaNizzahon* and his other writings. He is "the only medieval Ashkenazi Jew known to have commented on the [Maimonidean] principles of Judaism." He introduced the *Guide of the Perplexed* to the Jews of central and eastern Europe.[20] As a Maimonidean, Mühlhausen believed that Judaism was a set of truth-claims about God. What linked Israel to God was the knowledge (or "cognition") of God as contained in the Torah and given expression in Rabbinic Judaism. The decovenantalization of circumcision that is implicit in Maimonides has become explicit in the *Sefer HaNizzahon*. When Mühlhausen proposed that Judaism "is dependent not on circumcision but on the heart," we may be sure that he meant what he said.

Circumcision Is Not Essential to Jewishness

The Talmud and the post-talmudic legal tradition recognize the Jewishness of a native-born Jewish male who remains uncircumcised. Such a man, known as an 'arel ("a foreskinned man"), is regularly associated by the Mishnah with the tamei, the person who is ritually impure. (Ritual impurity is typically caused by leprosy, sexual discharge, or contact with a corpse.) Impurity is a legal impairment, to be sure, preventing entrance into the Temple and contact with holy things, but does not in the slightest affect the Jewishness of the person involved. On the contrary, the capacity to become impure implies membership within the people of Israel, since gentiles, at least in rabbinic theory, cannot become impure. A priest who is foreskinned, like a priest who is impure, may not eat of the holy offerings and may not minister at the altar, but he otherwise is a priest. A foreskinned priest is allowed to sprinkle the purifying waters of the red heifer on the impure, and a foreskinned lay Israelite may be purified from corpse impurity by being sprinkled (Numbers 19). The presence of a foreskin does not prevent a Jewish man from marrying and having a family.[21]

Neither the Mishnah nor the Yerushalmi asks or explains why these priests and Israelites remain uncircumcised. In two passages, the Bavli suggests that these men are left intact because their older brothers had died as a result of their circumcision. On the assumption that circumcision would endanger their lives as well, they were never circumcised and grew into adulthood as foreskinned Jews. They are not "apostates" or the sons of apostates; they are innocent and faithful Jews afflicted by some medical condition (hemophilia, for example) that does not allow them to be circumcised. The Bavli says explicitly that such a man is a "Jew of good standing" and this attitude is given canonical expression in the medieval law codes.[22] Since the Bavli does not advance this explanation in connection with all the passages that speak of the foreskinned Jew, Rabbenu Tam, a well-known talmudist of the twelfth century, suggests that some of these passages might better be understood as referring to a man who was left uncircumcised out of "fear of the pain of circumcision." Even such a man, Rabbenu Tam explains, is not to be considered an apostate since his "heart is directed at heaven." He merely is terrified at the prospect of circumcision.[23] In any case, we see that Jewish law recognizes the Jewishness of a native-born Jewish man who is not circumcised, at least if his failure to be circumcised was the consequence of a reasonable circumstance and not of apostasy and rebellion. Such a man is indeed a Jew in good standing and a full member of the Jewish polity. No doubt Maimonides and Mühlhausen, if asked for evidence that circumcision is not essential to Jewishness, would have cited this halakhic tradition for support.[24]

I have emphasized that when the Talmud speaks of foreskinned Jews, it is speaking of native-born Jews. Mühlhausen too, as is evident from the Christian question to which he is responding ("Women, who have no circumcision, do not have the status of Jews"), is speaking of native-born Jews. The rabbinic legal tradition that speaks of foreskinned Jewish men; the Christian tradition that uses the non-circumcision of women as an opportunity for anti-Jewish polemic; Maimonides in his implicit decovenantalization of circumcision; and Mühlhausen in his explicit decovenantalization of circumcision— none of these is speaking of converts or conversion to Judaism. But, we may ask, if Judaism is a theology "dependent not on circumcision but on the heart," may we logically conclude that gentile men can convert to Judaism even without circumcision? By believing in God, Torah, and Israel, by accepting the truth-claims of Judaism, and by rejecting their gentile past, cannot gentile men convert to Judaism even without circumcision, or, in fact, any other ritual marker? Who needs the ritual if Judaism is a theology? A Maimonidean conception of Judaism should minimize the significance of circumcision not only for the native born but also for those who would convert to Judaism. This conclusion is logical, reasonable, and consistent with the data, but wrong.

Maimonides states explicitly that a male convert to Judaism must be circumcised. "A proselyte who is entering the community of Israel requires circumcision first." "When a gentile wishes to enter the covenant and to be gathered up under the wings of the divine presence and accepts under oath the yoke of the Torah, he requires circumcision, immersion, and the sprinkling of sacrificial blood."[25] While it is clear that Maimonides requires converts to be circumcised, what is not clear is the function of the circumcision in the conversion process. Maimonides' careful formulation in the first citation seems to imply that circumcision is a necessary precondition for conversion, while his careful formulation in the second citation seems to imply that circumcision is a means by which conversion is effected.[26] Logically, if Judaism is just a theology or primarily a theology, a gentile man should be able to convert to Judaism without being circumcised, but Judaism is not just a theology. Even Maimonides has to allow some room for ethnicity, descent, and "peoplehood," in his construction of Jewish identity, and circumcision is necessary as a sign of belonging to the people.[27]

Indeed, all medieval jurists agree that circumcision is required for conversion, even if they disagree among themselves on the precise function of circumcision in the conversion process. Thus, the medieval jurists debate the proper method for converting a gentile man who had already been circumcised in his gentile state—an Arab, for example. Some jurists argued, "there is no way to alter his condition," that is, that such a man cannot be converted to Judaism. These scholars believe that circumcision is a means by which conversion is effected; since the circumcised gentile cannot be circumcised again, he cannot be converted to Judaism. Other jurists argued that he can be converted through "the shedding of a drop of covenantal blood" from the place where the foreskin once had been. These scholars also believe that conversion is effected through proper circumcision, except that they believe that shedding covenantal blood is an acceptable substitute. In contrast, a third group of jurists argued that the circumcised gentile could be converted just as he is. In their mind, apparently, circumcision is a necessary precondition for conversion, no more; since the circumcised gentile has already had his foreskin removed, he has fulfilled the condition, and the conversion process can continue. This debate is interesting and important, but what matters for our purposes is the fact that all medieval jurists demand the circumcision of gentile men who would convert to Judaism.[28] Classical rabbinic law tolerates native-born Jewish men who are foreskinned much more readily than it tolerates converts to Judaism who are foreskinned.[29] We may safely assume that Mühlhausen, too, shared this view.[30]

For native-born Jews, circumcision, at least in the classical halakhic tradition, is not a sacrament and is not essential to salvation or to membership in the synagogue community. Circumcision is not baptism. Popular piety and medieval mysticism invested circumcision with sacramental powers, as we saw in chapter 1, but the legal tradition did not. When Mühlhausen said that an uncircumcised Jew was still a Jew, he had the rabbinic legal tradition behind him. When he said that Jewishness depended on proper belief, he had Maimonides behind him.

The Exemption of Women and the Exemption of Men

Mühlhausen writes: "The commandment of circumcision does not pertain to women; likewise they [women] have the commandment of the sacrifice after childbirth, which does not pertain to men." Women's inability to fulfill the commandment of circumcision is no more portentous than men's inability to fulfill the commandment of bringing the required sacrifice after childbirth, a commandment that applies only to the parturient (Leviticus 12:6).[31] Exemption from some of the commandments, Mühlhausen seems to be suggesting, is normal and unexceptional. As Maimonides demonstrates in his *Book of the Commandments,* no individual Jew is obligated, or has ever been obligated, to observe all 613 commandments. Many of the positive commandments apply only to specific people under specific circumstances. So, concludes Mühlhausen, the exemption of women from some of the commandments, including the commandment of circumcision, says nothing about their Jewishness.

If no individual Jew observes, or has ever observed, all 613 commandments, who then does observe them? Neither Maimonides nor Mühlhausen addresses this question, perhaps because the answer is obvious. It is the people of Israel as a whole. This idea is given beautiful expression by R. Hayyim ibn Attar (1696–1743), a talmudist, mystic, and holy man. He is best known for his *Or haHayyim,* "The Light of Life," a large commentary on the Torah that he published in Livorno, Italy, in 1741/42 en route from his native Morocco to the land of Israel.[32] He is buried in the old Jewish cemetery on the Mount of Olives in Jerusalem, and his tomb is to this day a site of pilgrimage and prayer. On the verse *And the children of Israel did everything just as the Lord commanded Moses* (Exodus 39:32), he writes as follows:

> Here Scripture has made the fulfillment of the Torah depend on the concerted action of the entire people, and has shown that the children of Israel earn merit [in God's eyes] one for the other. The Torah was given so as to be fulfilled through the entire people of Israel, each one acting to the best of his ability and therefore earning merit one for the other. . . . God has commanded 613 commandments, but it is impossible that a person will be found who is able to observe them all. And this is the proof: priest, Levite, Israelite, and women. There are positive commandments that apply to the priests, and no Israelite has the ability to do them. There are commandments for Israelites that do not apply to priests; likewise for Levites, and likewise for women. What ability does a single person have to observe them [all]? . . . Certainly the Torah is fulfilled [only] by the concerted action of the entire people, and they earn merit one from the other.
>
> This is what Scripture means when it says here *The children of Israel did everything just as the Lord commanded.* It considers together all of them and their work. Even though some of them brought contributions

and others did the work, Scripture says about the entire people that they did it all.[33]

The construction of the Tabernacle in the wilderness was a communal enterprise for the children of Israel. Some contributed gold, some contributed silver, others contributed precious cloths. Some did the actual labor on the Tabernacle, its implements and equipment, and the priestly vestments. Who gets the credit for this immense project? It is the people of Israel, the people as a whole, even though no single Israelite in fact did it all. Similarly, R. Attar says, the observance of the commandments of the Torah is a communal enterprise. No one Jew observes all the commandments, since some commandments are incumbent only on priests, others only on Levites, others only on Israelites, and others only on women. Who then observes all the commandments of the Torah? It is the people of Israel, the people as a whole.[34]

Commandments That Apply to Women

All three of Mühlhausen's main points derive from Maimonides: Jewishness is defined by belief; circumcision is not essential to Jewishness; men and women alike are exempt from some of the positive commandments. The latter two points had ample warrant within the halakhic tradition, as we have seen, and therefore passed without much notice. Not so the claim that Jewishness is a function of belief, which, notwithstanding its impeccable Maimonidean pedigree, was a radical interpretation of Judaism. The philosophers who succeeded Maimonides argued with him at length over this very point. Later readers of Mühlhausen were struck by his sharp and unambiguous formulation "faith is dependent not on circumcision but on the heart." Nineteenth-century reformers, who wanted to do away with circumcision, looked at Mühlhausen as one of their own and cited his formulation as evidence that even within traditional Judaism, circumcision was not all that important.[35] We shall return to these reformers in the concluding chapter.

An anonymous seventeenth- or eighteenth-century Hebrew manuscript provides further evidence for the radicalness of Mühlhausen's formulation. This manuscript contains notes on the Torah derived from various sources, including Mühlhausen's *Sefer HaNizzahon*. On Gene-

sis 17:10, *Every male among you shall be circumcised,* the manuscript
provides the following:

> The nations of the world say that [Jewish] women do not have the status
> of Jews since they are not circumcised. Answer them that circumcision is
> one commandment of the [many] commandments of the Torah. There-
> fore, someone who observes all the other commandments, even though he
> does not observe the commandment of circumcision, nevertheless has a
> share in the world to come and has the status of a Jew—for example,
> someone whose [elder] brothers died as a result of circumcision. So too
> women, even though they are not circumcised, inasmuch as they observe
> the commandments that apply to women, they have the status of Jews.[36]

The author of this manuscript has followed Mühlhausen, but only in
part. Mühlhausen is the source for the question that the gentiles ask as
well as the answer that the Jews are to give. The gentiles ask whether
women are really Jews since they are not circumcised. Of course they
are, is the reply, since circumcision is no more important than any other
commandment. Jewishness does not depend on circumcision. Here, as
proof of this position, the author adduces the man who remains uncircumcised because his older brothers had died of the procedure. His Jewishness is beyond question, and therefore so too is a woman's.

If Jewishness does not depend on circumcision, on what does it depend? Mühlhausen had answered very clearly: on faith. The author of
the manuscript omits this answer, probably because he found it too radical. Perhaps he sensed the potentially antinomian undercurrent that
would so appeal to the Reformers a century or two later. Instead he substitutes a much safer answer: Jewishness is a function of the observance
of commandments. Women have the status of Jews by observing the
commandments that "apply to them." This might mean simply what
Maimonides meant when he enumerated the positive commandments
that apply to women (and to men). Or, perhaps the author is referring
to the commandments of menstrual purity, separating the priestly offering from the bread dough *(hallah),* and the lighting of the Sabbath
lamps. These three were widely regarded as "women's commandments,"[37] not because they were imposed solely on women but because
their observance was generally the domain of women. In any case,
Mühlhausen would certainly have disagreed with the last sentence of
this paraphrase. Mühlhausen, following Maimonides, says that membership within the people of Israel depends on faith; this author thinks
that it depends on the observance of the commandments.

Conclusions

In this chapter, as in the previous, we have seen how Maimonides provides the intellectual framework for those who would explain the non-circumcision of Jewish women. In the previous chapter, the Maimonidean framework was circumcision as moral perfection; in this chapter, the framework is circumcision as just another commandment.

Genesis 17 shows that circumcision is not just another commandment. It is an obligation under the covenant between God and Israel; it is a sign of the covenant; it *is* the covenant. Unlike every other commandment, it is done once only. Therefore it required some intellectual derring-do for Maimonides to downplay the covenantal value of circumcision, but this is what he did. As a sign of the covenant, circumcision establishes a mark on the bodies of those who believe in the unity of God. It does not affect the relationship of the individual with God any more than does any other commandment. What makes a Jew a Jew, says Maimonides, is belief in God and belief in the other essentials of Judaism. Maimonides thus decovenantalizes circumcision, removing it from any position of centrality and prominence in the pantheon of the commandments.

Within this Maimonidean structure R. Yom-Tov Lipmann Mühlhausen creates an ingenious answer to the Christian argument based on the non-circumcision of women. No individual Jew, male or female, observes, or is obligated to observe, all 613 commandments. The exemption of women from the commandment of circumcision is no more significant than the exemption of men from the commandment to bring a sacrifice to the temple after childbirth. Jewish women, like Jewish men, find their place as Jews through proper faith in God, for it is faith, not the observance of ritual ("works") that is the essence of all religion.

Mühlhausen was no "feminist"; he shared his contemporaries' low view of women.[38] His goal was not to argue for equality between men and women but to beat back a Christian anti-Jewish argument. And this he did.

CHAPTER 8

The Celebration of Womanhood

As with every chapter of Jewish history, this rite [circumcision] is dwelt upon when worthy of remark . . . its prominence as a religious observance means a disparagement of all female life, unfit for offerings, and unfit to take part in religious services; incapable of consecration. The circumcision of the heart even, which women might achieve, does not render them fit to take an active part in any of the holy services of the Lord.

Elizabeth Cady Stanton, The Woman's Bible

The previous two chapters were devoted to unfolding and unpacking Maimonides' views of circumcision. Maimonides argues that circumcision reduces male lust and is a sign of membership for those who belong to the league of the believers in the unity of God. Nothing in a woman's experience corresponds to circumcision because nothing in a woman's experience needs to correspond to circumcision. Only men are circumcised because only men need circumcision. Circumcision is a commandment like any other commandment; it is not covenantal and does not affect an individual's relationship with God any more than any other commandment. In this chapter I elaborate a non-Maimonidean perspective. Circumcision is indeed covenantal, and indeed establishes a bodily connection between a male Jew and God. Women do not need to be circumcised because the female experience includes an analogue to circumcision. Men have circumcision; women have menstruation. The central author to be considered here is R. Joseph Bekhor Shor.

R. Joseph Bekhor Shor

R. Joseph Bekhor Shor ("Joseph, a first-born bull," a name derived
from Deuteronomy 33:17), who lived in Orleans in the middle of the
twelfth century, is best known for his commentary on the Torah, which
shows him to have been both an independent thinker and an ardent
polemicist. As a result of his dedication to the "simple" or "plain"
meaning of Scripture, he often rejected the explanations of the Midrash
and Talmud, advancing his own instead. But far more pointed than his
rejection of traditional rabbinic interpretations was his polemic against
Christian interpretations of the Torah. In dozens of passages, Bekhor
Shor explicitly and unambiguously condemns the Christians for their
ignorant, perverse, and stupid readings of Scripture.[1] Both his intellectual independence and his anti-Christian perspective are evident in his
commentary on Genesis 17:11, which runs as follows:

> *And that shall be the sign of the covenant between me and you:*
>   A mark and a sign that I am the master and you are my slaves. The seal
> of the sign of the covenant is in a hidden place that is not seen, so that the
> nations of the world should not say concerning Israel: they are maimed.
> Since God commanded the males, and not the females, we may deduce
> that God commanded to seal the covenant on the place of maleness. And
> the blood of menstruation that women observe by telling their husbands
> of the onset of their periods—this for them is covenantal blood.[2]

I shall discuss each of these four sentences in turn.

In the opening sentence Bekhor Shor argues that circumcision is a
sign of servitude, akin to the marks or brands that were affixed to
slaves. Earlier in his commentary, Bekhor Shor had explained:

> *And I shall place my covenant between me and you* by placing a seal on
> your flesh, to be a mark that you are my slave . . . just as slaves have a seal
> on their clothes in order to show that they are slaves and under the con-
> trol of their masters. . . . Here too the Holy One, blessed be he, placed a
> seal on our flesh, because we are his slaves, in a place that a person can-
> not remove and cast off from himself.[3]

Certainly the best-known example of slave marking is the piercing of
the ear of the Hebrew slave, prescribed by Exodus 21:5–6. Unlike a
mark on clothing, which can be easily removed and cast off, circumcision is corporeal and permanent.[4]

Bekhor Shor immediately senses a problem with his explanation:
how can a hidden sign function as a marker of slavery? The main pur-

pose of marking slaves was to enhance their identifiability and to rein-
force their subordinate status, but how can a hidden mark perform either of these tasks? Bekhor Shor replies that "The seal of the sign of the
covenant is in a hidden place that is not seen, so that the nations of the
world should not say concerning Israel: they are maimed." In branding
his slaves, God had to choose a hidden mark, because otherwise the
gentiles would taunt the Jews as maimed, disfigured.

Bekhor Shor assumes that the only permanent way to mark the body
(tattooing being forbidden by Leviticus 19:28) is to cut it, but he realizes that any such cutting could be construed as a mutilation. Earlier in
his commentary, Bekhor Shor had explained:

> And be perfect: Do not think in your heart that you will be maimed on ac-
> count of this, like a person part of whose hand or foot has been cut off
> and is maimed as a result. You will not be deemed maimed [because of
> your circumcision] but perfect and whole . . . everywhere in Scripture the
> word *perfect* implies the absence of a deficiency.[5]

Bekhor Shor explains that the commandment of circumcision is introduced with the phrase *be perfect* in order to prevent circumcision from
being construed as a mutilation. Circumcision is not an act of mutilation; a circumcised man is not "missing something." The Midrash had
already commented that the foreskin is a "blemish" in God's eyes,
whose removal perfects the body.[6] Circumcision is an act of perfecting.
Bekhor Shor further argues that the removal of the foreskin assists the
male to accomplish his procreative task:

> I will make you exceedingly numerous: [God says this] so that you should
> not say "perhaps circumcision will hinder me from ejaculating [lit: seed-
> ing]." Not only will it not hinder, but it will assist (in ejaculation), be-
> cause sometimes the foreskin hinders the semen so that it does not shoot
> forth like an arrow, but now there will be no hindrance, and thereby *I will
> make* your seed *numerous*.[7]

Eleven hundred years before Bekhor Shor, Philo had advanced precisely
the same argument: that circumcision enhances fertility by removing
obstacles from the semen's path.[8] We may safely assume that Bekhor
Shor did not know Philo's work, and that he arrived at the same idea
independently. Far from causing a blemish or being a mutilation, circumcision is a perfection of God's work.

The gentiles, of course, are not convinced by any of this. In their eyes
circumcision is mutilation. Because the gentiles (mis)construe circumcision as a mutilation, Bekhor Shor argues, God ordained that this sign of

servitude be impressed on a hidden part of the body, and thereby also become an aid to procreation. Circumcision is hidden not in the sense that it is secret but in the sense that it is private. An act that could be viewed as a mutilation should not flaunted before the eyes of other men.

There is a remarkable parallel on this point between Bekhor Shor and Rupert of Deutz (ca. 1075–1129), an important Christian theologian and scriptural commentator. One of Rupert's goals is to refute the Jewish interpretation of Scripture. Throughout his extensive writings Rupert returns to this subject in order to defend the truth of the Christian faith.[9] Rupert devotes three long passages to circumcision and its replacement by baptism. The first passage is from his most important work, *On the Holy Trinity and Its Works,* a massive study of the history of salvation, which includes a running commentary on almost the entire Christian Old Testament. It was written in Liège (Belgium) between 1112 and 1116, hence a generation or so before Bekhor Shor. The second long passage on circumcision is in his *Commentary on John,* written at the same time (1114–16) as his magnum opus, and the third is in *The Ring; or, a Dialogue between a Christian and a Jew,* written in 1126 in Deutz (a small town near Cologne).[10] In all three passages, which closely parallel one another, Rupert argues in good Pauline fashion that Abraham's circumcision was the sign of the covenant, not the covenant itself. It was, as Paul said in Romans 4:11, *the seal of the righteousness which he had by faith.* The real covenant was God's promise that through Abraham's seed all the nations of the world would be blessed. This promise was fulfilled, of course, by the arrival of Jesus. Corporeal circumcision for a Christian is tantamount to a denial of Christ, because circumcision is a sign of faith in a forthcoming redeemer, but Christians believe that the redeemer has already come. Hence, concludes Rupert, Christians reject circumcision of the body and believe, as Paul said, *If you be circumcised Christ will be of no advantage to you* (Galatians 5:2).

While developing this argument, Rupert anticipates an objection. If Abraham's circumcision was a sign of his faith, why was the sign placed on a secret part of the body? Rupert explains:

> Now it is asked: why in such a place, in such a part of the body, did our father Abraham accept the seal of righteousness by faith? If indeed, the Jew says, the branding of circumcision was given [to Abraham] as a seal or as a sign of righteousness, why was it not given rather in some part or member of the body that is bare, so that it would always be evident? I may answer this inept little objection in a rather childish way: because if

God had placed the sign of circumcision on the nose or the lip, or all the more so on the ear or on the eye, this cursed blemish would certainly have disfigured the human face![11]

After presenting this jocular explanation, Rupert develops the "real" explanation. The faith of which circumcision is a sign or a seal was Abraham's faith that through his seed all the nations of the world would be blessed. And what body-part better represents the divine promise and the human expectation of this seed, than the generative organ through which the seed flows?[12]

Both Rupert, following Christian tradition, and Bekhor Shor, following rabbinic tradition, call circumcision a "seal";[13] both follow the verse in Genesis 17 and call it a "sign." For Rupert circumcision is a sign of righteousness (or "justification") by faith; for Bekhor Shor it is a sign of servitude. As a "sign," circumcision would seem to confer no theological benefits in and of itself; it refers to, and is a manifestation of, something else, something outside itself. Rupert is explicit on this point; circumcision is not the covenant between God and Abraham but only the *sign* of the covenant. Both Rupert and Bekhor Shor are now troubled by the same problem: how can circumcision function as a sign when it is hidden? A sign should be public, but circumcision is private. Why? Rupert puts this objection in the mouth of a Jew, probably because Christians knew that Jews had always emphasized that circumcision was not "just" a sign but that it also conferred some physical or moral or spiritual benefit.

Rupert argues that circumcision had to be performed on a hidden part of the body because it is a "cursed blemish" or "wound" that disfigures the body, and such disfigurement should be kept hidden. Bekhor Shor argues that circumcision had to be performed on a hidden part of the body because otherwise the gentiles (Rupert, for example) would have said that it disfigures the body. To avoid arousing hostile comment from outsiders, God commanded that the sign of circumcision be hidden. Rupert claims that this explanation is rather silly, and perhaps in his eyes it *was* silly, but it was advanced with all seriousness by other Christian thinkers.[14] Rupert, through his Jewish interlocutor, calls circumcision a "branding" or an "act of branding," which parallels Bekhor Shor's interpretation of circumcision as a mark of divine ownership and servile status. In response to Rupert's assertion that physical circumcision is (just) a mutilation and a branding, Bekhor Shor argues that it confers physical benefits by aiding procreation. Perhaps, too, Bekhor Shor's emphasis on the permanence and the corporeality of circumcision ("in a place that a person cannot remove and cast off from himself") is intended not only to highlight circumcision's utility as a religious marker but also to argue for its superiority over baptism. Circumcision is a mark on the body; baptism is not.[15] The physical effect of circumcision is permanent; the physical effect of baptism is transitory. I freely admit that these correspondences are not sufficient to "prove" that Bekhor Shor was inspired by Rupert or had Rupert in mind when he penned his commentary on Genesis 17, but they are suggestive, especially in light of the other intersections between the commentaries of Rupert and Bekhor Shor.[16]

Even if Bekhor Shor was inspired by Rupert in his discussion of the "disfiguring" quality of circumcision, when he turns to the gender implications of circumcision he leaves Rupert behind. Although many other Christian theologians of the eleventh and twelfth centuries used the non-circumcision of women as an anti-Jewish argument, as we saw in chapter 3, Rupert was not among them. He is not troubled by God's command to Abraham to impress the seal of faith only on the males, nor does he exploit the absence of circumcision from women as an anti-Jewish argument. Bekhor Shor's consideration of the gender question was a response, then, not to Rupert but to the general chorus of Christian anti-Jewish polemicists. Bekhor Shor first raises the gender issue with the unremarkable observation "Since God commanded the males, and not the females, we may deduce that God commanded to seal the covenant on the place of maleness." This sentence is loosely based on the talmudic comment that Scripture implies that circumcision is to be performed "on the place where maleness and femaleness are recognized as different."[17] Bekhor Shor's originality and brilliance are evident, however, in the next sentence. "And the blood of menstruation that women observe by telling their husbands of the onset of their periods—this for them is covenantal blood."

In a feat of intellectual daring and independence Bekhor Shor argues that the blood of menstruation, or, more accurately, the blood of menstruation within the context of the observance of the Jewish rules of menstrual purity and impurity, is the female analogue to male circumcision. If Bekhor Shor is carrying forward his interpretation of male circumcision as a sign of servitude to God, this argument should be interpreted to mean that a woman's observance of the regimen of menstrual purity converts her blood into a sign of servitude to God. That is, the blood itself is of no more significance than is circumcision itself. I suppose this interpretation is possible, but I think that it is not likely, because the phrase used by Bekhor Shor, "covenantal blood," implies that the blood itself is significant. If the blood of menstruation is the blood of the covenant, we may presume that the blood of circumcision is too. As I outlined in chapter 1, by the time of Bekhor Shor, circumcision blood was regularly conceived as "the blood of the covenant," and all sorts of salvific and healing powers were attributed to it, as indeed to circumcision itself. And if the blood of circumcision is the blood of the covenant, we may conclude that circumcision is *itself* the covenant. This conclusion conflicts with Bekhor Shor's earlier explanation of circumcision as a "sign." Either Bekhor Shor did not notice the inconsistency between his two explanations, or perhaps he was willing to adopt two different approaches, one to explain the circumcision of men, and the other to explain the non-circumcision of women.

Throughout rabbinic literature, both ancient and medieval, the menstruant and her blood are routinely invoked as paradigms of impurity. By treating menstrual blood as covenantal, Bekhor Shor has inverted the symbolism regnant in rabbinic discourse: from impurity to purity, from negative to positive. Bekhor Shor was able to accomplish this because of his rationalist reading of the Torah's rules regarding impurity.[18] According to Bekhor Shor, impurity is not a metaphysical or irrational category; it is not "dangerous" or demonic, and it has nothing to do with death or the sin of Adam and Eve. On the contrary, impurity is entirely physical and comprehensible. "Impure" is the Torah's synonym for dirty, disgusting, and stinking. Animal corpses are impure because they are malodorous and disgusting; impure animals, says Bekhor Shor, are disgusting.[19] Similarly, Bekhor Shor explains, "according to reason, neither menstrual nor non-menstrual blood renders a woman impure to her husband; rather it is the stink that comes out from her body with the blood."[20] The word that I have translated "stink" does not necessarily refer to a malodorous quality; here it is more likely to refer to the abstract state of being disgusting.[21] Menstrual blood itself is just blood, but it has a disgusting quality (says Bekhor Shor) that is the source of its impurity. In contrast, other kinds of female bleeding (says Bekhor Shor) are not disgusting; this allows Bekhor Shor to explain why some female blood is pure, and other female blood is impure. By arguing that menstrual blood is not in and of itself impure, Bekhor Shor can then advance the radical idea that menstrual blood can, when properly treated, become the blood of the covenant.

As I discussed briefly in chapter 1, it is also possible that Bekhor Shor deduced his explanation from the Torah itself. Leviticus 12 details the rules governing the purity and impurity of the parturient. The Torah speaks of the *blood of purification*, thus suggesting that not all female genital bleeding is impure. Leviticus 12 also seems to establish a parallel between the purification of the mother (to take place on the fortieth day after the birth of a son) and the circumcision of the boy on his eighth day of life. By reading Leviticus 12 in conjunction with Genesis 17, Bekhor Shor may have deduced that if circumcision is the covenantal ritual for the infant boy, then the purification ritual must be the covenantal ritual for his mother. By properly observing the restrictions associated with the impurity caused by menstruation and parturition, and by properly purifying themselves afterwards, Jewish women are not simply observing a divine requirement; they are embodying the covenant between God and Israel.

Nizzahon Yashan

Bekhor Shor's argument reappears in *Sefer Nizzahon*, "The Book of Victory" (or perhaps better, "The Book of Polemic"). This anonymous book, which is sometimes called *Nizzahon Vetus* ("The Old *Nizzahon*"), in order to distinguish it from later books of the same name (notably the work of Mühlhausen discussed in the previous chapter), is one of the longest and most detailed anti-Christian polemics of the high Middle Ages, a veritable encyclopedia of Jewish anti-Christian lore. In 245 paragraphs it disputes Christian interpretations of the Hebrew Bible, and attacks Christian theology, morals, and practices. It was written in Germany around the year 1300.[22] On the question of the non-circumcision of women, the author writes as follows:

> The heretics [i.e., Christians] ask: We baptize both males and females and in that way we accept our faith, but in your case only men are circumcised, not women. One can respond: Women are accepted [as Jews] because of their menstrual blood, since they guard themselves and exercise care with themselves.[23]

In spite of some syntactical ambiguities in the last sentence, the meaning is clear enough. We have here a slightly watered-down version of Bekhor Shor's explanation, and we may be sure that *Nizzahon*, either directly or indirectly, drew on Bekhor Shor. According to *Nizzahon*, the boundary marker for Jewish women, corresponding to circumcision for Jewish men and baptism for Christians, is menstrual blood. The blood has this effect when women "guard themselves and exercise care with themselves," that is, when they carefully follow the regimen of the menstrual prohibitions. The author of the *Nizzahon* cannot quite bring himself to say that the observance of these rules endows menstrual blood with covenantal value. Bekhor Shor was more radical than the author of the *Nizzahon*.

R. Yair ben Shabbetai da Correggio

An argument similar to that of Bekhor Shor is advanced by R. Yair ben Shabbetai da Correggio in his *Herev Piphioth*, "A Two-Edged Sword."[24] Written in Hebrew in northern Italy in the 1560s, the *Two-Edged Sword* is a dialogue between "a gentile" and "a Hebrew" on a range of theological topics, including the messiah, divine providence, life after death, fate, and free will. Needless to say, the gentile upholds the New Testament and the Christian tradition, while the Hebrew attacks them both, upholding the Hebrew Bible and rabbinic tradition. Needless to say, too, the Hebrew always gets the last word in the argument and is clearly "the winner."

Chapter 13 is devoted to two topics: reward in the hereafter, and circumcision. The gentile argues that the Torah of Moses knows nothing about immortality of the soul or reward in the hereafter, unlike the Prophets and the New Testament, which allude frequently to these ideas. As proof of the Torah's ignorance of immortality and the hereafter, the gentile adduces circumcision:

> This [the Torah's ignorance of the hereafter] is evident in connection with the covenant of circumcision. This is the most important [or: severe] commandment in the Torah of Moses, and yet God, may he be blessed, did not on its account promise to our father Abraham immortal life. And if it is impossible to acquire human perfection without it, why were not Adam, Seth, Enoch, Methuselah, Noah, and the other early righteous men commanded about it? And furthermore: how do women merit [eternal life]? Is it right in God's eyes for their souls to be lost?[25]

The questions asked by the gentile interlocutor were asked by Justin Martyr fourteen hundred years earlier, but the argument is somewhat different. Justin had sought to prove that circumcision was not a necessary concomitant of righteousness, and two of his proofs were the non-circumcision of the antediluvian worthies and the non-circumcision of women.[26] The gentile in *A Two-Edged Sword*, however, is seeking to prove that the Torah neither promises nor confers spiritual rewards in the hereafter. Even circumcision does not guarantee eternal life. The non-circumcision of the worthies of ancient times and of women in all times proves that non-circumcision is no barrier to immortality, hence that circumcision cannot confer immortality. Reward in the hereafter is gained only through belief in Christ. This is the gentile's argument.

The Hebrew responds. The Torah, indeed the entire Hebrew Bible, if read and interpreted properly, promises rewards in the hereafter not only to righteous Jews but also to the people of Israel as a whole. Circumcision, too, confers eternal life and attests to the eternal connection between God and the people of Israel, for it is *an eternal covenant* (Genesis 17:7). The worthies before Abraham were not given the commandment of circumcision because God wanted Abraham, the father of the chosen people, to be the first to be so commanded. Nevertheless, they also have a share in the world to come through God's grace and mercy. Women as well have a share in the world to come:[27]

> And women too merit to walk in the Garden of Eden as the reward for the observance of even[28] one of the commandments, and all the more so, if they observe the three commandments that were given specifically to them, namely, menstruation, *hallah,* and the lighting of the [Sabbath] lamp. And if a woman did not attain [the age] to observe a single one of them, or if a youth dies before the proper time for his circumcision, they have not as a result left the category of Israel,[29] because the Lord through his mercy and loving-kindness will rescue the souls of the unfortunate from the punishment of Gehenna.

Correggio is exploiting a logical flaw in the gentile's argument. From the true proposition "circumcision bestows immortal life," we cannot conclude that "the absence of circumcision prevents immortal life," because there may well be other avenues to immortal life aside from circumcision. In the case of women, Correggio argues, there are indeed two other avenues. The first of these is the observance of commandments, especially the three commandments that are traditionally the domain of women: the regimen of menstrual purity and impurity, the separation of the priestly offering *(hallah)* from bread dough, and the ritual lighting of the lamps for the Sabbath and holidays.[30] By observing these "women's" commandments, a woman gains her share in the world to come. The second avenue is God's mercy and kindness. If a girl dies in childhood so that she never attains the age of majority, never marries, never runs a home, hence never observes any of the three women's commandments, she is in the same situation as the boy who dies in infancy before his eighth day: both of them, like the worthies who lived before the time of Abraham, depend on God's mercy and loving-kindness to attain a place in the Garden of Eden. Since the Lord is merciful and full of loving-kindness, our confidence is justified.[31]

Like Mühlhausen, Correggio argues that the observance of commandments is the woman's analogue to male circumcision. Unlike Mühlhausen, however, Correggio sees circumcision as the most important commandment, or at least as a commandment of special import. Hence Correggio emphasizes that in the life-experience of Jewish women three commandments are typically and classically theirs, and these are the functional equivalent to the uniquely male commandment of circumcision. Like Bekhor Shor, Correggio also sees the observance of the regimen of menstrual purity and impurity as an analogue to circumcision, but Bekhor Shor is far more radical than Correggio. Bekhor Shor singles out the menstrual regimen as *the* analogue to circumcision and emphasizes the covenantal quality of menstrual blood, parallel to the covenantal quality of circumcision blood. These striking points are absent from *A Two-Edged Sword*.[32]

The Blood of the Covenant

Bekhor Shor's explanation for the non-circumcision of women is predicated on the fact that the blood of circumcision is covenantal, indeed that the shedding of blood is the main point of the ritual. It is the blood of the covenant that gives circumcision its theological power and turns a surgical procedure into a religiously efficacious ritual. As I explained above in chapter 1, in the Bible and in the Talmud the essential act of circumcision is the removal of the foreskin; the blood that is shed during circumcision is either ignored completely or treated as the inevitable, if insignificant, byproduct of cutting skin. The blood of circumcision ascends to ideological prominence only in the eighth century (approximately), as attested in the *Pirqei de Rabbi Eliezer,* "the chapters of Rabbi Eliezer." According to this text, the blood of circumcision, together with the blood of the Paschal sacrifice, protected the Israelites from the plague of the first-born and brought about the redemption from Egypt. The blood of Abraham's circumcision entered the ground precisely where the altar would later be built and where the blood of the sin offerings would be poured. These two bloods, the blood of Abraham's circumcision and the blood of the sin offerings, atone for the sins of Israel. The blood of circumcision having become significant, its disposal also became an important question. *Pirqei de Rabbi Eliezer* itself endorses the custom of burying the severed foreskin and the blood, and other texts describe other customs as well.[33] This is the trajectory on which we can situate Bekhor Shor's audacious equation of menstrual blood with circumcision blood. If circumcision is simply the excision of the foreskin, there is nothing in the female experience that can serve as an analogue to it. But if circumcision is understood primarily as a means for releasing blood, the female experience certainly has an analogue. Bekhor Shor concludes that the blood of menstruation, like the blood of circumcision, is covenantal.

Roads Not Taken

Modern anthropologists and psychologists have observed that the genital bleeding caused by the circumcision of men is the mirror image of the menstruation of women. Men's bleeding is artificial (or "cultural") and controlled; women's is natural and uncontrollable. Men's bleeding is covenantal, powerful, and status-enhancing; women's is impure, dangerous, and status-limiting. Men's bleeding is an occasion of public rejoicing; women's an occasion of private shame. And so on. "Menstrual blood is the symbolic inversion of circumcision."[34]

Without reading any of the anthropology textbooks that would be written centuries later Bekhor Shor intuits a relationship between menstruation and circumcision, but he understands that relationship as homology rather than inversion. Fully aware of all the negative associations of menstruation and menstrual blood in rabbinic Judaism, Bekhor Shor nevertheless argues that the purification regimen observed by married Jewish women gives their menstrual blood the same covenantal value as the blood of circumcision. Bruno Bettelheim, a modern anthropologist/psychologist, agrees with Bekhor Shor that there is close correspondence, almost parallelism, between menstruation and circumcision, even if Bekhor Shor assigns primacy of meaning to circumcision and Bettelheim assigns primacy of meaning to menstruation. Bekhor Shor understands menstruation (or, more accurately, purification from menstruation) as an analogue to circumcision, while Bettelheim understands circumcision as an analogue to menstruation. Awed and overwhelmed by the procreative power of women, Bettelheim says, men attempted in their own feeble way to mimic and arrogate to themselves the reproductive processes of women, and among these ways was the artificial genital bleeding induced by circumcision. We might almost say that in this view circumcision is the result of menstruation envy.[35] Since the Torah ascribes the origin of circumcision to a command from God to Abraham, Bettelheim's argument obviously goes well beyond what Bekhor Shor or any other traditional rabbi could have said, but in his own way Bekhor Shor was just as radical and just as perceptive.

If we seek uniquely feminine analogues to circumcision, another obvious candidate is childbirth. As I discussed in chapter 1, Genesis 17 itself seems to suggest, implicitly and obliquely to be sure, that circumcision and childbirth parallel each other. In that chapter God establishes a covenant between himself and Abraham, a covenant that is to be carried forward to Abraham's offspring. God changes Abram's name to Abraham and enjoins upon him and his sons the commandment of circumcision. God changes Sarai's name to Sarah and promises that she will give birth to a son. Under the terms of the covenant, Abraham will become potent and Sarah fertile. Circumcision is the instrument by which Abraham achieves potency, and childbirth is the manifestation of Sarah's newfound fertility. Sarah's childbirth is the consequence of, and analogue to, Abraham's circumcision.[36] As I discussed in chapter 3, several medieval Christian thinkers understood childbirth for women and circumcision for men as parallel. Before a sinful humanity could achieve atonement for Original Sin through faith in Christ, men were punished and atoned by circumcision, and women were punished and perhaps atoned by childbirth.[37] Circumcision and childbirth are parallel. They are parallel, too, in that each of them inevitably entails the loss of blood.

Why didn't Bekhor Shor adduce childbirth as the feminine covenantal analogue to circumcision? We can only speculate, of course. Perhaps he simply didn't think of it. Or perhaps he accepted rabbinic culture's view of childbirth as a woman's obligation to her husband, not as act of independent fulfillment. As the Mishnah explains, "The commandment *be fruitful and multiply* applies to men and not to women." A man is obligated to procreate and his wife is obligated to assist him. She fulfills no commandment on her own by bearing a child. The Talmud records dissident opinions on this subject, to be sure, some sages arguing that the commandment of procreation was incumbent on both men and women.[38] By the time of Bekhor Shor, however, this debate had long since been settled: normative law determined that women are not obligated to procreate. If childbirth is not a commandment for women, it can scarcely be a covenantal act. And so Bekhor Shor had to look elsewhere.

There is yet another road not taken. Several anthropologists have observed that in Islamic society the closest feminine analogue to male circumcision is the ritualized rupturing of the bride's hymen on the wedding night.[39] In many medieval Jewish communities, too, the deflowering of the bride on the wedding night was almost a public affair. The groom would emerge from the bridal chamber carrying the bloodstained sheet, and in front of the assembled crowd would recite a benediction over wine, a benediction over spices, and then a special benediction that in highly poetic and allusive language praises the virginity of the bride and her chastity. This ceremony is first attested in approximately the ninth century, but was widely practiced in the medieval Jewish world. In Christian countries, the public ceremony gradually disappeared and was replaced by the private recitation of the benediction by the groom either just after or just before the copulation; by early modern times the benediction fell out of use entirely. In Islamic countries, despite the opposition of Maimonides, the ceremony persisted for centuries, probably because Islamic society itself celebrated bridal virginity in loud and public ways.[40] The parallels between circumcision and defloration are apt: a unique event, genital pain, genital bleeding, benedictions, and communal celebration. The parallel goes even further: in literary form and style the "benediction over the tokens of virginity" resembles the benediction recited at circumcisions.[41] In more recent times, the parallel has resurfaced. In 1974 a Jewish feminist created quite a stir when she suggested that as a rite of entry to the Jewish people baby girls should have their hymens ruptured by a needle, parallel to the circumcision of boys.[42]

Why didn't Bekhor Shor adduce bridal defloration as the feminine covenantal analogue to circumcision? Again, we can only speculate. Perhaps he simply didn't think of it. Or, if we seek a more substantive answer, perhaps Bekhor Shor accepted rabbinic culture's view of marital intercourse as a religious obligation for the husband, not the wife. He is fulfilling a commandment by having intercourse with her, whereas she is not fulfilling a commandment by having intercourse with him (except in the most general sense of fulfilling her wifely duty). As an analogue to circumcision, Bekhor Shor wants a sacred act that women are obligated to perform not just because of biological or social destiny but also because of a commandment of the Torah. In Bekhor Shor's world, a Jewish woman was expected to be a virgin at her wedding and to bear her husband's children; no doubt she enjoyed social status and respectability for conforming to these expectations, but, technically speaking, she was not fulfilling a commandment by either action.

This brings us back to Bekhor Shor's answer, menstruation. A woman does not fulfill any religious obligation by menstruating or by ceasing to menstruate. However, a married woman who carefully keeps track of her menstrual periods, informs her husband of her status, and then carefully follows the rabbinic regimen of purification is fulfilling her duty as enjoined upon her in the Torah. Her righteous behavior not only protects her husband from sin but also is meritorious in itself, because the commandment to maintain separation between a menstruant and her husband, as stated in Leviticus 18:19 and elaborated in rabbinic law, is incumbent upon both him and her.[43]

We cannot call Bekhor Shor a "feminist." True, Bekhor Shor argues that Jewish women have a uniquely feminine analogue to the uniquely masculine ritual of circumcision. This argument is remarkable in and of itself. But he, a citizen of the twelfth century, cannot yet conceive of women as autonomous and independent persons who have a place in the covenant on their own and on their own terms. For Bekhor Shor, a Jewish woman is a married woman, subordinate to a man. Her blood becomes covenantal when she informs her husband of the onset of her period. Bekhor Shor, then, is working within the decidedly anti-feminist conceptual framework that I discussed at length in chapter 5: Jewish women are subordinate to Jewish men, and they derive and express their Jewishness through their relationship with Jewish men.

For contemporary Jews, however, a Jewish woman is not necessarily a married woman and does not need to inform her husband or her partner of anything in order to find her way in the covenant. Hence some contemporary Jewish thinkers have argued that menstruation itself should be conceived as covenantal, and menstrual blood as covenantal blood. The regimen of purification does not endow menstruation with covenantal value; rather, a woman's very bloodiness embodies the covenant. Monthly purification in the *miqveh* is not (just) for the purpose of making her sexually available to her husband but (also) to enhance her own connection, as a bloody woman, with God. These thinkers argue further that in the second paragraph of the Grace after Meals, women, too, can thank God for the "covenant you have sealed in our flesh," since the bloody flesh of women embodies the covenant with God no less than the circumcised flesh of men.[44] Here, then, is a "feminist" expression of Bekhor Shor's idea; it is "feminist" in that it is predicated on the assumption that Jewish women in their own right are, and ought to be, full members of the covenant, with rights and privileges equal to those of men. This was a path that Bekhor Shor himself could not take.

Challenges to the Circumcision of Jewish Men

For is not all that one does to children, force?—
That is, except what Religion does to children.

        Gotthold Ephraim Lessing, *Nathan the Wise*

This chapter is a brief foray into the nineteenth, twentieth, and early twenty-first centuries. In antiquity and the Middle Ages, Christian writers had used the non-circumcision of Jewish women as an argument against the circumcision of Jewish men. This argument returned in the middle of the nineteenth century, this time in the hands of Jewish reformers, who zealously campaigned against the necessity for circumcision. In the twentieth and twenty-first centuries, many contemporary Jews are disturbed by the lack of parity in the treatment Jewish newborns. For them, the absence of any ceremony or ritual marking the birth of a baby girl, the absence of anything equivalent to the *berit* for boys, is a major problem and a major challenge. Some as a consequence have urged that the circumcision of boys be eliminated or at least much reduced in emphasis; others have urged the creation of rituals celebrating the birth of baby girls. The non-circumcision of women remains, then, a problem on the contemporary Jewish agenda.

Also looming on the horizon is the challenge to the Jewish circumcision of males posed by the non-Jewish (generally Islamic) circumcision of women. As Western governments have moved to outlaw the circumcision of women, the question has been asked: why is the genital mutilation of men tolerated, while the genital mutilation of women is prohibited? The goal of the questioners is not to legalize female genital mutilation but to outlaw male circumcision, on the grounds that it too is a genital mutilation. This argument can be refuted, to be sure, but the argument is real, and future defenders of Jewish circumcision will need to deal with it. Hence both the non-circumcision of Jewish women and the circumcision of non-Jewish women challenge the circumcision of Jewish men.

1843 and Beyond

The Jewish circumcision wars of modern times began in Germany, in Frankfurt-am-Main, in 1843. On February 8th of that year, the city health department, in response to the recent deaths of some infant Jewish boys, caused, it was said, by their circumcision, issued an order requiring medical supervision of all circumcisions. Most striking was the language of the order, which was phrased in such a way as to suggest that Jewish parents could decide whether they wanted their sons circumcised. In the spring, a member of the Jewish community, a banker named Flersheim, refused to allow his newborn son to be circumcised, all the while insisting that he himself remain, and that his son be enrolled as, a member in good standing of the community. In July, a Jewish group calling itself the Frankfurt Reform Association published a brief manifesto against circumcision arguing that membership in the Jewish community has nothing to do with the observance, or lack of observance, of circumcision. In response to these challenges, the traditionalists rallied to the defense of circumcision, threatening Herr Flersheim and his son with full or partial expulsion from the community, petitioning the municipal and state governments not to allow the advocates of Reform to invent a circumcision-free Judaism, and calling on the agencies of state to compel Jewish fathers to have their sons circumcised. The traditionalists were led by the chief rabbi of the community, Rabbi Solomon Abraham Trier, who, assisted by two other communal rabbis, quickly solicited and published a collection of legal briefs ("responsa") by twenty-eight of the leading rabbis of central Europe. All of the responsa, to a greater or lesser degree, upheld the importance of circumcision and denounced the actions of the Reform Association. And thus the battle was joined.[1]

The battle began in 1843 and continued in the following decades. Between 1843 and 1860, at least twenty German-Jewish fathers refused to have their sons circumcised but insisted that their sons nevertheless be registered as Jews. Throughout the 1840s, rabbis, physicians, and scholars published numerous books and articles on the subject of circumcision. Even among those who defended the practice, there were vigorous debates on the techniques that were to be employed and on the means of complying with the newly emerging demands for medical probity. In 1866 sixty-six Jewish physicians in Vienna signed a statement against circumcision; their reasoning included the argument that circumcision weakens Jewish men, making them prone to "Jewish diseases" and shorter lived than their Christian countrymen.[2] Circumcision was a major topic of discussion at the Jewish conferences held in Leipzig in 1869 and in Augsburg in 1871. The participants, most of whom were advocates of "moderate," not "radical," Reform, recognized that circumcision was indeed of "supreme importance" in Judaism, yet concluded that "a boy born of a Jewish mother who has not been circumcised . . . must be considered a Jew and treated as such in all ritual matters."[3] Similarly the American Reform rabbinic conference held in Philadelphia in 1869 resolved that "The male child of a Jewish mother is . . . to be considered a Jew by descent even though he be uncircumcised."[4] The American Reform rabbinic conferences of 1891 and 1892 went even further, declaring that gentiles may be admitted as proselytes into the Jewish fold "without any initiatory rite, ceremony, or observance whatever."[5] By the end of the nineteenth century, the circumcision controversy had reached Eastern Europe. A conference of Orthodox rabbis in St. Petersburg was devoted to the subject, as I shall discuss in a moment. In October 1908 the superintendents of the Jewish cemetery of Warsaw were shocked to discover that a deceased ten-month-old boy who had been brought in for burial had not been circumcised. The father of the child said that he did not regard this "barbaric ritual" as either sacred or necessary; after much discussion among the rabbis and the leaders of the community, the dead boy was circumcised and buried in the Jewish cemetery.[6]

The war over circumcision was part of the larger war between Reform and Orthodox, as the two movements would come to be called. The prayerbook, the synagogue service, the architecture of the synagogue, head-covering for men, the belief in a messiah and the hope for the restoration of the Temple in Jerusalem, the Sabbath restrictions, the food laws, the authority of the Talmud—all these and more were intensely debated between the rival camps, first in Western Europe and then, before very long, in America and Eastern Europe as well. The setting for these debates was the "Emancipation," that is, the emergence of the Jews from the closed communities of the Middle Ages and their entrance into the new European societies that were being shaped by na-

tionalism, industrialization, and urbanization. The advocates of Reform enthusiastically supported the integration of the Jews into their
new social and national settings, while the advocates of Orthodoxy
insisted on the primacy of Jewish ritual and Jewish difference. There
was great variety of opinion within each of these camps, to be sure, with
divisions between radical and moderate Reform, and between radical and moderate Orthodox.[7] In chapter 6, we met Rabbi Samson
Raphael Hirsch, one of the leaders of moderate (or "neo") Orthodoxy
in Germany.

The advocates of Orthodoxy quickly and correctly realized that the
battle with Reform was not just over this ritual, that tenet, or this custom. The battle was over Judaism itself: did modern Jews have the
right—indeed, the duty—to redefine, reinvent, and reform Judaism, as
Reform insisted? Or, as the Orthodox argued, were modern Jews, living
in a time of growing assimilation and religious indifference, ever more
obligated to remain faithful custodians of the sacred legacy that they
had received from prior generations? In response to the Reform challenge, the first instinct of the Orthodox was to magnify the importance
of everything that was attacked. No law or ritual was too small to defend, because in the edifice of Judaism every brick is sacred and im-
mutable; "anything new is prohibited by the Torah."[8] The great irony,
of course, is that this attitude itself was new. Earlier generations of rabbinic leaders, not confronted by the likes of Reform, never had to work
out a theory of the immutability of Judaism's practices and beliefs. The
Orthodox had to invent a tradition by which to defend tradition.[9]

The irony of novelty in defense of tradition is evident in the Orthodox defense of circumcision. In July 1843, in the midst of the circumcision controversy in Frankfurt, the supplement to the *Frankfurt Journal*
published an unsigned piece by an opponent of Reform. The author
writes: "Through the repudiation of circumcision, a Jew ceases to be a
Jew. Without circumcision, no Judaism is possible, because it is dogma,
not ritual."[10] This defense of circumcision is thoroughly novel. No Jewish legal text had said that "through the repudiation of circumcision, a
Jew ceases to be a Jew." Such a Jew, of course, is a sinner, perhaps an
apostate, but no authoritative legal text had excluded such a Jew from
Judaism or Jewishness. In the second sentence the author clearly assimilates Judaism to Christianity and circumcision to baptism. Just as there
is no Christianity without baptism, there is no Judaism without circumcision, because baptism and circumcision are not mere "rituals" or
"ceremonies"; they are essential parts of the truth-claims or "dogmas"

that Christianity and Judaism advance.[11] Christians assumed from an early moment in the history of Christianity that Jewish circumcision was analogous to Christian baptism, but, as I discussed in chapter 1, the interpretation of circumcision as a sacrament does not appear in Jewish sources until the high Middle Ages. Even then this view becomes common only in popular piety and esoteric mysticism, not in the legal tradition. So, in his defense of circumcision, this writer in the *Frankfurt Journal* has misrepresented the Jewish legal tradition and has adopted a reading of circumcision that has more in common with Christian interpretations than with normative rabbinic law. All this in the name of tradition!

The novelty of the traditionalists' position is well illustrated by the following story told by Rabbi Joseph B. Soloveitchik (1903–1993), the preeminent leader of modern Orthodoxy in the United States in the second half of the twentieth century. The hero of the story is R. Joseph Soloveitchik's grandfather, R. Hayyim Soloveitchik (1853–1918), the head of the talmudic academy of Volozhin and, one could argue, the outstanding talmudist of his day. R. Hayyim Soloveitchik was known as R. Hayyim of Brisk (Brest-Litovsk). Here is the story:

> Once R. Hayyim of Brisk was attending a conference of outstanding Torah scholars in St. Petersburg. The item on the agenda was the question of uncircumcised infants—should their names be entered in the official registers of the Jewish community? All of the rabbis declared: "It is certainly forbidden to register them, for they are not circumcised." Through this tactic they hoped to compel the assimilationists to circumcise their sons. R. Hayyim arose and said, "My masters, please show me the Halakhah [Jewish law] which states that one who is not circumcised is not a member of the Jewish people. I am aware that a person who is not circumcised may not partake of the sacrifices or the heave offering, but I am unaware that he is devoid of the holiness belonging to the Jewish people. To be sure, if he comes of age and does not circumcise himself he is liable to *karet*.[12] However, he who eats blood [non-kosher meat] and he who violates the Sabbath are also liable to *karet*. Why then do you treat the uncircumcised infant so stringently and the Sabbath violator so leniently? On the contrary, this infant has not as yet sinned at all, except that his father has not fulfilled his obligation."[13]

Here ends the story. R. Joseph Soloveitchik comments: "From a political and practical perspective, and as an emergency measure, no doubt the majority was correct. However, on the basis of pure Halakhah, R. Hayyim was correct." Sixty years or so after the circumcision controversy had erupted in Frankfurt in 1843, it reached the Czarist empire in the east. Here again the defenders of tradition wanted to adopt a rigorist position. They were opposed by R. Hayyim, who was certainly a traditionalist himself but not a practical man. He was a legal scholar, not a community leader.[14] The law is the law, he argued, and misrepresentation of the law is not justified by even the most urgent social and political pressures. An uncircumcised male Jew is a Jew according to Jewish law, R. Hayyim ruled, and from the perspective of Jewish law R. Hayyim was certainly correct. Nevertheless, as R. Joseph Soloveitchik comments at the end of the narrative, from the perspective of the needs of the hour, R. Hayyim may well have been wrong.

I turn now to the arguments of the Reformers and return to our theme. Five days after the defender of circumcision had declared in the pages of the *Frankfurt Journal* that "without circumcision no Judaism is possible," the advocates of Reform responded with a broadside of their own. They offered five arguments to prove that a Jew does not enter into Judaism through circumcision. The first four, which are of varying quality, need not detain us here; the fifth, however, is full of interest:

> By what means, then, [if one becomes a Jew through circumcision,] do our daughters enter into Judaism? The truth is that, according to the principles of the Mosaic faith, birth makes one into a Jew, and that the offspring of Jewish parents belongs to the Jewish religious community even if he should not observe a single ritual commandment—so long as he does not deny the fundamental doctrine of the one sole God and revelation.[15]

Circumcision cannot be the portal into Jewishness, say the Reformers, because if so how do women become Jews? The non-circumcision of women proves that the circumcision of men cannot have a sacramental function. The circumcision of an eight-day-old boy does not turn him into a Jew. What does turn him into a Jew is his descent. The offspring of Jewish parents automatically at birth belong to the Jewish community. The observance, or lack of observance, of any of the ritual commandments, including circumcision, has nothing do with membership in the Jewish people and the Jewish community. A born Jew remains a member of the Jewish community so long as he or she does not reject the fundamental tenets of monotheism and revelation.

The idea that descent is the primary determinant of Jewishness allowed the Reformers not only to do away with the necessity of circumcision but also to ameliorate women's status in Jewish society and law. At the Frankfurt rabbinical conference of 1845, Rabbi S. Adler introduced a motion "to declare the female portion of Israel's communion equal with the male sex in all respects of religious obligation and privilege." The matter was duly referred to a committee, which at the rabbinical conference of 1846 recommended that "women be counted whenever a quorum is needed at the divine service."[16] Similarly these same rabbinical conferences also spent much time discussing the amelioration of women's status in the rabbinic laws of marriage and divorce. So, when the Reformers in 1843 adduced the non-circumcision of women as evidence that Jewish men too did not need to be circumcised, they were not merely scoring a point against the traditionalists. The "women's question" was on their agenda; the Jewishness of women and of men was equally determined by descent.[17]

The Reformers' position stands in dialectical tension with that of Maimonides and Mühlhausen, which I discussed in the previous chapter. Like Maimonides and Mühlhausen before them, the Reformers downplay the significance of circumcision for Jewish identity. Indeed, Mühlhausen explicitly argues that circumcision does not confer Jewishness, and that the absence of circumcision does not contraindicate Jewishness. On this point both Mühlhausen and the Reformers are in agreement and are supported by the normative halakhic tradition, as evidenced by R. Hayyim of Brisk. What, then, makes a Jew a Jew? Mühlhausen, following Maimonides, argued that the answer is faith, for Judaism is a religion of faith, not works. The Reformers, at least not here, did not want to take this route, because they knew that on theological grounds too they would never be able to pass muster. They were willing to allow that the denial of two core doctrines, monotheism and revelation, put one outside the Jewish religious community, but they were not willing to assign proper faith a central place in defining the boundaries of the community. Instead, they played up what Maimonides and Mühlhausen had played down: descent. By arguing that the Jewishness of those born to Jewish parents (or, more accurately, those born to a Jewish mother) is determined solely by birth, the Reformers assured for themselves a place within the normative Jewish community in spite of their innovative theology and praxis.

Many of the rabbis represented in Rabbi Trier's anthology ignored the Reformers' five arguments, but some responded to them seriatim. Both the Reformers and the traditionalists were oblivious to the debates that had come before them; neither realized that they were replaying a debate that reached back approximately seventeen hundred years. The Reformers did not realize that Justin Martyr in the second century, Cyprian in the third, the *Dispute between the Church and the Syna-*

gogue in the fifth, and many later Christian writers as well, had used the non-circumcision of women as an argument against Jewish circumcision.[18] The traditionalists did not realize that many medieval Jewish polemicists and apologists had already responded to this argument.[19] Like R. Jacob Anatoli and Menahem before them, some traditionalists argued that the circumcision of men indicates their social and religious primacy within the Jewish polity, and that the absence of circumcision from women betokens their second-tier status.[20] What seemed reasonable to R. Jacob Anatoli in the thirteenth century still seemed reasonable to these German rabbis in the middle of the nineteenth.

Parity between Boys and Girls, Men and Women

Contemporary Jews, certainly in the United States and in other western countries, and to a lesser degree in Israel too, are far more gender conscious and egalitarian than Reform Jews had been in nineteenth-century Germany. Many of these Jews are rankled by the disparity in the treatment of newborn boys and girls: boys are dramatically and publicly welcomed into the people of Israel by their circumcision and the attendant festivities, while girls . . .

Jewish opponents of circumcision use this disparity as one of their arguments. The Jewish circumcision ritual, they say, is so irredeemably androcentric that it can no longer be tolerated. They argue for the creation of circumcision-less *berit* ceremonies for boys and/or genderneutral covenant ceremonies for boys and girls.[21] The first attempt to create such a ritual with such a purpose was undertaken by Joseph Johlson (1777–1851) in Frankfurt in the fateful year 1843. Johlson, a teacher in a Jewish school that was allied with the Friends of Reform, supported the anti-circumcision cause. In a book on circumcision that he published pseudonymously, Johlson argued that the circumcision of Jewish boys was neither desirable nor necessary and for the first time sketched out a script for a gender-neutral ceremony that would celebrate the arrival of all newborn Jews. As might be expected, the ceremony is basically the standard *berit* ritual minus any reference to circumcision or blood.[22] The Jewish opponents of circumcision in Frankfurt in 1843 still have their followers today.

Most contemporary Jews, however, no matter how great their feminist ardor, are not (yet) willing to dispense with the circumcision of boys. Instead they have invested much energy in creating ceremonies to

celebrate the birth of Jewish girls. Unlike Johlson and his latter-day followers, these ritual innovators are basically traditionalists. They do not
question the circumcision of boys; they hope rather to create a ceremony for girls that is as weighty and impressive as is the circumcision of
boys. As traditionalists, they look to the past for inspiration, and Jewish
history preserves some traces of gender-neutral birth celebrations. In
medieval Spain and Provence, the births of boys and girls seem to have
been celebrated equally with a week-long celebration, known as the
shevua ha ben ("the week of the son") for boys, and the *shevua ha bat*
("the week of the daughter") for girls.[23] Jewish communities of the vil-
lages and towns of southern Germany and Austria celebrated the
Hollekreisch, a folk ritual practiced in the home in which the secular or
common name was bestowed on the baby, the sacred or Hebrew name
having been bestowed earlier either at the *berit* (for boys) or at a synagogue service (for girls). The *Hollekreisch,* first attested in the fifteenth
century, was still being celebrated in the rural areas of Germany before
the Second World War.[24] Some Jewish communities had celebrations
specifically for girls, frequently called *simhat bat* or *zeved bat*. Here,
then, is warrant for the public communal celebration of the birth of
girls, alongside the public communal celebration of the birth of boys.
But, of course, none of these pre-modern celebrations was born out of a
need or desire for gender "equality." In pre-modern Jewish societies, the
secondary status of girls and women was natural and self-evident, and
these birth celebrations were no threat to the social order. The modern
impulse is different, however; modern Jews want to celebrate the birth
of girls in such a way so as to demonstrate that girls are as valued and as
important as boys. The egalitarian impulse is modern.

The egalitarian impulse has led sections of contemporary Jewish society to treat girls and women "the same" as boys and men, wherever
possible, that is, to extend to females the same religious habits and pre-
rogatives that previously had been the exclusive domain of males. The
assumption is that real Judaism is the Judaism long practiced by boys
and men and long withheld from girls and women. By giving females
access to the treasures that once had been the exclusive domain of
males, the egalitarian impulse can be satisfied. Thus the *bat mitzvah* celebration for girls, first instituted by Rabbi Mordecai M. Kaplan in New
York in 1922 for his daughter Judith, has become almost as common as
the *bar mitzvah* celebration for boys. In many circles a woman wears a
kippah (a head-covering, often shaped like a beanie, worn to show rev-
erence for God), wraps herself in a *tallit* (prayer shawl), and dons *tefillin*

(phylacteries), just as men do. The exemption of women from the obligation to observe positive commandments that must be observed at specific times, an exemption that I discussed in chapter 5, has been circum-
vented by the Conservative movement in Judaism, which has in effect
declared that men and women can be said to be equally bound to observe all the commandments.[25] And, of course, women can become, and
have become, rabbis.

Here is a particularly interesting example of this egalitarian impulse
in German Jewry of the modern period, an example that is close to our
theme. German Jewish communities had the custom of taking a piece of
the swaddling cloth that had been wrapped around a boy at his circumcision, preferably a piece of cloth that had been stained by circumcision
blood, and using it to create an elaborately decorated Torah binder that
would later be presented to the synagogue in a public ceremony.[26]
Thousands of such *wimpel*s are extant in museums and private collections, the oldest of them from the sixteenth century, the most recent
from the years just before the Holocaust. A rather plain and unassum-
ing one was donated to the synagogue of Budyne (or Budin) in northern
Bohemia by Sara Gellner in honor of her daughter Rachel, who had
been born 10 Tammuz 5687 (July 10, 1927). I am not sufficiently expert
in the history of the *wimpel* to be able to say that this is the first *wimpel*
ever to have been created in honor of the birth of a daughter, but I can
say with confidence that this *wimpel* is highly unusual. One would like
to know more about this mother and daughter, but, even in the absence
of additional information, it is hard to resist the conclusion that the
egalitarian impulse in the 1920s apparently reached even the small Jewish community of Budyne in northern Bohemia. Even if Rachel Gellner
could not be welcomed into the covenant with a *berit*, her mother saw
to it that her arrival would be celebrated with a *wimpel*.[27]

How, then, do we satisfy the egalitarian impulse in the case of circumcision? No one suggests that little girls should be excised or circumcised, because such genital mutilation has no warrant whatever in the
Jewish tradition and, no less important, is regarded in the West with re-
vulsion. It is also unlawful. Nevertheless, we understand what impelled
one Jewish feminist in the 1970s to suggest that an appropriate birth
ceremony for a girl would be to rupture her hymen with a sterilized needle. Such an act would strike a blow against the cult of virginity, which
lives on in traditional society and is a powerful agent in the social control of young women, and would give girls an impressive, bloody, surgical act mimicking the circumcision of boys.[28] As far as I know, this sug-

gestion has never actually been implemented, and there are no signs that it will ever be implemented; in fact when first published it was met by shock and derision. But the origins of the idea are clear; if circumcision is the archetypal Jewish birth ceremony, what can we do for girls? We can easily rewrite some of the prayers just as Johlson did in 1843, and just as many contemporary Jews do, in order to create a gender-neutral ritual appropriate for girls, but such a bloodless ceremony cannot pack the emotional wallop of a circumcision. Some have sought to anchor their ceremonies in symbolism that is more naturally associated with women, such as the moon or water; here, at least, we are closer to the feminine, but we are further from circumcision.[29]

One feminist scholar has advocated a different approach. Like the opponents of circumcision, she is much disturbed by the irredeemable androcentrism of the traditional circumcision ceremony. Unlike the opponents, however, she is loath to surrender circumcision because of her commitment to Jewish tradition and continuity. Her solution: perform circumcision privately on the eighth day, in the presence of the parents, the circumciser, the baby, and no one else, and hold a public celebration and baby naming on or about the thirtieth day, a gender-neutral celebration that can avoid any overtones or trappings of a circumcision.[30] This elegant solution accomplishes several goals at once. By separating the circumcision from the public celebration, it deflects attention from the former and bestows it on the latter. It satisfies the egalitarian impulse for a gender-neutral ritual and yet is respectful of traditional practice. In some communities in America this suggestion is being followed.[31]

Female Genital Mutilation and Male Circumcision: A Case of Moral Relativism?

Opposition to circumcision continues still. In the United States and other western countries, even in Israel, there is a small but vocal anti-circumcision movement.[32] The goal of these opponents, both Jewish and non-Jewish, is to prohibit all circumcisions except those necessary on medical grounds. They would eliminate not only routine neonatal circumcision, which is still relatively common in the United States, but also the Jewish and Islamic circumcision of boys. One of their arguments, which is directly related to our theme, runs as follows: the circumcision of men is no less a genital mutilation than is the circumcision of women; the defense of Jewish male circumcision by appeal to "tradition" is no more compelling than the defense of female circumcision by appeal to "tradition"; just as right-minded people oppose the circumcision of women, they should also oppose the circumcision of men.[33]

As I discussed in chapter 2, throughout Africa and the Near East, females are "excised" or "circumcised," that is, all or part of the external genitalia (including the clitoris) is surgically removed. This practice, called by its opponents female genital mutilation (FGM), is popularly associated with Islam, and many of its practitioners are convinced that it is required by Islam, just like the circumcision of men. This belief is incorrect, or at least is not justified historically, but historical accuracy does not much matter on this point, since the practice has become an established tradition in these societies, no matter whether its origin is Islamic, pre-Islamic, or non-Islamic. For a long time the circumcision of women in Africa and the Near East was a subject of concern only for Christian missionaries and colonial governments. The former railed against it, and the latter attempted from time to time to abolish it. Just as, for example, the British colonial regime in India in 1829 abolished *suttee,* the burning of widows, on the grounds that a civilized empire cannot abide such a practice, the British colonial regime in Kenya in the first part of the twentieth century attempted to abolish female circumcision. The campaign in India against *suttee* was ultimately successful, but the campaign in Kenya against female circumcision was not. An important apologist for the ritual was Jomo Kenyatta, whom we met briefly in chapter 2. Kenyatta argued that the African circumcision of females should be no more offensive to westerners than the Jewish circumcision of males. Kenyatta writes: "The real anthropological study, therefore, is to show that clitoridectomy, like Jewish circumcision, is a mere bodily mutilation which, however, is regarded as a *conditio sine qua non* of the whole teaching of tribal law, religion, and morality."[34] Like Jewish circumcision, African circumcision should not be dismissed as "a mere bodily mutilation"; it is essential to group identity, Kenyatta argues, specifically "tribal law, religion, and morality." Hence Africans should not be expected to give up female circumcision any more than Jews would be expected to give up male circumcision.

When Kenyatta wrote his apologia in 1938, few Kenyans were living in the West. Few Africans had emigrated to the countries of their colonial masters, and few Muslims had left the Near East and South Asia for homes in the West. For westerners, the circumcision of women was an issue—if it was seen as an issue at all—that affected people far away and, from the imperialist colonialist perspective, people that did not matter much (dark-skinned colonial subjects—women at that). But in the last decades of the twentieth century, this situation has changed dramatically. Many thousands of African immigrants have arrived in France, England, the United States, and other western countries, as well as many thousands of Muslims from the Near East and South Asia. Many of these immigrants have brought with them their ancestral customs, including the circumcision of women. What was once far away is now uncomfortably close. The result has been that the United States, France, and Canada have declared female circumcision illegal; those who excise a girl are subject to prosecution and imprisonment. (Female circumcision is now illegal in Kenya too.)[35] At this point, the opponents of male circumcision ask: if it is a criminal act to excise a girl, why shouldn't it be a criminal act to circumcise a boy? This question has not yet elicited much comment in the Jewish community, but defenders of Jewish circumcision will need to deal with it.[36] I shall return to this point in a moment.

Conclusions

Opposition to Jewish circumcision has a long history. In antiquity two monarchs, one Greek and one Roman, outlawed Jewish circumcision and persecuted those Jews who violated the prohibition. From the second century BCE to the fifth century CE, Greek and Roman poets, philosophers, and essayists mocked Jewish circumcision. Out of fear of ridicule or persecution, or perhaps out of a desperate desire to belong to general society, some Jews in antiquity attempted to hide their own circumcision or refrained from circumcising their sons.[37] Christian opposition to circumcision took on a theological cast. Christians argued that the Jews misinterpreted their own Torah, for God wanted not the literal or "carnal" circumcision of the Jews but the spiritual circumcision of the Christians. This argument, shaped in large part by the letters of Paul, remained the mainstay of Christian anti-circumcision polemic for centuries.

In the nineteenth century, the Jewish discourse concerning circumcision changed, and for the first time since the Roman period, Jews began to question, and even oppose, circumcision.[38] For some, opposition to circumcision was simply the first step toward baptism and leaving the Jewish community. For others, however, opposition to circumcision was part of a newly emerging program to *reform* Judaism. Circumcision, the food laws, and many other traditional ritual observances were to be jettisoned in order to make Judaism modern and respectable. The goal of the reformers was not to destroy Judaism, they argued, but to save it, to make it attractive to the new generations of bourgeois, urban, and educated Jewry who, to be blunt, wanted a Judaism that resembled Protestant Christianity. Heretofore in Jewish history, the rejection of the ritual laws was a sign of social deviance, perhaps apostasy; now it was a sign of a new era in the history of Judaism: the age of Reform. The advocates of reform debated among themselves which rituals should be retained and which rejected, and what form the old rituals should receive. Circumcision figured prominently in these debates, but in the end the intellectual leaders of Reform, a few radical voices aside, could never quite bring themselves to reject circumcision outright. Circumcision endured as a sign of Jewishness and Jewish identity even among Reform circles.

As we have seen in this chapter, one of the arguments advanced by the advocates of Reform against traditional circumcision was based on the non-circumcision of women. Surely newborn boys are Jews by birth just as newborn Jewish girls are. The non-circumcision of girls shows that the circumcision of boys cannot be essential to their Jewishness. The advocates of Reform did not realize that they were presenting a version of a classic Christian argument. Christians used the argument to prove that circumcision had nothing to do with righteousness before God, or to prove that Christianity, which baptized both girls and boys, was superior to Judaism. Reform Jews used the argument to prove that circumcision was a ritual like any other, which could be skipped or omitted without affecting the Jewishness of the individual. Such arguments can still be heard within the Jewish community of the United States and even of Israel.

With the rise of sexual egalitarianism in the last decades of the twentieth century, traditionalist Jews have become increasingly bothered by the disparity in the ritual treatment of newborn Jewish boys and newborn Jewish girls. These traditionalists advocate not the cessation of circumcision for boys but the creation of a ritual for girls that will somehow correspond to the circumcision of boys. The search for an appropriate ritual continues.

The setting for the debate about Jewish circumcision has also changed markedly since the nineteenth century. On the one hand, in the United States neonatal circumcision is routine; the percentage of male newborns who are circumcised has declined in recent decades from the eighty-percent range to the sixty-percent range, but still this is a very high number indeed. Never before have Jews lived in a non-Muslim country in which male circumcision is so widely practiced by broad reaches of the population. Clearly in this environment, Jewish circumcision is perfectly acceptable.

On the other hand, in recent decades there has been a backlash against routine neonatal circumcision, including Jewish circumcision; its opponents have advanced many arguments, and I shall consider briefly three of them here. First, they argue that circumcision provides no statistically meaningful medical benefits, or that whatever medical benefit it provides is so small as to be offset by the costs and risks of the procedure itself. Second, they have argued that circumcision is a mutilation and an affront to body integrity. Third, they ask, why does western society allow the circumcision of boys but condemn and prohibit the circumcision of girls? These are powerful arguments indeed, but none of them is cogent.

First, whether circumcision provides statistically significant medical benefit—whether for the male himself or for his female sexual partner—is endlessly debated. Current research suggests that circumcision does provide some statistically meaningful protection against the transfer of the virus that causes AIDS and does reduce the incidence of cervical cancer in female sexual partners;[39] whether such protection is sufficiently great so as to justify routine neonatal circumcision is a question for social policy analysts to ponder. In any case, the Jewish argument for circumcision has not turned on its putative health benefits, even if Philo in the first century argued that circumcision is indeed medically advantageous, and even if Jewish circumcision became medicalized in the course of the nineteenth century. Surely Genesis 17 did not ordain male circumcision for the Israelites as a public health measure, just as Leviticus 11 did not prohibit the eating of swine and shellfish as a public health measure. The logic of these commandments lies elsewhere.

Second, does male circumcision constitute a mutilation? The answer of course is that mutilation is in the eye of the beholder. Many cultures practice all kinds of bodily modifications; some are regarded in the West as mutilations, some not. In the West we have our own kinds of mutilations that we prefer not to regard as mutilations. For example, an outside observer could argue that we regularly perform a form of female genital mutilation in the United States. True, we do not excise the clitoris but we do excise the uterus. Each year in the United States more than 600,000 women undergo a hysterectomy; about one third of women in the United States have had a hysterectomy by age 60.[40] These numbers far exceed the comparable statistics of any other industrialized country. We have been culturally conditioned not to regard this as mutilation, but someone who has not been so conditioned could make a reasonable argument that this extraordinary rate of hysterectomy is a form of female genital mutilation. Is male circumcision, then, a mutilation? Only if we will it so.

Third, opponents of male circumcision assume parity between male circumcision, which is tolerated, and female circumcision, which is proscribed. However, if we may believe the opponents of female genital mutilation, there is no parity. In the extreme forms of female circumcision, virtually all of the external genitalia are cut off. The male analogue to this is not the circumcision of the foreskin but the removal of the penis. A clitoridectomy means that a woman will not be able to experience sexual pleasure. Even if Maimonides is correct that male circumcision reduces male sexual pleasure, no one denies that circumcised men experience sexual pleasure. And further, in many cases the extreme forms of female circumcision not only remove pleasure but substitute pain in its stead. The act of intercourse is extremely painful for the excised woman; even urination and menstruation can be difficult. Female circumcision substantially compounds the danger and pain of childbirth. Hence in their surgical aspects the two procedures differ markedly one from the other. If we may believe the opponents of female genital mutilation, the differences between male circumcision and female circumcision are real, and can legitimately be used to justify the prohibition of the latter, certainly in its extreme form, even by those who tolerate or support the former.[41]

The theme of this book has been the challenge to the circumcision of Jewish men posed by the non-circumcision of Jewish women. If circumcision is an important, even essential, marker of Jewishness, why do Jewish women not possess this mark or any functional equivalent? As we have seen, medieval Jewish sources adopt different strategies in answering this question: some concede that circumcision is indeed essential to Jewishness, while others contend that circumcision has no greater or lesser role in the determination of Jewishness than any other commandment. Among those who affirm the high value of circumcision, some (R. Jacob ben Abba Mari Anatoli, Menahem) argue that the absence of circumcision from women betokens their second-tier status in Judaism, while others (R. Joseph Bekhor Shor) argue that Jewish women are marked by some uniquely feminine sign analogous to circumcision. Among those who limit the value of circumcision, some argue that the purpose of circumcision is to reduce male lust, and consequently that circumcision has nothing to do with women (Maimonides, by implication), while others (R. Lipmann Mühlhausen, developing a Maimonidean idea) argue that circumcision is no more significant than any other commandment and that Jewishness is a function of faith. Thus was met the challenge of the non-circumcision of women in the Middle Ages.

Notes

ABBREVIATIONS

Rabbinic Texts

Note: rabbinic texts are generally cited according to the following paradigm: name of work (sometimes abbreviated), name of section or tractate, section number, and page number in the indicated edition. All of the following editions have been reprinted frequently.

AdRN	*Avoth de Rabbi Nathan,* Fathers according to Rabbi Nathan. Ed. Solomon Schechter. Vienna, 1887.
B	Babylonian Talmud (Bavli). Vilna: Romm, 1880–86.
Genesis Rabbah	Ed. J. Theodor and H. Albeck. Berlin, 1912–36.
Leviticus Rabbah	Ed. M. Margulies. Jerusalem, 1953–60.
M	Mishnah. Ed. H. Albeck. Jerusalem: Bialik Institute, 1952–58.
Mekhilta HR	Ed. H. S. Horovitz and I. A. Rabin. Frankfurt, 1931.
Mekhilta L	Ed. Jacob Lauterbach. Philadelphia: Jewish Publication Society, 1933–35.
PdRE	Pirqei de Rabbi Eliezer. Ed. David Luria. Warsaw, 1852.
Sifra on Leviticus	Ed. I. H. Weiss. Vienna, 1862.

Sifra on Leviticus F	For the opening sections of the Sifra I have also used the edition of L. Finkelstein. 5 vols. New York: Jewish Theological Seminary, 1983–90.
Sifrei on Deuteronomy	Ed. L. Finkelstein. Berlin, 1939.
Sifrei on Numbers	Ed. H. S. Horovitz. Leipzig, 1917.
T	Tosefta. Ed. Saul Lieberman. New York: Jewish Theological Seminary, 1955–88 (for the orders Zeraim through Nashim and the first three tractates of Neziqin). Ed. M. S. Zuckermandel. Passewalk, 1877–81, frequently reprinted (for the rest of Neziqin and the orders Qodashim and Toharot).
TK	*Tosefta Ki-Fshutah: A Comprehensive Commentary on the Tosefta.* By Saul Lieberman. New York: Jewish Theological Seminary, 1955–88. 10 vols. (Hebrew).
Y	Yerushalmi (Talmud of the Land of Israel). Cited according to the pagination of the first edition, Venice, 1523–24.

Patristic Sources

CCCM	Corpus Christianorum Continuatio Mediaevalis. Turnhout: Brepols, 1966–.
CCSL	Corpus Christianorum Series Latina. Turnhout: Brepols, 1954–.
CPL	Clavis Patrum Latinorum, ed. Eligius Dekkers, 3rd ed. Steenbrugis: in Abbatia Sancti Petri/Brepols, 1995.
CPPM	Clavis Patristica Pseudepigraphorum Medii Aevi, 2: *Theologica Exegetica.* Ed. Iohannis Machielsen. Turnhout: Brepols, 1994.
CSCO	Corpus Scriptorum Christianorum Orientalium.
CSEL	Corpus Scriptorum Ecclesiasticorum Latinorum.
GCS	Die griechischen christlichen Schriftsteller der ersten drei Jahrhunderte. Leipzig: Hinrichs, 1897–1969.
PG	Patrologiae cursus completus, series graeca. Ed. J.-P. Migne. 161 vols. in 166 pts. Paris, 1857–66.
PL	Patrologiae cursus completus, series latina. Ed. J.-P. Migne. 221 vols. in 222 pts. Paris, 1844–80.

Other

CCAR   Central Conference of American Rabbis.

PREFACE

1. Orenstein, *Lifecycles*, 55. Bibliographical information for this and all subsequent references is in the bibliography.

2. In some times and places women assimilated the male perspective so that men's construction of women became women's construction of themselves (just as colonialized peoples often absorb as their own the views of their colonialist oppressors). For example, R. Abraham Gombiner (ca. 1637–1683, in Poland) reports that women are in the habit of leaving the synagogue when the Torah is read (*Magen Avraham* on Orah Hayyim 282, sec. 6). In other words, the women of seventeenth-century Poland had accepted and internalized the male determination that women are exempt from the study of Torah. This is a telling piece of information, but I know of nothing like it that will reveal women's attitudes toward circumcision.

3. I am a historian interested in the history of Judaism; I see this book as a specimen of intellectual history. For examples of approaches that I do not follow, see Anidjar, "On the (Under)Cutting Edge," and Pippin and Aichele, "The Cut That Confuses." Jacques Derrida has written a series of autobiographical reflections entitled *Circumfession* that revolve around several key themes, one of them being circumcision, both his own and that of all male Jews; see Bennington and Derrida, *Jacques Derrida*.

4. Between my stints at Williams College and in Jerusalem, I published my "Why Aren't Jewish Women Circumcised?" my first foray into the subject of this book.

CHAPTER 1: A CANONICAL HISTORY OF JEWISH CIRCUMCISION

1. Montaigne, *Journal de voyage*, ed. Dédéyan, 213–16; for ease of reference I have numbered the paragraphs. The translation is that of Frame, *Montaigne's Travel Journal*, 80–82, slightly modified; cf. Trechmann, *Diary of Montaigne's Journey*, 133–36. For discussions of Montaigne's account of circumcision, see Boon, "Circumscribing Circumcision," esp. 568–73; S. Cohen, "Between Judaism and Christianity," 307–8; Bonfil, *Jewish Life*, 250–54; Frojmovic, "Christian Travelers," 130–34.

2. Luke 1:59–63 and 2:21.

3. Boon, "Circumscribing Circumcision," 570–72, notes that Montaigne's *Travel Diary* is much interested in social and religious diversity.

4. Well observed by Frojmovic, "Christian Travelers," 133. In the second paragraph, which I have omitted, Montaigne compares the disorder of the synagogue service to that of Calvinist churches: "They pay no more attention to their prayers than we do to ours."

5. Montaigne, *Essays* 1:55, "On Smells," in Screech, *Essays of Montaigne*, 353–54, "which convinces me of the truth of what is said about the invention of

odours and incense in our Churches (a practice so ancient and so widespread among all nations and religions): that it was aimed at making us rejoice, exciting us and purifying us so as to render us more capable of contemplation." This passage is adduced by many editors of the *Travel Journal*, e.g., Dédéyan, 216 n. 456. On circumcision as a "mystery" see below, note 149 and chapter 3 at note 48.

6. Montaigne, *Essays* 2:12, "An Apology for Raymond Sebond," in Screech, *Essays of Montaigne*, 646.

7. Montaigne, *Essays* 2:12, "An Apology for Raymond Sebond," in Screech, *Essays of Montaigne*, 647–48. On Muslim circumcision, see the picaresque tale about one Giuseppe in Montaigne, *Journal de voyage*, ed. Dédéyan, 285–86 [Frame, *Montaigne's Travel Journal,* 123–24], discussed by Boon, "Circumscribing Circumcision," 568–69.

8. Montaigne, *Essays* 3:5, "On Some Lines of Vergil," in Screech, *Essays of Montaigne*, 993; book 3 of the essays was first published in 1588. This passage is adduced by many editors of the *Travel Journal* and by Frojmovic, "Christian Travelers," 133 n. 12.

9. On scholarly discussions of circumcision in the sixteenth and seventeenth centuries, see Shapiro, *Shakespeare and the Jews*, 114–21. Nineteenth- and early twentieth-century scholarship is summarized in detail in Gray, "Circumcision." More recent work is readily available in any bibliographical database (e.g., WorldCat [FirstSeach], ATLA Religion Database).

10. Boon, "Circumscribing Circumcision," 562. (The ellipsis after "stoicism" is in the original.)

11. Hence I do not discuss here the so-called Apocrypha and Pseudepigrapha; Philo (see below, chapter 2); Josephus (see S. Cohen, "Respect for Judaism"); the New Testament (see below, chapter 3); Greek and Latin authors (see S. Cohen, *Beginnings of Jewishness,* 39–49); Samaritans; Karaites; Christian Jews; etc. A full and detailed history of Jewish circumcision remains to be written. Recent treatments include *Encyclopaedia Judaica*, s.v. "circumcision"; Eilberg-Schwartz, "Fruitful Cut"; Hoffman, *Covenant of Blood;* Gollaher, *Circumcision,* 6–30 (heavily indebted to Eilberg-Schwartz and Hoffman); Goldberg, *Jewish Passages,* 28–76. Hoffman's book contains numerous errors of omission and commission (some of which are noted below) and should be used with great care. Gollaher may well be one of "the new enemies of circumcision"; see Levenson, "New Enemies."

12. For a detailed exposition of the classic view (Genesis 17 is composite, written by P in response to the destruction, new emphasis on circumcision as symbol of Jewish identity in the Diaspora), see Grünwaldt, *Exil und Identität*. For a discussion of Genesis 17 within the context of priestly ideology, see Fox, "Sign of the Covenant," 586–96; Eilberg-Schwartz, "Fruitful Cut," with the critique of Goldberg, "Cambridge in the Land of Canaan." On circumcision in the Bible and ancient Near East, see Sasson, "Circumcision in the Ancient Near East"; Fox, "Sign of the Covenant"; and Hall, "Circumcision," 1025–27.

13. Perhaps because of the Christian self-conception as a "new covenant," there has been much scholarly discussion of the precise meaning of *berit* in

the Bible. See, e.g., Mendenhall and Herion, "Covenant"; Haran, "'Berit' Covenant."

14. Fox, "Sign of the Covenant," 587–88, writes: "The designation of circumcision as a covenant is a synecdoche for covenantal obligation. . . . The sentence may be translated 'this is the aspect of my covenant that *you* shall keep.'" If this is right, the second formulation is the same as the first.

15. I follow Fox, "Sign of the Covenant," 595.

16. See, e.g., Song of Songs Rabbah 1.15 13a.: "Israel is distinct through its hair style, circumcision, and fringes." Whether these three really made Jews distinct in the ancient world is not clear; see S. Cohen, *Beginnings of Jewishness*, 28–34.

17. Mellinkoff, *Mark of Cain*.

18. Isaac, "Circumcision as a Covenant Rite"; essential background in the classic article of Bickerman, "'Couper une alliance'." With Genesis 15, cf. Jeremiah 34:18–20. The parallel between cutting an animal and cutting the foreskin suggests that circumcision is akin to a sacrifice, a notion that is also implicit in Exodus 4 and Leviticus 12, as we shall see.

19. See below, chapter 2, for references and discussion.

20. See ibn Ezra's short commentary on Exodus 4:25; see also the novellae of R. Nissim of Gerona (known as the RaN) on B. Nedarim 32a and the comment of R. Yom Tov Lipmann Heller (the *Tosafot Yom Tov*) on M. Niddah 5.3. In medieval Europe, the baby about to be circumcised was dressed up and paraded about "like a bridegroom"; see Horovitz, ed., *Mahzor Vitry*, 626; R. Jacob HaGozer, *Kelalei HaMilah*, in Glassberg, *Zichron Berit*, 63–64 and 114; Goldin, "Role of Ceremonies."

21. See below, chapter 2, note 12.

22. This is the argument of Eilberg-Schwartz, "Fruitful Cut," and Hoffman, *Covenant of Blood*, 80, both following the lead of Nancy Jay.

23. If, as Eilberg-Schwartz argues, circumcision is a celebration of patriliny, Ishmael either should have been left uncircumcised or should not have been thrown out of the house; this is the objection of Goldberg "Cambridge in the Land of Canaan," 17 n. 44; see also Goldberg, *Jewish Passages*, 36–38. Eilberg-Schwartz, "Fruitful Cut," 148, admits that for Ishmael circumcision is about fertility, nothing more.

24. On the matrilineal principle, see below, the end of chapter 5.

25. Genesis 49:5–7 is a definite improvement.

26. The Midrash suggests that Dinah may have wanted to remain with Shechem; see below, chapter 6. For a modern feminist Midrash on the story of Dinah, see, e.g., Seltzer, "Rape of Dinah."

27. On the rewriting of Genesis 34 in Jewish texts of the Hellenistic period, see S. Cohen, *Beginnings of Jewishness*, 123 n. 37; Kugel, "Story of Dinah."

28. M. Nedarim 3.11; see below. On the foreskin as a source of shame, see also Joshua 5:9.

29. M. Yevamot 8:1; see below.

30. For recent discussion and bibliography, see Propp, *Exodus 1–18*, ad loc.

31. The apotropaic power of circumcision is commented upon by Origen, *Against Celsus* 5.48, in Chadwick, trans., *Origen contra Celsum*, 302 (followed

by Ambrose, Epistle 72.6 [PL 16:1245b]); Tertullian, *Against the Jews* 2.10 [CCSL 2:1343] (Jews say that a child must be circumcised on the eighth day "because of the threat of death"); Hizquni on Exodus 4:25.

32. See, e.g., Loewenstamm, *Evolution of the Exodus Tradition*, 202–4, and Levenson, *Death and Resurrection,* 48–52.

33. Ezekiel 28:10; 31:18; 32:19–32.

34. The benedictions appear at T. Berakhot 6.13 37; B. Shabbat 137b; and parallels. Flusser and Safrai, "Who Sanctified the Beloved?" 52–53, argue that "destruction" here means not "hell" but "evil," or "the sway of the kingdom of evil." I am not convinced; as Flusser and Safrai well know, *shahat,* destruction, is a common rabbinic synonym for Gehenna, and in a time when neonatal mortality was a common fact of life, a prayer that circumcision should save a baby (who might die before being able to perform any of the other *mitzvoth*) from punishment in the hereafter makes perfect sense. See Wolfson, "Circumcision and the Divine Name," 80 n. 7.

35. Genesis Rabbah 48.8 483; and numerous parallels. See Ginzberg, *Legends of the Jews,* 5:267 n. 318; and Wolfson, "Circumcision and the Divine Name," 80 n.6.

36. Tanhuma (nidpas) on Genesis 17, Lekh Lekha 20.

37. R. Ovadyah Seforno writes as follows in his commentary on Leviticus 12:3, "*He shall be circumcised on the eighth day.* Because [by] then the impure menstrual blood, from which the fetus is nourished in its mother's womb, is fully digested, and the child is pure so as to enter the holy covenant." Similar comment by Luzzato apud Trier, *Rabbinische Gutachten*, 89. Contrast Sifra, *Tazria* on Lev. 12:2 (58a W): "[only] *she shall be impure*—but her offspring is not impure."

38. Genesis 34:4 and 27 (see above); Isaiah 52:1; Ezekiel 44:7; M. Yevamot 8.1; and elsewhere. See below, chapter 7 at note 21.

39. Herodotus 2.37.2. This Herodotean passage is often translated as if it were dealing with cleanliness (the Egyptians "practice circumcision for the sake of cleanliness"), but this translation is misleading, because the Greek words that Herodotus uses *(kathareiotês* and *katharos)* refer not just to cleanliness but also to purity. The context of the passage shows that "purity" is the primary reference, for the paragraph opens with the words "They [the Egyptians] are God-fearing beyond measure, more than all other people." As part of their veneration for their gods, they are circumcised, so as to be pure/clean. There is a similar ambiguity in a passage of Philo; see below, chapter 2, note 28.

40. For example, see Maimonides, *Book of Commandments* (discussed below in chapter 7); R. Eliezer of Metz, *Sefer Yere'im ha Shalem*, no. 402, 2.223a, ed. Schiff; Frankel, *Mahazor leShavuot,* 630, note to line 1.

41. For a good summary and discussion of the rabbinic material, see Rubin, *Beginning of Life,* 77–121.

42. Izates, prince of Adiabene, is circumcised by the court physician in order to convert to Judaism (Josephus, *Jewish Antiquities* 20.46).

43. Josephus, *Jewish Antiquities* 13.257–58 and 13.318–19; *Vita* 112–13 and 149–54.

44. Conversion of children: M. Ketuvot 1:2, 3:1, 4:3; B. Ketuvot 11a; B. Yevamot 60b; Y. Qiddushin 4:1 65b. Circumcision of slaves even against their will: B. Yevamot 48a and Y. Yevamot 8:1 8d.

45. T. Avodah Zarah 3:13 464Z; B. Avodah Zarah 27a; Y. Yevamot 8:1 9a.

46. T. Avodah Zarah 3:12 464Z; see S. Cohen, *Beginnings of Jewishness*, 226–28.

47. Origen, *Against Celsus* 5.47, in Chadwick, trans., *Origen contra Celsum*, 301: "anyone who is circumcised [for one purpose] is entirely different from one who is circumcised for another purpose. For the purpose and law and intention of the man who performs the circumcision put the thing into a different category . . . Thus circumcision is different according to the different doctrines of the people who practice the rite."

48. Full documentation in S. Cohen, *Beginnings of Jewishness*, chap. 7.

49. See below, chapter 6, note 31, and chapter 7, note 28.

50. This is the position of the Samaritans; see Rubin, "Study of Change," 94 n. 57.

51. In the original: *yaroq*; alternative translation: yellow.

52. T. Shabbat 15(16).8 70–71 (with numerous parallels).

53. Preuss, *Medizin*, 285; Rubin, *Beginning of Life*, 93 n. 84.

54. On these disabilities, see Rubin, *Beginning of Life*, 85 n. 38. See references and discussion below, chapter 7, at note 22.

55. T. Shabbat 15(16).9 71–72 (and numerous parallels). Medieval jurists debated the normative law that was to be derived from the talmudic discussion; see, e.g., Lewin, *Otzar Hageonim Shabbat*, part 1, sec. 386–95, pp. 124–28, and part 2, sec 310, pp. 84–86. See below, chapter 7, note 28.

56. AdRN A 1.2 6b.

57. It is based on Exodus 2:2 and 6. See Ginzberg, *Legends of the Jews*, 5:399 n.51, and Jacobson, *Commentary on Pseudo-Philo's Liber Antiquitatum Biblicarum*, 1:425.

58. See Genesis Rabbah 11.6 94 and 46.3 460; Ginzberg, *Legends of the Jews*, 5:268 n. 318. See below, chapter 5, note 51.

59. Kister, "He Was Born Circumcised," 12–16.

60. The classic discussion is Preuss, *Biblisch-talmudische Medezin*, 278–89.

61. M. Shabbat 19.2. That circumcision overrides the Sabbath is also assumed by John 7:22–23.

62. M. Shabbat 19.6.

63. Bryk, *Circumcision in Man and Woman*, 122, gives a list of various procedures affecting the foreskin; of these, at least eight could be called "circumcision."

64. Jeremiah 9:24–25; Steiner, "Incomplete Circumcision."

65. Jubilees 15:33, as translated by Vanderkam, *Book of Jubilees*, 94.

66. The translation is not certain. R H. Charles and C. Rabin translate, "But I warn you that the sons of Israel will not keep this rule, neither will they circumcise their sons in accordance with this law; for, though circumcised themselves, they will neglect the circumcision of their sons, and the miscreants ("sons of Beliar"), all of them, will leave their sons uncircumcised, just as they were

born." See Sparks, *Apocryphal Old Testament,* 56. In this rendering the author of Jubilees is attacking not two groups but one.

67. 1 Maccabees 1:11–15.

68. B. Yevamot 71b. On *peri'ah,* see S. Cohen, *Beginnings of Jewishness,* 225 n. 66, and "Bernard Gui," 307–11.

69. Hall, "Epispasm"; Rubin, "Stretching the Foreskin"; Rubin, *Beginning of Life,* 100–2. The idea that *peri'ah* was instituted in the Hellenistic or Roman period in order to counter epispasm has a long history. See J. Bergson, cited by M. Steinschneider apud Glasberg, *Beschneidung,* 152–53 n. 1 and 263; Reggio apud Preuss, *Biblisch-talmudische Medezin,* 281; Kohler, "Circumcision," 93. *Peri'ah* may be either a rabbinic invention or a pre-rabbinic procedure that the rabbis endorsed and made normative. Muslim circumcision apparently does not include *peri'ah:* Steinschneider apud Glasberg, *Beschneidung,* 256 and 263. The difficulty of epispasm after a rabbinic circumcision is well illustrated in a memorable scene of the movie *Europa, Europa.*

70. B. Shabbat 133b. Preuss does not cite any non-rabbinic evidence for the healing power of suctioning, nor can I find anything relevant in Majno, *Healing Hand.*

71. B. Shabbat 110b. Preuss does not cite any non-rabbinic evidence for the medical use of cumin, nor can I find anything relevant in Majno, *Healing Hand.*

72. "'Dragon's blood' is dark or blood-red gum of a species of palm . . . which was commonly applied by Jews to heal the wound of circumcision." Trachtenberg, *Devil and the Jews,* 151 n. 34.

73. M. Shabbat 19.3.

74. Jubilees 15; Philo: see below, chapter 2; Josephus, *Jewish Antiquities* 1.214.

75. In some versions: R. Yosi the Galilean.

76. R. Yom Tov Lipmann Heller (1579–1654), author of the *Tosafot Yom Tov,* understands the Mishnah as follows: "Great is circumcision, for Moses the righteous, on account of [the delay of only] one full hour, was not given a reprieve [from punishment] on its account." The Mishnah is alluding, of course, to the story in Exodus 4.

77. Some versions have "Rabbi Meir."

78. M. Nedarim 3.11.

79. T. Nedarim 2.5–7 105 (and parallels). These statements have been interpolated into some versions of the Mishnah from the Tosefta; see Lieberman TK Nedarim 425.

80. Dwelling in the land of Israel (T. Avodah Zarah 4.3 466Z; Sifrei Deuteronomy 80 146F), observance of the Sabbath (Y. Berakhot 1.5 3c and parallels), and wearing *tzitzit* (Sifrei Numbers 115 126H; B. Menahot 43) are also said to equal all the (other) commandments of the Torah. Jeremiah 33:25, *but for my covenant . . . I would not have appointed the ordinances of Heaven and earth,* which is applied to circumcision in the Tosefta, is elsewhere applied to the Torah (B. Pesahim 68b) and the *ma'amadot,* the stations of lay Israelites who read the Torah at the times of the sacrifices (B. Megillah 31b). I am puzzled by Mekhilta Pisha 18 1.165L, 72H–R, which explicitly declares that circumcision does *not* equal the sum of all the other commandments.

81. See Bavli and Yerushalmi on M. Shabbat 19 and M. Nedarim 3.11.

82. Romans 4:3, citing Genesis 15:6.

83. For the anti-Christian character of Rabbi's statement, see the note in the Soncino translation of the Talmud; see also Urbach, *Sages*, 296.

84. Schäfer, "Bar Kokhba Revolt and Circumcision." By "hellenizers" I mean of course "radical hellenizers"; surely the Hasmoneans and the rabbinic sages were "hellenized" too.

85. The exception, of course, is the Septuagint of Exodus 4.

86. The Mishnah on circumcision: M. Shabbat 19 (see above) and M. Nedarim 3:11. The benediction at the circumcision ceremony: T. Berakhot 6:13 37 (and parallels; see note 34 above). Paeans of praise: see above. Discussions of Exodus 4: Y. Nedarim 3.14 38b, B. Nedarim 31b-32a. The only possible exception is T. Nedarim 2.6 105, cited above, which asserts "Great is circumcision, for it equals in value all the [other] commandments of the Torah," and cites as proof the verse *This is the blood of the covenant which the Lord [now makes with you concerning all these commands]* (Exodus 24:8). I do not think that this passage necessarily implies a theology of "the blood of the covenant." The sages may have simply understood the verse as follows: the covenant between the Lord and Israel that involves blood—in other words, the covenant of circumcision—concerns all the commandments, that is, is equivalent to all the other commandments. In a forthcoming study of the exegesis of Exodus 24:8, David Biale, following Hoffman, sees a theology of circumcision blood in this exegesis, but I am not convinced.

87. This crucial point is obscured by Hoffman; see my "Brief History."

88. Herr, "Pirkei de-Rabbi Eliezer." I cite the English translation of Friedlander, *Pirke de Rabbi Eliezer.*

89. PdRE 29, Friedlander trans., 210, Luria ed., 65a.

90. PdRE is followed here by Targum Jonathan on Exodus 12:13. The verb *pasahti* (Exodus 12:13), usually translated "I shall pass over," was taken by PdRE, as well as Targum Onkelos here, Targum Jonathan here, and Targum Jonathan on Ezekiel 16:6, to mean "I shall spare," or "I shall pity." See also Rashi on Exodus 12:13.

91. Propp, *Exodus*, 238–39.

92. Onkelos, Neofiti, Jonathan, and the Fragmentary Targums are almost identical on this verse. See Drazin, *Targum Onkelos to Exodus*, 73 nn. 31 and 32, and McNamara, *Aramaic Bible . . . Exodus*, 24–25 and 172–73 with accompanying notes.

93. I assume here, following Shinan, "Relationship," that Targum Jonathan is dependent on PdRE. Circumcision blood also is prominent in the Midrash Tanhuma, another text of this same period; see my "Brief History."

94. Zohar 3.14a in Tishby, *Wisdom of the Zohar*, 3:1180–81.

95. On circumcision as sacrifice: Rubin, *Beginning of Life*, 102–3 and 116; Goldin, "Role of Ceremonies," 167–71; Wolfson, *Circle in the Square*, 33 n. 26.

96. PdRE 10, Friedlander trans., 72, Luria ed., 26b.

97. PdRE 29, Friedlander trans., 204, Luria ed., 64a. Another passage reflecting the idea that circumcision is sacrifice: PdRE 29, Friedlander trans., 207–8, Luria ed., 65a–b.

98. Genesis Rabbah 47.7 475; 48.4 480; 63.13 698.

99. M. Ta'anit 4.1

100. Tur Yoreh De'ah 265, near the end, citing R. Isaac b. Abba Mari of Marseille (ca. 1120–90).

101. Krohn, *Bris Milah*, 114–16

102. PdRE 29, Friedlander trans., 212, Luria ed., 66a; Targum Jonathan on Numbers 23:10, in Clarke, *The Aramaic Bible . . . Numbers*, 256. Targum Jonathan may again be dependent on PdRE.

103. Lewin, *Otzar HaGeonim Shabbat*, sec. 380–84, pp. 122–24; Hoffman, *Covenant of Blood*, 103–5; Rubin, *Beginning of Life*, 104–6; Weisberg, *Otzar HaBerit*, 1:152–53; 2:294–97.

104. Hamburger, *Wormser Minhagbuch*, 2:72, and nn. 93 and 97. Jewish museums around the world display cups whose inscriptions attest that they were intended for this purpose.

105. Yaakov ha Gozer in Glassberg, *Zichron berit*, 61, discussed by Gross, "Blood Libel."

106. Hamburger, *Wormser Minhagbuch*, 2:72, with note 104.

107. Weber, *Mappot*; Hamburger, *Shorshei Minhag Ashkenaz*, 2:322–604.

108. *Sefer Zekher David*, by David Zakut Modena of Modena (printed Livorno 1837, by Eliezer Menahem Ottolenghi; preface dated 1805), part 1, chap. 70, p. 187a

109. Taz-Magen David on Shulhan Arukh Orah Hayyim 584.4.

110. Wertheimer, *Abudraham HaShalem*, 350, quoted by R. Moshe Isserles on Shulhan Arukh Yoreh De'ah 265.1. These divergent customs and their history await investigation. The Mahzor Vitry, 626, says that a circumciser should wash his hands before making the benedictions, but the text does not specify washing the mouth too.

111. See Frojmovic, "Christian Travelers," 133 (234) n. 9, citing the *Sod HaShem* of David Lida (1680). According to David Zakut Modena, *Sefer Zekher David*, 1.65 (see note 108 above), in the name of R. Jonah the Physician, experienced circumcisers ask to be buried with the foreskins that they have accumulated, because the foreskins are an "amulet" *(segulah)* that keep away dangerous spirits in the afterworld. Furthermore, "it is a sign of good fortune for a circumciser if the number of children that he has circumcised equals the numerical value of his name." Perhaps this is the mysterious number to which Montaigne alludes. (I regret that I do not have access to *Sefer Zekher David* when writing this note and so cannot verify this citation; I am relying on Greenwald, *Zokher haBerit* 59a para. 3.)

112. B. Shabbat 137b and parallels; see above note 48.

113. PdRE 48, Friedlander trans., 378, Lurie ed. 114b According to this source, Moses's "real" name was Yekutiel.

114. The *siddurim* of R. Amram and R. Saadiah Gaon; see discussion in Rubin, *Beginning of Life*, 111–12.

115. R. Yaakov haGozer (ca. 1230), *Kelalei haMilah*, in Glassberg, *Zichron Berit*, 88.

116. Lewin, *Otzar HaGeonim Berakhot*, pp. 119–20, nos. 336–38, and *Otzar HaGeonim Eruvin*, pp. 30–32, nos. 83–87; responsa 57 of R. Natronai

Gaon, in Brody ed., 1:164. Discussion in Zimmels, *Magicians,* 163 n 151; Sperber, *Customs of Israel,* 60–66; Ta-Shema, *Franco-German Ritual,* 327–35; Rubin, *Beginning of Life,* 108 n. 191. The dates given in parentheses for the *geonim* are the dates of their ascension to the leadership of the academy, as established by Brody, *Geonim,* 344–45. R. Yaakov HaGozer cites the *Maaseh Ha-Geonim,* "The Legal Precedents of the Geonim," as his source; I cannot find this citation in the extant text as edited by Epstein-Freimann (there is something similar on p. 60; see Sperber, *Custom,* 62 n. 5), nor can I find any other reference to R. Sherira in this connection. Hoffman, *Covenant of Blood,* 84–87, argues that a cup of wine was present, untouched and unblessed, in the circumcision ceremony of the talmudic period; this is fantasy, perhaps nonsense.

117. Wedding benedictions: B. Ketuvot 7b–8a. For another connection between circumcision and wedding ceremonies, see note 20 above. In the geonic period wine was introduced also to the ceremony of the redemption of the firstborn: Lewin, *Otzar HaGeonim Pesahim,* no. 362, p. 131, discussed by Ta-Shema, *Franco-German Ritual,* 340ff. For a survey of the use of wine in Jewish ceremonial, see Ginzberg, *Responsa,* 111–16.

118. Wine gladdens the heart: Psalms 104:15. Wine in the sacrificial cult: Leviticus 23:13; Numbers 15:1–12; Numbers 28–29.

119. M. Berakhot 8:1 with the Talmudim ad loc.; M. Pesahim 10; B. Pesahim 106a.

120. In other words, at this stage of development the cup of wine is not an iconic representation of blood and has nothing to do with blood, pace Hoffman.

121. In particular the *geonim* and their medieval continuators debated who, if anyone, was to drink the cup of wine if a circumcision was celebrated on a fast day. One text that is part of this discussion is mistranslated and misconstrued by Hoffman, *Covenant of Blood,* 86–87. Discussion in Sperber, *Customs of Israel,* 60–66 (followed by Goldberg, *Jewish Passages,* 45–47), and Grossman, *Pious and Rebellious,* 322–23.

122. As far as I have been able to determine, the earliest source to state explicitly that the infant receives wine during the recitation of Ezekiel 16:6 is the *Mahzor Vitry,* ed. Horovitz, 626–27. (The core of the *Mahzor Vitry* ascends to the early twelfth century, but the text was much expanded and interpolated in its transmission.) Another early attestation is the *Sefer HaManhig* of R. Abraham b. Nathan of Lunel (ca. 1200), ed. Raphael, 2:580. The juxtaposition of wine and Ezekiel 16:6 did not become universal immediately; thus, for example, in the *Shibboley HaLeqet* (187a) of R. Tzidqiyah b. Avraham ha Rofe, written in Rome ca. 1240, the baby is given a few drops to drink, and the prayer for the baby's welfare is recited, but there is no mention whatever of Ezekiel 16:6. The introduction of Ezekiel 16:6 at last provides Hoffman some support for his thesis that the cup of wine is an iconic representation of the blood of the infant; see Hoffman, *Covenant of Blood,* 91. Where Hoffman errs is the dating; the cup of wine becomes an icon for circumcision blood only in Europe in the high Middle Ages, not before.

123. Responsum of R. Kohen Tzedeq in Lewin, *Otzar HaGeonim Shabbat,* no. 383, p. 123. (Brody, *Geonim,* 344–45, lists two *geonim* named Kohen

Tzedeq, one of whom is to be dated to 841 and the other to 926.) The gaon is actually responding to two questions, the first about the disposition of the blood in sand (earth) or water (see note 103 above), and the second about bringing the baby to the synagogue for circumcision. The extant responsum deals only with the former question. It is possible, therefore, that the response "it doesn't matter and there is no prohibition one way or another that would impel us to order you to change your customs" applies only to the matter of sand vs. water, and that the *gaon* completely ignores the question about the synagogue.

124. Rubin, *Beginning of Life*, 100–101; Zimmels, *Magicians*, 161 n. 127; Weisberg, *Otzar HaBerit*, 1:115 and 2:270–71; Goldberg, *Jewish Passages*, 43–44. Synagogal circumcision is probably to be connected also with the custom of pouring circumcision blood in the earth; the only place that has earth sacred enough for such an act would be the synagogue.

125. At the door of the synagogue: Spitzer, *Sefer Maharil*, 486 n. 3; Hamburger, *Wormser Minhagbuch*, 2:64 nn. 7–8. In front of the ark: Goldin, "Ceremonies," 166–67 and 171.

126. Bonfil, *Jewish Life*, 250, assumes that up until the sixteenth century circumcision in the synagogue would have been the norm, and that a changed perception of the sanctity of the synagogue led to the transference of the circumcision ritual from the synagogue to the home. I prefer to assume that circumcision in the home had always been the norm in many communities, and that the move to the synagogue was the innovation.

127. Preference for a minyan: PdRE 18 (19), Friedlander trans., 127, Luria ed., 44b, and Lewin, *Otzar HaGeonim Shabbat*, no. 418, p. 137, citing R. Tzemah b. Paltoi (ca. 872). Discussion in Rubin, *Beginning of Life*, 97–98; Weisberg, *Otzar HaBerit*, 1:122 and 2:271–72. The presence of a prayer quorum is not a requirement; if a quorum cannot be assembled, the circumcision is performed nonetheless.

128. The fullest and best discussion of the *sandaq/ba'al berit* is now Baumgarten, "Circumcision and Baptism." German-speaking Jews used the term *Kevater* or *Gevatter*, "godfather," for the man, and *Kevaterin*, "godfatheress," for the woman.

129. *Sefer Maharil Minhagim: Hilkhot Milah* 1, in Spitzer *Sefer Maharil*, 476. The vocalization *sandiq* (instead of the common *sandaq*) is implied by the *yud* between the *dalet* and *qof*.

130. The equation of circumcision with incense was, no doubt, suggested to the Maharil by texts such as Genesis Rabbah 47.7 475 (cited below, note 136); Tanhuma nidpas Vayera 2, Tanhuma-Buber Vayera 4 (1.42b), followed by Aggadat Bereishit 19; and Numbers Rabbah 14:12 62c, ed. Vilna.

131. PdRE 29 end, Friedlander trans., 213–14 (slightly modified), Luria ed., 66b. This passage of the PdRE is cited with approval in a responsum attributed to R. Sherira Gaon (968) in Lewin, *Otzar HaGeonim Shabbat*, no. 424, p. 139.

132. Lewin, *Otzar HaGeonim Shabbat*, no. 425, p. 139; Rubin, *Beginning of Life*, 95–96; Goldberg, *Jewish Passages*, 41–43.

133. See Rubin, *Beginning of Life*, 114–17.

134. PdRE 29, Friedlander trans. 207–8 (slightly modified), Luria ed., 65a–b.

135. Lewin, *Otzar HaGeonim Shabbat*, 123, no. 383; see above note 103. On fragrant herbs at a circumcision ceremony, see Weisberg, *Otzar HaBerit*, 1:154, and Shamash, "What Is the Source of the Custom?"

136. R. Tzidqiyah b. Avraham haRofe, *Shibboley HaLeqet*, 188a, ed. Buber. He credits his brother with the explanation that the custom has its origins in Genesis Rabbah 47.7 475: "R. Aibu said: When Abraham circumcised those that were born in his house, he set up a hillock of foreskins; the sun shone upon them and they putrefied, and their odor ascended before the Holy one, blessed be He, like sweet incense and like an *olah*, which is whole burnt by fire."

137. On myrtle and herbs at a wedding ceremony see, e.g., Maimonides, *Hilkhot Ishut* 10.5, cited by Shamash, "What Is the Source of the Custom?" On myrtle as protection against demons, see Lauterbach, "Origin and Development," 392–401. *Ashkenazic* Jews, that is, descendants of the Jews of northern and eastern Europe, do not have the custom of sniffing fragrant herbs at either a wedding or a circumcision, but many *Sephardim* do; see *Shulhan Arukh, Yoreh De'ah* 265.1.

138. See above, note 35.

139. Lewin, *Otzar HaGeonim Shabbat*, no. 420, p. 138; a slightly different formulation in no. 419, p. 137. For discussion, see Ginzberg, *Legends of the Jews*, 6:341 n. 118; Zimmels, *Magicians*, 161 n 123; Lieberman, "Some Aspects of After Life," 525–27; Wolfson, "Circumcision and the Divine Name," 79 n. 5.

140. For this interpretation, see the *Perishah* on Tur Yoreh De'ah, 353 n. 10. A slight emendation would yield "his father will have knowledge of that child and will recognize him" (reading *umavkhin leh avuha* instead of *umavkhin leh le-avuha*), which would seem to make much better sense. But the transmitted text is supported by several sources cited by Lewin, *Otzar HaGeonim Shabbat*, 138 n. 1.

141. *Teshuvot Rashi*, no. 40, ed. Elfenbein; the source is R. Isaac b. Moses of Vienna (ca. 1180–1250), *Or Zarua* 2.26c–d sec. 104. A shortened version of the responsum appears in R. Jacob HaGozer, *Kelalei HaMilah*, in Glassberg, *Zikhron Berit Larishonim*, 126–28. Among the respondents is R. Natan b. Yehiel of Rome, author of the *Arukh*.

142. The source is R. Isaac b. Moses of Vienna (see previous note); his teacher is R. Simha b. Samuel of Speyer, on whom see Urbach, *Tosaphists*, 411–20.

143. A Karaite source claims that post-mortem circumcision was done by the midwife; see Lewin, *Otzar HaGeonim Shabbat*, 138 n. 3, and Lieberman, "Some Aspects of After Life," 526 n. 94.

144. Ibn Ezra on Genesis 17:14 in *Mikra'ot Gedolot Haketer*, ed. Menahem Cohen, 154.

145. Lasker, "Original Sin," 130 n. 21, even suggests that post-mortem circumcision is based on the concept of original sin. Perhaps. Two medieval versions of R. Nahshon's responsum have the gaon say that the dead baby is circumcised "in order that he should not come to the other world without the seal" (Lieberman, "Some Aspects of After Life," 525 nn. 90–91 and 526 n. 97; Wolfson, "Circumcision and the Divine Name," 79 n. 5). "Seal," of course, was a common Christian term for baptism, but I am not sure whether the Hebrew

word "seal" necessarily implies a sacramental understanding of circumcision akin to baptism; Lieberman assumes that it does.

146. Hill and Stasiak, "Limbo."

147. *Tur* and *Shulhan Arukh, Yoreh De'ah* 263. Maimonides does not mention it.

148. Tanner, *Decrees*, 1:540–42. The key part of the text is: "hec [sacramenta] vero nostra et continent gratiam et ipsam digne suscipientibus conferunt ... inter hec sacramenta tria sunt, baptismus, confirmatio et ordo, que characterem, id est spirituale quoddam signum a ceteris distinctivum, imprimunt in anima indelebile." The editors note that these definitions derive from Thomas Aquinas. Aquinas explains "grace" and "character" in his *Summa Theologiae* 3a.62 and 63.

149. Boyarin, *Radical Jew*, 126–30, flirts with the idea that a zoharic theology of circumcision may have been current already in the time of Paul. Similarly, Smith, *Clement*, 181–83, thinks that the understanding of circumcision as a "mystery" may date back to the first or second century CE. The Tanhuma calls circumcision a "mystery," but what that might mean I do not know; see Tanhuma (nidpas) Lekh Lekha 19; Tanhuma Lekh Lekha 23, ed. Buber.

150. Wolfson, *Circle in the Square* 33.

151. Wolfson, *Circle in the Square* 38.

152. Wolfson, "Circumcision and the Divine Name."

153. Wolfson, *Circle in the Square*, 44.

154. Whether the Zohar in this matter has been influenced by Christianity, I leave for others to determine. Christian influence is more apparent in R. Hasdai Crescas (ca. 1340–ca. 1410), who believes that circumcision is the remedy to "original sin." Lasker is not sure whether Crescas has been influenced by Christianity on this point, but I do not see how this explanation can be denied; see Lasker "Original Sin," and *Refutation*, 32 with n. 28, and 100 n. 5. George Barton apud Gray, "Circumcision," 680, writes, "Jewish writers contend that it [circumcision] is not a sacrament, in the sense in which Baptism and Communion are sacraments to the Christian. But it is clear that, although no mystic character is attached to it, and no doctrine of a mysterious change in the nature of the recipient is built upon it, it does hold, when viewed as a distinctly Jewish rite of fundamental importance to the Jewish faith, much the same place outwardly that the sacraments have held in Christianity." Both Barton and his unidentified Jewish interlocutors were correct. In the halakhic tradition circumcision (of the native born) is not a sacrament and is not like baptism; in the mystical tradition (unbeknownst to Barton), and to some degree in the "popular" religion as well (witness post-mortem circumcision), circumcision certainly does resemble baptism and can be construed as a sacrament.

155. Cahana, *Maharam*, 2:149, no. 155. Discussion in Hoffman, *Covenant of Blood*, 196–207; Grossman, *Pious and Rebellious*, 321–22; Baumgarten, "Circumcision and Baptism," 119–22.

156. Baumgarten, "Circumcision and Baptism," 120 (233) n. 33, against Hoffman.

157. Cahana, *Maharam* 2:149, no. 156.

158. Cahana, *Maharam* 2:262, no. 211 = Maharil, *Hilkhot Milah*, 1, in Spitzer ed., *Sefer Maharil*, 476

159. See below, chapter 4, note 7.

160. *Davar shebiqedushah*. Source of phrase: B. Megillah 23b and elsewhere.

161. The term is *arelah*; see Eliezer Ben-Yehuda, *Dictionary*, 9:4734.

CHAPTER 2: WERE JEWISH WOMEN EVER CIRCUMCISED?

The source of the epigraph is Schalom Ben-Chorin, in *Geschichte-Tradition-Reflexion: Festschrift für Martin Hengel I: Judentum* (Tübingen: Mohr Siebeck, 1996), 568: "Das antike Hebräertum war eine sakramentale Männergemeinschaft, gekennzeichnet durch die Beschneidung des männlichen Gliedes. . . . Es gibt kein vergleichsweises Sakrament für die neugeborenen Mädchen, was auf den patriarchalischen Grundcharakter des Judentums hinweist."

1. The fullest survey of contemporary practice (and sharpest polemic against it) is Hosken, *Hosken Report*. From the abundant bibliography, the following may be mentioned: *Encyclopaedia of Islam*, 4:913–14, s.v. *khafd*; Hicks, *Infibulation*; Lightfoot-Klein, *Prisoners of Ritual*; Walker and Parmar, *Warrior Marks*; Toubia, *Female Genital Mutilation*; Cloudsley, *Women of Omdurman*; Talle, "Transforming Women." I do not know of any reliable historical study of the subject. Hosken's historical introduction is filled with numerous inaccurate statements; she relies completely on secondary and tertiary sources, and, as she herself realizes, such sources are simply not reliable.

2. Kenyatta, *Facing Mount Kenya*, 130–54; see discussion in Murray-Brown, *Kenyatta*, 155–71, 222–23, and 388–89. Similar to Kenyatta and just as disingenuous is Bouhdiba, *Sexuality in Islam*, 176: "Excision of girls must not be confused with clitoridectomy. The former is tolerated [the removal of the semi-prepuce, which covers the upper part of the clitoris], the latter strictly prohibited." On p. 184 Bouhdiba confesses that excision, "despite the canonical regulations is very often simply a clitoridectomy."

3. Talle, "Transforming Women," 99–103.

4. In his discussion of female circumcision, Bryk, *Circumcision in Man and Woman*, 275, lists eight different possible procedures. Some of these procedures are better designated "excision" rather than "circumcision."

5. Rowlandson, *Women and Society*, 99–100, no. 78. Knight, "Curing Cut," 330–31, discusses a text of the Middle Kingdom that may mention the circumcision of women, but the translation is uncertain.

6. That female circumcision is a relatively late importation into Egypt is suggested by Montserrat, "*Mallocouria*," 47–48. Montserrat, *Sex and Society*, 45, writes that "it seems improbable that female genital mutilation . . . was widespread in Graeco-Roman Egypt."

7. Brooten, *Love between Women*, 162–71; Knight, "Curing Cut," 322–28. On clitoridectomy as a standard medical procedure in nineteenth-century Europe and America, see Laqueur, " 'Amor Veneris'," 113ff ("The Clitoris as a Social Problem"); the chapter on clitoridectomy in Wallerstein, *Circumcision:*

An American Health Fallacy, and Gollaher, *Circumcision: A History of the World's Most Controversial Surgery,* 187–207.

8. Berkey, "Circumcision Circumscribed," esp. 22–27.

9. Hosken, *Hosken Report,* 6, "Infibulation (Pharaonic circumcision) . . . today is performed only by Moslems." *Encyclopaedia of Islam,* 4:913–14, s.v. *khafd.*

10. Berkey, "Circumcision Circumscribed," 20.

11. Berkey, "Circumcision Circumscribed," 30. On Islamic circumcision in general, see *Encyclopedia of Islam,* s.v. *khafd* and *khitan;* Kister, "Circumcision in Hadith."

12. For example, Bouhdiba, *Sexuality,* 182; Crapanzano, "Rite of Return," 25; Kennedy, "Circumcision and Excision," esp. 177–82. See above, chapter 1 at note 21.

13. Kennedy, "Circumcision and Excision," 185.

14. Or, in the formulation of Kennedy, "Circumcision and Excision," 186–87, the male ritual emphasizes ego-enhancement, while the female ritual emphasizes punishment and social control. See also Kister, "Circumcision in Hadith," 23. Critics of female circumcision see the practice primarily as a vehicle for the subjugation and subordination of women; see, for example, Hosken, *Hosken Report,* passim.

15. Glassberg, *Zichron,* part 3, 203, suggests that the text is a tacit polemic against female circumcision, but this is unlikely.

16. B. Yevamot 46a and 71a; compare also B. Bava Qamma 88a with the Tosfaot s.v. *sheken eynah bemilah.*

17. Goitein, *Mediterranean Society,* 3: *The Family,* 233: "Female circumcision, practiced among Copts, is unknown in Judaism." On Richard Burton's view of the matter, see the appendix to this chapter.

18. Strabo 17.2.5, p. 824 (M. Stern, *Greek and Latin Authors,* no. 124).

19. Strabo 16.2.37, p. 761 (M. Stern, *Greek and Latin Authors,* no. 115).

20. Strabo 16.4.9, p. 771 (M. Stern, *Greek and Latin Authors,* no. 118).

21. Strabo 16.4.17, p. 776.

22. Contrast Diodorus of Sicily 3.32.4 (cited by Jones in the Loeb edition of Strabo at 16.4.10), who clearly implies that more skin is removed from one who is *kolobos* than from one who is merely circumcised (the opposite of Strabo): *Koloboi* "have all the part that is merely circumcised by the others cut off with razors in infancy."

23. It is likely that the "Jewishness" of the Beta Israel is a function of political and religious strife in Ethiopia from the fourteenth to the sixteenth century; see Kaplan, *Beta Israel,* esp. 53–78.

24. Ullendorff, *Ethiopia,* 108. Female excision by the Beta Israel is also mentioned by Leslau, *Falasha Anthology,* xvii.

25. Schäfer, *Judeophobia,* 248 n. 15, is puzzled by Strabo. Lieu, "Circumcision, Women, and Salvation," 360, and Schiffman, *Who Was a Jew?* 84 n. 35, simply dismiss Strabo as erroneous, a judgment that was already reached by Cornelius à Lapide (1567–1637), *Commentaria in Pentateuchum,* 171. Montserrat, *Sex and Society,* 42, observes that Strabo is also mistaken about universal childrearing and male circumcision in Egypt.

26. In addition to the passage cited above, see Strabo apud Josephus, *Jewish Antiquities* 14.118 (M. Stern, *Greek and Latin Authors*, no. 105).

27. Philo, *On the Special Laws* 1.1–11, as translated by Colson in the Loeb Classical Library (vol. 7, pp. 101–7). For discussion, see Collins, "Symbol of Otherness," 171–76; Hecht, "Exegetical Contexts"; Barclay, "Paul and Philo," 538–43; Niehoff, "Circumcision as a Marker of Identity."

28. "Purity" is a more likely translation than "cleanliness;" see above, chapter 1, note 39.

29. Philo explicitly uses the metaphor of Deuteronomy 10:16 in *On the Special Laws* 1:304–6. For this motif in Philo, see Le Déaut, "Le thème de la circoncision du coeur, 187–89.

30. Barclay, "Paul and Philo," 539, understands Philo's argument here as metaphorical; Goodenough, *Introduction to Philo Judaeus*, 156, understands it as physical.

31. Philo, *Questions and Answers on Genesis* 3.46–52, trans. Ralph Marcus in the Loeb edition, supp. vol. 1, 240–54.

32. Philo, *Questions and Answers on Genesis* 3.47, trans. Ralph Marcus in the Loeb edition, supp. vol. 1, 241–42.

33. On the comparison and contrast with Egyptian practice, see Hecht, "Exegetical Contexts," 77–78.

34. Philo follows the common Greek view that menstrual fluid is the stuff out of which the fetus is created; see Marcus's note "c" on p. 242. On this view, see Dean-Jones, *Women's Bodies*, 200–209.

35. Sly, *Philo's Perception of Women*.

36. The only Philonic passage that associates circumcision with the election of Israel is *Questions on Genesis* 3.49, trans. Marcus, 249; this association is not typical of Philo's thought. See Hecht, "Exegetical Contexts," 63 and 67–68; Birnbaum, *Place of Judaism*, 125–26, 155–56, and 158; Niehoff, "Circumcision as a Marker of Identity," 95 and 101. In *Questions on Exodus* 2.2, Philo says that the "proselyte" is the one "who circumcises not his uncircumcision but his desires and sensual pleasures" (trans. Marcus); the intent of this remark is not clear and is widely debated. See Birnbaum, *Place of Judaism*, 200; S. Cohen, *Beginnings of Jewishness*, 152 n. 41; Barclay, "Paul and Philo," 542–43 n. 9.

37. For a good survey of the subject, see Collins, "Symbol of Otherness."

38. Josephus, *Jewish Antiquities* 1.192.

39. Hall, "Epispasm."

40. Philo, *On the Migration of Abraham* 92.

41. Niehoff, "Circumcision as a Marker of Identity, " 97 n. 28, is not convinced by this suggestion.

42. Richard Francis Burton, *The Book of the Thousand Nights and a Night* (Benares: printed by the Kamashastra Society for the Burton Club, 1885; frequently reprinted), 5:279.

43. For a full discussion of the work of R. Gershom, see Grossman, *Early Sages*, 106–74.

44. Richard F. Burton, *Personal Narrative of a Pilgrimage to Al-Madinah and Meccah*, ed. Isabel Burton, 2 vols. (London: Tylston and Edwards, 1893; repr. New York: Dover, 1964), 2:19–20 n. 2.

45. See, for example, Elizabeth Gould Davis, *The First Sex* (Baltimore: Penguin, 1972), 15, cited with approval by Hosken, *Hosken Report,* 77.

CHAPTER 3: CHRISTIAN QUESTIONS, CHRISTIAN RESPONSES

The source of the epigraph is John Milton, *Complete Poems and Major Prose,* ed. Merritt Hughes (Indianapolis: Bobbs-Merrill/Odyssey Press, 1957), 81.

1. For a good discussion of these passages, see, for example, Hall, "Circumcision," part C; Betz, "Beschneidung"; and Horn, "Der Verzicht auf die Beschneidung."

2. For a classic exposition of spiritual circumcision, see Origen, *Commentary on Romans* 2.12–13 (PG 14:898–913), and *Homilies on the Hexateuch: Homily 3 on Genesis: On the Circumcision of Abraham* (GCS 29:39–50 [*Origenes Werke,* 6]); discussion in Niehoff, "Circumcision as a Marker of Identity," 108–14.

3. On circumcision of the heart in Philo and Paul, see Barclay, "Paul and Philo," 542–55. On "spiritual circumcision" in the Septuagint, Qumran, and the Targumim, see Le Déaut, "Le thème de la circoncision du coeur."

4. See, for example, Justin Martyr, *Dialogue with Trypho* 19, in Falls-Halton, *Justin Martyr,* 31–32.

5. Romans 3:30, 4:9; Galatians 2:7. See Marcus, "Circumcision and the Uncircumcision." This usage may also be attested in Ignatius; see S. Cohen, "Judaism without Circumcision." This usage is also attested in M. Nedarim 3.11; see below, chapter 4, text following note 5.

6. Hunt, "*Colossians* 2:11–12."

7. In my interpretation of this much-discussed passage, I follow Martin, "Covenant of Circumcision." On the circumcision of the gentile slave, see Genesis 17:12–13.

8. This point is the centerpiece of Boyarin, *A Radical Jew.*

9. Cf. Ilan, *Jewish Women in Greco-Roman Palestine,* 165–66, n. 26; Setzer, "Excellent Women."

10. Martin, "Covenant of Circumcision," 121–22; this explanation is similar to that of Augustine (see below, chapter 5, note 100). The common scholarly view that "there is no male or female" was part of a fixed baptismal formula inherited by Paul, not invented by him; against this view, see Martin, "Covenant of Circumcision," 111–15.

11. See Lieu, "Circumcision, Women, and Salvation," 368–69, for a good critique of scholars who see Paul as a crusader for women's equality. See also Ilan, *Jewish Women in Greco-Roman Palestine,* 9–10.

12. Schreckenberg, *Christlichen Adversus-Judaeos-Texte.* For other surveys of Christian polemic against Judaism, see Williams, *Adversus Judaeos* (which itself is a specimen of anti-Jewish literature); Browe, *Die Judenmission im Mittelalter,* 99–110; Blumenkranz, *Les auteurs chrétiens latins;* Baron, *Social and Religious History of the Jews,* 9:288–29; Dahan, *Les intellectuals chrétiens* and *La polémique chrétienne.* On the polemic against circumcision, see Blumenkranz, *Judenpredigt Augustins,* 145–48. In the twelfth century (or perhaps the thirteenth) there was a major shift in the strategy and methods of anti-Jewish

polemic; see Funkenstein, "Changes in Christian Anti-Jewish Polemics"; J. Cohen, *The Friars and the Jews*, 21–32; Chazan, *Daggers of Faith*; and Lasker, "Jewish-Christian Polemics at the Turning Point."

13. About Christian literature in Syriac, Coptic, Armenian, Arabic, and other "ethnic" languages, I know even less than I do about Christian literature in Greek and Latin.

14. Justin Martyr, *Dialogue with Trypho* 23.4–5 (PG 6:528); I have slightly modified the translation of Falls, *Writings of Saint Justin Martyr*, 183 (= Falls-Halton, *Justin Martyr*, 38). Justin's arguments against circumcision appear chiefly in sections 16–24; see also 29, 41, and 46. For discussion, see Niehoff, "Circumcision as a Marker of Identity," 105–8. On Justin's debt to Paul, see Werline, "The Transformation of Pauline Arguments."

15. Justin Martyr, *Dialogue with Trypho* 16.2 (Falls-Halton, *Writings of Saint Justin Martyr*, 27).

16. For Justin's connections with Hellenistic Judaism and Philo, see Runia, *Philo in Early Christian Literature*, 97–105, and Niehoff, "Circumcision as a Marker of Identity," 105 n. 46. On the non-circumcision of women as a Jewish anti-circumcision argument combated by Philo, see above, chapter 2, note 41.

17. Lieu, "Circumcision, Women, and Salvation," 359, notes the absence of this argument from subsequent Christian thinking about the Law. Among the Greeks the argument first recurs (as far as I can determine) in the *Refutation of Jewish Error* by Gennadios II Scholarios, Patriarch of Constantinople (1464), a man who knew Latin and Latin theology (he translated Aquinas into Greek). See Petit, *Oeuvres complètes de Gennade Scholarios*, 3: *Oeuvres polémiques*, 274, ll. 31–32.

18. Cyprian *Ad Quirinum* 1.8 (CCSL 3,1:12). The Latin is "tunc quod illud signaculum feminis non proficit, signo autem Domini omnes signantur"; some testimonia read not *feminis* but *seminis*, which would yield: "That sign [that is, the sign of physical circumcision] is of no use to the seed [that is, the infant]." If this is the correct reading, I do not understand Cyprian's argument. I was first referred to this text by Lieu, "Circumcision, Women, and Salvation," 359 n. 5.

19. *Tractatus de Circumcisione* 1.3.1 (PL 11:345a–354b [CCSL 22:24]): "Solet enim magnis cum vociferationibus saepe jactare, hanc esse gentis suae nobilitatem, hanc coelestis sacramenti virtutem, hanc aeternae vitae legitimam genetricem, hanc perpetuam futuri regni consortem, sine qua nemo possit omnino ad Dei notitiam pervenire."

20. See above, chapter 1, at note 74 and following.

21. *Tractatus de Circumcisione* 1.3.2 (CCSL 22:24). "Circumcisio est, fratres, in damnum rotundi vulneris ferro circulata cicatrix." My translation is really a paraphrase. In his note in CCSL, Löfstedt compares Gregorius Iliberritanus, "circumcisionem esse circumductum ferro vulnus quo aliquid amputatur" (CCSL 69:27).

22. *Tractatus de Circumcisione* 1.3.9 (CCSL 22:26).

23. *Tractatus de Circumcisione* 1.3.21 and 23 (CCSL 22:29).

24. *Tractatus de Circumcisione* 1.3.19 (CCSL 22:28). On Mary's conception of Christ through her ear, see the helpful note of Bigelmair, *Zeno von Verona*, 165 n.1.

25. *Contra Iudeos, Collectio Veronensis* in CCSL 87:105 (ca. 400 CE; cf. CPPM 2:1261); Zacchaeus Christianus, in PL 20:1122b (fifth century); Isidore of Seville (ca. 560–636), *Liber de Variis Quaestionibus adversus Iudeos* 53.2–3, in Vega and Anspach, *Isidori . . . Liber de Variis Quaestionibus,* 159. That Christian women too can be circumcised by the true circumcision of Christianity is one of the points of the *De Vera Circumcisione,* attributed to Jerome but written by Eutropius Presbyter (fl. ca. 400); see PL 30:194–217 (in some printings 188–210), with the bibliographical note in CPL 197, no. 566.

26. *De Altercatione Ecclesiae et Synagogae: Dialogus,* in PL 42:1131–40. On this text, see Juster, *Les juifs dans l'empire romain,* 1:73–74; Williams, *Adversus Judaeos,* 321–38; Blumenkranz, *Les auteurs chrétiens ,* 39–42; Schreckenberg, *Adversus Judaeos Texte,* 1:354; Krauss-Horbury, *Jewish-Christian Controversy,* 49–50; CPL 201, no. 577; and CPPM 88–90, no. 163.

27. For artistic depictions of *Synagoga* and *Ecclesia,* see Schreckenberg, *Jews in Christian Art,* 31–74.

28. PL 42:1134; Williams, *Adversus Judaeos,* 329.

29. Justin Martyr, *Dialogue with Trypho* 24.1.

30. Brooten, *Women Leaders in the Ancient Synagogue,* 57–72.

31. The same argument appears in Zeno of Verona, *Tractatus* 1.3.8 (CCSL 22:25).

32. Learned clerics: Abulafia, *Christians and Jews in the Twelfth-Century Renaissance,* 124–26 (citing Abelard, Guibert of Nogent, Peter Alphonsi, and Rupert of Deutz; I shall return to Abelard below). Mystics: Hildegard of Bingen, *Scivias* 2.3.29 (PL 197:464 [CCCM 43:152]), "I have given the circumcision of one member to the males of the nation of Abraham, but in my Son I have imposed the circumcision of all members on the men and women of all peoples." On Hildegard, see further below, note 66. Merchants: Limor, "Missionary Merchants."

33. Gutwirth, "Gender, History, and the Judeo-Christian Polemic."

34. Apparently based on a Christian reading of Psalms 51:9.

35. Limor, *Disputation zu Ceuta* 137–138. The crucial line runs "scis quia mulieres non circumdebantur, et ideo necesse erat ut aliquit commune historialiter esset et appareret, unde utriusque sexus humanum genus salvari posset." The same argument, in almost the same words, appears in the disputation of Mallorca in 1286 (Limor, *Disputation* 186).

36. Petrus Alphonsi, *Dialogue,* in PL 157:658c–d, written between 1106 (the date of his conversion to Christianity) and 1110.

37. In the following pages I do not pretend to give a complete survey of Christian views of biblical and Jewish circumcision, a work remaining to be written. A large body of evidence that I have completely ignored and that also awaits full documentation is the corpus, both written and artistic, of Christian reflections on the circumcision of Jesus (see fig. 2). On the artistic representations of this circumcision, see Schreckenberg, *Jews in Christian Art,* 144–46; Steinberg, *Sexuality of Christ,* 49–64 and passim; and Blumenkranz, *Le juif médiéval au miroir de l'art chrétien,* 81–82, figs. 87–88.

38. The two classic second-century defenses of Christian "orthodoxy" are

Irenaeus, *Against the Heretics,* and Tertullian, *Against Marcion;* each of them defends circumcision as having been commanded by God. See Irenaeus 3.9–12 (PG 7:868–910), especially 3.11.11 (PG 7:905), and 5.22 (PG 7:1182–84); and Tertullian, *Against Marcion* 5.4 (CCSL 1:671–75), especially 5.4.11 (CCSL 1:674), "circumcisio et praeputiatio uni deo deputabantur." For a beautiful Christian defense of circumcision, heavily indebted to Origen, see Ambrose, epistle 72 (PL 16:1243–51 [epistle 69, CSEL 82:178–92]). Willet, *Hexapla,* 193–95, written in the early seventeenth century, is still well within this patristic framework.

39. The following citations are illustrative, not exhaustive. A sign: Irenaeus, *Against the Heresies* 4.16 (PG 7:1015); Origen, *Commentary on* Romans 2.12–13 (PG 14:898–913); Aphrahat in Neusner, *Aphrahat,* 22 and 24; John of Damascus, *Exposition of Faith* (= *On the Orthodox Faith*) 4.25 (PG 94:1212–16). To separate the Israelites from wicked pagans: Irenaeus 3.11.11 (PG 7:905); Theodoret, *Questions on Genesis* 69 (PG 80:177, where it is *quaestio* 68) and *Questions on Joshua* 3 (PG 80:465–68); *Dialogue between Athanasius and Zacchaeus* 125 (Conybeare ed., 61–62); pseudo Gregory of Nyssa, *Testimonies against the Jews* (PG 46:220A); Gennadios II Scholarios, in Petit, *Oeuvres complètes,* 3: *Oeuvres polémiques,* 275. To inhibit intermarriage: John Chrysostom, *Homilies on Genesis* 39.4 (PG 53:366); Peter Abelard, *Dialogue,* trans. Payer, 47 (PL 178:1623d). To provide Abraham's children with a sign: Eusebius. *Preparation for the Gospel* 7.8.24 309d–310a (GCS 43, 1:374); cf. *Demonstration of the Gospel* 1.6.5 and 1.6.11 (PG 22:49–53). To make it easier for Jesus to prove that he was a Jew: Theophylactus, *Exposition of* Acts (PG 125:609 and 908); Peter Alphonsi, *Dialogue* (PL 157:658d). To facilitate the recognition of Israelite corpses: Millás Vallicrosa, "Tratado anónimo," 14–15. (This tract is of the early thirteenth century; see Schreckenberg, *Christlichen Adversus-Judaeos-Texte* , 3:54). Following a suggestion of Millás Vallicrosa, 6, Baron suggests that this explanation derives from a lost Jewish Midrash; see his *Social and Religious History of the Jews,* 5:346, n. 51. But it is more likely that the explanation derives from the reality of warfare between Muslims and Christians. The explanation also appears in Muslim sources; see Kister, "'And He Was Born Circumcised'," 11 n. 8.

40. Objection: Epistle of Barnabas 9; Celsus in Origen, *Against Celsus* 1.22 and 5.41 (in Chadwick ed., *Origen contra Celsum,* 21–22 and 297). Response: Theodoret, *Questions on Genesis* 69 (PG 80:177); Aphrahat in Neusner, *Aphrahat and Judaism,* 25. Willet, *Hexapla in Genesin,* 199, follows Theodoret rather than Herodotus.

41. Epistle of Barnabas 9; Justin Martyr, *Dialogue with Trypho* 16 (PG 6:509) and 19 (PG 6:516); Tertullian, *Against the Jews* 2.10–3.13 (CCSL 2:1343–47), esp. 3.4 and 3.7 (1345).

42. Mellinkoff, *The Mark of Cain,* 92–98, citing Isidore of Seville, Rabanus Maurus, Remigius of Auxerre, Bruno of Asti, and others.

43. Cornelius à Lapide, *Commentaria in Pentateuchum* 171. See chapter 5 below for the Jewish version of this explanation.

44. Actually, Greek Christian writers completely ignored the non-circumci-

sion of women, neither using it as an anti-Jewish argument (see above note 17) nor seeing it as a problem that required discussion.

45. A note in PG 94:1212, apparently by Michael Le Quien (1661–1733), editor of the works of John of Damascus, confirms that it is Augustine who marks the shift in Latin thinking.

46. *De Nuptiis et Concupiscentia* 2.11.24 (PL 44:450 [CSEL 42:277]).

47. Cf. *City of God* 16.27 (PL 41:506–7 [CCSL 48:531–32]). For other passages, see the index in PL 46:166–67, s.v. "circumcisio."

48. *Moralia in Iob, praefatio* 4.3 (PL 75:635 [CCSL 143:160]).

49. *Summa Theologiae* 3a.70.4, translated by Cunningham, *Thomas Aquinas*, 166–69. For discussion, see Schenk, "Covenant Initiation."

50. From antiquity to modern times, various Christian groups have practiced circumcision and have in consequence been denounced as "heretics." On antiquity, see, for example, Klijn and Reinink, *Patristic Evidence for Jewish Christian Sects*, index, s.v. "circumcision." In the Middles Ages, for example, the Pasagini (or Passagii) were alleged to argue that just as circumcision was necessary for the purification from original sin in the time before Jesus, it still remained necessary even after the advent of Jesus, since Jesus nowhere is said to have abrogated it. See Praepositinus, *Summa contra Haereticos* 7.4, in Garvin-Corbett, *Summa*, 121; Newman, *Jewish Influence on Christian Reform Movements*, 261–65; S. Cohen, "Between Judaism and Christianity," 315. Some eastern churches, notably the Ethiopian and the Coptic, practiced (still practice?) circumcision, and they felt the need to apologize for their custom when confronted by western Christians; see, for example, the statement of Michael, metropolitan of Damietta (twelfth century) in Burmester, "Sayings," 113–14 (in the Arabic) and 123–24 (in English translation): "We do not consider that the prepuce is impure and that circumcision is pure, only he who does it [circumcision] among us [Copts] does it for the sake of custom, and not on account of the Jewish law, since we do not perform it on the eighth day nor at any definite time, and also we do not perform it after Baptism."

51. Ambrose, *On Abraham* 2.11.78 (PL 14:493–94 [CSEL 32,1:630–31]), follows Philo in explaining why God commanded only the males and is not based on an Augustinian conception of circumcision.

52. The following discussion is representative, not exhaustive. Schenk, "Covenant Initiation," 576–77, discusses Robert Kilwardby (d. 1279), a commentator on the Sentences of Peter Lombard, who collects additional explanations.

53. *Sententiarum Liber* 4.1.7 (PL 192:840–41) [= *Sententiarum Liber* 4.1.8 (editio Bonaventuriana 2:237)].

54. Peter is anticipated here by Peter Alphonsi, *Dialogue* (PL 157:659: "Quod autem circumcisionem, salvationis causam esse dixisti, utique circumcisio tantum causa non fuit ejus rei, imo etiam fides bona, sacrificia atque opera recta, et post datam circumcisionem, et antea, sicut patet in Adam, Seth, Enoch, Mathusale, Noe et Sem, Job et sociis ejus atque Judaicis mulieribus, qui omnes sine circumcisione, fide recta salvati sunt, ac bonis operibus") and followed by Raymond Martin (1220–1286), *Pugio Fidei* 786. As the editors of Lombard

note, this explanation also appears in the *Glossa Ordinaria* (PL 113:125) and the *Summa sententiarum* (PL 171:1148b and 176.119c).

55. *Sententiarum Liber* 4.1.8 (PL 192:841 [= *Sententiarum Liber* 4.1.9.3 (editio Bonaventuriana, 2:238)]).

56. *Summa Theologiae* 3a.70.2, trans. Cunningham, *Thomas Aquinas,* 161.The same tradition is attested by Radulphus Ardens (twelfth century), *Homily on the Circumcision of the Lord* (PL 155:1725).

57. *Commentary on Romans* 4:11 (PL 178:844b–d [CCCM 11:130]).

58. The same explanation is advanced in Abelard's *Dialogue,* where it is placed in the mouth of the Jewish speaker (!). See Payer, *Dialogue* 50–51 (PL 178:1624). A similar explanation appears in *Aliquot Quaestionum Liber: Quaestio XV: De Redemptione humana* (PL 93:476), which is ascribed to Bede but which is really a product of the school of Anselm of Laon (d. 1117); see CPPM, 133, no. 400, and p. 135.

59. First Timothy 2:15 "Yet woman will be saved through bearing children" suggests that women are indeed saved by childbirth from the effects of original sin, but the verse was (and is) interpreted in different ways; see Porter, "What Does It Mean to Be 'Saved by Childbirth'?" and Köstenberger, *Women in the Church.*

60. *Commentary on Romans* 4:11 (PL 178:844d [CCCM 11:130–31]).

61. *Commentary on Romans* 4:11 (PL 178:844d–845a [CCCM 11:131]).

62. A slightly different version of this explanation is also advanced by Thomas Aquinas, *Summa Theologiae* 3a.70.2, trans. Cunningham, 161: "Circumcision as an institution was reserved for males, and wisely so, since it was a sign of the faith of Abraham who believed he would be the father of the promised Christ."

63. *Scivias* 2.3.21 (PL 197:460 [CCCM 43:147]). For a slightly different translation, see Hart, *Hildegard,* 177.

64. The crucial line runs "nam mulier non est circumcidenda, quia maternum tabernaculum latet in corpore ejus, nec tangi potest nisi ut caro carnem constringit." The first edition of the *Scivias,* printed by Jacob Faber in 1513 and followed by the Patrologia Latina, reads "nec tangi potest tactu exteriori," which I assume is a "correction" by Faber to soften Hildegard's graphic sexual imagery. Such editorial "improvements" can be found throughout Faber's edition; see CCCM 43:lvii, the introduction to the *Scivias* by A. Führkötter.

65. *Scivias* 2.6.76–77 (CCCM 43:290–91), cited and discussed by Børresen, "God's Image," 225.

66. Baptism has replaced circumcision: *Scivias* 2.3.16 (PL 197:459 [CCCM 43:144–45]), and *Scivias* 2.3.29 (PL 197:464 [CCCM 43:152]), cited above in note 32. Circumcision's role in fighting the devil, *Scivias* 2.3.19 (PL 197:460 [CCCM 43:146, trans. Hart, 176]): "The warning of the holy spirit first threatened him through Noah, afterwards circumcision struck him in the jaw through Abraham, and then the church bound him in the end of time."

67. "Baptismus operatur apud nos, quod agebat circumcisio apud vos," says Gilbert Crispin to his Jewish disputant in his *Disputatio Iudaei [Continuatio]* 26, in Abulafia, *Works,* 60.

CHAPTER 4: FROM RETICENCE TO POLEMIC

1. T. Shabbat 15(16).9 71 and parallels.

2. The parallel between the foreskin of fruit trees and the foreskin of humans is developed at length by Eilberg-Schwartz, "Fruitful Cut."

3. This question appears at the parallel passage in Genesis Rabbah 46.5 463 and 46.13 470. Glassberg long ago suggested that Genesis 17:14 is a tacit polemic against female circumcision, but this is unlikely because female circumcision was unknown in the ancient Near East; see above, chapter 2, note 15.

4. M. Nedarim 3:11. "May × be as forbidden to me as a sacrificial offering" is my paraphrase of the mishnaic *qonam*. For a full explanation, see Benovitz, *Kol Nidre*, 111–26.

5. Such a man is a Jew in good standing; see my brief discussion of this point in chapter 1 above, and the fuller discussion in chapter 7 below. If a male Jew is uncircumcised as a result of heresy or apostasy, the legal consequences may be different; see the concluding chapter below.

6. B. Avodah Zarah, 27a. I translate the text edited by Abramson, *Tractate 'Abodah Zarah*, 24b, which differs in several small points from the standard text.

7. Medieval scholars debate which of the two positions is normative law: Spiegel, "Woman as Ritual Circumciser"; Fishman "A Kabbalistic Perspective," 241–42; Sperber, *Minhagei Yisrael*, 4.8–9; and Baumgarten, "Circumcision and Baptism," 122. Ilan, *Jewish Women in Greco-Roman Palestine*, 182, argues (on the basis of T. Shabbat 15.8) that women in rabbinic society often performed the circumcision of infants (cf. 1 Maccabees 1.60–61; 2 Maccabees 6.10; 4 Maccabees 4.25).

8. Elsewhere in the Talmud a woman's exemption from circumcision is a function of the fact that she is physically unable to be circumcised. See above, chapter 2, note 16.

9. See now the discussion of Levine, "A Woman Resembles Someone Who Has Been Circumcised," who surveys the history of the interpretation of this phrase.

10. See the commentary of R. Abraham ben David of Posquieres ad loc. in Schreiber ed., *Commentary on the Treatise of Abodah Zarah*, 58. In B. Bekhorot, 41a, s.v. *eyn lakh mum*, Rashi says "the place of femininity is like a blemish [or: defect]."

11. See the talmudic summaries of R. Isaac Alfasi (known as the Rif) and R. Asher (known as the Rosh), end of Shabbat, chap. 19.

12. B. Yevamot 46a.

13. For full discussion see S. Cohen, *Beginnings of Jewishness*, 219–21.

14. See the Midrash cited above in chapter 1, note 89.

15. Thus Rashi. The Meiri quotes the view that they are the wives of the patriarchs (Sarah, Rebecca, Rachel, and Leah).

16. B. Yevamot 46b.

17. See below, chapter 5, note 85.

18. On the differing functions of neonatal and conversionary circumcision, see above, chapter 1, note 49; and below, chapter 6, note 31; and chapter 7,

note 28. On the sacramental and non-sacramental character of circumcision, see above, chapter 1

19. In his rabbinic commentary on Philo's *Questions on Genesis*, Belkin transcribes 3.47, the passage cited above at the end of chapter 2 and cited again below in chapter 6, but can find no parallel from rabbinic sources; see Belkin, *The Midrash of Philo*, 280. Alexander Goldfahn long ago suggested that the midrashic passages cited above at notes 1 and 3 were intended as a response to Justin; see Golfahn, *Justinus Martyr*, 54. Perhaps.

20. Maier, *Jüdische Auseinandersetzung*; Boyarin, *Dying for God*; Niehoff, "Circumcision, as a Marker of Identity," 91 n. 6.

21. See above, chapter 1, at note 83.

22. Why, then, did Christian anti-Jewish writers use the non-circumcision of women as an argument? Were they in favor of gender equality? No, they were not. They were simply scoring points. See the final paragraphs of chapter 3 above.

23. "Fiunt non nascuntur Christiani": Tertullian, *Apology* 18.4 (PL 1:378 [CCSL 1:118]); "de Iudaeo Iudaeus nascitur": Ambrosiaster, *Quaestiones veteris et novi testamenti* 81 (PL 35:2274 [CSEL 50:137]). Both Ambrosiaster and I leave aside converts to Judaism.

24. M. Qiddushin 4:1; M. Bikkurim 1:4, as analyzed by S. Cohen, *Beginnings of Jewishness*, chap. 10. The tension within rabbinic Judaism between Israel as a descent group and Israel as a "religion" is a major focus of Porton, *The Stranger within Your Gates*.

25. This view is disputed by Ambrosiaster, who realized that circumcision was not baptism (PL 35:2274 [CSEL 50:137–38]): "de Iudaeo Iudaeus nascitur, non enim, sicut quibusdam videtur, quia circumcisio facit Iudaeum. Circumcisio enim signum Iudaismi est, non Iudaismus."

26. On Jewish women in the Middle Ages, see Finkelstein, *Jewish Self-Government*, 378–79; Falk, "Status of Women"; Grossman, "Connection between Law and Economy"; and above all Grossman, *Pious and Rebellious*. On the presence of women at the circumcision ceremony, see above, chapter 1, note 155.

27. Saadia Gaon, *The Book of Beliefs and Opinions* 3.7, in Rosenblatt, *Saadia Gaon*, 158.

28. See my discussion of all these points in chapter 1 above.

29. I am *not* arguing that these developments typified European Jewry *only*; some of these developments clearly are true for non-European communities too, but these are not my concern.

30. Lasker, *Jewish Philosophical Polemics*, 13–20, lists forty-one different medieval Jewish anti-Christian works. For even fuller lists, see Rosenthal, "Anti-Christian Polemics," and Krauss-Horbury, *Jewish-Christian Controversy*, 201–61. On this literature in general, see Baron, *Social and Religious History of the Jews*, 9:293–97; Krauss-Horbury, *Jewish-Christian Controversy*; Trautner-Kromann, *Shield and Sword*; Chazan, *Daggers of Faith*; Lasker, "Jewish-Christian Polemics at the Turning Point."

31. On the Official family and their polemical activity, see Rosenthal's introduction to his edition of *Yosef HaMeqanne*; Trautner-Kromann, *Shield*

and Sword, 90–101; and Krauss-Horbury, *Jewish-Christian Controversy*, 150–53.

32. Cf. Isaiah 44:18.

33. Rosenthal, *Sefer Joseph Hamekane*, 72, no. 72, prints *me'ir*, which is a misprint for *me'id*.

34. Rosenthal, *Sefer Joseph Hamekane*, 72 no. 72. This argument also appears in the commentary on Leviticus 12:3 by R. Hayyim Paltiel (ca. 1300) in Lange, *Commentary*, 394.

35. This argument was already known to Origen and Jerome, who explain that the true circumcision of the heart means the circumcision of both the spirit (beliefs, thoughts, emotions) and the flesh (actions); see Origen, *Homily on Genesis* 3.5 (GCS 29:44), and *Commentary on Romans* 2.13 (PG 14:908), discussed by Niehoff, "Circumcision as a Marker of Identity," 110; Jerome, *Commentary on Ezekiel* 13 (PL 25:432 [CCSL 75:649–50]). I have explained R. Joseph's argument in the light of R. Joseph Kimhi, *Sefer Haberit* 26a–b in Talmage, *Book of the Covenant*, 48.

CHAPTER 5: THE CELEBRATION OF MANHOOD

The source of the epigraph is the speech "Is It a Crime for a Citizen of the United States to Vote?" given by Susan B. Anthony in response to her arrest on the charge of voting illegally in the federal elections of 1872.

1. On Jacob Anatoli, see Saperstein, *Jewish Preaching, 1200–1800*, 111–13. On anti-Christian polemic in Anatoli, see Saperstein, "Christians and Christianity in the Sermons of Jacob Anatoli." reprinted as chapter 5 in his *"Your Voice Like a Ram's Horn,"* and Krauss-Horbury, *Jewish-Christian Controversy*, 102 n. 4. On the date of the *Malmad*, see Saperstein, "Christians and Christianity in the Sermons of Jacob Anatoli," 237 n. 3 [= *"Your Voice Like a Ram's Horn,"* 57 n.3].

2. Anatoli, *Malmad Hatalmidim* 15a–b.

3. Saperstein, "Christians and Christianity in the Sermons of Jacob Anatoli," 230 [= *"Your Voice Like a Ram's Horn,"* 64].

4. Anatoli, *Malmad Hatalmidim* 15b–16a. This passage of Anatoli is cited with approval by R. Aharon HaKohen of Lunel, *Orhot Hayyim*, Laws of Circumcision 1.1. (vol. 2, p. 3, ed. Schlesinger) and the *Kol Bo* sec. 73, Laws of Circumcision.

5. *Mitzvot aseh shehazeman gerama*, usually translated "time-bound positive commandments."

6. Lit., "from one end of heaven to the other," based on Deuteronomy 4:32.

7. Anatoli, *Malmad Hatalmidim* 16a.

8. See the appendix to chapter 6 below.

9. Rosenthal, "Religious Disputation," 61.

10. Rosenthal, "Jewish Critique," 134. Rosenthal assumes that the author of this anonymous work is R. Joseph Official himself ("Jewish Critique," 123), but I see no indication of this in the text. An abbreviated version of Menahem's argument appears in the commentary on Leviticus 12:3 by R. Hayyim

Paltiel (ca. 1300), in Lange, *Torah Commentaries of R. Hayim Paltiel,* 394. The anti-Christian polemics of R. Hayyim, and their relationship with the Official polemicists, remain to be investigated. On R. Hayim's interest in refuting "heretics," see Lange, *Torah Commentaries of R. Hayim Paltiel,* 233.

11. On circumcision as a tax, see B. Avodah Zarah 10b.

12. B. Bava Metzia 59a and Sanhedrin 107a.

13. See below, note 50.

14. B. Berakhot 17a (cited by Rosenthal, "Jewish Critique," 134 n. 57), where the context is merit for the world to come; the identical words are ascribed by B. Sotah 21a to Ravina, where the context is the protective power of merit. Berakhot 17a does not say explicitly that these words are the reply of R. Hiyya; perhaps Rav answers his own question.

15. M. Qiddushin 1.7 (B. Qiddushin 29a; Y. Qiddushin 58b).

16. The Talmud does not clarify this point, which is discussed at length by the medieval commentators.

17. B. Qiddushin 29a; Y. Qiddushin 1.7 61a; T. Qiddushin 1.11 279; and parallels. Obligations of a father to his daughter are stated in M. Ketuvot 4.4–6.

18. B. Qiddushin 31b; Y. Qiddushin 1.7 61a; partial parallel in T. Qiddushin 1.11 279 and elsewhere.

19. T. Qiddushin 1.11 279; Y. Qiddushin 1.7 61a–b. In B. Qiddushin 30b and Sifra on Leviticus 19:2 this qualification is attached to the obligation of *fear,* which I do not understand. In B. Qiddushin 35a the same qualification is presented in a different context

20. Widowed or divorced: Y. Qiddushin 1.7 61b. Divorced: B. Qiddushin 30b. (For the same idea, see M. Bava Qamma 8.4.) Husband does not object: a reasonable deduction made by R. Shabbtai b. Meir Hacohen of Vilna in the *Siftei Kohen* on *Yoreh Deʿah* 240.17.

21. B. Qiddushin 33b–34a; Y. Qiddushin 1.7 61c; T. Qiddushin 1:10 279. My translation is an explanatory paraphrase.

22. See Leviticus 23:42; Leviticus 23:40; Leviticus 23:24; Numbers 15:38; Deuteronomy 6:8.

23. See Deuteronomy 6:9; Deuteronomy 22:8; Exodus 23:4 and Deuteronomy 22:1–3; Deuteronomy 22:6–7.

24. M. Berakhot 3.3 (B. Berakhot 20a–b; Y. Berakhot 3 6b).

25. This argument is explicit in B. Berakhot 20b and implicit in Y. Berkahot 3 6b.

26. Rovner, "Rhetorical Strategy."

27. B. Qiddushin 34a.

28. That the principle is descriptive rather than prescriptive is agreed by historians, like Ilan, *Jewish Women in Greco-Roman Palestine,* 176–84, and Safrai, "*Mitzva* Obligation," 233–34, and rabbis, like Berman, "Status of Women in Halakhic Judaism," 11–13, and Dorff, "Custom Drives Jewish Law on Women."

29. An explanation similar to Anatoli's is advanced by R. David b. Joseph Abudraham (Spain, fourteenth century), in Ehrenreich, *Sefer Abudarham [sic],* 108, and Wertheimer, *Abudraham Hashalem,* 25 and 42. Perhaps Anatoli was

the source for Abudraham. Both were anticipated by R. Joseph Bekhor Shor's commentary on Leviticus 23:42 (Nebo, *Commentary of R. Joseph Bekhor Shor on the Torah*, 226–27).

30. B. Hagigah 4a and parallels.

31. Fishman, "A Kabbalistic Perspective on Gender-Specific Commandments." The work is the *Sefer Haqanah*.

32. Berman, "Status of Women in Halakhic Judaism," 12, citing Rabbi Emanuel Rackman. This is not much different from R. Joseph Bekhor Shor; see chapter 8 below.

33. For a good discussion, see Biale, *Women and Jewish Law*, 10–43; Baskin, *Midrashic Women*, 80–81. Berman, "Status of Women in Halakhic Judaism," 16–17, suggests that the rabbinic goal was to exempt a woman from any obligation that would necessarily interfere with her role as wife and mother; this is excellent, and not much different from Anatoli.

34. Plaskow, *Standing Again at Mount Sinai*.

35. M. Hagigah 1.1.

36. B. Hagigah 2a–3a.

37. The Hebrew terms are *adam, nefesh, ish, me-akheha, ezrah*.

38. Man or woman: Exodus 21:28–29, Leviticus 13:29 and 38, 20:27; Numbers 5:6 and 6:2; Deuteronomy 17:2, 29:17. Son or daughter: Exodus 21:31; Deuteronomy 5:14, 12:8, 13:7, 16:11, and 14.

39. For a full collection of the material, and a valiant attempt to discover consistency and rationality in it, see Chernick, "*ish* as Man and Adult." Chernick's study would have been improved by a parallel treatment of the terms *anashim* [men], *ezrah*, and *Israel*. The Midrash's inconsistency is noted by Harris, *How Do We Know This?* 23, but see Elman's strictures in "Small Scale of Things," 64–65. The equation of women with men in the laws of damages is stated in Mekhilta on Exodus 21:18, Neziqin 6 269H–R = 3.51L; T. Bava Qamma 1.3 2; and parallels.

40. Sifra Qedoshim parashah 10 91b. I translate the text of Finkelstein, *Codex Assemani*, 409.

41. Israel: Sifra Ahare Mot pereq 10 84a; Ahare Mot parashah 8 84c; Ahare Mot pereq 11 84c; Emor parashah 7 98a. Native *(ezrah)*: Sifra Ahare Mot pereq 7 83a and pereq 13 86c.

42. Sifrei Numbers 39 43H and 43 49H. Exegesis of the same pattern occurs in Sifrei Numbers 117 137H and Sifrei Deuteronomy 149 204F.

43. Sifrei Numbers 109 112H (on the word *qahal*) and 111 118H (on the word *'edah*).

44. Sifra Vayiqra parshata 2 4bW [2.19–20F].

45. Sifra Tzav parashah 11 39a–b.

46. Leviticus 23:42 and Sifra Emor pereq 17.9 103a. The reading "to exclude women" is confirmed by Finkelstein, *Codex Assemani*, 460, and various testimonia. However, there is a variant reading "to include women," and the medieval commentators had difficulty in reconciling the conflicting traditions in the exegesis of this verse. See Sifrei on Numbers 112 119H; B. Sukkah 28a, and B. Qiddushin 34a.

47. M. Sanhedrin 10.1. On women as Israel, see M. Terumot 8.12 and Niddah 4.2.

48. See J. Tabory, "Benedictions of Self-Identity."

49. Wagenseil, *Tela Ignea Satanae,* 471. On Johann Wagenseil (1633–1705), see Krauss-Horbury, *Jewish-Christian Controversy,* 142–44; for estimates of his character, see 142 n. 89.

50. Anatoli, *Malmad Hatalmidim* 25b. On the question in general, see Horowitz, "Image of God"; a comprehensive study of the subject is needed. On Christian thinkers, see below.

51. AdRN A 2 6b, citing Genesis 1:24. That this midrash is a response to Christian argumentation is suggested by Ginzberg, *Legends of the Jews,* 5:268 n. 318; see above, chapter 1 note 58. On this midrash's conception of the image of God, see Smith, *Studies in the Cult of Yahweh,* 1:120 n. 20, and Goshen-Gottstein, "Body as Image," 175.

52. T. Berakhot 6.18 38. The text appears with minor variations in Y. Berakhot 9.2 13b (12b).

53. By happy coincidence, the English word "boor" is a homonym of the Hebrew word *boor,* which appears here, but the words are distinct. The root meaning of English "boor" is "farmer" (Dutch *boer*), and belongs to the lexical family of words like "pagan," "rustic," "country-bumpkin," and the like. The root meaning of the Hebrew word *boor* is "outsider" (from Aramaic *bera,* outside), that is, outside the city, outside the academy, outside civilization.

54. B. Menahot 43b–44a. According to the vulgate printed editions of the Bavli, a slave is lower than a woman; according to the Munich manuscript of the Bavli, a woman is lower than a slave. According to other readings, the text is not saying that one is lower than the other.

55. Smith, *Studies in the Cult of Yahweh,* 1:150–60.

56. See Lieberman, *Tosefta Ki-fshutah,* 1:121.

57. Wertheimer, *Abudraham Hashalem,* 41–42; Ehrenreich, *Sefer Abudarham,* 170.

58. The same explanation appears in Tur, Orah Hayyim 46.4, which is approximately contemporary with Abudraham.

59. Austria: R. Joseph b. Moses, *Leqet Yosher,* in Freimann, *Leqet Yosher* 7. Provence: Jochnowitz, "'. . . Who Made Me a Woman'." These and other sources are discussed by J. Tabory, "Benedictions of Self-Identity."

60. For an expanded and more detailed version of the following discussion, see my "'Your Covenant That You Have Sealed in Our Flesh'."

61. B. Berakhot 48b.

62. The name of this obscure rabbi is transmitted in various forms in the manuscripts: Pelomi, Peloma. The vocalization is uncertain.

63. For example, see Rashi here and R. Hai Gaon in Lewin, *Otzar Hageonim: Berakhot,* 83, no. 234. For full discussion, see Lieberman, *TK Sotah,* 707–10.

64. M. Nedarim 3:11; Y. Nedarim 3.14 38b; B. Shabbat 132a and 133a; B. Pesahim 69b; B. Yevamot 5b.

65. I follow the reading of various medieval testimonia; this reading is en-

dorsed by Lieberman, *TK Berakhot,* 38. The vulgate printed editions read: "For
R. Hannanel said in the name of Rav: whoever does not say covenant, Torah,
and kingdom has [nevertheless] fulfilled his obligation." As Rabbinowicz remarks in the *Diqduqei Soferim,* this reading is not as smooth as the alternative
because R. Hisda needs to adduce an injunction before the fact, not permission
after the fact, in support of his position, but this is supplied by the reading that
I have followed.

66. B. Berakhot 49a.

67. The covenant of circumcision, however, does apply to male slaves:
M. Bava Qamma 1:3; B. Gittin 23b; B. Qiddushin 41b.

68. I follow the commentary of the Rashba.

69. M. Berakhot 3:3.

70. I translate the version of R. Amram; for a large collection of variants, see
Finkelstein, "Birkat Ha-mazon," 247–49.

71. See, for example, Birnbaum, *Daily Prayer Book,* 829–30.

72. The Yerushalmi has no doubt that the verse applies to women too:
Y. Berakhot 3 6b. On the Bavli's question, see Lieberman, *TK Berakhot,* 83.

73. As the biblical story about the daughters of Zelophehad abundantly attests, Numbers 27 and 36.

74. B. Berakhot 48b–49a; see above.

75. Tosafot, Berakhot 20b, s.v. *nashim;* see also Tosafot Harosh.

76. Perhaps in their support the Tosafot would adduce Rav, who clearly felt
that "covenant" excludes women. But support such as this is a two-edged
sword. First, according to the vulgate reading—perhaps the reading that the
Tosafot had—Rav validated, at least after the fact, the recitation of the Grace
after Meals without the mention of "covenant." This ruling completely undercuts the Tosafot's argument. Second, the Talmud rejects Rav, implying that
Rav's concern is not valid. This too undercuts the Tosafot's argument.

77. Lewin, *Otzar Hageonim: Berakhot,* 49–50, no. 123; Tosafot, Arakhin
3a, s.v. *mezamnot;* Meiri on Berakhot, 48b; the gloss of R. Moses Isserles on
Shulhan Arukh Orah Hayyim 187.3 (and see the Magen Avraham ad loc.).

78. On these tendencies, see Grossman, *Pious and Rebellious,* 309–42.

79. Y. Berakhot 1 3d; cf. T. Berakhot 3.9 14. In fact, even in the Bavli, if we
exclude the comment of Pelomi and the explanation for Rav's behavior, there is
no sign that "covenant" refers to circumcision.

80. I translate the version of R. Saadyah Gaon as presented by Finkelstein,
"Birkat Ha-Mazon," 247–49, who also assembles numerous variants. R.
Saadyah was a champion of Babylonian Judaism, but his Siddur follows the rite
of Eretz Israel.

81. Asaf, "From the Prayer Book of the Land of Israel," 129. Similarly, the
medieval poetical expansions of the Grace after Meals assume that the word
berit in the second paragraph means "covenant," not "circumcision." See
Habermann, "Poetical Blessings," and Ratzhabi, "New Poetical Blessings."

82. Sifra Behuqotai pereq 8 112c.

83. Mekhilta Bahodesh 7 230, ed. Horovitz-Rabin. In the parallels the inclusion of women is ambiguous. The Covenant of Damascus 12.12 prohibits an
Israelite owner from selling to gentiles "his [male] slave or his female slave, be-

cause they entered with him into the covenant of Abraham." For this author even the covenant of Abraham can include women.

84. See, for example, B. Berakhot 16b bottom (a prayer that entered the siddur); B. Gittin 23b; T. Berakhot 3.7 13–14; T. Sanhedrin 11:4 431; M. Bava Qamma 1.2 is ambiguous (see 1.3).

85. Well noted by Safrai, "*Mitzva* Obligation," 228–30.

86. Mekhilta Bahodesh 2 207HR and parallels; cf. also Mekhilta Bahodesh 2 209HR.

87. Mekhilta Bahodesh 3 214HR and parallels.

88. B. Yevamot 46b.

89. Grossman, *Pious and Rebellious*, 356 and 507, citing a study by Hava Frankel-Goldschmidt.

90. Circumcision as a celebration of maleness is discussed by Eilberg-Schwartz, "Fruitful Cut," 167–74; Hoffman, *Covenant of Blood*, passim; Baskin, *Midrashic Women*, 18–22.

91. The fundamental "otherness" of women in rabbinic Judaism is the theme of Baskin, *Midrashic Women*.

92. In modern times when traditionalist thinkers explain why women do not have a covenantal mark, they advance a version of Anatoli's or Menahem's explanation, even without having read Anatoli or Menahem. See, for example, David Zakut Modena, *Sefer Zekher David*, 200a (on this book, see above, chapter 1, note 108); various responsa in Trier, *Rabbinische Gutachten* (see the concluding chapter below, note 20). In general the argument that women are meant solely to attain merit through their husbands and sons is explicitly defended even today by some adherents of Haredi Orthodoxy. See, for example, Washofsky, "Responsa and Rhetoric," 391–93, an analysis of R. Yechiel Michael Tykocinski, *Ha'isha al pi torat yisrael* (Jerusalem 1920). Tykocinski's pamphlet is an elaborate polemic against granting women the right to vote in the Jewish community of mandate Palestine. Marriage manuals given to Haredi brides before their wedding exhort the woman to remember that her task is to facilitate acts of piety by her husband.

93. The medieval commentaries debate whether circumcision is in fact a positive commandment that needs to be observed at a specific time. It certainly would seem to be, but why then does the Talmud seek out a special scriptural source to exclude women from this commandment (that is, to exclude women from the obligation of having their sons circumcised)? Should they not have been excluded by the general principle? See Tosafot on B. Qiddushin 29a, s.v. *oto*, and Urbach, *Arugot Habosem*, 3:187 n. 45.

94. Ortner, *Making Gender*, 23; later in the book (139–72 and 174–77) Ortner concedes that there may be exceptions to the pattern.

95. Birnbaum, *Daily Prayer Book*, 427–28. It is striking that the *Sabbath and Festival Prayer Book* (New York: Rabbinical Assembly and United Synagogue, 1946), edited by Robert Gordis and filled with studied and deliberate alterations of the traditional text, retained this prayer intact.

96. And Muslims too, if I may trust my limited knowledge about Islam. Some scholars have argued that rabbinic misogyny and androcentrism are the result of Hellenistic influence; see Baskin, *Midrashic Women*, 36–40. I realize

that in some times and places ancient society may well have been less androcentric than I am allowing here, but this does not affect my main point.

97. On classical Athens, see Patterson, *"Attikai,"* and Loraux, *Children of Athena*, 116–23, esp. 119 ("there is no such thing as a 'female citizen,' any more than there is a 'female Athenian' ").

98. Diogenes Laertius *Lives of the Philosophers* 1.33. I omit "first," "next," and "third" from the translation.

99. See J. Tabory, "Benedictions of Self-Identity."

100. Augustine argues that the Pauline declaration "there is no longer Jew or Greek, there is no longer slave or free, there is no longer male and female," means that all such distinctions have been removed from the unity of faith; in the course of normal life and mortal existence, however, such distinctions still exist and matter. See Augustine, *Exposition on Galatians* 28 (PL 35:2125 [CSEL 84:93]). This explanation may be politically incorrect, but it makes sense out of Paul. See above, chapter 3, note 10.

101. Martyrdom of Pionios 3.6, ed. Robert, 22.

102. Celsus in Origen, *Against Celsum* 3.44, in Chadwick, *Origen contra Celsum*, 158.

103. "In multis iuris nostri articulis deterior est condicio feminarum quam masculorum," Digest 1.5.9 (Papinian).

104. Gregory of Tours, *Histories* 8.20, in *Gregorii Episcopi Turonensis Libri Historiarum X*, ed. Bruno Krusch and Wilhelm Levison, Monumenta Germaniae Historica, Scriptores Rerum Merovingicarum I,1 (Hannover: Hahn, 1951), 386–87.

105. I am aware, of course, that rabbinic literature frequently uses the word *adam* to mean "a man," because for the rabbis a plain ungendered person is a man. As a result rabbinic usage can pair *adam* and woman as contrasting categories (e.g., M. Avodah Zarah 2.1). This usage, which is occasionally offset by passages that use *adam* to include women (e.g., M. Sanhedrin 7.4), is not surprising and does not affect my point. Scriptural usage of the term *adam* is never construed as excluding women, although it is sometimes construed as excluding gentiles. Genesis Rabbah 21.2 199 affirms that the scriptural locution *Adam* can include Eve.

106. One wonders why they did not cite Numbers 31:35. See the commentary of R. Hizqiyah b. Manoah (known as Hizquni) on Genesis 1:26 and Rosenthal, *Sefer Yosef Hameqane*, sec. 39, pp. 55–56.

107. Fleischer, "Are Women Human?"

108. Børresen, "God's Image, Man's Image?" Contemporary debate animates Horowitz, "Image of God in Man."

109. Willet, *Hexapla* (1611 edition), 205, as cited by Shapiro, *Shakespeare and the Jews*, 263 n. 32. The 1605 edition has a different formulation on 198–99: "Though the males only were circumcised, because the beginning of generation, and so of originall corruption was from them, yet it served also for the signe of the covenant for the female sexe, because the woman is of the man, as the Apostle saith, 1. Cor. 11.8, and so was circumcised in the man."

110. S. Cohen, *Beginnings of Jewishness*, chap. 9

111. I am not suggesting that Genesis 17 is the source of the matrilineal

principle; at most it, and other biblical passages, might be a source concerning the offspring of slave women, but from slave women to free women is a big step.

CHAPTER 6: THE REDUCTION OF LUST
AND THE UNMANNING OF MEN

The epigraph is discussed in the appendix to this chapter.

1. Philo, *Questions and Answers on Genesis* 3.47, in Marcus, *Philo Questions . . . Genesis*, 241–42. See above, chapter 2, at note 32.

2. Sly, *Philo's Perception*, 201–7 and 219–21; Stowers, *Rereading Romans*, 42–82; Satlow, "Try to Be a Man."

3. Or, if he does, I cannot find it either in Philo or in Sly, *Philo's Perception*.

4. Sly, *Philo's Perception*, 48, citing *On the Special Laws* 1:200ff.

5. Philo here uses "woman" as a synonym for "female principle."

6. *Guide of the Perplexed* 3.49, in Pines, *Guide*, 609–11. For discussion, see J. Stern, "Maimonides on Circumcision" from whom I have learned much.

7. *Guide of the Perplexed* 3.49 and 3.35, in Pines, *Guide*, 606 and 538.

8. B. Meʿilah 17a suggests that ancient critics of circumcision argued that it weakens the body, but I do not know any other ancient evidence for such a stance; in any case B. Meʿilah 17a is not Maimonides' source, since it suggests that circumcision weakens the entire body, not merely the sexual function. In the nineteenth century, Jewish critics of circumcision argued that circumcision weakens the Jewish male body; see below, the concluding chapter, note 2.

9. *Guide of the Perplexed* 3.33, in Pines, *Guide*, 532. On this theme in general, see Rosner, *Sex Ethics in the Writings of Moses Maimonides*.

10. There is nonetheless some support in the halakhic tradition for the position that the foreskin is not a blemish *(mum)*; see Lieberman, *TK Nedarim*, 7:424.

11. Genesis Rabbah 46.10 467.

12. Manicure: Genesis Rabbah 46.4 461 (see note 58 below); fig: Genesis Rabbah 46.1 458.

13. Genesis Rabbah 11.6 94–95.

14. Saadia Gaon, *Book of Beliefs and Opinions* 3.10, in Rosenblatt, *Saadia Gaon*, 177.

15. *Guide of the Perplexed* 2.28, in Pines, *Guide*, 336.

16. Maimonides' emphasis on "at birth" perhaps anticipates the objection that Muslims are circumcised and yet are sexually promiscuous (at least in Jewish eyes). Since their circumcision is not "at birth," their organ is not weakened as much as the Jewish one. Cf. John Bulwer, *View of the People* (published in 1654), 368: "Moses Egyptius [Maimonides] saith, that Circumcision helpeth to bridle and restraine inordinate lust and concupiscence of the flesh, but the contrary doth appeare; for no Nation is more given to carnall lust than the Egyptians, Saracens, and Turkes that are Circumcised."

17. Tanhuma, Lekh-Lekha 5 on Genesis 12:11.

18. Genesis Rabbah 80.11 966.

19. Judith Hauptman claims to find this same attitude in B. Yevamot 34b: the comment of a female character in a rabbinic story "fits well with the general

observation of the rabbis that non-Jewish men, in contradistinction to Jewish men, are sexually promiscuous and hence more competent. It also suggests that women enjoy sex, with non-Jewish men in particular." See Hauptman, *Rereading the Rabbis,* 144. The female character's comment, alas, is very ambiguous and Hauptman's interpretation is not the only, or the most plausible, one.

20. In a note to his Hebrew translation of the *Guide,* J. Kafah (Kafih) suggests that Maimonides indeed is referring to the woman's pleasure, but I find this unlikely, because Maimonides is clearly focusing on the effects of circumcision on the person who is circumcised, namely, the man. I am grateful to my friend David Sklare for verifying that nothing in Maimonides' Arabic implies that the subject is the pleasure of the woman. See Kafah, *Maimonides: Guide,* 398 n. 73.

21. *Guide of the Perplexed* 3.49, in Pines, *Guide,* 609–10.

22. J. Stern, "Maimonides on Circumcision," 139; Novak, "Treatment of Islam," esp. 235–40 and 244–46.

23. J. Stern, "Maimonides on Circumcision," 140–41; Novak, "Treatment of Islam," 240–43.

24. See J. Stern, "Maimonides on Circumcision," 144–46, for some speculation on this point.

25. J. Stern, "Maimonides on Circumcision," 142.

26. Augustine has the same idea. He explains the circumcision of Abraham's descendants as follows: "Men cannot be joined together for the sake of any religion, whether true or false, unless they are bound together by having in common some visible signs or rituals" ("In nullum autem nomen religionis, seu verum, seu falsum, coagulari homines possunt, nisi aliquo signaculorum vel sacramentorum visibilium consortio colligentur") (Augustine, *Contra Faustum* 19.11, in PL 42:355, cited by Thomas Aquinas, *Summa Theologiae* 3a.70.2, in Cunningham ed., *Summa Theologiae,* 57:160–61).

27. Maimonides, introduction to the Mishneh Torah, in Kafah, *Mishneh Torah,* 1:59.

28. Maimonides, introduction to the Mishneh Torah, in Kafah, *Mishneh Torah,* 1:76. On this placement of the laws of circumcision, see Twersky, *Introduction to the Code of Maimonides,* 283–84.

29. The phrase *berit milah* appears only twice in the entire Mishneh Torah. (The wonders of computer technology allow me to make this claim with some confidence.) The first is *Laws of Blessings* 2.3, in Kafah, *Mishneh Torah,* 2:501, regarding the Grace after Meals; the second is *Laws of Forbidden Intercourse* 13.2, regarding the conversion of gentiles.

30. B. Berakhot 48b–49a (see above, chapter 5, note 64); Mishneh Torah, *Laws of Circumcision* 3.9, in Kafah, *Mishneh Torah,* 2:476. In his note ad loc., Kafah notices that Maimonides is more specific than his talmudic source. Maimonides follows the talmudic source in his *Laws of Blessings* 2.3, in Kafah, *Mishneh Torah,* 2:501. My translation of Maimonides follows Twersky, *Introduction to the Code of Maimonides,* 152.

31. See *Laws of Forbidden Intercourse* 13.1–4, and J. Stern's discussion, "Maimonides on Circumcision," 137. This distinction is also made, apparently independently of Maimonides, by R. Moshe ben Yosef Schick (1807–1879),

She'elot u Teshuvot Maharam Schick, Yoreh De'ah 245, who cites Nachmanides (1194–1270) for support (see below, chapter 7 for discussion).

32. R. Eliezer ben Samuel of Metz, *Sefer Yere'im HaShalem* 223a.

33. *Sefer ha Hinuch, Lekh Lekha,* in Chavel, *Sefer HaHinukh,* 56.

34. R. Joseph Karo, *Shulhan Arukh, Yoreh De'ah,* 260.

35. *Guide of the Perplexed* 3.35, in Pines, *Guide,* 537.

36. I am not convinced by J. Stern, "Maimonides on Circumcision," 148–50, who has forgotten to cite *The Book of Commandments.*

37. See *Laws of Marriage (Hilkhot Ishut)* 14, *Laws of Forbidden Intercourse (Hilkhot Issure Biah)* 21, and *Laws of Temperaments (Hilkhot Deot)* 3.2, 4.19, and 5.4. Excerpts from all these are assembled by Rosner, *Sex Ethics in the Writings of Maimonides.* At the request of the vizier, Maimonides wrote an entire treatise *On Cohabitation* (Rosner, *Sex Ethics,* 11–40).

38. Saperstein, *Decoding the Rabbis,* 98. In the following excerpt I follow Saperstein's translation except that I have replaced Saperstein's "uncircumcized" with "foreskinned," and have added the last line on the basis of Saperstein, "The Earliest Commentary on the Midrash Rabbah," 296. In the paragraph after the close of our excerpt, R. Isaac cites the Midrash on Genesis 34:26 that Maimonides had cited.

39. Saperstein, *Decoding the Rabbis,* 94, argues that R. Isaac is more extreme on this point than Maimonides, but I do not see any difference.

40. This contrast is (what I take to be) the main point of Boyarin, *Unheroic Conduct.*

41. The question is well posed by Saperstein, *Decoding the Rabbis,* 100. Saperstein believes that liaisons between Jewish men and Christian women were more common than liaisons between Christian men and Jewish women.

42. B. Eruvin 19a. I read *de-meshukha arlato.* A more natural reading would be *de-mashkhah arlato,* "since she has stretched his foreskin."

43. Genesis Rabbah 48.8 483 and parallels. See above, chapter 1, note 35.

44. Hall, "Epispasm," and Rubin, "The Stretching of the Foreskin."

45. Actually, the talmudic passage is from the beginning of the second chapter of Eruvin, not the end of the first, and the motif of Abraham sitting at the entrance to Gehenna is from Genesis Rabbah 48.8, not the Babylonian Talmud. Our author is writing from memory.

46. *Sefer Maharil, Liqutim,* in Spitzer, *Maharil,* 624.

47. Little is known of R. Isaac of Weida, who was appointed a regional rabbi by the bishop of Mainz in 1385; see Yuval, *Scholars in Their Time,* 150; Maimon, *Germania Judaica* 3,1.227 (s.v. "Dieburg)" and 3,2.871 (s.v. "Miltenberg") and 1558 (s.v. "Weida").

48. Satlow, "Try to Be a Man"; S. Stern, *Jewish Identity in Early Rabbinic Writings,* 23–26.

49. Boyarin, *Unheroic Conduct,* 239.

50. Bebel, *Facetiae* 1.2, in Bebermeyer, *Bebels Facetien,* 5 (the original Latin) = Wesselski, *Heinrich Bebels Schwänke,* vol. 1, p. 5 (a reprint of the German translation of 1558). On the life and writings of Heinrich Bebel (1472–ca. 1518), see Wesselski's introduction, i–xxviii. My attention was first drawn to

this story by Hsia, "Witchcraft, Magic, and the Jews," 427, who, however, has mistranslated the punch-line.

51. Browne, *Pseudodoxia Epidemica* 202, cited with approval by Bulwer, *A View of the People of the Whole World,* 378 (who expands on this theme). My attention was first drawn to Browne by Shapiro, *Shakespeare and the Jews,* 37.

52. Bartholinus, *De Morbis Biblicis* 88.

53. [Münster], *Messias* 2–3. My attention was first directed to this text by Hsia, "Witchcraft, Magic, and the Jews," 428 (who cites the original Latin).

54. [Münster], *Messias* 8–9.

55. Berger, *Jewish-Christian Debate,* 340 (note on *Nizzahon* chap. 238, which is Münster's source); Rogoff, "Is the Jew White?"; Brodkin, *How Jews Became White.*

56. B. Horayot 13a.

57. Eilberg-Schwartz, *God's Phallus,* 170–74. I do not consider here Eilberg-Schwartz's analysis (151–62) of this motif in the Hebrew Bible, which also does not convince me. If I read Boyarin correctly, his thesis is different from that of Eilberg-Schwartz. When Boyarin writes that "Premodern Jewish male subjects frequently perceived themselves as femminized [*sic*; "culturally constructed as women"], in part because of their circumcision" (*Unheroic Conduct,* 240), he means that they are "femminized" in the eyes of gentiles according to the canons of western Christian culture (more clearly, *Unheroic Conduct,* 210–11), not that they are "femminized" in their own eyes by the canons of Jewish culture. Or does Boyarin agree with Eilberg-Schwartz that the rabbis were "femminized" in their own eyes? If so, I disagree with him too.

58. Genesis Rabbah 46.4 461. I alluded to this text above in my discussion of Maimonides (see note 12).

59. Eilberg-Schwartz, *God's Phallus,* 171–72.

60. This is one of the main points of D. Stern, *Parables in Midrash.*

61. Bynum, *Jesus as Mother,* 110–69 ("Jesus as Mother and Abbot as Mother"), esp. 139–46, 160–62, 167–68.

62. Baron, *Social and Religious History of the Jews,* 11:154.

63. Johnson, "Myth of Jewish Male Menses"; and Resnick, "Medieval Roots of the Myth of the Jewish Male Menses," both with bibliography. Discussion in Marienberg, *Niddah,* 56–61. The source quoted is in Johnson, "Myth of Jewish Male Menses," 293–94.

64. See, for example, Fabre-Vassas, *The Singular Beast,* 112–19; Shapiro, *Shakespeare and the Jews,* 120.

65. Gilman, *Freud, Race, and Gender,* 49–92 (the quote is from 81); Boyarin, *Unheroic Conduct,* 210–20 (and passim); Geller, "Paleontological View of Freud's Study of Religion." This fascinating and important material awaits full historical treatment.

66. *Guide of the Perplexed* 3.48, in Pines, *Guide,* 600.

67. See the passages cited and discussed by Kellner, "Philosophical Misogyny in Medieval Jewish Philosophy," 121 (*Guide of the Perplexed* 1.17; 3.8, 37, and 48).

68. Miriam, sister of Moses, attained the highest level of cognition of God; see *Guide of the Perplexed* 3.51, in Pines, *Guide,* 627–28, citing B. Moed Qatan

28a. Maimonides maintains that, in general women, like children and fools, have limited intellectual capacity: *Guide of the Perplexed* 1.33, in Pines, *Guide,* 71; *Guide of the Perplexed* 1.35, in Pines, *Guide,* 81; *Mishneh Torah Laws of Repentance* 10.1 and 5. For discussion, see Kellner, "Philosophical Misogyny in Medieval Jewish Philosophy," 124–27.

69. Kellner, "Philosophical Misogyny in Medieval Jewish Philosophy," 122–24.

70. For biography, see Rosenbloom, *Tradition in an Age of Reform,* 39–120.

71. Rosenbloom, *Tradition in an Age of Reform,* 123–43 ("The Maimonidean Mantle").

72. Hirsch, *Horeb* chap. 36, in Grunfeld, *Samson Raphael Hirsch Horeb,* 1:170, para. 263.

73. Rosenbloom, *Tradition in an Age of Reform,* 267. For Hirsch on circumcision, see Rosenbloom, *Tradition in an Age of Reform,* 266–73 and Grunfeld, *Samson Raphael Hirsch Horeb,* 1:cxi–cxx. Did Hirsch know Philo?

74. Hirsch, *Commentary* on Leviticus 23:43, in Levy, *Pentateuch . . . Hirsch* 3.2.712.

75. Hirsch, *Collected Writings,* 8:83–137 ("The Jewish Woman"). Note especially 86: "The Jewish maiden becomes a mature human being, a full-fledged adult Jew, only once she has a husband"; this statement seems be an inversion of B. Yevamot 63a.

76. Hirsch makes the same point in his *Commentary* on Genesis 17:15, in Levy *Pentateuch . . . Hirsch* 1:305.

77. Hirsch's paean to the merit of righteous women recurs in *Collected Writings,* 8:117–24. The concept derives from B. Sotah 11b.

78. Much in the Hirschian tradition is Susser, "Covenant of Circumcision," 44. Hirsch's position has become commonplace in traditional Orthodox circles; see, for example, D. Cohen, *Celebrating Your New Jewish Daughter,* 19 (neither Cohen nor her respondent realize that they are discussing Hirsch's view). Cf. Kass, *Beginning of Widsom,* 314 n. 23, "[circumcision is] a taming of maleness, putting men into the service of the (more traditionally womanly) work of child rearing."

79. Antonelli, *Image,* xxii.

80. Antonelli, *Image,* xxviii–xxx.

81. Antonelli, *Image,* 271 (emphasis in original).

82. Slightly earlier in her discussion, not quoted here, Antonelli cites Maimonides' first explanation of circumcision.

83. B. Avodah Zarah 27a; see above, chapter 4, note 6.

84. Her dismissal of the view that "one must have a member to be a member" is directed at Eilberg-Schwartz, *The Savage in Judaism,* 145.

85. Goldingay, "Significance of Circumcision," 16.

86. Anticipate Maimonides: Abraham ibn Ezra (1089–1164), *Yesod Mora* 7.7, in Cohen-Simon, *Yesod Mora,* 140–41 (inspired by B. Sukkah 52a); Judah HaLevi (ca. 1075–1141), *Kuzari* 1:115. Follow Maimonides: see the sources collected by Glassberg, *Zichron Berit larishonim,* 3:211–20.

87. For an excellent recent biography of Spinoza, see Nadler, *Spinoza: A Life.* Spinoza's impact on the shaping of modern Jewish identities is the subject of

Smith, *Spinoza, Liberalism, and the Question of Jewish Identity.* On the Marrano background to Spinoza's thought, see Yovel, *Spinoza and Other Heretics.*

88. Spinoza, *Theological-Political Treatise* 3, trans. Shirley, *Spinoza Tractatus,* 99.

89. Spinoza, *Theological-Political Treatise* 3, trans. Shirley, *Spinoza Tractatus,* 100.

90. The Latin reads "nisi fundamenta suae religionis eorum animos effoeminarent." "Did not the principles of their religion make them effeminate" is the translation of Wernham, *Benedict de Spinoza: The Political Works,* 63.

91. On Spinoza's "Zionism," see Yovel, *Spinoza and Other Heretics,* 190–93.

92. Smith, *Spinoza, Liberalism, and the Question of Jewish Identity,* 101–2.

93. Geller, "A Paleontological View of Freud's Study of Religion," 59, writes of Spinoza "tying together circumcision, the persistence of the Jews, and effeminacy." Gilman, *Freud, Race, and Gender,* 57, writes of "Spinoza's often cited comments on the centrality of circumcision for the definition of the feminized Jewish male."

CHAPTER 7: TRUE FAITH AND THE EXEMPTION OF WOMEN

The source of the epigraph is Eliezer Berkovits, *Jewish Women in Time and Torah* (Hoboken, N.J.: Ktav, 1990), 5.

1. Maimonides, *Sefer HaMitzvot,* end of the positive commandments, trans. Chavel, *The Commandments,* 1:257–58 (slightly modified).

2. Actually, one of the sixty applies only to male priests: the commandment to bless the people of Israel (no. 26). Other medieval thinkers discussed the conditional or contingent nature of many of the commandments; see, for example, Abraham ibn Ezra, *Yesod Mora* 4, in Cohen-Simon, *Yesod Mora,* 114–18; Bekhor Shor on Deuteronomy 10:12, in Nebo, *Commentary of R. Joseph Bekhor Shor on the Torah,* 325.

3. Maimonides, *Sefer HaMitzvot,* end of the positive commandments, trans Chavel, *Commandments,* 1:260 (slightly modified).

4. The New Jewish Publication Society version notes that the "exact meaning and connection of vv. 11–12" are "uncertain." The translators also suggest that the verb should be construed as second-person feminine rather than as first-person masculine, but this is not our concern.

5. For these two readings of Zechariah 9:11, see the commentaries of (or ascribed to) Rashi, Ibn Ezra, and Radaq, ad loc.

6. Leviticus Rabbah 6:5 141 and Leviticus Rabbah 19:6 439.

7. Mekhilta on Exodus 12:6, *Bo* 5, 14HR, 1.33–34L.

8. Both men and women, of course, are obligated to observe the negative commandments also, but these are, by definition, acts of abnegation. In any case, all of them apply to women (as well as men) except three: see negative commandments nos. 43, 44, and 166, in Chavel, *Commandments,* 2:41–42 and 160–61, based on M. Qiddushin 1.7.

9. For what it is worth, I note that Maimonides nowhere cites the Mekhilta (note 7 above) that includes the citation from Zechariah 9:11. Instead he cites the version of Exodus Rabbah 19:6 that omits Zechariah 9:11. See Halkin and Hartman, *Crisis and Leadership,* 17–18; Maimonides, *Guide of the Perplexed* 3.46, in Pines, *Guide,* 585.

10. On Mühlhausen (also spelled Muehlhausen or Muelhausen), see M. Breuer, in Maimon, *Germania Judaica,* 3:1129–31; Ta-Shema, "Muelhausen, Yom Tov Lipmann." Talmage, introduction to his "*Sefer ha-Nissahon* of R. Yom Tov Lipmann Mühlhausen"; Yuval, "Kabbalisten, Ketzer und Polemiker," esp. 160–62; the classic study is Kaufman, *R. Yom Tov Lipmann Mühlhausen.* See also Krauss-Horbury, *Jewish-Christian Controversy,* 223–25. On Mühlhausen's communal activities, see Yuval, *Scholars in Their Time,* index, s.v. "Mühlhausen." Breuer places the composition of *Sefer HaNizzahon* in Krakow; the common opinion places it in Prague. On Mühlhausen as philosophical polemicist, see Lasker, "Philosophical Polemics in Ashkenaz," 206–10. On Mühlhausen's debt to Maimonides, see below.

11. Mühlhausen, *Nizzahon,* sec. 21, in Talmage, "*Sefer ha-Nissahon* of R. Yom Tov Lipmann Mühlhausen," 19. This passage is cited by David Zakut Modena, *Zekher David,* chap. 74, p. 200a. The last sentence (lit.: "save his body") is omitted in Hackspan's edition but is supplied by Wagenseil in Talmage, "*Sefer ha-Nissahon* of R. Yom Tov Lipmann Mühlhausen," 224.

12. Other passages in which *emunah* would seem to mean "religion" are *Nizzahon,* sec. 8 (p. 13), 259 (p. 140), 272 (p. 149), 288 (pp. 158 and 159), and 348 (p. 193).

13. The similarity of Mühlhausen's argument to Romans 4:9–10 was noticed by Joseph de Voisin, who in 1651 annotated and edited the *Pugio Fidei* of Raymond Martin. (His annotations were included in Carpzov's edition of 1688, which I have used.) See Voisin, *Observationes* 174, in Martin, *Pugio Fidei.* On the quality of Voisin's annotations, see Moore, "Christian Writers on Judaism," 208–9.

14. Mühlhausen, *Nizzahon,* sec. 209 (p. 117).

15. See S. Cohen, "Were Pharisees and Rabbis the Leaders of Communal Prayer and Torah Study in Antiquity?" 101–2, with bibliography.

16. Krauss-Horbury, *Jewish-Christian Controversy,* 224 n. 84.

17. Mühlhausen, *Nizzahon,* sec. 76 (p. 46).

18. Kellner, *Dogma in Medieval Jewish Thought,* 16. It is of no concern here whether "these foundations" are the entire set of thirteen principles or only a subset of them.

19. This is the theme of Kellner, *Dogma in Medieval Jewish Thought.*

20. Mühlhausen a Maimonidean: Lasker, "Philosophical Polemics in Ashkenaz," 200–201. Cites Maimonides: Mühlhausen, *Nizzahon,* introduction (p. 50 in the Hebrew page numeration); Talmage, *Apples of Gold,* 401–2. The only Ashkenazi Jew: Kellner, *Dogma in Medieval Jewish Thought,* 196. Introduction of the *Guide:* Ta-Shema, "Muelhausen," 500.

21. M. Pesahim 5:3 and 6:6; Yevamot 8:1 ('*arel* has wife and children); Zevahim 2:1 and 3:6, Menahot 1:2; Talmudim ad loc.; B. Hagigah 4b; Y. Pesahim

8:8 36b bottom. In theory gentiles are outside the rabbinic purity system, but de facto the rabbis attributed to gentiles a statutory degree of impurity.

22. B. Hulin 4b-5a (*yisrael ma'alya hu*) and B. Avodah Zarah 27a. See also Shulhan Arukh, Yoreh De'ah 2.7 and 264.1; Hoshen Mishpat 34.21. On the likelihood that the man is suffering from hemophilia, see Rosner, "Hemophilia in Classic Rabbinic Texts."

23. Tosafot B. Hagigah 4b, s.v. *demarbeh;* Zevahim 22b, s.v. *'arel;* Tosafot HoRosh B. Yevamot 70a, s.v. *he'arel.* Why wasn't he circumcised as an infant before he could develop his terror of circumcision? Perhaps his father was terrified too and therefore left him uncircumcised. Rabbenu Tam does not explain this point.

24. As indeed was done by the author of MS Oxford Bodleian Heb. 2074; see below.

25. Maimonides, *Laws of Circumcision,* 1.7 (some texts read "a gentile who is entering the community" but the meaning is the same no matter whether we read "gentile" or "proselyte"); *Laws of Forbidden Intercourse* 13.4.

26. See discussion in J. Stern, "Maimonides on Circumcision."

27. See my discussion in chapter 6 above, esp. note 25; in general, see Kellner, *Maimonides on the Jewish People.*

28. B. Shabbat 135a. First position, *eyn lo taqqanah:* see the commentary of Rabbenu Hannanel (printed on B. Shabbat 135b); a fuller version of Rabbenu Hannanel is cited by R. Jacob ben Asher in Tur, Yoreh De'ah 268. Rabbenu Nissim of Gerona (known as the Ran) on Shabbat 135a (see pp. 53b–54a in the Rif, s.v. *u le inyan ger*) attributes this view to Rabbenu Tam; see the Hiddushei Hagahot on the Tur. Second position, requires *hattafat dam berit:* see Halakhot Gedolot, ed. Hildesheimer (1972) 1:216 n. 35. Third position, he can be converted as he is: see Rabbenu Tam as cited in Tosafot Shabbat 135a, s.v. *lo nehlequ,* and Yevamot 46b, s.v. *de rabbi yosi.* Modern talmudists continue this debate; see the responsum of R. Moses Schick cited above in chapter 6, note 31; the responsum of R. Yehiel Jacob Weinberg cited in the next note; and, in a different rhetorical vein, Sagi and Zohar, *Conversion to Judaism.*

29. In modern times several jurists have addressed the question of converting a gentile man to Judaism who, for medical reasons, is unable to be circumcised. See, for example, R. Yehiel Jacob Weinberg (1885–1966), *Seridei Esh,* vol. 2, no. 102 (old numeration), vol. 2, no. 67 (new numeration).

30. I have dilated on this point because in the nineteenth century, advocates of Reform cited Mühlhausen in support of positions that Mühlhausen himself would have rejected. In 1843 Bar Amithai (a pseudonym for Joseph Johlson; see below, concluding chapter, note 22) adduced Mühlhausen in support of the position that newborn boys can be left uncircumcised and not forfeit their claims to Jewishness or their membership in the Jewish community. See Bar Amithai, *Ueber die Beschneidung in historischer und dogmatischer Himsicht,* 13. Mühlhausen might have agreed with this view in theory but would have disagreed in practice, arguing that an uncircumcised Jew of this kind is by definition an apostate who does not believe properly and whose membership in the community therefore is indeed compromised. In 1892 American Reformers adduced Mühlhausen in support of their conclusion that male con-

verts to Judaism do not require circumcision; see Central Conference of American Rabbis, *Yearbook 1891–92*, 67 and 99 (both with errors), and Solomon Freehof in Jacob and Zemer, *Conversion to Judaism*, 165–66. We may safely assume that Mühlhausen would have rejected this conclusion in both theory and practice.

31. Maimonides, *The Book of the Commandments*, positive commandment 76 (Chavel, *Commandments*, 1:88).

32. *Encyclopedia Judaica*, 3:833–35, s.v. "Attar, Hayyim ben Moses."

33. *Or haHayyim* on Exodus 39:32, in Bloom, ed., *Or haHayyim: Exodus* 170. (The *Or haHayyim* is printed in many rabbinic bibles.)

34. I would add: the people of Israel synchronically (that is, all the people of Israel alive at any one time, considered collectively) and diachronically (that is, all the people of Israel across time, considered collectively).

35. See note 30 above.

36. Codex Oxford Bodl. Heb. no. 2074, as published by Gellis, *Tosafot HaShalem*, 5:194. For information about this manuscript, see Beit-Arié, *Catalogue of the Hebrew Manuscripts in the Bodleian Library, Supplement*, 382–83.

37. M. Shabbat 2.6; see below, chapter 8, note 30.

38. Mühlhausen, *Nizzahon*, 8 (p. 12), 96 (p. 57), and 340 (p. 189).

CHAPTER 8: THE CELEBRATION OF WOMANHOOD

The source of the epigraph is Elizabeth Cady Stanton, *The Woman's Bible*, 2 vols. (New York: European Publishing Co., 1895–98; repr. New York: Arno Press, 1974), 1:75, comment on Exodus 4:24–26.

1. On R. Joseph Bekhor Shor (also known as R. Joseph ben Isaac of Orleans), see Urbach, *The Tosaphists*, 1:132–40. On his Torah commentary, see Smalley, *Study of the Bible in the Middle Ages*, 152–53 (by Louis Rabbinowitz). On his anti-Christian polemics, see Kamin, "R. Joseph Bekhor Shor's Polemic against Allegory"; Krauss-Horbury, *Jewish-Christian Controversy*, 85; and S. Cohen, "Does Rashi's Torah Commentary Respond to Christianity?" On the polemical background, see Grossman, "Jewish-Christian Polemic," 29–31. Touitou, "Rashi and His School," 242–44, recognized the anti-Christian intent of Bekhor Shor's comment on Genesis 17:11.

2. R. Joseph Bekhor Shor, commentary on Genesis 17:11, in Nebo, *Commentary of R. Joseph Bekhor Shor on the Torah*, 29; and M. Cohen, *Mikra'ot Gedolot* 1:155. This passage is attributed to R. Eleazar of Worms (known as the Roqeah) in *Sefer Hatzi Menashe*, ed. Menashe Grossberg (London, 5661 [1901], repr. Brooklyn, 5752 [1992]), 16, reprinted in Gellis, *Tosafot Hashalem*, 2:90. This attribution is almost certainly wrong; the comment is far more congruent with the style of Bekhor Shor than that of the Roqeah, and also it is absent from Konyefsky, *Rokeach. . . Braishith*, 145–52. I assume here that the passage is indeed by R. Joseph Bekhor Shor and that it became attributed to R. Eleazar Roqeah by mistake. (My thanks to Ivan Marcus for helping me to sort this out.)

3. R. Joseph Bekhor Shor, commentary on Genesis 17:2, in Nebo, *Commentary of R. Joseph Bekhor Shor on the Torah*, 29; and M. Cohen, *Mikra'ot Gedolot*, 1:153.

4. The Talmud, too, refers to identifying marks worn by slaves (B. Shabbat 57b–58a; see Lieberman, *Tosefta Ki-Fshuta* 3:74 on T. Shabbat 5.7 21). Mühlhausen as well argues that "the mark of circumcision is a sign that we are the slaves of God"; I do not know whether Mühlhausen read Bekhor Shor. See Mühlhausen, *Nizzahon*, sec. 20 (p. 19).

5. R. Joseph Bekhor Shor, commentary on Genesis 17:1, in Nebo, *Commentary*, 29; and M. Cohen, *Mikra'ot Gedolot*, 1:153.

6. See Genesis Rabbah 46.1 458 (on Genesis 17:1), and chapter 6 above, note 12.

7. R. Joseph Bekhor Shor, commentary on Genesis 17:2, in Nebo, *Commentary*, 29; and M. Cohen, *Mikra'ot Gedolot*, 1:153.

8. See chapter 2 above, at note 27 (Philo's fourth explanation).

9. The standard study of Rupert in English is van Engen, *Rupert of Deutz*, whose chronology I follow. On Rupert's polemical interest in Judaism, see van Engen, *Rupert of Deutz*, 241–48.

10. Rupertus Tuitiensis [Rupert of Deutz], *De Trinitate* 5.31–33 (PL 167: 394–97 [CCCM 21: 365–68]); *In Iohannis Evangelium* 3 (PL 169:308–13 [CCCM 9:140–46]); *Anulus, sive Dialogus inter Christianum et Judaeum* 1 (PL 170:561–68 [Haacke, *Ruperti Abbati Tuitiensis Anulus*,185–93]).

11. Rupertus Tuitiensis [Rupert of Deutz], *De Trinitate* 5.31 (PL 167:395a–b [CCCM 21:365]).

12. The parallel passages omit the jocular explanation and develop only the serious or "real" explanation; see *Commentaria in Iohanni Evangelium* 3 (PL 169:309–10 [CCCM 9:142]); and *Anulus, sive Dialogus inter Christianum et Judaeum* 1 (PL 170:564, Haacke, *Ruperti Abbati Tuitiensis Anulus*, 187–88]). These texts as well put the question in the mouth of the Jews.

13. Rupert is inspired, of course, by Romans 4:11; Bekhor Shor is inspired by B. Shabbat 137b and the second paragraph of the Grace after Meals.

14. Pelagius *Commentary on Romans* 2:26, in de Bruyn, *Pelagius's Commentary on St. Paul's Epistle to the Romans*, 76: "The reason they [the Israelites] were marked in that particular part of the body is, first of all, so that another part which was open to public view might not be disabled or defaced." Zacharias Chrysopolitanus (ca. 1152) took both of Rupert's explanations seriously; see PL 186:77b.

15. Cf. the statement of Jacob Anatoli, *Malmad Hatalmidim* 15a–b, cited in chapter 5 above, note 2.

16. On some of these other intersections see Kamin, "R. Joseph Bekhor Shor's Polemic against Allegory," 379–84.

17. B. Shabbat 108a; Genesis Rabbah 46.5 463; and parallels.

18. Bekhor Shor's approach may well have been inspired by Rashbam (R. Shmuel b. Meir, ca. 1080–1160), as is well noted by Touitou (citing Rashbam on Leviticus 11:34–38). On the impurity of the menstruant in rabbinic Judaism, see now Marienberg, *Niddah: Lorsque les juifs conceptualisent la menstruation*.

19. Regarding human corpses, Bekhor Shor adopts a different tack; human corpses are deemed impure in order to prevent worship of, or disrespect toward, the dead—or both. See Bekhor Shor on Numbers 19:2, in Nebo, *Commentary*, 274 (inspired in part by M. Yadayim 4.6).

20. Bekhor Shor on Leviticus 12:4, in Nebo, *Commentary*, 196. For other examples of Bekhor Shor's rationalization of the purity rules, noted by Nebo, *Commentary*, 9, see Bekhor Shor's commentary on Leviticus 11:8, 14:40, and 15:31 (Nebo, *Commentary*, 194, 201, and 204).

21. The word is *zihum*, which can indeed refer to a metaphysical quality ("corruption"), as in B. Yevamot 103b and parallels, "when the serpent had intercourse with Eve, he cast corruption *(zuhama)* into her," but here Bekhor Shor is using it in a physical sense, following B. Niddah 65b.

22. The standard treatment in English is Berger, *Jewish-Christian Debate*. See also Trautner-Kromann, *Shield and Sword*, 102–16; and Krauss-Horbury, *Jewish-Christian Controversy*, 246–47.

23. *Nizzahon Vetus* (or *Nizzahon Yashan*) para. 237, in Berger, *Jewish-Christian Debate*, 224, and in Breuer, *Sefer Nizzahon Yashan*, 192.

24. On R. Yair ben Shabbetai and the *Herev Piphioth*, see Rosenthal's introduction to his edition of the book, and Krauss-Horbury, *Jewish-Christian Controversy*, 217.

25. Rosenthal, *Herev Piphioth*, 73.

26. Justin Martyr *Dialogue with Trypho* 19 and 33, cited by Rosenthal, *Herev Piphioth*, 73 n. 2.

27. Rosenthal, *Herev Piphioth*, 77.

28. Rosenthal prints *yod-vav-peh-yod* followed by the abbreviation sign; this is certainly a mistake, whether by Correggio, the copyist, or Rosenthal I cannot say. Surely the text should read *aleph-peh-yod*, a standard abbreviation for *afilu*, "even."

29. Or, perhaps, "the collectivity of Israel," or "the people of Israel" (Heb. *kelal yisrael*). I am tempted to use Solomon Schechter's wonderful phrase "catholic Israel."

30. M. Shabbat 2.6.

31. Correggio's last sentence is based on Psalms 72:13 and Isaiah 63:7.

32. I do not know whether Correggio knew either Bekhor Shor or Mühlhausen; neither appears on Correggio's list of works cited (Rosenthal, *Herev Piphioth*, 15).

33. See chapter 1, notes 102–7.

34. Eilberg-Schwartz, *The Savage in Judaism*, 184. This idea is developed by Archer, "'In Thy Blood Live'," and "Bound by Blood," and by Hoffman, *Covenant of Blood*.

35. Bettelheim, *Symbolic Wounds*, esp. 154–206.

36. See chapter 1 above, at note 22.

37. See chapter 3 above, note 58 re Abelard.

38. M. Yevamot 6:6; B. Yevamot 65b; Hauptman, *Rereading the Rabbis*, 130–46.

39. Bouhdiba, *Sexuality in Islam*, 186; Crapanzano, "Rite of Return," 20.

40. Langer, *Worship*, 60–73.

41. Well noted by Langer, *Worship*, 61.

42. Gendler, "Sarah's Seed." See below, concluding chapter, note 28.

43. See, for example, *Sefer ha Hinukh* nos. 181 and 207.

44. Shevitz, "Covenant of the Flesh"; and Seidenberg, "Brit Taharah," who might have profitably cited Bekhor Shor. On "the covenant you have sealed in our flesh," see my discussion in chapter 5 above.

CONCLUSION

The source of the epigraph is Gotthold Ephraim Lessing, *Nathan the Wise*, act IV, scene 2: "Denn ist Nicht Alles, was man Kindern thut, Gewalt?—Zu sagen: ausgenommen, was die Kirch' an Kindern thut."

1. Trier, *Rabbinische Gutachten;* Meisl, "Zur Geschichte der jüdischen Reformbewegung." Philipson, *Reform Movement in Judaism,* 131–39; Katz, *Divine Law in Human Hands,* 320–56, and cf. 357–402; Meyer, *Response to Modernity,* 122–23. The fullest discussion is now Judd, *German Jewish Rituals,* chap. 1, summarized in her "Circumcision and Modern Jewish Life."

2. Hirsch, "66 Wiener Aerzte," esp. 118–20; *Referate . . . der ersten israelitischen Synode,* 196–97.

3. Plaut, *Rise of Reform Judaism,* 211; cf. Central Conference of American Rabbis *Yearbook,* 5651 [1890–91], 115.

4. Central Conference of American Rabbis *Yearbook,* 5651 [1890–91], 120.

5. Central Conference of American Rabbis, *Yearbook,* 5653 [1892–93], 36.

6. Bacon, "Circumcision Controversy." Analogous incidents had occurred earlier in Hannover in 1870 and Vienna in 1872; see Judd, *German Jewish Rituals,* chap. 2.

7. The standard modern history of Reform is Meyer, *Response to Modernity.*

8. This is the slogan associated with R. Moshe Sofer, known as the Hatam Sofer (1762–1839).

9. See Silber, "Emergence of Ultra-Orthodoxy," a wonderful article.

10. *Frankfurter Journal, Beilage* no. 183 (July 5, 1843): "durch das Nichtanerkennen der Beschneidung hört der Jude auf, Jude zu seyn; ohne Beschneidung ist kein Judenthum möglich, denn das ist Dogma und nicht Ritual."

11. In his previous sentence the author explicitly compares Judaism to Christianity: "in der jüdischen Religion eben so gut wie in der christlichen ein Unterschied zwischen *Dogma* und *Ceremonie* zu machen ist."

12. *Karet,* usually translated "extirpation," is the punishment of being "cut off" from one's people. What exactly this means is not clear and was debated by rabbinic exegetes.

13. Soloveitchik, *Halakhic Man,* 90. I have slightly modified Kaplan's translation.

14. I say this even though in 1892, when the Czarist government closed the yeshiva of Volozhin, which he had headed, R. Hayyim became the community rabbi of Brisk (Brest-Litovsk). I do not know the date of this conference; perhaps it was occasioned by the circumcision controversy of 1908 in Warsaw (see note 6 above).

15. *Frankfurter Journal, Beilage* no. 188 (July 10, 1843): "Wodurch treten denn die Töchter in das Judenthum ein? Die Wahrheit ist, dass, nach den Principien des mosaischen Glaubens, die Geburt zum Juden macht und dass der von jüdischen Eltern Erzeugte zur jüdischen Religionsgesellschaft gehört, selbst

wenn er kein einziges Ceremonialgebot beobachten sollte, so lange er nicht die Grundlehre von einem einzigen Gotte und die Offenbarung läugnet."

16. Central Conference of American Rabbis, *Yearbook*, 5651 [1890–91], 93 and 99.

17. Similarly Holdheim, *Ueber die Beschneidung zunächst in religiös-dogmatischer Beziehung*, 8–10, is at pains to argue that even in terms of biblical religion, women and men alike belong to the religious community by virtue of their birth. Holdheim rejects the idea that men entered the community through circumcision and that women entered through their relationship with an Israelite male. All of this is quite remarkable given the Reform tendency to emphasize Judaism's status as a religion, and to deemphasize Judaism's status as a people or ethnicity.

18. Rabbi Jakob Bamberger of Worms, in Trier, *Rabbinische Gutachten*, 162, sensed the affinity between the Reformers' arguments and Paul, but did not realize that the closest analogy to the Reformers' arguments comes from the church fathers.

19. To be sure, not all of these texts had been published by 1843.

20. See the responsa of Rabbi Adler of Hannover; Rabbis S. Fürst of Heidelberg and H. Traub of Mannheim; and Rabbi Leopold Schott of Randegg in Trier, *Rabbinische Gutachten*, 11, 198, and 226–27; this also seems to be the point of Rabbi Felsenstein of Hanau and Rabbi Löwenstein of Gailingen in Trier, *Rabbinische Gutachten*, 21 and 177. On R. Jacob ben Abba Mari Anatoli and Menahem, see chapter 5 above.

21. See, for example, Goldman, *Questioning Circumcision*, and at www .circumcision.org; Pollack, "Redefining the Sacred"; and Karsenty, "A Mother Questions Brit Milla."

22. Bar Amithai, *Ueber die Beschneidung;* Meyer, "The First Identical Ceremony." Bar Amithai is a pseudonym for Joseph Johlson; see Meyer, *Response to Modernity*, 123.

23. The evidence is circumstantial. Tosefta Megillah 3.15 357 (and parallels) has a reference to *shevua ha ben*, which in context may well mean "the circumcision celebration." See the discussion in Rubin, *Beginning of Life*, 117–19. However R. Isaac ibn Ghiyyat (1038–1089) and R. Moses ben Nahman (1194–1270, known as Nahmanides), both of Spain, preserve a variant reading that contrasts the *shevua ha ben* with the *shevua ha bat*. In this case, the former cannot mean "the circumcision celebration," and the parallel phrases would seem to refer respectively to week-long celebrations of the births of boys and girls. The evidence is assembled by Lieberman TK 5.1186–87, whence Hoffman, *Covenant of Blood*, 177–79. This reading is also cited by the *Orhot Hayyim* of R. Aharon Ha Cohen of Lunel (early 1300s), 2.14, ed. Schlesinger. I deduce that in Spain and Provence, the births of boys and girls were celebrated with weeklong festivities.

24. The fullest discussion of the *Hollekreisch* (both spelling and etymology are debated) is Hamburger, *Shorshei Minhag Ashkenaz*, 1:415–55; the fullest discussion in English is Pollack, *Jewish Folkways in Germanic Lands*, 27–28; Omi, "Jewish Women's Naming Rites," 145–47. In 1998 my wife, Miriam, had the good fortune of meeting a woman who had attended the *Hollekreisch* celebrating the birth of Miriam's mother in Friedberg, Germany, in 1921.

25. The circumvention has occurred in stages. In the 1970s Rabbi Joel Roth argued that women could be admitted to the Rabbinical School of the Jewish Theological Seminary if they accepted an obligation to pray akin to that of men. Recently Judith Hauptman has argued that in fact women and men are equally obligated to pray, and that women do not need any special ritual act in order to make themselves like men. See Hauptman, "Women and Prayer."

26. See above, chapter 1, note 107.

27. Weber ed., *Mappot*, 166–67, no. 29, and p. 172. The full name of the town is Budyne nad Ohri. The author of the catalogue entry for this *wimpel*, Eva Frojmovic, correctly notes its importance. The family name on the *wimpel* is Nellner (with a *nun*, not a *gimel)*, but Frojmovic notes that Nellner is not a known family name, whereas there was a Gellner family in the town in the 1930s. Hence the *nun* must be a mistake for a *gimel* (evidence for Hebrew illiteracy?). Hamburger, *Shorshei* 2:537, also notes that this *wimpel* is "unusual." No doubt the preparation and presentation of this *wimpel* were facilitated by the fact that in Bohemia the link between *wimpel* and circumcision had weakened, so that *wimpel*s were presented to synagogues there upon all sorts of occasions, not just circumcisions; see Hamburger, *Shorshei Minhag Ashkenaz*, 2:420. Perhaps this was under Italian influence, since Italian *wimpel*s never had any connection with *berit* or childbirth (Hamburger, *Shorshei Minhag Ashkenaz*, 2: 414–18 and 535–36).

28. Gendler, "Sarah's Seed." Knight, "Curing Cut," 336–38, argues that a ritualized rupturing of the hymen (in ancient Egypt) may have been the ultimate source for the later practice of female circumcision.

29. See "Welcoming Children into Name and Covenant," chapter 3 in Orenstein, *Lifecycles* (contributions by Laura Geller and Shulamit Magnus), as well as Magnus, "Re-Inventing Miriam's Well," esp. 341. For a collection of ceremonies celebrating the birth of girls, see, for example, D. Cohen, *Celebrating Your New Jewish Daughter*. For discussion, see Goldberg, *Jewish Passages*, 67–76; Omi, "Naming Rites;" Millen, *Women, Birth and Death*, 70–108.

30. Shulamit Magnus in Orenstein, *Lifecycles,* 68–69. An analogue to this suggestion might be the *simhat betulim,* the public celebration on the display of the tokens of a bride's virginity (see above, chapter 8, note 40). This practice has long since fallen into desuetude; what was once public is now private.

31. So I have been informed by various (non-Orthodox) rabbis.

32. For an assessment of contemporary arguments against circumcision, see Gilman, "Decircumcision: The First Aesthetic Surgery," and Levenson, "New Enemies of Circumcision." On the anti-circumcision movement in Israel, see Tabory and Erez, "Circumscribed Circumcision." Opponents of circumcision are well represented on the Internet.

33. These arguments are developed forcefully by Sami A. Aldeeb Abu-Sahlieh, "To Mutilate in the Name of Jehovah or Allah," which is available on various Internet sites; they are developed briefly by Gollaher, *Circumcision: A History of the World's Most Controversial Surgery,* 205, among others.

34. Kenyatta, *Facing Mount Kenya,* 133.

35. "In Kenyan Family, Ritual for Girls Still Divides," *New York Times,* January 6, 2002; "In Africa, Girls Fight a Painful Tradition"; *New York Times,*

January 3, 2004; "Genital Cutting Shows Signs of Losing Favor in Africa," *New York Times*, Tuesday June 8, 2004. In general, see Rahman and Toubia, *Female Genital Mutilation*.

36. See Levenson, "The New Enemies of Circumcision"; Francine Klagsbrun, in *Moment* (April 1997): 22.

37. See above, chapter 1, notes 69 and 84.

38. Hughes, "Distinguishing Signs," 22 n. 62, argues that some members of the Jewish community of Trapani (in Sicily) were trying at the beginning of the fifteenth century to withhold circumcision from their sons yet remain Jews. This is an error; she has misread the document that she cites. The only post-Hellenistic, pre-modern Jewish critique of Jewish circumcision of which I am aware is in *Kol Sakhal*, "The Voice of a Fool," which argues that male gentiles should be allowed to convert to Judaism even without circumcision; see Fishman, *Shaking the Pillars of Exile*, 150.

39. See, for example, the news stories collected at www.geocities.com/HotSprings/2754/, accessed on June, 8, 2004.

40. www.4woman.gov/faq/hysterectomy.htm#2, accessed on June 8, 2004.

41. I have bracketed these sentences with the words "if we may believe the opponents of female genital mutilation," because western discourse about female circumcision has been shaped exclusively by its opponents. However, as Shweder observes, opponents of the ritual have no clinical evidence to support their claim that female circumcision causes a life of pain for its recipients or endangers their health. On the contrary, circumcised African women report that they do enjoy sex, and there is no statistical evidence that they suffer from higher rates of miscarriage or disease than non-circumcised women. Perhaps, concludes Shweder, our abhorrence of African female genital mutilation is a function of our own western conception of the clitoris as the focal point of female sexual pleasure, and we should not impose our conceptions on others. See Shweder, "'Female Genital Mutilation.'" If this be true—and I leave this for others to determine—the horror stories told by the opponents of female circumcision have no greater statistical validity than the horror stories told by the opponents of male circumcision. Perhaps, then, an argument could be made for moral parity between female circumcision and male circumcision, not in order to proscribe them both but in order to tolerate them both (this indeed seems to be Shweder's position).

Bibliography

Abramson, Shraga, ed. *Tractate ʿAbodah Zarah of the Babylonian Talmud MS. Jewish Theological Seminary.* New York: Jewish Theological Seminary, 1957 (Hebrew).

Abulafia, Anna Sapir. *Christians and Jews in the Twelfth-Century Renaissance.* London: Routledge, 1995.

Abulafia, Anna Sapir, and G. R. Evans, ed. *The Works of Gilbert Crispin.* London and New York: Oxford University Press, 1986.

Anatoli, Jacob ben Abba Mari. *Malmad Hatalmidim.* Lyck: M'kize Nirdamim, 1866 (Hebrew).

Anidjar, Gil. "On the (Under)Cutting Edge: Does Jewish Memory Need Sharpening?" In *Jews and Other Differences: The New Jewish Cultural Studies,* ed. Jonathan Boyarin and Daniel Boyarin, 360–96. Minneapolis: University of Minnesota Press, 1997.

Antonelli, Judith S. *In the Image of God: A Feminist Commentary on the Torah.* Northvale, N.J.: Jason Aaronson, 1995.

Archer, Leonie. "Bound by Blood: Circumcision and Menstrual Taboo." In *After Eve: Women, Theology, and the Christian Tradition,* ed. Janet M. Soskice, 38–61. London: Marshall Pickering/Collins, 1990.

———. "'In Thy Blood Live': Gender and Ritual in the Judaeo-Christian Tradition." In *Through the Devil's Gateway: Women, Religion, and Taboo,* ed. Alison Joseph, 22–49. London: SPCK, 1990.

Asaf, Simha. "From the Prayer Book of the Land of Israel." In *Sefer Dinaburg: Studies Offered to Ben Zion Dinaburg,* ed. Y. Baer et al., 116–31. Jerusalem: Qiryat Sefer, 1949 (Hebrew).

Bacon, Gershon. "Religious Coercion, Freedom of Expression and Modern Jewish Identity in Poland: I. L. Peretz, Sholem Asch and the 'Circumcision Scandal' in Warsaw, 1908." In *From Vilna to Jerusalem: Studies in the History and Culture of the Jews of Eastern Europe Offered to Prof. Shmuel*

Werses, edited by David Asaf et al., 167–85. Jerusalem: Magnes Press, 2002 (Hebrew).

Bar Amithai [Joseph Johlson, pseud.]. *Ueber die Beschneidung in historischer und dogmatischer Himsicht.* Frankfurt: Hermann, 1843.

Barclay, John. "Paul and Philo on Circumcision." *New Testament Studies* 44 (1998): 536–56.

Baron, Salo. *A Social and Religious History of the Jews.* 2nd ed. 18 vols. New York: Columbia University Press, 1953–83.

Bartholinus, Thomas. *De Morbis Biblicis, Miscellanea Medica.* 2nd ed. Frankfurt am Main: Danielis Paullus, 1672.

Baskin, Judith. *Midrashic Women: Formations of the Feminine in Rabbinic Literature.* Hanover, N.H., and London: Brandeis University Press/University Press of New England, 2002.

Baumgarten, Elisheva. "Circumcision and Baptism." In *The Covenant of Circumcision,* ed. Elizabeth Wyner Mark, 114–27. Hanover, N.H.: Brandeis University Press/University Press of New England, 2003.

Bebermeyer, Gustav, ed. *Heinrich Bebels Facetien.* Bibliothek des literarischen Vereins in Stuttgart 276. Leipzig: Hiersemann, 1931.

Beit-Arié, Malachi, and R. A. May. *Catalogue of the Hebrew Manuscripts in the Bodleian Library: Supplement of Addenda and Corrigenda.* Oxford: Clarendon Press, 1994.

Belkin, Samuel. *The Midrash of Philo . . . 1: Genesis II–XVII.* Edited by E. Hurvitz. New York: Yeshiva University Press, 1989 (Hebrew).

Bennington, Geoffrey, and Jacques Derrida. *Jacques Derrida,* trans. G. Bennington. Chicago: University of Chicago Press, 1993

Benovitz, Moshe. *Kol Nidre: A Study of Rabbinic Votive Institutions.* Brown Judaic Studies 315. Atlanta: Scholars Press, 1998.

Berger, David. *The Jewish-Christian Debate in the High Middle Ages: A Critical Edition of Nizzahon Vetus.* Philadelphia: Jewish Publication Society, 1979.

Berkey, Jonathan. "Circumcision Circumscribed: Female Excision and Cultural Accommodation in the Medieval Near East." *International Journal of Middle East Studies* 28 (1996): 19–38.

Berman, Saul. "The Status of Women in Halakhic Judaism." *Tradition* 14, no. 2 (Fall 1973): 5–28.

Bettelheim, Bruno. *Symbolic Wounds: Puberty Rites and the Envious Male.* Rev. ed. New York: Collier, 1962.

Betz, Otto. "Beschneidung." *Theologische Realenzyklopädie* 5 (1980): 719–22.

Biale, Rachel. *Women and Jewish Law.* New York: Schocken, 1984.

Bickerman, Elias. "'Couper une alliance'." In his *Studies in Jewish and Christian History,* pt. 1, 1–32. Leiden: Brill, 1976.

Bigelmair, Andreas. *Des heiligen Bischofs Zeno von Verona Traktate.* Bibliothek der Kirchenväter, Reihe 2, Band 10. Munich: Kösel & Pustet, 1934.

Birnbaum, Ellen. *The Place of Judaism in Philo's Thought: Israel, Jews, and Proselytes.* Brown Judaic Studies 290. Atlanta: Scholars Press, 1996.

Birnbaum, Philip. *Daily Prayer Book Ha-Siddur Ha-Shalem.* New York: Hebrew Publishing, 1949.

Bloom, A, ed. *Sefer Or haHayyim al haTorah*. Jerusalem: A. Bloom, 5789 [1989].

Blumenkranz, Bernhard. *Les auteurs chrétiens latins du moyen age sur les juifs et le judaïsme*. Paris: Mouton, 1963.

———. *Die Judenpredigt Augustins*. Basel, 1946; repr. Paris: Études Augustiniennes, 1973.

———. *Le juif médiéval au miroir de l'art chrétien*. Paris: Études Augustiniennes, 1966.

Bonfil, Robert. *Jewish Life in Renaissance Italy*, trans. Anthony Oldcorn. Berkeley and Los Angeles: University of California Press, 1994.

Boon, James A. "Circumscribing Circumcision/Uncircumcision: An Essay amidst the History of Difficult Description." In *Implicit Understandings: Observing . . . the Encounters between Europeans and Other Peoples in the Early Modern Era*, ed. Stuart Schwartz, 556–85. Cambridge: Cambridge University Press, 1994.

Børresen, Kari Elisabeth. "God's Image, Man's Image? Patristic Interpretation of Gen. 1,27 and I Cor. 11,7," and "God's Image: Is Woman Excluded? Medieval Interpretations of Gen. 1,27 and I Cor. 11,7." In *Image of God and Gender Models in Judaeo-Christian Tradition*. ed. K. E. Børresen, 188–207 and 208–27. Oslo: Solum, 1991.

Bouhdiba, Abdelwahab. *Sexuality in Islam*, trans. Alan Sheridan. London: Routledge & Kegan Paul, 1985.

Boyarin, Daniel. *Dying for God*. Stanford: Stanford University Press, 1999.

———. *A Radical Jew: Paul and the Politics of Identity*. Berkeley and Los Angeles: University of California Press, 1994.

———. *Unheroic Conduct: The Rise of Heterosexuality and the Invention of the Jewish Man*. Berkeley and Los Angeles: University of California Press, 1997.

Breuer, Mordechai. *Sefer Nizzahon Yashan*. Ramat Gan: Bar Ilan University Press, 1978.

Brodkin, Karen. *How Jews Became White Folks and What That Says about Race in America*. New Brunswick, N.J.: Rutgers University Press, 1998.

Brody, Robert. *The Geonim of Babylonia and the Shaping of Medieval Jewish Culture*. New Haven: Yale University Press, 1998.

Brooten, Bernadette. *Love between Women: Early Christian Responses to Female Homoeroticism*. Chicago: University of Chicago, 1996.

———. *Women Leaders in the Ancient Synagogue*. Brown Judaic Studies 36. Chico, Calif.: Scholars Press, 1982.

Broshi, Magen. *The Damascus Document Reconsidered*. Jerusalem: Israel Exploration Society, 1992.

Browe, Peter. *Die Judenmission im Mittelalter und die Päpste*. Miscellanea Historiae Pontificiae 6. Rome, 1942; repr. Rome: Università Gregoriana Editrice, 1973.

Browne, Thomas. *Pseudodoxia Epidemica; or, Enquiries into Very Many Received Tenents [sic] and Commonly Presumed Truths*. London: T. H. for Edward Dod, 1646. Microfilm repr., Early English Books, 1641–1700, no. 810:20. Ann Arbor: University Microfilms, 1978.

Bruyn, Theodore de. *Pelagius's Commentary on St. Paul's Epistle to the Romans*. Oxford: Clarendon, 1993.

Bryk, Felix. *Circumcision in Man and Woman*, trans. David Berger. New York: American Ethnological Press, 1934.

B[ulwer], J[ohn]. *A View of the People of the Whole World*. London: William Hunt, 1654. Microfilm repr., Early English Books, 1641–1700, no. 839:1. Ann Arbor: University Microfilms, 1978.

Burmester, O. H. E. "The Sayings of Michael, Metropolitan of Damietta," *Orientalia Christiana Periodica* 2 (1936).

Bynum, Caroline Walker. *Jesus as Mother: Studies in the Spirituality of the High Middle Ages*. Berkeley and Los Angeles: University of California Press, 1982.

Cahana, I. [Itzhak] Z. *Rabbi Meir ben Barukh (Maharam) of Rottenburg: Responsa, Rulings and Customs*. 3 vols. Jerusalem: Mossad HaRav Kook, 1957–62 (Hebrew).

Chavel, Charles [Hayim], ed. *Sefer HaHinukh*. 5th ed. Jerusalem: Mosad HaRav Kook, 5722 [1962]. Frequently reprinted.

———. *The Commandments: Sefer Ha-Mitzvoth of Maimonides*. 2 vols. London and New York: Soncino Press, 1967.

Chadwick, Henry, trans. *Origen contra Celsum*. Cambridge: Cambridge University Press, 1965.

Chazan, Robert. *Daggers of Faith: Thirteenth-Century Christian Missionizing and Jewish Response*. Berkeley and Los Angeles: University of California Press, 1989.

Chernick, Michael. "*ish* as Man and Adult in the Halakhic Midrashim," *Jewish Quarterly Review* 73 (1982–83): 254–80.

Clarke, Ernest G., ed. *The Aramaic Bible*, 4: *Targum Neofiti 1 Numbers and Targum Pseudo-Jonathan Numbers*. Edinburgh: T. & T. Clark, 1995.

Cloudsley, Anne. *Women of Omdurman: Life, Love and the Cult of Virginity*. London: Ethnographica, 1983.

Cohen, Debra Nussbaum. *Celebrating Your New Jewish Daughter. Creating Jewish Ways to Welcome Baby Girls into the Covenant: New and Traditional Ceremonies*. Woodstock, Vt.: Jewish Lights Publishing, 2001.

Cohen, Jeremy. *The Friars and the Jews*. Ithaca, N.Y.: Cornell University Press, 1982.

Cohen, Joseph, and Uriel Simon. *R. Abraham ibn Ezra Yesod Mora ve-Sod Torah*. Ramat Gan: Bar Ilan University Press, 2002 (Hebrew).

Cohen, Menachem, ed. *Mikra'ot Gedolot Haketer: Genesis, Part 1*. Ramat Gan: Bar Ilan University, 1997 (Hebrew).

Cohen, Shaye J. D. *The Beginnings of Jewishness*. Berkeley and Los Angeles: University of California, 1999.

———. "Between Judaism and Christianity: The Semicircumcision of Christians according to Bernard Gui, His Sources, and R. Eliezer of Metz," *Harvard Theological Review* 94 (2001): 285–321.

———. "A Brief History of Jewish Circumcision Blood." In *The Covenant of Circumcision*, ed. Elizabeth Wyner Mark, 30–42. Hanover, N.H.: Brandeis University Press/University Press of New England, 2003.

———. "Does Rashi's Torah Commentary Respond to Christianity? A Comparison of Rashi with Rashbam and Bekhor Shor." In *The Idea of Biblical Interpretation: Essays in Honor of James Kugel,* ed. H. Najman and J. H. Newman, 449–72. Leiden: Brill, 2004.

———. "Judaism without Circumcision and 'Judaism' without 'Circumcision' in Ignatius." *Harvard Theological Review* 95 (2002): 395–415.

———. "Respect for Judaism by Gentiles in the Writings of Josephus," *Harvard Theological Review* 80 (1987): 409–30.

———. "Were Pharisees and Rabbis the Leaders of Communal Prayer and Torah Study in Antiquity?" In *Evolution of the Synagogue: Problems and Progress,* ed. H. C. Kee and L. H. Cohick, 89–105. Harrisburg, Pa.: Trinity Press International, 1999.

———. "Why Aren't Jewish Women Circumcised?" *Gender and History* 9 (1997): 560–78.

———. "'Your Covenant That You Have Sealed in Our Flesh': Women, Covenant, and Circumcision." In *Louis H. Feldman Festschrift* (forthcoming).

Collins, John J. "A Symbol of Otherness: Circumcision and Salvation in the First Century." In *To See Ourselves as Others See Us,* ed. J. Neusner and E. Frerichs, 163–86. Chico, Calif.: Scholars Press, 1985. Reprinted in Collins, *Seers, Sybils, and Sages in Hellenistic-Roman Judaism.* Leiden: Brill, 1997.

Colson, F. H. trans. and ed., with G. H. Whitaker. *The Works of Philo.* Loeb Classical Library. Cambridge, Mass: Harvard University Press, and London: Heinemann, 1929–62.

Crapanzano, Vincent. "Rite of Return: Circumcision in Morocco." *The Psychoanalytic Study of Society* 9 (1981): 15–36.

Cunningham, J. J. *St. Thomas Aquinas Summa Theologiae,* vol. 57. New York: McGraw-Hill, and London: Eyre & Spottiswoode, 1975.

Dahan, Gilbert. *Les intellectuals chrétiens et les juifs au moyen âge.* Paris: Éditions du Cerf, 1990.

———. *La polémique chrétienne contre le judaisme au moyen âge.* Paris: Albin Michel, 1991.

Dean-Jones, Lesley A. *Women's Bodies in Classical Greek Science.* Oxford: Clarendon, 1994.

Dédéyan, Charles, ed. *Montaigne: Journal de voyage en Italie par la Suisse et l'Allemagne.* Paris: Société les Belles Lettres, 1946.

Dorff, Elliot. "Custom Drives Jewish Law on Women." *Conservative Judaism* 49, no. 3 (Spring 1997): 3–21.

Drazin, Israel. *Targum Onkelos to Exodus.* [Hoboken, N.J.]: Ktav, and Denver: Center for Judaic Studies, University of Denver, 1990.

Ehrenreich, Ch. L., ed. *Sefer Abudarham* [sic] *von Rabbi David Abudraham.* Cluj-Klausenburg: Weinstein & Friedmann, 1927 (Hebrew).

Eilberg-Schwartz, Howard. "The Fruitful Cut." In his *The Savage in Judaism,* 141–76. Bloomington: Indiana University Press, 1990.

———. *God's Phallus and Other Problems for Men and Monotheism.* Boston: Beacon Press, 1994.

Elman, Yaakov. "The Small Scale of Things: The World before the Genizah." *Proceedings of the American Academy for Jewish Research* 63 (1997–2001): 49–85.

van Engen, John H. *Rupert of Deutz.* Berkeley and Los Angeles: University of California Press, 1983.

Fabre-Vassas, Claudine. *The Singular Beast: Jews, Christians, and the Pig.* New York: Columbia University Press, 1997.

Falk, Zeev. "The Status of Women in the Communities of Ashkenaz and France in the Middle Ages. *Sinai* 48 (5721 [1961]): 361–67 (Hebrew).

Falls, Thomas, trans. *St. Justin Martyr: Dialogue with Trypho.* Rev. Thomas Halton. Washington, D.C.: Catholic University of America Press, 2003.

———. *Writings of Saint Justin Martyr.* Fathers of the Church 6. New York: Christian Heritage, 1948

Finkelstein, Louis, ed. "The Birkat Ha-Mazon." *Jewish Quarterly Review* 19 (1928–29): 211–62.

———. *Jewish Self-Government in the Middle Ages.* New York: Jewish Theological Seminary, 1924; repr. New York: Feldheim, 1964.

———. *Sifra or Torat Kohanim according to Codex Assemani LXVI.* New York: Jewish Theological Seminary, 1956.

Fishman, Talya. "A Kabbalistic Perspective on Gender-Specific Commandments." *AJS Review* 17 (1992): 199–245.

———. *Shaking the Pillars of Exile: "Voice of a Fool," an Early Modern Jewish Critique of Rabbinic Culture.* Stanford: Stanford University Press, 1997.

Fleischer, Manfred P. "Are Women Human?" *Sixteenth Century Journal* 12 (1981): 107–20.

Flusser, David, and Shmuel Safrai. "Who Sanctified the Beloved in the Womb?" *Immanuel* 11 (1980): 46–55.

Fox, Michael V. "The Sign of the Covenant: Circumcision in the Light of the Priestly 'ot Etiologies." *Revue Biblique* 81 (1974): 557–96.

Frame, Donald, trans. *Montaigne's Travel Journal.* San Francisco: North Point Press, 1983.

Frankel, Yonah, ed. *Mahazor leShavuot lefi minhag beney Ashkenaz.* Jerusalem: Koren, 5760 [2000].

Friedlander, Gerald, trans. *Pirkê de Rabbi Eliezer.* London, 1916; repr. New York: Hermon, 1965.

Frojmovic, Eva. "Christian Travelers to the Circumcision." In *The Covenant of Circumcision,* ed. Elizabeth Wyner Mark, 128–41. Hanover, N.H.: Brandeis University Press/University Press of New England, 2003.

Funkenstein, Amos. "Changes in Christian Anti-Jewish Polemics in the Twelfth Century," In his *Perceptions of Jewish History,* 172–201. Berkeley and Los Angeles: University of California Press, 1993.

Garvin, Joseph, and James Corbett. *The Summa Contra Haereticos Ascribed to Praepositinus of Cremona.* Publications in Medieval Studies 15. Notre Dame: University of Notre Dame Press, 1958.

Geller, Jay. "A Paleontological View of Freud's Study of Religion: Unearthing the *Leitfossil* Circumcision." *Modern Judaism* 13 (1993): 49–70.

Gellis, Jacob, ed. *Tosafot HaShalem: Otzar Perushe Ba'alei haTosaphot.* 10 vols.

Jerusalem: Ariel United Israel Institutes/Mifal Tosafot Hashalem, 5742–
[1982–] (Hebrew).

Gendler, Mary. "Sarah's Seed: A New Ritual for Women." *Response* 24 (Winter
1974–75): 65–75.

Gilman, Sander L. "Decircumcision: The First Aesthetic Surgery." *Modern Judaism* 17, no. 3 (1997): 201–10.

———. *Freud, Race, and Gender.* Princeton: Princeton University Press, 1993.

Ginzberg, Louis. *The Legends of the Jews.* 7 vols. Philadelphia: Jewish Publication Society, 1909–38. Frequently reprinted.

———. *The Responsa of Professor Louis Ginzberg.* Ed. David Golinkin. New
York and Jerusalem: Jewish Theological Seminary, 1996.

Glasberg, A., ed. *Die Beschneidung in ihrer geschichtlichen, ethnographischen,
religiosen und medicinischen Bedeutung.* Berlin: M. Poppelauer's Buchhandlung [Poppelauer is pasted over the name of the original publisher, which apparently was C. Boas], 1896

Glassberg, Jacob. *Zichron berit larishonim.* 3 parts (paginated consecutively);
parts 1 and 2 are in Hebrew, part 3 is in German. Krakow: Fischer 1892.
Parts 1 and 2 were reprinted in Jerusalem, 5782 [1982].

Goitein, S. D. *A Mediterranean Society,* 3: *The Family.* Berkeley and Los Angeles: University of California Press, 1978.

Goldberg, Harvey. "Cambridge in the Land of Canaan: Descent, Alliance, Circumcision, and Instruction in the Bible." *Journal of the Ancient Near Eastern Society* 24 (1996): 9–34.

———. *Jewish Passages: Cycles of Jewish Life.* Berkeley and Los Angeles: University of California Press, 2003.

Goldfahn, Alexander. *Justinus Martyr und die Agada.* Breslau: H. Skutsch, n.d.
[1873].

Goldin, Simha. "The Role of Ceremonies in the Socialization Process: The Case
of the Jewish Communities of Northern France and Germany in the Middle
Ages." *Archives de Sciences Sociales des Religions* 95 (1996): 163–78.

Goldingay, John. "The Significance of Circumcision." *Journal for the Study of
the Old Testament* 88 (2000): 3–18.

Goldman, Ronald. *Questioning Circumcision: A Jewish Perspective.* Boston:
Vanguard Publications 1998.

Gollaher, David L. *Circumcision: A History of the World's Most Controversial
Surgery.* New York: Basic Books, 2000.

Goodenough, Erwin. *An Introduction to Philo Judaeus.* 2nd ed. Oxford: Blackwell, 1962.

Goshen-Gottstein, A. "The Body as Image of God in Rabbinic Literature." *Harvard Theological Review* 87 (1994): 171–95.

Gray, L. H., et al. "Circumcision." In *Encyclopedia of Religion and Ethics,* ed.
James Hastings, vol. 3 (1924): 659–80

Greenwald, Asher Anshel. *Sefer Zokher ha Berit.* Uzhorod-Ungvar: MS Gellis,
[5]691 [1931]; repr. Jerusalem [5]746 [1996] (Hebrew).

Gross, Abraham. "The Blood Libel and the Blood of Circumcision: An Ashkenazic Custom That Disappeared in the Middle Ages. *Jewish Quarterly Review* 86 (1995): 171–74.

Grossman, Avraham. "The Connection between Law and Economy in the Status of the Jewish Woman in Early Ashkenaz." In *Religion and Economy: Connections and Interactions,* ed. Menahem Ben-Sasson, 139–59. Jerusalem: Zalman Shazar Center for Jewish History, 1995 (Hebrew).

———. *The Early Sages of Ashkenaz.* Jerusalem: Magnes, 1981 (Hebrew).

———. "The Jewish-Christian Polemic and Jewish Bible Exegesis in Twelfth-Century France." *Zion* 51 (1986): 29–60.

———. *Pious and Rebellious: Jewish Women in Europe in the Middle Ages.* Jerusalem: Shazar Center for Jewish History, 2001 (Hebrew).

Grunfeld, I., trans. *Samson Raphael Hirsch Horeb.* 2 vols. London: Soncino Press, 1962.

Grünwaldt, Klaus. *Exil und Identität: Beschneidung, Passa, und Sabbat in der Priesterschrift.* Frankfurt: Hain, 1992.

Gutwirth, E. "Gender, History, and the Judeo-Christian Polemic." In *Contra Judaeos,* ed. Ora Limor and Guy G. Stroumsa, 257–78. Texts and Studies in Medieval and Early Modern Judaism 10. Tübingen: Mohr-Siebeck, 1996.

Haacke, Rhabanus, ed. *Ruperti Abbati Tuitiensis Anulus.* In Maria Lodovica Arduini. *Ruperto di Deutz e la controversia tra Cristiani ed Ebrei nel secolo XIII,* 175–273. Studi Storici, fasc. 119–21. Rome: Istituto Storico Italiano, 1979.

Habermann, A. M. "Poetical Blessings after Meals." *Yediot ha-makhon le-heqer ha-shirah ha-ivrit* 5 (1939): 43–105 (Hebrew).

Halkin, Abraham, and David Hartman, ed. and trans. *Crisis and Leadership: Epistles of Maimonides.* Philadelphia: Jewish Publication Society, 5745 [1985].

Hall, Robert G. "Circumcision." *Anchor Bible Dictionary,* vol. 1, 1025–31.

———. "Epispasm and the Dating of Ancient Jewish Writings." *Journal for the Study of the Pseudepigrapha* 2 (1988): 71–86.

Hamburger, Benjamin, and Erich Zimmer, eds. *Wormser Minhagbuch des R. Jousep (Juspa) Schammes.* 2 vols. Jerusalem: Makhon Yerushalayim, 1992;

Hamburger, Benjamin S. *Shorshei Minhag Ashkenaz* [The Origins of Ashkenazic Custom]. 2 vols. Bnei Berak: Moreshet Ashkenaz Institute, 5755 [1995] and 5760 [2000].

Haran, Menahem. "The 'Berit' Covenant: Its Nature and Ceremonial Background." In *Tehillah le-Moshe: Biblical and Judaic Studies in Honor of Moshe Greenberg,* ed. Mordechai Cogan, Barry L. Eichler, and Jeffrey H. Tigay, 203–20. Winona Lake, Ind.: Eisenbrauns, 1997.

Harris, Jay. *How Do We Know This? Midrash and the Fragmentation of Modern Judaism.* Albany: State University of New York Press, 1995.

Hart, Columba, and Jane Bishop, trans. *Hildegard of Bingen Scivias.* The Classics of Western Spirituality. New York: Paulist Press, 1990.

Hauptman, Judith. *Rereading the Rabbis: A Woman's Voice.* Boulder, Colo.: Westview Press, 1998.

———. "Women and Prayer: An Attempt to Dispel Some Fallacies." *Judaism* 42 (1993): 94–103.

Hecht, Richard D. "The Exegetical Contexts of Philo's Interpretation of Circumcision." *Nourished with Peace: Studies in Hellenistic Judaism*, ed. F. Greenspahn et al., 51–79. Chico, Calif.: Scholars Press, 1984.

Herr, Moshe D. "Pirkei de-Rabbi Eliezer." *Encyclopedia Judaica* 13 (1972): 558–60.

Hicks, Esther. *Infibulation: Female Mutilation in Islamic Northeastern Africa*. New Brunswick, N.J.: Transaction, 1993.

Hill, P. J., and K. Stasiak. "Limbo." *New Catholic Encyclopedia*, 2nd ed. 8 (2003): 590–91.

Hirsch, Naftali. "66 Wiener Aerzte contra die Beschneidung." *Jeschurun: Zeitschrift zur Förderung jüdischen Geistes und jüdischen Lebens* 15 (5629 [Jan.–Mar. 1869]): 101–38.

Hirsch, Samson Raphael. *The Collected Writings*, 8: *Mensch-Yisroel: Perspectives on Judaism*. New York and Jerusalem: Philipp Feldheim for the Rabbi Dr. Joseph Breuer Foundation, 1995.

Hoffman, Lawrence. *Covenant of Blood: Circumcision and Gender in Rabbinic Judaism*. Chicago: University of Chicago Press, 1996.

Holdheim, Samuel. *Ueber die Beschneidung zunächst in religiös-dogmatischer Beziehung*. Schwerin: Kürchner, 1844.

Horn, Friedrich. "Der Verzicht auf die Beschneidung im frühen Christentum." *New Testament Studies* 42 (1996): 479–505.

Horovitz, Simeon, ed. *Mahzor Vitry*. Repr. Jerusalem: Alef Publishing, 1963.

Horowitz, Maryanne C. "The Image of God in Man—Is Woman Included?" *Harvard Theological Review* 72 (1979): 175–206.

Hosken, Fran. *The Hosken Report: Genital and Sexual Mutilation of Females*. 4th rev. ed. [Lexington, Mass.]: Women's International News Network, 1993.

Hsia, Ronnie Po-Chia. "Witchcraft, Magic, and the Jews in Late Medieval and Early Modern Germany." In *From Witness to Witchcraft: Jews and Judaism in Medieval Christian Thought*, ed. Jeremy Cohen, 419–33. Wolfenbütteler Mittelalter-Studien 11. Wiesbaden: Harrassowitz, 1996.

Hughes, Diane Owen. "Distinguishing Signs: Ear-Rings, Jews and Franciscan Rhetoric." *Past and Present* 112 (1986): 3–59.

Hunt, J. P. T. "Colossians 2:11–12, The Circumcision/Baptism Analogy, and Infant Baptism." *Tyndale Bulletin* 41 (1990): 227–44.

Ilan, Tal. *Jewish Women in Greco-Roman Palestine*. Texte und Studien zum antiken Judentum 44. Tübingen: Mohr-Siebeck, 1995.

Isaac, Erich. "Circumcision as a Covenant Rite." *Anthropos* 59 (1964): 444–56.

Jacob, Walter, and Moshe Zemer, eds. *Conversion to Judaism in Jewish Law*. Tel Aviv and Pittsburgh: Freehof Institute of Progressive Halakhah, 1994.

Jacobson, Howard. *A Commentary on Pseudo-Philo's Liber Antiquitatum Biblicarum*. 2 vols. Arbeiten zur Geschichte des antiken Judentums und des Urchristentums 31. Leiden: E. J. Brill, 1996.

Jochnowitz, George. "'. . . Who Made Me a Woman'." *Commentary* 71, no. 4 (April 1981): 63–64.

Johlson, Joseph. See Bar Amithai.

Johnson, Willis. "The Myth of Jewish Male Menses." *Journal of Medieval History* 24 (1998): 273–95.

[Josephus, Flavius.] *Josephus in Nine Volumes.* Ed. and trans. H. St. J. Thackeray, Ralph Marcus, Allen Wikgren, and Louis H. Feldman. Loeb Classical Library. Cambridge, Mass.: Harvard University Press, and London: Heinemann, 1926–65.

Judd, Robin Esther. "Circumcision and Modern Jewish Life: A German Case Study, 1843–1914." In *The Covenant of Circumcision,* ed. Elizabeth Mark, 142–55. Hanover, N.H.: Brandeis University Press/University Press of New England, 2003.

———. "German Jewish Rituals, Bodies, and Citizenship." PhD dissertation, University of Michigan, 2000.

Juster, Jean. *Les juifs dans l'empire romain.* 2 vols. Paris: P. Geuthner, 1914.

Kafah, Joseph, trans. *Maimonides: Mishneh Torah, Edited according to Yemenite Manuscripts with an Extensive Commentary.* 22 vols. Qiryat Ono: Mekhon Mishnat HaRambam, 5744 [1984]–5757 [1997] (Hebrew).

———. *Moses Maimonides: Guide of the Perplexed.* Jerusalem: Mossad HaRav Kook, 1972 (Hebrew).

Kahana. See Cahana, I. Z.

Kamin, Sarah. "R. Joseph Bekhor Shor's Polemic against Allegory," *Jerusalem Studies in Jewish Thought* 3 (5744 [1984]): 367–92. Reprinted in her *Jews and Christians Interpret the Bible.* Jerusalem: Magnes Press, 1991 (Hebrew).

Kaplan, Steven. *The Beta Israel (Falasha) in Ethiopia.* New York: New York University Press, 1992.

Karsenty, N. "A Mother Questions Brit Milla." *Humanistic Judaism* 6 (1988): 14–21.

Kass, Leon R. *The Beginning of Wisdom: Reading Genesis.* New York: Free Press, 2003.

Katz, Jacob. *Divine Law in Human Hands.* Jerusalem: Magnes Press, 1998.

Kaufman [Kofman], Yehudah. *R. Yom Tov Lipmann Mühlhausen.* New York: n.p. 1927 (Hebrew).

Kellner, Menachem Marc. *Dogma in Medieval Jewish Thought: From Maimonides to Abravanel.* Littman Library of Jewish Civilization. Oxford and New York: Oxford University Press, 1986.

———. *Maimonides on Judaism and the Jewish People.* Albany: State University of New York Press, 1991.

———. "Philosophical Misogyny in Medieval Jewish Philosophy: Gersonides v. Maimonides." *Jerusalem Studies in Jewish Thought* 14 (1998): 113–28.

Kennedy, John G. "Circumcision and Excision in Egyptian Nubia." *Man* 5 (1970): 175–91.

Kenyatta, Jomo. *Facing Mount Kenya: The Tribal Life of the Gikuyu.* London: Secker and Warburg, 1953 (first ed., 1938).

Kister, M. J. "'. . . And He Was Born Circumcised . . .': Some Notes on Circumcision in Hadith." *Oriens* 34 (1994): 10–30.

Klijn, A. F. J. and G. J. Reinink. *Patristic Evidence for Jewish-Christian Sects. Novum Testamentum* supp. 36. Leiden: Brill, 1973.

Knight, Mary. "Curing Cut or Ritual Mutilation? Some Remarks on the Practice of Female and Male Circumcision in Graeco-Roman Egypt." *Isis* 92 (2001): 317–38.

Kohler, Kaufmann. "Circumcision." *Jewish Encyclopaedia* 4 (1903): 92–96.

Konyevsky, Chaim, ed. *Rokeach: A Commentary on the Bible by R. Elazar of Worms*, 1: *Braishith*. Bnei Brak, Israel: 1986 (Hebrew).

Köstenberger, Andreas, Thomas Schreiner, and H. Scott Baldwin, eds. *Women in the Church: A Fresh Analysis of 1 Timothy 2:9–15*. Grand Rapids, Mich.: Baker Books, 1995.

Krauss, Samuel. *The Jewish-Christian Controversy from the Earliest Times to 1789*, ed. William Horbury. Texte und Studien zum antiken Judentum 56. Tübingen: Mohr-Siebeck, 1995.

Krohn, Paysach. *Bris Milah Circumcision—The Covenant of Abraham*. ArtScroll Mesorah Series. Brooklyn, N.Y.: Mesorah Publications, 1985.

Kugel, James L. "The Story of Dinah in the Testament of Levi." *Harvard Theological Review* 85 (1992): 1–34.

Lange, Yitzhak S. "The Commentaries of R. Hayyim Paltiel to the Pentateuch." *Tarbiz* 43 (1973–74): 231–34 (Hebrew).

———. *The Torah Commentaries of R. Hayim Paltiel*. Jerusalem, n.p., 5781 [1981] (Hebrew).

Langer, Ruth. *To Worship God Properly: Tensions between Liturgical Custom and Halakhah in Judaism*. Cincinnati: Hebrew Union College Press, 1998.

à Lapide, Cornelius. *Commentaria in Pentateuchum Mosis*. Antwerp: apud Meursios, 1630.

Laqueur, Thomas. "'Amor Veneris, vel Dulcedo Appeletur'." In *Zone: Fragments for a History of the Human Body*, ed. Michel Feher et al., part 3, 90–131. N.Y.: Urzone, 1989.

Lasker, Daniel J. "Jewish-Christian Polemics at the Turning Point: Jewish Evidence from the Twelfth Century." *HTR* 89 (1996): 161–73.

———. *Jewish Philosophical Polemics against Christianity in the Middle Ages*. New York: Ktav, 1977.

———. "Jewish Philosophical Polemics in Ashkenaz." In *Contra Iudaeos: Ancient and Medieval Polemics between Christians and Jews*, ed. Ora Limor and Guy Stroumsa, 195–213. Texts and Studies in Medieval and Early Modern Judaism 10. Tübingen: Mohr (Siebeck), 1996.

———. "Original Sin and Its Atonement according to Hasdai Crescas." *Daat: A Journal of Jewish Philosophy and Kabbalah* 20 (5748 [1988]): 127–35 (Hebrew).

———. *The Refutation of the Christian Principles by Hasdai Crescas*. Albany: State University of New York Press, 1992.

Lauterbach, Jacob Z. "The Origin and Development of Two Sabbath Ceremonies." *Hebrew Union College Annual* 15 (1940): 367–424.

Le Déaut, Roger. "Le thème de la circoncision du coeur." *Congress Volume, Vienna 1980*, 178–205. *Vetus Testamentum* supp. 32. Leiden: Brill, 1981.

Leslau, Wolf. *Falasha Anthology*. New Haven: Yale University Press, 1951.

Levenson, Jon. *The Death and Resurrection of the Beloved Son*. New Haven: Yale University Press, 1993.

———. "The New Enemies of Circumcision." *Commentary* 109 (March 2000): 29–36.

Levey, Samson. *The Aramaic Bible, 13: The Targum of Ezekiel*. Edinburgh: T. & T. Clark, 1987.

Levine, Yael. "'A Woman Resembles Someone Who Has Been Circumcised'." *Massekhet* (Jerusalem: Matan, The Torah Institute for Women) 2 (5764 [2004]): 27–45 (Hebrew)

Levy, Isaac, trans. *The Pentateuch Translated and Explained by Samson Raphael Hirsch*, 2nd ed., 5 volumes in 6. N.Y.: Judaica Press, 1971.

Lewin, B. M. *Otzar Hageonim*. 13 volumes. Haifa, 1928–43; repr. Jerusalem: Wagshall, 1984.

Lieberman, Saul. "Some Aspects of After Life in Early Rabbinic Literature." In *Harry Austryn Wolfson Jubilee Volume*, 495–532. Jerusalem: American Academy for Jewish Research, 1965.

Lieu, Judith M. "Circumcision, Women, and Salvation." *New Testament Studies*. 40 (1994): 358–70.

Lightfoot-Klein, Hanny. *Prisoners of Ritual: An Odyssey into Female Genital Circumcision in Africa*. New York: Haworth Press, 1989.

Limor, Ora. *Die Disputation zu Ceuta (1179) und Mallorca (1286)*. Quellen zur Geistesgeschichte des Mittlealters 15. Munich: Monumenta Germaniae Historica, 1994.

———. "Missionary Merchants: Three Medieval Anti-Jewish Works from Genoa." *Journal of Medieval History* 17 (1991): 35–51.

Loewenstamm, Samuel. *The Evolution of the Exodus Tradition,* trans. Baruch Schwartz. Jerusalem: Magnes Press, 1992.

Loraux, Nicole. *The Children of Athena,* trans. C. Levine. Princeton: Princeton University Press, 1993.

Magnus, Shulamit. "Re-Inventing Miriam's Well." In *The Uses of Tradition,* ed. Jack Wertheimer, 331–47. New York and Jerusalem: Jewish Theological Seminary, 1992.

Maier, Johann. *Jüdische Auseinandersetzung mit dem Christentum in der Antike*. Darmstadt: Wissenschaftliche Buchgesellschaft, 1982.

Maimon, Arye, et al. *Germania Judaica, Band 3, 1350–1519*. 2 vols. Tübingen: Mohr (Siebeck), 1987–95.

Majno, Guido. *The Healing Hand: Man and Wound in the Ancient World*. Cambridge, Mass: Harvard University Press, 1975; paperback edition, 1991.

Marcus, Joel. "The Circumcision and the Uncircumcision in Rome." *New Testament Studies* 35 (1989): 67–81.

Marcus, Ralph, trans. *Philo. . .Supplement I: Questions and Answers on Genesis*. Loeb Classical Library. Cambridge, Mass.: Harvard University Press, 1953; repr. 1971.

Marienberg, Evyatar. *Niddah: Lorsque les juifs conceptualisent la menstruation*. Paris: Les Belles Lettres, 2003.

Mark, Elizabeth W., ed. *The Covenant of Circumcision: New Perspectives on an Ancient Jewish Rite*. Hanover, N.H.: Brandeis University Press/University Press of New England, 2003.

Martin, Raymond. *Raymundi Martini Pugio Fidei cum observationibus Josephi de Voisin et introductione Jo. Benedicti Carpzovi.* Leipzig: Haeredes Friderici Lanckisi, 1688; repr. Farnborough, England: Gregg Press, 1967.

Martin, Troy. "The Covenant of Circumcision (Genesis 17:9–14) and the Situational Antitheses in Galatians 3:28." *Journal of Biblical Literature* 122 (2003): 111–25.

McNamara, Martin, and Robert Hayward and Michael Maher. *The Aramaic Bible*, 2: *Targum Neofiti: Exodus, Targum Pseudo-Jonathan: Exodus.* Edinburgh: T. & T. Clark, 1994.

Meisl, Josef. "Zur Geschichte der jüdischen Reformbewegung." *Monatsschrift für Geschichte und Wissenschaft des Judentums* 69 (1925): 41–46.

Mellinkoff, Ruth. *The Mark of Cain.* Berkeley and Los Angeles: University of California Press, 1981.

Mendenhall, George, and Gary Herion. "Covenant." *Anchor Bible Dictionary*, vol. 1: 1179–1202.

Meyer, Michael. "The First Identical Ceremony for Giving a Hebrew Name to Girls and Boys." *Journal of Reform Judaism* (Winter 1985): 84–87.

———. *Response to Modernity: A History of the Reform Movement in Judaism.* New York: Oxford University Press, 1988.

Millás Vallicrosa, José. "Un tratado anónimo contra los Judíos." *Sefarad* 13 (1953): 3–34.

Millen, Rochelle. *Women, Birth and Death in Jewish Law and Practice.* Hanover, N.H.: Brandeis University Press/University Press of New England, 2004.

Modena, David Zakut. *Sefer Zekher David.* Livorno: Eliezer Menahem Ottolenghi, 1837 (Hebrew).

Montserrat, Dominic. "*Mallocouria* and *Therapeuteria*: Rituals of Transition in a Mixed Society?" *Bulletin of the American Society of Papyrologists* 28 (1991): 43–49

———. *Sex and Society in Graeco-Roman Egypt.* London and New York: Kegan Paul, 1996.

Moore, George F. "Christian Writers on Judaism." *Harvard Theological Review* 14 (1921): 197–254.

[Moryson, Fynes.] *Shakespeare's Europe: A Survey of the Condition of Europe at the End of the 16th Century, being unpublished chapters of Fyne's Moryson's Itinerary (1617).* First published 1903; 2nd ed., New York: Benjamin Blom, 1967.

Mülhausen, R. Yom-Tov Lipmann. *Sefer Hanizzahon.* Altdorf-Nirenberg: T. Hackspan, 1644; repr. Jerusalem: Dinur Center, 1983, with prolegomenon by Frank Talmage (Hebrew).

[Münster, Sebastian.] *The Messias of the Christians and the Jewes; held forth in a discourse between a Christian, and a Iew obstinately adhering to his strange opinions . . . rendered into English by Paul Isaiah.* London: William Hunt, 1655. Microfilm repr., Early English Books, 1641–1700, no. 1707:17. Ann Arbor: University Microfilms International, 1986.

Murray-Brown, Jeremy. *Kenyatta.* New York: E. P. Dutton, 1973.

Nadler, Steven. *Spinoza: A Life.* Cambridge: Cambridge University Press, 1999.

Nebo, Yehoshafat, ed. *The Commentary of R. Joseph Bekhor Shor on the Torah.* Jerusalem: Mosad HaRav Kook, 1994 (Hebrew).

Neusner, Jacob. *Aphrahat and Judaism.* Studia Post-Biblica 19. Leiden: Brill, 1971.

Newman, Louis I. *Jewish Influence on Christian Reform Movements.* Columbia University Oriental Studies 23. New York: Columbia University Press, 1925.

Niehoff, Maren. "Circumcision as a Marker of Identity: Philo, Origen, and the Rabbis on Genesis 17:1–14." *Jewish Studies Quarterly* 10 (2003): 89–123.

Novak, David. "The Treatment of Islam and Muslims in the Legal Writings of Maimonides." In *Studies in Islamic and Judaic Traditions,* ed. W. Brinner and S. Ricks, 233–50. Atlanta: Scholars Press, 1986.

Omi [Morganstern Leissner]. "Jewish Women's Naming Rites and the Rights of Jewish Women." *Nashim* 4 (5762 [2001]): 140–77.

Orenstein, Debra, ed. *Lifecycles, 1: Jewish Women on Life Passages and Personal Milestones.* Woodstock, Vt.: Jewish Lights Publishing, 1994.

Ortner, Sherry. *Making Gender: The Politics and Erotics of Culture.* Boston: Beacon, 1996.

Patterson, Cynthia B. "*Attikai.*" *Helios* 13, no. 2 (1986): 49–67.

Payer, Pierre, trans. *Peter Abelard, A Dialogue of a Philosopher with a Jew and a Christian.* Toronto: Pontifical Institute of Mediaeval Studies, 1979.

[Peter Lombard]. *Magistri Petri Lombardi Sententiae in IV Libris Distinctae.* Spicilegium Bonaventurianum 4 and 5. Grottaferrata: Editiones Collegii S. Bonaventurae ad Claras Aquas, 1971–81.

Petit, Louis, X. A. Siderides, and Martin Jugie, eds. *Oeuvres complètes de Gennade Scholarios, 3: Oeuvres polémiques.* Paris: Maison de la bonne presse, 1930.

Philipson, David. *The Reform Movement in Judaism.* Repr. New York: Ktav [1967].

Philo. See Colson, F. H.

Pines, Shlomo, trans. *Moses Maimonides, The Guide of the Perplexed.* Chicago: University of Chicago Press, 1963.

Pippin, Tinia, and George Aichele. "The Cut That Confuses, or: In the Penile Colony." In *Culture, Entertainment and the Bible.* ed. George Aichele, 106–23. *Journal for the Study of the Old Testament* Supp. 309. Shefffield: Sheffield Academic Press, 2000.

Pirqei de Rabbi Eliezer. See Friedlander, Gerald.

Plaskow, Judith. *Standing Again at Mount Sinai.* San Francisco: Harper & Row, 1990.

Plaut, W. Gunther. *The Rise of Reform Judaism: A Sourcebook of Its European Origins.* New York: World Union for Progressive Judaism, 1963.

Pollack, Herman. *Jewish Folkways in Germanic Lands (1648–1806).* Cambridge, Mass.: MIT Press, 1971.

Pollack, Miriam. "Redefining the Sacred." In *Sexual Mutilations: A Human Tragedy,* ed. George Denniston and Marilyn Milos, 163–73. New York: Plenum Press, 1997.

Porter, Stanley E. "What Does It Mean to Be 'Saved by Childbirth' (1 Timothy 2.15)?" *Journal for the Study of the New Testament* 49 (1993): 87–102.

Porton, Gary. *The Stranger within Your Gates*. Chicago: University of Chicago Press, 1994.

Preuss, Julius. *Biblisch-talmudische Medezin*. Berlin, 1911; repr. New York: Ktav, 1971.

Propp, William H. C. *Exodus 1–18 : A New Translation with Introduction and Commentary*. Anchor Bible 2. New York: Doubleday, 1999.

Rahman, Anika, and Nahid Toubia. *Female Genital Mutilation: A Guide to Laws and Policies Worldwide*. London and New York: Zed Books, 2000.

Ratzhabi, Yehudah. "New Poetical Blessings after Meals." *Sinai* 54, no. 108 (5751 [1991]): 193–231 (Hebrew).

Referate über die der ersten israelitischen Synode zu Leipzig überreichten Anträge. Berlin: L. Gerschel, 1871.

Resnick, Irven. "Medieval Roots of the Myth of the Jewish Male Menses." *Harvard Theological Review* 93, no. 3 (July 2000): 241–64.

Rogoff, Leonard. "Is the Jew White? The Racial Place of the Southern Jew." *American Jewish History* 85 (1997): 195–230.

Rosenblatt, Samuel, trans. *Saadia Gaon, The Book of Beliefs and Opinions*. Yale Judaica Series 1. New Haven: Yale University Press, 1948.

Rosenbloom, Noah. *Tradition in an Age of Reform: The Religious Philosophy of Samson Raphael Hirsch*. Philadelphia: Jewish Publication Society, 1976.

Rosenthal, Judah. "Anti-Christian Polemics from its Beginnings to the End of the Eighteenth Century." *Aresheth: An Annual of Hebrew Booklore* 2 (1960): 130–79, and 3 (1961): 433–39 (Hebrew).

———. "A Religious Disputation between a Jewish Scholar called 'Menahem' and the Convert Pablo Christiani." In *Hagut Ivrit Ba Amerika*, ed. Menahem Zohori et al., vol. 3 of 3, 61–74. Tel Aviv: Yavneh, 1974.

———. *Sepher Joseph Hamekane*. Jerusalem: Mekize Nirdamim, 1970 (Hebrew).

———. "A Thirteenth-Century Jewish Critique of the New Testament." In *Studies in Jewish Bibliography, History and Literature in Honor of I. Edward Kiev*, ed. Charles Berlin, 123–39. New York: Ktav, 1971 (Hebrew).

———. *Yair ben Shabetay da Corregio Herev Piphioth*. Jerusalem: Mossad Harav Kook, 1958 (Hebrew).

Rosner, Fred. "Hemophilia in Classic Rabbinic Texts." *Journal of the History of Medicine and Allied Sciences* 49 (1994): 240–50.

———. *Sex Ethics in the Writings of Moses Maimonides*. New York: Bloch Publishing, 1974.

Rovner, J. "Rhetorical Strategy and Dialectical Necessity in the Babylonian Talmud. The Case of Kiddushin 34a–35a." *Hebrew Union College Annual* 65 (1994): 177–231.

Rowlandson, Jane. *Women and Society in Greek and Roman Egypt: A Sourcebook*. Cambridge: Cambridge University Press, 1998.

Rubin, Nissan. *The Beginning of Life: Rites of Birth, Circumcision and Redemption of the First-born in the Talmud and Midrash*. Israel: Hakkibutz Hameuchad, 1995 (Hebrew).

———. "*Brit Milah:* A Study of Change in Custom." In *The Covenant of Cir-*

cumcision, ed. Elizabeth W. Mark, 87–97. Brandeis University Press/University Press of New England, 2003.

———. "The Stretching of the Foreskin and the Enactment of *Peri'ah*." *Zion* 54 (1989): 105–17 (Hebrew).

Runia, David T. *Philo in Early Christian Literature: A Survey*. Assen: van Gorcum, 1993.

Safrai, Shmuel. "The *Mitzva* Obligation of Women in Tannaitic Thought." *Bar Ilan Annual* 26–27 (1995): 227–36 (Hebrew).

Sagi, Avi, and Zvi Zohar. *Conversion to Judaism and the Meaning of Jewish Identity*. Jerusalem: Bialik Institute and the Shalom Hartman Institute, 1994 (Hebrew).

Saperstein, Marc. "Christians and Christianity in the Sermons of Jacob Anatoli." *Jewish History* 6 (1992): 225–42.

———. *Decoding the Rabbis: A Thirteenth-Century Commentary on the Aggadah*. Cambridge, Mass.: Harvard University Press, 1980.

———. "The Earliest Commentary on the Midrash Rabbah." In *Studies in Medieval Jewish History and Literature*, ed. Isidore Twersky, 283–306. Cambridge, Mass.: Harvard University Press, 1979.

———. *Jewish Preaching, 1200–1800: An Anthology*. Yale Judaica Series 26. New Haven: Yale University Press, 1989.

———. *"Your Voice Like a Ram's Horn": Themes and Texts in Traditional Jewish Preaching*. Monographs of the Hebrew Union College 18. Cincinnati: Hebrew Union College Press, 1996.

Sasson, Jack M. "Circumcision in the Ancient Near East." *Journal of Biblical Literature* 85 (1966): 473–76.

Satlow, Michael. " 'Try to Be a Man': The Rabbinic Construction of Masculinity." *Harvard Theological Review* 89 (1996): 19–40.

Schäfer, Peter. "The Bar-Kokhba Revolt and Circumcision." In *Jüdische Geschichte in hellenistisch-römischer Zeit*, ed. Aharon Oppenheimer, 119–32. Schriften des Historischen Kollegs Kolloquien 44. Munich: Oldenbourg, 1999.

———. *Judeophobia: Attitudes toward the Jews in the Ancient World*. Cambridge, Mass.: Harvard University Press, 1997.

Schenk, Richard. "Covenant Initiation: Thomas Aquinas and Robert Kilwardby on the Sacrament of Circumcision." In *Hommage au professeur Jean-Pierre Torrell, O. P.* ed. Carlos-Josaphat Pinto de Oliveira, 555–93. Fribourg: Éditions Universitaires, 1992.

Schiffman, Lawrence. *Who Was a Jew?* New York: Ktav, 1985.

Schreckenberg, Heinz. *Die christlichen Adversus-Judaeos-Texte*. 3 vols. Frankfurt: Peter Lang, 1982–94.

———. *The Jews in Christian Art: An Illustrated History*. New York: Continuum, 1996.

Schreiber, Abraham, ed., *Commentary on the Treatise of Abodah Zarah by R. Abraham ben David of Posquieres*. New York: n.p., 1960 (Hebrew).

Screech, M. A., trans. and ed. *The Essays of Michel de Montaigne*. London: Allen Lane/Penguin, 1991.

Seidenberg, David. "Brit Taharah—Woman as Covenantal Body." *Sh'ma* 25 (January 20, 1995), 5–6.

Seltzer, Debra. "The Rape of Dinah." *Living Text: The Journal of Contemporary Midrash* 1 (July 1997): 5–11.

Setzer, Claudia. "Excellent Women: Female Witnesses to the Resurrection." *Journal of Biblical Literature* 116 (1997): 259–72.

Shamash, Abraham. "What Is the Source of the Custom of Sniffing a Myrtle at a Circumcision?" *Shma'tin* 37 [no. 129] (5760 [2000]): 66–71 (Hebrew).

Shapiro, James. *Shakespeare and the Jews.* New York: Columbia University Press, 1996.

Shevitz, Dan, and Amy Hill Shevitz. "The Covenant of the Flesh." *Reconstructionist* (Spring 1993): 25–27.

Shinan, Avigdor. "The Relationship between Targum Pseudo-Jonathan and Midrash Pirqe de-Rabbi Eliezer." In *Teuda 11: Studies in the Aggadic Midrashim,* ed. M. A. Friedman and M. B. Lerner, 231–43. Tel Aviv: Chaim Rosenberg School of Jewish Studies, Tel Aviv University, 1996.

Shirley, Samuel. *Baruch Spinoza Tractatus Theologico-Politicus.* 2nd ed. Leiden: Brill, 1991.

Shweder, Richard. "'What about Female Genital Mutilation?' and Why Understanding Culture Matters." In his *Why Do Men Barbecue?* 168–216. Cambridge, Mass: Harvard University Press, 2003.

Silber, Michael. "The Emergence of Ultra-Orthodoxy." In *The Uses of Tradition,* ed. Jack Wertheimer, 23–84. New York and Jerusalem: Jewish Theological Seminary, 1992.

Sly, Dorothy. *Philo's Perception of Women.* Brown Judaic studies 209. Atlanta: Scholars Press, 1990;

Smalley, Beryl. *The Study of the Bible in the Middle Ages.* Oxford: Blackwell, 1952.

Smith, Morton. *Clement of Alexandria and a Secret Gospel according to Mark.* Cambridge, Mass.: Harvard University Press, 1973.

———. *Studies in the Cult of Yahweh,* 2 vols., ed. Shaye J. D. Cohen. Religions in the Graeco-Roman World 130. Leiden: Brill, 1996.

Smith, Steven B. *Spinoza, Liberalism, and the Question of Jewish Identity.* New Haven: Yale University Press, 1997.

Soloveitchik, Joseph B. *Halakhic Man.* trans. Lawrence Kaplan. Philadelphia: Jewish Publication Society, 1983.

Sparks, H. F. D. *The Apocryphal Old Testament.* Oxford; Clarendon Press, 1984.

Sperber, Daniel. *Minhagei Yisrael* (Customs of Israel, vol. 1). Jerusalem: Mossad Harav Kook, 1989.

Spiegel, Yaakov. "Woman as Ritual Circumciser—the *Halakhah* and Its Development." *Sidra* 5 (1989) 149–57 (Hebrew).

Spitzer, Shlomoh. *The Book of Maharil: Customs by Rabbi Yaacov Mulin* [Molin]. Jerusalem: Machon Yerushalayim, 1989 (Hebrew).

Steinberg, Leo. *The Sexuality of Christ in Renaissance Art and in Modern Oblivion.* 2nd ed. Chicago: University of Chicago Press, 1996.

Steiner, Richard. "Incomplete Circumcision in Egypt and Edom." *Journal of Biblical Literature* 118 (1999): 497–505.

Stern, David. *Parables in Midrash.* Cambridge, Mass.: Harvard University Press, 1991.

Stern, Josef. "Maimonides on Circumcision." In *The Midrashic Imagination: Jewish Exegesis, Thought and History,* ed. Michael Fishbane, 131–54. Albany: State University of New York Press, 1993.

Stern, Menahem. *Greek and Latin Authors on Jews and Judaism.* 3 vols. Jerusalem: Israel Academy of Sciences, 1974–84.

Stern, Sacha. *Jewish Identity in Early Rabbinic Writings.* Arbeiten zur Geschichte des antiken Judentums und des Urchristentums 23. Leiden: Brill,1994.

Stowers, Stanley K. *A Rereading of Romans.* New Haven and London: Yale University Press, 1994.

Susser, Bernhard. "The Covenant of Circumcision." In Annette Weber et al., eds., *Mappot . . . Blessed Be Who Comes: The Band of Jewish Tradition,* 42–45. Osnabrück: Secolo Verlag, 1997.

Tabory, Ephraim, and Sharon Erez. "Circumscribed Circumcision: The Motivations and Identities of Israeli Parents Who Do Not Circumcise Their Sons." In *The Covenant of Circumcision,* ed. Elizabeth W. Mark, 161–76. Hanover, N.H.: Brandeis University Press/University Press of New England, 2003.

Tabory, Joseph. "The Benedictions of Self-Identity and the Changing Status of Women and of Orthodoxy." In *Kenishta: Studies of the Synagogue World,* ed. Joseph Tabory, 107–38. Bar-Ilan: Bar-Ilan University Press, 2001.

Tal, Shlomo. *Siddur Rinat Yisrael Nusah Ashkenaz.* Jerusalem: Moreshet, 5737 [1977] (Hebrew). Frequently reprinted.

Tal, Shlomo, with Amram Aburabia. *Siddur Rinat Yisrael Nusah Sephardim Veedot Hamizrah.* Jerusalem: Moreshet, 5736 [1976] (Hebrew). Frequently reprinted.

Talle, Aud. "Transforming Women into 'Pure' Agnates: Aspects of Female Infibulation in Somalia." in *Carved Flesh, Cast Selves: Gendered Symbols and Social Practices,* ed. Vigdis Broch-Due et al., 83–106. Oxford and Providence: Berg Publishers 1993.

Talmage, Frank [Ephraim]. *The Book of the Covenant and Other Writings [of R. Joseph Kimhi and R. David Kimhi].* Jerusalem: Mosad Bialik, 1974 (Hebrew)

———, ed. *The Sefer HaNizzahon of R. Yom Tov Lipmann Mühlhausen,* a facsimile of the first edition. Jerusalem: Merkaz Dinur, 1984. Hebrew

———. "*Sefer ha-Nissahon* of R. Yom Tov Lipmann Mühlhausen." In his *Apples of Gold in Settings of Silver: Studies in Medieval Jewish Exegesis,* ed. Barry D. Walfish, 319–56. Papers in Mediaeval Studies 14. Toronto: Pontifical Institute of Mediaeval Studies, 1999.

Tanner, Norman, ed. *Decrees of the Ecumenical Councils.* 2 vols. London: Sheed and Ward; Washington, D.C.: Georgetown University Press, 1990.

Ta-Shema, Israel. *Early Franco-German Ritual and Custom.* Jerusalem: Magnes Press, 1992. Hebrew.

———. "Muelhausen, Yom Tov Lipmann." *Encyclopedia Judaica* 12 (1972): 499–502.

Tishby, Isaiah. *The Wisdom of the Zohar.* trans. David Goldstein. Oxford University Press/Littman Library, 1989.

Toubia, Nahid. *Female Genital Mutilation: A Call for Global Action.* New York: Women Ink, 1993.

Touitou, Elazar. "The Method in Rashbam's Commentary on the Halakhic Parts of the Torah." *Milet: Everyman's University Studies in Jewish History and Culture* 2 (Tel Aviv 1985): 275–88 (Hebrew)

———. "Rashi and His School: The Exegesis of the Halakhic Part of the Pentateuch." In *Bar Ilan Studies in History 4: Medieval Studies in Honour of Avram Saltman,* 242–44. (Ramat-Gan: Bar-Ilan University Press, 1995) (Hebrew).

Trachtenberg, Joshua. *The Devil and the Jews.* New Haven: Yale University Press, 1943. Frequently reprinted.

Trautner-Kromann, Hanne. *Shield and Sword: Jewish Polemics against Christianity and the Christians in France and Spain from 1100–1500.* Texts and Studies in Medieval and Early Modern Judaism 8. Tübingen: Mohr-Siebeck, 1993.

Trechmann, E. J., trans. *The Diary of Montaigne's Journey to Italy.* London: Hogarth Press/Leonard and Virginia Woolf, 1929.

Trier, Salomon Abraham. *Rabbinische Gutachten über die Beschneidung.* Frankfurt: Bach, 1844.

Twersky, Isadore. *Introduction to the Code of Maimonides.* New Haven: Yale University Press, 1980.

Ullendorff, Edward. *Ethiopia and the Bible.* London: British Academy/Oxford University Press, 1968.

Urbach, Efraim [Ephraim]. *The Sages: Their Concepts and Beliefs,* trans. Israel Abrahams. Jerusalem: Magnes Press, 1979.

———. *Sefer Arugat Habosem, auctore R. Abraham b. R. Azriel.* 4 vols. Jerusalem: Mekize Nirdamim, 1939–63 (Hebrew).

———. *The Tosaphists: Their History, Writings, and Methods.* 5th ed. Jerusalem: Bialik Institute, 1986 (Hebrew).

Vanderkam, James C. trans. *The Book of Jubilees.* Corpus Scriptorum Christianorum Orientalium 511. Louvain: Peeters, 1989.

Vega, A. C. and A. F. Anspach, ed. *S. Isidori Hispalensis Episcopi Liber de Variis Quaestionibus.* Madrid: Typis Augustinianis Monasterii Escurialensis, 1940.

Wagenseil, Joh. Christopher. *Tela Ignea Satanae, Hoc Est Arcani et Horribiles Judaeorum Adversus Christum Deum et Christianam Religionem Libri Anecdotoi.* Altdorf: excudit Joh. Henricus Schönnerstaedt, 1681.

Walker, Alice, and Pratibha Parmar. *Warrior Marks: Female Genital Mutilation and the Sexual Blinding of Women.* New York: Harcourt Brace, 1993.

Wallerstein, Edward. *Circumcision: An American Health Fallacy.* New York: Springer, 1980.

Washofsky, Mark. "Responsa and Rhetoric." In *Pursuing the Text: Studies in*

Honor of Ben Zion Wacholder, ed. John Reeves and J. C. Kampen, 360–409. *Journal for the Study of the Old Testament*, Supp. 184. Sheffield: Sheffield Academic Press, 1994.

Weber, Annette, et al., eds. *Mappot . . . Blessed Be Who Comes: The Band of Jewish Tradition.* Osnabrück: Secolo Verlag, 1997.

Wegner, Judith. *Chattel or Person? The Status of Women in the Mishnah.* New York: Oxford University Press, 1988.

Weisberg, Yosef David. *Otzar HaBerit: Encyclopedia of the Laws and Customs of Brit Milah.* 4 vols. Jerusalem: Torat HaBerit Institute, 5746 [1986]–5762 [2002] (Hebrew).

Werline, Rodney. "The Transformation of Pauline Arguments in Justin Martyr's Dialogue with Trypho." *Harvard Theological Review* 92 (1999): 79–93.

Wernham, A. G. *Benedict de Spinoza The Political Works.* Oxford: Clarendon Press, 1958.

Wertheimer, Shelomo. *Abudraham Hashalem.* Jerusalem: Usha, 5723 [1963] (Hebrew).

Wesselski, Albert. *Heinrich Bebels Schwänke.* 2 vols. Munich and Leipzig: G. Müller, 1907.

Willet, Andrew. *Hexapla in Genesin: A Sixfold Commentarie upon Genesis.* John Leget, printer to the University of Cambridge, 1605.

Williams, A. Lukyn. *Adversus Judaeos.* Cambridge: Cambridge University Press, 1935.

Wolfson, Elliot. *Circle in the Square: Studies in the Use of Gender in Kabbalistic Symbolism.* Albany: State University of New York Press, 1995.

———. "Circumcision and the Divine Name: A Study in the Transmission of Esoteric Doctrine." *Jewish Quarterly Review* 78 (1987): 77–112.

Yovel, Yirmiyahu. *Spinoza and Other Heretics: The Marrano of Reason.* Princeton: Princeton University Press, 1989. Paperback edition, 1992.

Yuval, Israel J. "Kabbalisten, Ketzer und Polemiker: Das kulturelle Umfeld des Sefer ha-Nizachon von Lipman Mühlhausen." In *Mysticism, Magic, and Kabbalah in Ashkenazi Judaism.* ed. K. E. Grözinger and J. Dan, 155–71. Studia Judaica 13. Berlin: de Gruyter, 1995.

———. *Scholars in Their Time: The Religious Leadership of German Jewry in the Late Middle Ages.* Jerusalem: Magnes Press, 1988 (Hebrew).

Zimmels, H. J. *Magicians, Theologians, and Doctors. Studies in Folk-medicine and Folk-lore as Reflected in the Rabbinical Responsa.* London: E. Goldston, 1952.

General Index

Page numbers in italics *indicate an illustration.*

Index of Premodern Sources

Text: 10/13 Sabon
Display: Sabon
Indexer: Patricia Deminna
Compositor, printer, and binder: Sheridan Books, Inc.

DATE DUE
